THE POWER ELITE

THE
POWER
ELITE

C. WRIGHT MILLS

OXFORD   UNIVERSITY   PRESS

LONDON   OXFORD   NEW YORK

OXFORD UNIVERSITY PRESS

Oxford London New York
Glasgow Toronto Melbourne Wellington
Cape Town Ibadan Nairobi Lusaka Addis Ababa Delhi
Bombay Calcutta Madras Karachi Lahore Dacca
Kuala Lumpur Hong Kong Tokyo

Printed in the United States of America

Contents

THE POWER ELITE

1

The Higher Circles

THE powers of ordinary men are circumscribed by the everyday worlds in which they live, yet even in these rounds of job, family, and neighborhood they often seem driven by forces they can neither understand nor govern. 'Great changes' are beyond their control, but affect their conduct and outlook none the less. The very framework of modern society confines them to projects not their own, but from every side, such changes now press upon the men and women of the mass society, who accordingly feel that they are without purpose in an epoch in which they are without power.

But not all men are in this sense ordinary. As the means of information and of power are centralized, some men come to occupy positions in American society from which they can look down upon, so to speak, and by their decisions mightily affect, the everyday worlds of ordinary men and women. They are not made by their jobs; they set up and break down jobs for thousands of others; they are not confined by simple family responsibilities; they can escape. They may live in many hotels and houses, but they are bound by no one community. They need not merely 'meet the demands of the day and hour'; in some part, they create these demands, and cause others to meet them. Whether or not they profess their power, their technical and political experience of it far transcends that of the underlying population. What Jacob Burckhardt said of 'great men,' most Americans might well say of their elite: 'They are all that we are not.'[1]

The power elite is composed of men whose positions enable them to transcend the ordinary environments of ordinary men and women; they are in positions to make decisions having major consequences. Whether they do or do not make such decisions is less important than the fact that they do occupy such pivotal positions: their failure to act, their failure to make decisions, is itself an act that is often of greater consequence than the decisions they do make. For they are in command of the major hierarchies and organizations of modern society. They rule the big corporations. They run the machinery of the state and claim its prerogatives. They direct the military establishment. They occupy the strategic command posts of the social structure, in which are now centered the effective means of the power and the wealth and the celebrity which they enjoy.

The power elite are not solitary rulers. Advisers and consultants, spokesmen and opinion-makers are often the captains of their higher thought and decision. Immediately below the elite are the professional politicians of the middle levels of power, in the Congress and in the pressure groups, as well as among the new and old upper classes of town and city and region. Mingling with them, in curious ways which we shall explore, are those professional celebrities who live by being continually displayed but are never, so long as they remain celebrities, displayed enough. If such celebrities are not at the head of any dominating hierarchy, they do often have the power to distract the attention of the public or afford sensations to the masses, or, more directly, to gain the ear of those who do occupy positions of direct power. More or less unattached, as critics of morality and technicians of power, as spokesmen of God and creators of mass sensibility, such celebrities and consultants are part of the immediate scene in which the drama of the elite is enacted. But that drama itself is centered in the command posts of the major institutional hierarchies.

1

The truth about the nature and the power of the elite is not some secret which men of affairs know but will not tell. Such men hold quite various theories about their own roles in the sequence of event and decision. Often they are uncertain about their roles, and even more often they allow their fears and their hopes to affect their assessment of their own power. No matter how great their actual power, they tend to be less acutely aware of it than of the resistances of others to its use. Moreover, most American men of affairs have learned well the rhetoric of public relations, in some cases even to the point of using it when they are alone, and thus coming to believe it. The personal awareness of the actors is only one of the several sources one must examine in order to understand the higher circles. Yet many who believe that there is no elite, or at any rate none of any consequence, rest their argument upon what men of affairs believe about themselves, or at least assert in public.

There is, however, another view: those who feel, even if vaguely, that a compact and powerful elite of great importance does now prevail in America often base that feeling upon the historical trend of our time. They have felt, for example, the domination of the military event, and from this they infer that generals and admirals, as well as other men of decision influenced by them, must be enormously powerful. They hear that the Congress has again abdicated to a handful of men decisions clearly related to the issue of war or peace. They know that the bomb was dropped over Japan in the name of the United States of America, although they were at no time consulted about the matter. They feel that they live in a time of big decisions; they know that they are not making any. Accordingly, as they consider the present as history, they infer that at its center, making decisions or failing to make them, there must be an elite of power.

On the one hand, those who share this feeling about big historical events assume that there is an elite and that its power is great. On the other hand, those who listen carefully to the reports of men apparently involved in the great decisions often do not believe that there is an elite whose powers are of decisive consequence.

Both views must be taken into account, but neither is adequate. The way to understand the power of the American elite lies neither solely in recognizing the historic scale of events nor in accepting the personal awareness reported by men of apparent decision. Behind such men and behind the events of history, linking the two, are the major institutions of modern society. These hierarchies of state and corporation and army constitute the means of power; as such they are now of a consequence not before equaled in human history—and at their summits, there are now those command posts of modern society which offer us the sociological key to an understanding of the role of the higher circles in America.

Within American society, major national power now resides in the economic, the political, and the military domains. Other institutions seem off to the side of modern history, and, on occasion, duly subordinated to these. No family is as directly powerful in national affairs as any major corporation; no church is as directly powerful in the external biographies of young men in America today as the military establishment; no college is as powerful in the shaping of momentous events as the National Security Council. Religious, educational, and family institutions are not autonomous centers of national power; on the contrary, these decentralized areas are increasingly shaped by the big three, in which developments of decisive and immediate consequence now occur.

Families and churches and schools adapt to modern life; governments and armies and corporations shape it; and, as they do so, they turn these lesser institutions into means for their ends. Religious institutions provide chaplains to the armed forces where they are used as a means of increasing the effectiveness of its morale to kill. Schools select and train men for their jobs in corporations and their specialized tasks in the armed forces. The extended family has, of course, long been broken up by the industrial revolution, and now the son and the father are removed from the family, by compulsion if need be, whenever the army of the state sends out the call. And the symbols of all these lesser institutions are used to legitimate the power and the decisions of the big three.

The life-fate of the modern individual depends not only upon the family into which he was born or which he enters by marriage, but increasingly upon the corporation in which he spends the most alert hours of his best years; not only upon the school where he is educated as a child and adolescent, but also upon the state which touches him throughout his life; not only upon the church in which on occasion he hears the word of God, but also upon the army in which he is disciplined.

If the centralized state could not rely upon the inculcation of nationalist loyalties in public and private schools, its leaders would promptly seek to modify the decentralized educational system. If the bankruptcy rate among the top five hundred corporations were as high as the general divorce rate among the thirty-seven million married couples, there would be economic catastrophe on an international scale. If members of armies gave to them no more of their lives than do believers to the churches to which they belong, there would be a military crisis.

Within each of the big three, the typical institutional unit has become enlarged, has become administrative, and, in the power of its decisions, has become centralized. Behind these developments there is a fabulous technology, for as institutions, they have incorporated this technology and guide it, even as it shapes and paces their developments.

The economy—once a great scatter of small productive units in autonomous balance—has become dominated by two or three hundred giant corporations, administratively and politically interrelated, which together hold the keys to economic decisions.

The political order, once a decentralized set of several dozen states with a weak spinal cord, has become a centralized, executive establishment which has taken up into itself many powers previously scattered, and now enters into each and every cranny of the social structure.

The military order, once a slim establishment in a context of distrust fed by state militia, has become the largest and most expensive feature of government, and, although well versed in smiling public relations, now has all the grim and clumsy efficiency of a sprawling bureaucratic domain.

In each of these institutional areas, the means of power at the disposal of decision makers have increased enormously; their central executive powers have been enhanced; within each of them modern administrative routines have been elaborated and tightened up.

As each of these domains becomes enlarged and centralized, the consequences of its activities become greater, and its traffic with the others increases. The decisions of a handful of corporations bear upon military and political as well as upon economic developments around the world. The decisions of the military establishment rest upon and grievously affect political life as well as the very level of economic activity. The decisions made within the political domain determine economic activities and military programs. There is no longer, on the one hand, an economy, and, on the other hand, a political order containing a military establishment unimportant to politics and to money-making. There is a political economy linked, in a thousand ways, with military institutions and decisions. On each side of the world-split running through central Europe and around the Asiatic rimlands, there is an ever-increasing interlocking of economic, military, and political structures.[2] If there is government intervention in the corporate economy, so is there corporate intervention in the governmental process. In the structural sense, this triangle of power is the source of the interlocking directorate that is most important for the historical structure of the present.

The fact of the interlocking is clearly revealed at each of the points of crisis of modern capitalist society—slump, war, and boom. In each, men of decision are led to an awareness of the interdependence of the major institutional orders. In the nineteenth century, when the scale of all institutions was smaller, their liberal integration was achieved in the automatic economy, by an autonomous play of market forces, and in the automatic political domain, by the bargain and the vote. It was then assumed that out of the imbalance and friction that followed the limited decisions then possible a new equilibrium would in due course emerge. That can no longer be assumed, and it is not assumed by the men at the top of each of the three dominant hierarchies.

For given the scope of their consequences, decisions—and indecisions—in any one of these ramify into the others, and hence top decisions tend either to become co-ordinated or to lead to a commanding indecision. It has not always been like this. When numerous small entrepreneurs made up the economy, for example, many of them could fail and the consequences still remain local; political and military authorities did not intervene. But now, given political expectations and military commitments, can they afford to allow key units of the private corporate economy to break down in slump? Increasingly, they do intervene in economic affairs, and as they do so, the controlling decisions in each order are inspected by agents of the other two, and economic, military, and political structures are interlocked.

At the pinnacle of each of the three enlarged and centralized domains, there have arisen those higher circles which make up the economic, the political, and the military elites. At the top of the economy, among the corporate rich, there are the chief executives; at the top of the political order, the members of the political directorate; at the top of the military establishment, the elite of soldier-statesmen clustered in and around the Joint Chiefs of Staff and the upper echelon. As each of these domains has co-incided with the others, as decisions tend to become total in their consequence, the leading men in each of the three domains of power—the warlords, the corporation chieftains, the political directorate—tend to come together, to form the power elite of America.

2

The higher circles in and around these command posts are often thought of in terms of what their members possess: they have a greater share than other people of the things and experiences that are most highly valued. From this point of view, the elite are simply those who have the most of what there is to have, which is generally held to include money, power, and prestige—as well as all the ways of life to which these lead.[3] But the elite are not simply those who have the most, for they could not 'have the most' were it not for their positions in the great institutions. For such institutions are the necessary bases of power, of wealth, and of prestige, and at the same time, the chief means of exercising power, of acquiring and retaining wealth, and of cashing in the higher claims for prestige.

By the powerful we mean, of course, those who are able to realize their will, even if others resist it. No one, accordingly, can be truly powerful unless he has access to the command of major institutions, for it is over these institutional means of power that the truly powerful are, in the first instance, powerful. Higher politicians and key officials of government command such institutional power; so do admirals and generals, and so do the major owners and executives of the larger corporations. Not all power, it is true, is anchored in and exercised by means of such institutions, but only within and through them can power be more or less continuous and important.

Wealth also is acquired and held in and through institutions. The pyramid of wealth cannot be understood merely in terms of the very rich; for the great inheriting families, as we shall see, are now supplemented by the corporate institutions of modern society: every one of the very rich families has been and is closely connected—always legally and frequently managerially as well—with one of the multi-million dollar corporations.

The modern corporation is the prime source of wealth, but, in latter-day capitalism, the political apparatus also opens and closes many avenues to wealth. The amount as well as the source of income, the power over consumer's goods as well as over productive capital, are determined by position within the political economy. If our interest in the very rich goes beyond their lavish or their miserly consumption, we must examine their relations to modern forms of corporate property as well as to the state; for such relations now determine the chances of men to secure big property and to receive high income.

Great prestige increasingly follows the major institutional units of the social structure. It is obvious that prestige depends, often quite decisively, upon access to the publicity machines that are now a central and normal feature of all the big institutions of modern America. Moreover, one feature of these hierarchies of corporation, state, and military establishment is that their top positions are increasingly interchangeable. One result of this is the accumulative nature of prestige. Claims for prestige, for example, may be initially based on military roles, then expressed in and augmented by an educational institution run by corporate executives, and cashed in, finally, in the political order, where, for General Eisenhower and those he represents, power and prestige finally meet at the very peak. Like wealth and power, prestige tends to be cumulative: the more of it you have, the more you can get. These values also tend to be translatable into one another: the wealthy find it easier than the poor to gain power; those with status find it easier than those without it to control opportunities for wealth.

If we took the one hundred most powerful men in America, the one hundred wealthiest, and the one hundred most celebrated away from the institutional positions they now occupy, away from their resources of men and women and money, away from the media of mass communication that are now focused upon them—then they would be powerless and poor and uncelebrated. For power is not of a man. Wealth does not center in the person of the wealthy. Celebrity is not inherent in any personality. To be celebrated, to be wealthy, to have power requires access to major institutions, for the institutional positions men occupy determine in large part their chances to have and to hold these valued experiences.

3

The people of the higher circles may also be conceived as members of a top social stratum, as a set of groups whose members know one another, see one another socially and at business, and so, in making decisions, take one another into account. The elite, according to this conception, feel themselves to be, and are felt by others to be, the inner circle of 'the upper social classes.'[4] They form a more or less compact social and psychological entity; they have become self-conscious members of a social class. People are either accepted into this class or they are not, and there is a qualitative split, rather than merely a numerical scale, separating them from those who are not elite. They are more or less aware of themselves as a social class and they behave toward one another differently from the way they do toward members of other classes. They accept one another, understand one another, marry one another, tend to work and to think if not together at least alike.

Now, we do not want by our definition to prejudge whether the elite of the command posts are conscious members of such a socially recognized class, or whether considerable proportions of the elite derive from such a clear and distinct class. These are matters to be investigated. Yet in order to be able to recognize what we intend to investigate, we must note something that all biographies and memoirs of the wealthy and the powerful and the eminent make clear: no matter what else they may be, the people of these higher circles are involved in a set of overlapping 'crowds' and intricately connected 'cliques.' There is a kind of mutual attraction among those who 'sit on the same terrace'—although this often becomes clear to them, as well as to others, only at the point at which they feel the need to draw the line; only when, in their common defense, they come to understand what they have in common, and so close their ranks against outsiders.

The idea of such ruling stratum implies that most of its members have similar social origins, that throughout their lives they maintain a network of informal connections, and that to some degree there is an interchangeability of position between the various hierarchies of money and power and celebrity. We must, of course, note at once that if such an elite stratum does exist, its social visibility and its form, for very solid historical reasons, are quite different from those of the noble cousinhoods that once ruled various European nations.

That American society has never passed through a feudal epoch is of decisive importance to the nature of the American elite, as well as to American society as a historic whole. For it means that no nobility or aristocracy, established before the capitalist era, has stood in tense opposition to the higher bourgeoisie. It means that this bourgeoisie has monopolized not only wealth but prestige and power as well. It means that no set of noble families has commanded the top positions and monopolized the values that are generally held in high esteem; and certainly that no set has done so explicitly by inherited right. It means that no high church dignitaries or court nobilities, no entrenched landlords with honorific accouterments, no monopolists of high army posts have opposed the enriched bourgeoisie and in the name of birth and prerogative successfully resisted its self-making.

But this does *not* mean that there are no upper strata in the United States. That they emerged from a 'middle class' that had no recognized aristocratic superiors does not mean they remained middle class when enormous increases in wealth made their own superiority possible. Their origins and their newness may have made the upper strata less visible in America than elsewhere. But in America today there are in fact tiers and ranges of wealth and power of which people in the middle and lower ranks know very little and may not even dream. There are families who, in their well-being, are quite insulated from the economic jolts and lurches felt by the merely prosperous and those farther down the scale. There are also men of power who in quite small groups make decisions of enormous consequence for the underlying population.

The American elite entered modern history as a virtually unopposed bourgeoisie. No national bourgeoisie, before or since, has had such opportunities and advantages. Having no military neighbors, they easily occupied an isolated continent stocked with natural resources and immensely inviting to a willing labor force. A framework of power and an ideology for its justification were already at hand. Against mercantilist restriction, they inherited the principle of *laissez-faire;* against Southern planters, they imposed the principle of industrialism. The Revolutionary War put an end to colonial pretensions to nobility, as loyalists fled the country and many estates were broken up. The Jacksonian upheaval with its status revolution put an end to pretensions to monopoly of descent by the old New England families. The Civil War broke the power, and so in due course the prestige, of the ante-bellum South's claimants for the higher esteem. The tempo of the whole capitalist development made it impossible for an inherited nobility to develop and endure in America.

No fixed ruling class, anchored in agrarian life and coming to flower in military glory, could contain in America the historic thrust of commerce and industry, or subordinate to itself the capitalist elite—as capitalists were subordinated, for example, in Germany and Japan. Nor could such a ruling class anywhere in the world contain that of the United States when industrialized violence came to decide history. Witness the fate of Germany and Japan in the two world wars of the twentieth century; and indeed the fate of Britain herself and her model ruling class, as New York became the inevitable economic, and Washington the inevitable political capital of the western capitalist world.

4

The elite who occupy the command posts may be seen as the possessors of power and wealth and celebrity; they may be seen as members of the upper stratum of a capitalistic society. They may also be defined in terms of psychological and moral criteria, as certain kinds of selected individuals. So defined, the elite, quite simply, are people of superior character and energy.

The humanist, for example, may conceive of the 'elite' not as a social level or category, but as a scatter of those individuals who attempt to transcend themselves, and accordingly, are more noble, more efficient, made out of better stuff. It does not matter whether they are poor or rich, whether they hold high position or low, whether they are acclaimed or despised; they are elite because of the kind of individuals they are. The rest of the population is mass, which, according to this conception, sluggishly relaxes into uncomfortable mediocrity.[5]

This is the sort of socially unlocated conception which some American writers with conservative yearnings have recently sought to develop.* But most moral and psychological conceptions of the elite are much less sophisticated, concerning themselves not with individuals but with the stratum as a whole. Such ideas, in fact, always arise in a society in which some people possess more than do others of what there is to possess. People with advantages are loath to believe that they just happen to be people with advantages. They come readily to define themselves as inherently worthy of what they possess; they come to believe themselves 'naturally' elite; and, in fact, to imagine their possessions and their privileges as natural extensions of their own elite selves. In this sense, the idea of the elite as composed of men and women having a finer moral character is an ideology of the elite as a privileged ruling stratum, and this is true whether the ideology is elite-made or made up for it by others.

In eras of equalitarian rhetoric, the more intelligent or the more articulate among the lower and middle classes, as well as guilty members of the upper, may come to entertain ideas of a counter-elite. In western society, as a matter of fact, there is a long tradition and varied images of the poor, the exploited, and the oppressed as the truly virtuous, the wise, and the blessed. Stemming from Christian tradition, this moral idea of a counter-elite, composed of essentially higher types condemned to a lowly station, may be and has been used by the underlying population to justify harsh criticism of ruling elites and to celebrate utopian images of a new elite to come.

The moral conception of the elite, however, is not always merely an ideology of the overprivileged or a counter-ideology of the underprivileged. It is often a fact: having controlled experiences and select privileges, many individuals of the upper stratum do come in due course to approximate the types of character they claim to embody. Even when we give up—as we must—the idea that the elite man or woman is born with an elite character, we need not dismiss the idea that their experiences and trainings develop in them characters of a specific type.

* See below, FOURTEEN: The Conservative Mood.

Nowadays we must qualify the idea of elite as composed of higher types of individuals, for the men who are selected for and shaped by the top positions have many spokesmen and advisers and ghosts and make-up men who modify their self-conceptions and create their public images, as well as shape many of their decisions. There is, of course, considerable variation among the elite in this respect, but as a general rule in America today, it would be naïve to interpret any major elite group merely in terms of its ostensible personnel. The American elite often seems less a collection of persons than of corporate entities, which are in great part created and spoken for as standard types of 'personality.' Even the most apparently free-lance celebrity is usually a sort of synthetic production turned out each week by a disciplined staff which systematically ponders the effect of the easy ad-libbed gags the celebrity 'spontaneously' echoes.

Yet, in so far as the elite flourishes as a social class or as a set of men at the command posts, it will select and form certain types of personality, and reject others. The kind of moral and psychological beings men become is in large part determined by the values they experience and the institutional roles they are allowed and expected to play. From the biographer's point of view, a man of the upper classes is formed by his relations with others like himself in a series of small intimate groupings through which he passes and to which throughout his lifetime he may return. So conceived, the elite is a set of higher circles whose members are selected, trained and certified and permitted intimate access to those who command the impersonal institutional hierarchies of modern society. If there is any one key to the *psychological* idea of the elite, it is that they combine in their persons an awareness of impersonal decision-making with intimate sensibilities shared with one another. To understand the elite as a social class we must examine a whole series of smaller face-to-face milieux, the most obvious of which, historically, has been the upper-class family, but the most important of which today are the proper secondary school and the metropolitan club.[6]

5

These several notions of the elite, when appropriately understood, are intricately bound up with one another, and we shall use them all in this examination of American success. We shall study each of several higher circles as offering candidates for the elite, and we shall do so in terms of the major institutions making up the total society of America; within and between each of these institutions, we shall trace the interrelations of wealth and power and prestige. But our main concern is with the power of those who now occupy the command posts, and with the role which they are enacting in the history of our epoch.

Such an elite may be conceived as omnipotent, and its powers thought of as a great hidden design. Thus, in vulgar Marxism, events and trends are explained by reference to 'the will of the bourgeoisie'; in Nazism, by reference to 'the conspiracy of the Jews'; by the petty right in America today, by reference to 'the hidden force' of Communist spies. According to such notions of the omnipotent elite as historical cause, the elite is never an entirely visible agency. It is, in fact, a secular substitute for the will of God, being realized in a sort of providential design, except that usually non-elite men are thought capable of opposing it and eventually overcoming it.*

The opposite view—of the elite as impotent—is now quite popular among liberal-minded observers. Far from being omnipotent, the elites are thought to be so scattered as to lack any coherence as a historical force. Their invisibility is not the invisibility of secrecy but the invisibility of the multitude. Those who occupy the formal places of authority are so check-mated—by other elites exerting pressure, or by the public as an electorate, or by constitutional codes—that, although there may be upper classes, there is no ruling class; although there may be men of power, there is no power elite; although there may be a system of stratification, it

---

* Those who charge that Communist agents have been or are in the government, as well as those frightened by them, never raise the question: 'Well, suppose there are Communists in high places, how much power do they have?' They simply assume that men in high places, or in this case even those in positions from which they might influence such men, do decide important events. Those who think Communist agents lost China to the Soviet bloc, or influenced loyal Americans to lose it, simply assume that there is a set of men who decide such matters, actively or by neglect or by stupidity. Many others, who do not believe that Communist agents were so influential, still assume that loyal American decision-makers lost it all by themselves.

has no effective top. In the extreme, this view of the elite, as weakened by compromise and disunited to the point of nullity, is a substitute for impersonal collective fate; for, in this view, the decisions of the visible men of the higher circles do not count in history.*

Internationally, the image of the omnipotent elite tends to prevail. All good events and pleasing happenings are quickly imputed by the opinion-makers to the leaders of their own nation; all bad events and unpleasant experiences are imputed to the enemy abroad. In both cases, the omnipotence of evil rulers or of virtuous leaders is assumed. Within the nation, the use of such rhetoric is rather more complicated: when men speak of the power of their own party or circle, they and their leaders are, of course, impotent; only 'the people' are omnipotent. But, when they speak of the power of their opponent's party or circle, they impute to them omnipotence; 'the people' are now powerlessly taken in.

More generally, American men of power tend, by convention, to deny that they are powerful. No American runs for office in order to rule or even govern, but only to serve; he does not become a bureaucrat or even an official, but a public servant. And nowadays, as I have already pointed out, such postures have become standard features of the public-relations programs of all men of power. So firm a part of the style of power-wielding have they become that conservative writers readily misinterpret them as indicating a trend toward an 'amorphous power situation.'

But the 'power situation' of America today is less amorphous than is the perspective of those who see it as a romantic confusion. It is less a flat, momentary 'situation' than a graded, durable structure. And if those who occupy its top grades are not omnipotent, neither are they impotent. It is the form and the height of the

---

* The idea of the impotent elite, as we shall have occasion to see, in ELEVEN: The Theory of Balance, is mightily supported by the notion of an automatic economy in which the problem of power is solved for the economic elite by denying its existence. No one has enough power to make a real difference; events are the results of an anonymous balance. For the political elite too, the model of balance solves the problem of power. Parallel to the market-economy, there is the leaderless democracy in which no one is responsible for anything and everyone is responsible for everything; the will of men acts only through the impersonal workings of the electoral process.

gradation of power that we must examine if we would understand
the degree of power held and exercised by the elite.

If the power to decide such national issues as are decided were
shared in an absolutely equal way, there would be no power
elite; in fact, there would be no *gradation* of power, but only a
radical homogeneity. At the opposite extreme as well, if the power
to decide issues were absolutely monopolized by one small group,
there would be no gradation of power; there would simply be this
small group in command, and below it, the undifferentiated, dominated masses. American society today represents neither the one
nor the other of these extremes, but a conception of them is none
the less useful: it makes us realize more clearly the question of the
structure of power in the United States and the position of the
power elite within it.

Within each of the most powerful institutional orders of modern
society there is a gradation of power. The owner of a roadside
fruit stand does not have as much power in any area of social or
economic or political decision as the head of a multi-million-dollar
fruit corporation; no lieutenant on the line is as powerful as the
Chief of Staff in the Pentagon; no deputy sheriff carries as much
authority as the President of the United States. Accordingly, the
problem of defining the power elite concerns the level at which
we wish to draw the line. By lowering the line, we could define
the elite out of existence; by raising it, we could make the elite
a very small circle indeed. In a preliminary and minimum way,
we draw the line crudely, in charcoal as it were: By the power
elite, we refer to those political, economic, and military circles
which as an intricate set of overlapping cliques share decisions
having at least national consequences. In so far as national events
are decided, the power elite are those who decide them.

To say that there are obvious gradations of power and of opportunities to decide within modern society is not to say that the
powerful are united, that they fully know what they do, or that
they are consciously joined in conspiracy. Such issues are best
faced if we concern ourselves, in the first instance, more with
the structural position of the high and mighty, and with the consequences of their decisions, than with the extent of their aware-

ness or the purity of their motives. To understand the power elite, we must attend to three major keys:

I. One, which we shall emphasize throughout our discussion of each of the higher circles, is the psychology of the several elites in their respective milieux. In so far as the power elite is composed of men of similar origin and education, in so far as their careers and their styles of life are similar, there are psychological and social bases for their unity, resting upon the fact that they are of similar social type and leading to the fact of their easy intermingling. This kind of unity reaches its frothier apex in the sharing of that prestige that is to be had in the world of the celebrity; it achieves a more solid culmination in the fact of the interchangeability of positions within and between the three dominant institutional orders.

II. Behind such psychological and social unity as we may find, are the structure and the mechanics of those institutional hierarchies over which the political directorate, the corporate rich, and the high military now preside. The greater the scale of these bureaucratic domains, the greater the scope of their respective elite's power. How each of the major hierarchies is shaped and and what relations it has with the other hierarchies determine in large part the relations of their rulers. If these hierarchies are scattered and disjointed, then their respective elites tend to be scattered and disjointed; if they have many interconnections and points of coinciding interest, then their elites tend to form a coherent kind of grouping.

The unity of the elite is not a simple reflection of the unity of institutions, but men and institutions are always related, and our conception of the power elite invites us to determine that relation. Today in America there are several important structural coincidences of interest between these institutional domains, including the development of a permanent war establishment by a privately incorporated economy inside a political vacuum.

III. The unity of the power elite, however, does not rest solely on psychological similarity and social intermingling, nor entirely on the structural coincidences of commanding positions and interests. At times it is the unity of a more explicit co-ordination. To say that these three higher circles are increasingly co-ordinated, that this is *one* basis of their unity, and that at times—as during the

wars—such co-ordination is quite decisive, is not to say that the
co-ordination is total or continuous, or even that it is very sure-
footed. Much less is it to say that willful co-ordination is the sole
or the major basis of their unity, or that the power elite has
emerged as the realization of a plan. But it is to say that as the
institutional mechanics of our time have opened up avenues to
men pursuing their several interests, many of them have come to
see that these several interests could be realized more easily if
they worked together, in informal as well as in more formal ways,
and accordingly they have done so.

6

It is not my thesis that for all epochs of human history and in
all nations, a creative minority, a ruling class, an omnipotent elite,
shape all historical events. Such statements, upon careful examination, usually turn out to be mere tautologies,[7] and even when
they are not, they are so entirely general as to be useless in the
attempt to understand the history of the present. The minimum
definition of the power elite as those who decide whatever is
decided of major consequence, does not imply that the members
of this elite are always and necessarily the history-makers; neither does it imply that they never are. We must not confuse the
conception of the elite, which we wish to define, with one theory
about their role: that they are the history-makers of our time. To
define the elite, for example, as 'those who rule America' is less to
define a conception than to state one hypothesis about the role
and power of that elite. No matter how we might define the elite,
the extent of its members' power is subject to historical variation.
If, in a dogmatic way, we try to include that variation in our generic definition, we foolishly limit the use of a needed conception.
If we insist that the elite be defined as a strictly coordinated class
that continually and absolutely rules, we are closing off from our
view much to which the term more modestly defined might open
to our observation. In short, our definition of the power elite cannot properly contain dogma concerning the degree and kind of
power that ruling groups everywhere have. Much less should it
permit us to smuggle into our discussion a theory of history.

During most of human history, historical change has not been
visible to the people who were involved in it, or even to those

enacting it. Ancient Egypt and Mesopotamia, for example, endured for some four hundred generations with but slight changes in their basic structure. That is six and a half times as long as the entire Christian era, which has only prevailed some sixty generations; it is about eighty times as long as the five generations of the United States' existence. But now the tempo of change is so rapid, and the means of observation so accessible, that the interplay of event and decision seems often to be quite historically visible, if we will only look carefully and from an adequate vantage point.

When knowledgeable journalists tell us that 'events, not men, shape the big decisions,' they are echoing the theory of history as Fortune, Chance, Fate, or the work of The Unseen Hand. For 'events' is merely a modern word for these older ideas, all of which separate men from history-making, because all of them lead us to believe that history goes on behind men's backs. History is drift with no mastery; within it there is action but no deed; history is mere happening and the event intended by no one.[8]

The course of events in our time depends more on a series of human decisions than on any inevitable fate. The sociological meaning of 'fate' is simply this: that, when the decisions are innumerable and each one is of small consequence, all of them add up in a way no man intended—to history as fate. But not all epochs are equally fateful. As the circle of those who decide is narrowed, as the means of decision are centralized and the consequences of decisions become enormous, then the course of great events often rests upon the decisions of determinable circles. This does not necessarily mean that the same circle of men follow through from one event to another in such a way that all of history is merely their plot. The power of the elite does not necessarily mean that history is not also shaped by a series of small decisions, none of which are thought out. It does not mean that a hundred small arrangements and compromises and adaptations may not be built into the going policy and the living event. The idea of the power elite implies nothing about the process of decision-making as such: it is an attempt to delimit the social areas within which that process, whatever its character, goes on. It is a conception of who is involved in the process.

The degree of foresight and control of those who are involved in decisions that count may also vary. The idea of the power elite does not mean that the estimations and calculated risks upon which decisions are made are not often wrong and that the consequences are sometimes, indeed often, not those intended. Often those who make decisions are trapped by their own inadequacies and blinded by their own errors.

Yet in our time the pivotal moment does arise, and at that moment, small circles do decide or fail to decide. In either case, they are an elite of power. The dropping of the A-bombs over Japan was such a moment; the decision on Korea was such a moment; the confusion about Quemoy and Matsu, as well as before Dienbienphu were such moments; the sequence of maneuvers which involved the United States in World War II was such a 'moment.' Is it not true that much of the history of our times is composed of such moments? And is not that what is meant when it is said that we live in a time of big decisions, of decisively centralized power?

Most of us do not try to make sense of our age by believing in a Greek-like, eternal recurrence, nor by a Christian belief in a salvation to come, nor by any steady march of human progress. Even though we do not reflect upon such matters, the chances are we believe with Burckhardt that we live in a mere succession of events; that sheer continuity is the only principle of history. History is merely one thing after another; history is meaningless in that it is not the realization of any determinate plot. It is true, of course, that our sense of continuity, our feeling for the history of our time, is affected by crisis. But we seldom look beyond the immediate crisis or the crisis felt to be just ahead. We believe neither in fate nor providence; and we assume, without talking about it, that 'we'—as a nation—can decisively shape the future but that 'we' as individuals somehow cannot do so.

Any meaning history has, 'we' shall have to give to it by our actions. Yet the fact is that although we are all of us within history we do not all possess equal powers to make history. To pretend that we do is sociological nonsense and political irresponsibility. It is nonsense because any group or any individual is limited, first of all, by the technical and institutional means of power at its command; we do not all have equal access to the means of power that now exist, nor equal influence over their use. To pretend that 'we' are all history-makers is politically irresponsible because it obfuscates any attempt to locate responsibility for the consequential decisions of men who do have access to the means of power.

From even the most superficial examination of the history of the western society we learn that the power of decision-makers is first of all limited by the level of technique, by the *means* of power and violence and organization that prevail in a given society. In this connection we also learn that there is a fairly straight line running upward through the history of the West; that the means of oppression and exploitation, of violence and destruction, as well as the means of production and reconstruction, have been progressively enlarged and increasingly centralized.

As the institutional means of power and the means of communications that tie them together have become steadily more efficient, those now in command of them have come into command of instruments of rule quite unsurpassed in the history of mankind. And we are not yet at the climax of their development. We can no longer lean upon or take soft comfort from the historical ups and downs of ruling groups of previous epochs. In that sense, Hegel is correct: we learn from history that we cannot learn from it.

For every epoch and for every social structure, we must work out an answer to the question of the power of the elite. The ends of men are often merely hopes, but means are facts within some men's control. That is why all means of power tend to become ends to an elite that is in command of them. And that is why we may define the power elite in terms of the means of power—as those who occupy the command posts. The major questions about the American elite today—its composition, its unity, its power— must now be faced with due attention to the awesome means of power available to them. Caesar could do less with Rome than Napoleon with France; Napoleon less with France than Lenin with Russia; and Lenin less with Russia than Hitler with Germany. But what was Caesar's power at its peak compared with the power of the changing inner circle of Soviet Russia or of America's temporary administrations? The men of either circle can cause great cities to be wiped out in a single night, and in a few weeks turn continents into thermonuclear wastelands. That the facilities of power are enormously enlarged and decisively centralized means that the decisions of small groups are now more consequential.

But to know that the top posts of modern social structures now permit more commanding decisions is not to know that the elite who occupy these posts are the history-makers. We might grant that the enlarged and integrated economic, military, and political structures are shaped to permit command decisions, yet still feel that, as it were, 'they run themselves,' that those who are on top, in short, are determined in their decisions by 'necessity,' which presumably means by the instituted roles that they play and the situation of these institutions in the total structure of society.

Do the elite determine the roles that they enact? Or do the roles that institutions make available to them determine the power of the elite? The general answer—and no general answer is sufficient—is that in different kinds of structures and epochs elites are quite differently related to the roles that they play: nothing in the nature of the elite or in the nature of history dictates an answer. It is also true that if most men and women take whatever roles are permitted to them and enact them as they are expected to by virtue of their position, this is precisely what the elite need *not* do, and often do not do. They may call into question the structure, their position within it, or the way in which they are to enact that position.

Nobody called for or permitted Napoleon to chase *Parlement* home on the 18 *Brumaire,* and later to transform his consulate into an emperorship.[9] Nobody called for or permitted Adolf Hitler to proclaim himself 'Leader and Chancellor' the day President Hindenburg died, to abolish and usurp roles by merging the presidency and the chancellorship. Nobody called for or permitted Franklin D. Roosevelt to make the series of decisions that led to the entrance of the United States into World War II. It was no 'historical necessity,' but a man named Truman who, with a few other men, decided to drop a bomb on Hiroshima. It was no historical necessity, but an argument within a small circle of men that defeated Admiral Radford's proposal to bomb troops before Dienbienphu. Far from being dependent upon the structure of institutions, modern elites may smash one structure and set up another in which they then enact quite different roles. In fact, such destruction and creation of institutional structures, with all their means of power, when events seem to turn out well, is just what is involved in 'great leadership,' or, when they seem to turn out badly, great tyranny.

Some elite men *are*, of course, typically role-determined, but others are at times role-determining. They determine not only the role they play but today the roles of millions of other men. The creation of pivotal roles and their pivotal enactment occurs most readily when social structures are undergoing epochal transitions. It is clear that the international development of the United States to one of the two 'great powers'—along with the new means of annihilation and administrative and psychic domination—have made of the United States in the middle years of the twentieth century precisely such an epochal pivot.

There is nothing about history that tells us that a power elite cannot make it. To be sure, the will of such men is always limited, but never before have the limits been so broad, for never before have the means of power been so enormous. It is this that makes our situation so precarious, and makes even more important an understanding of the powers and the limitations of the American elite. The problem of the nature and the power of this elite is now the only realistic and serious way to raise again the problem of responsible government.

7

Those who have abandoned criticism for the new American celebration take readily to the view that the elite is impotent. If they were politically serious, they ought, on the basis of their view, to say to those presumably in charge of American policy:[10]

'One day soon, you may believe that you have an opportunity to drop a bomb or a chance to exacerbate further your relations with allies or with the Russians who might also drop it. But don't be so foolish as to believe that you really have a choice. You have neither choice nor chance. The whole Complex Situation of which you are merely one balancing part is the result of Economic and Social Forces, and so will be the fateful outcome. So stand by quietly, like Tolstoy's general, and let events proceed. Even if you did act, the consequences would not be what you intended, even if you had an intention.

'But—if events come out well, talk as though you had decided.

For then men have had moral choices and the power to make them
and are, of course, responsible.

'If events come out badly, say that *you* didn't have the real
choice, and are, of course, not accountable: *they*, the others, had
the choice and they are responsible. You can get away with this
even though you have at your command half the world's forces
and God knows how many bombs and bombers. For you are, in
fact, an impotent item in the historical fate of your times; and
moral responsibility is an illusion, although it is of great use if handled in a really alert public relations manner.'

The one implication that can be drawn from all such fatalisms
is that if fortune or providence rules, then no elite of power can
be justly considered a source of historical decisions, and the idea—
much less the demand—of responsible leadership is an idle and an
irresponsible notion. For clearly, an impotent elite, the plaything
of history, cannot be held accountable. If the elite of our time do
not have power, they cannot be held responsible; as men in a difficult position, they should engage our sympathies. The people of
the United States are ruled by sovereign fortune; they, and with
them their elite, are fatally overwhelmed by consequences they
cannot control. If that is so, we ought all to do what many have in
fact already done: withdraw entirely from political reflection and
action into a materially comfortable and entirely private life.

If, on the other hand, we believe that war and peace and slump
and prosperity are, precisely now, no longer matters of 'fortune' or
'fate,' but that, precisely now more than ever, they are controllable,
then we must ask—controllable by whom? The answer must be:
By whom else but those who now command the enormously enlarged and decisively centralized means of decision and power?
We may then ask: Why don't they, then? And for the answer to
that, we must understand the context and the character of the
American elite today.

There is nothing in the idea of the elite as impotent which
should deter us from asking just such questions, which are now
the most important questions political men can ask. The American
elite is neither omnipotent nor impotent. These are abstract abso-
lutes used publicly by spokesmen, as excuses or as boasts, but in
terms of which we may seek to clarify the political issues before
us, which just now are above all the issues of responsible power.

There is nothing in 'the nature of history' *in our epoch* that rules out the pivotal function of small groups of decision-makers. On the contrary, the structure of the present is such as to make this not only a reasonable, but a rather compelling, view.

There is nothing in 'the psychology of man,' or in the social manner by which men are shaped and selected for and by the command posts of modern society, that makes unreasonable the view that they do confront choices and that the choices they make—or their failure to confront them—are history-making in their consequences.

Accordingly, political men now have every reason to hold the American power elite accountable for a decisive range of the historical events that make up the history of the present.

It is as fashionable, just now, to suppose that there is no power elite, as it was fashionable in the 'thirties to suppose a set of ruling-class villains to be the source of all social injustice and public malaise. I should be as far from supposing that some simple and unilateral ruling class could be firmly located as the prime mover of American society, as I should be from supposing that all historical change in America today is merely impersonal drift.

The view that all is blind drift is largely a fatalist projection of one's own feeling of impotence and perhaps, if one has ever been active politically in a principled way, a salve of one's guilt.

The view that all of history is due to the conspiracy of an easily located set of villains, or of heroes, is also a hurried projection from the difficult effort to understand how shifts in the structure of society open opportunities to various elites and how various elites take advantage or fail to take advantage of them. To accept either view—of all history as conspiracy or of all history as drift—is to relax the effort to understand the facts of power and the ways of the powerful.

8

In my attempt to discern the shape of the power elite of our time, and thus to give a responsible meaning to the anonymous 'They,' which the underlying population opposes to the anonymous 'We,' I shall begin by briefly examining the higher elements which most people know best: the new and the old upper classes of local society and the metropolitan 400. I shall then outline the world of the celebrity, attempting to show that the prestige system of American society has now for the first time become truly national in scope; and that the more trivial and glamorous aspects of this national system of status tend at once to distract attention from its more authoritarian features and to justify the power that it often conceals.

In examining the very rich and the chief executives, I shall indicate how neither 'America's Sixty Families' nor 'The Managerial Revolution' provides an adequate idea of the transformation of the upper classes as they are organized today in the privileged stratum of the corporate rich.

After describing the American statesman as a historical type, I shall attempt to show that what observers in the Progressive Era called 'the invisible government' has now become quite visible; and that what is usually taken to be the central content of politics, the pressures and the campaigns and the congressional maneuvering, has, in considerable part, now been relegated to the middle levels of power.

In discussing the military ascendancy, I shall try to make clear how it has come about that admirals and generals have assumed positions of decisive political and economic relevance, and how, in doing so, they have found many points of coinciding interests with the corporate rich and the political directorate of the visible government.

After these and other trends are made as plain as I can make them, I shall return to the master problems of the power elite, as well as take up the complementary notion of the mass society.

What I am asserting is that in this particular epoch a conjunction of historical circumstances has led to the rise of an elite of power; that the men of the circles composing this elite, severally and collectively, now make such key decisions as are made; and that, given the enlargement and the centralization of the means of power now available, the decisions that they make and fail to make carry more consequences for more people than has ever been the case in the world history of mankind.

I am also asserting that there has developed on the middle levels of power, a semi-organized stalemate, and that on the bottom level there has come into being a mass-like society which has little resemblence to the image of a society in which voluntary associations and classic publics hold the keys to power. The top of the American system of power is much more unified and much more powerful, the bottom is much more fragmented, and in truth, impotent, than is generally supposed by those who are distracted by the middling units of power which neither express such will as exists at the bottom nor determine the decisions at the top.

2

Local Society

In every town and small city of America an upper set of families stands above the middle classes and towers over the underlying population of clerks and wage workers. The members of this set possess more than do others of whatever there is locally to possess; they hold the keys to local decision; their names and faces are often printed in the local paper; in fact, they own the newspaper as well as the radio station; they also own the three important local plants and most of the commercial properties along the main street; they direct the banks. Mingling closely with one another, they are quite conscious of the fact that they belong to the leading class of the leading families.

All their sons and daughters go to college, often after private schools; then they marry one another, or other boys and girls from similar families in similar towns. After they are well married, they come to possess, to occupy, to decide. The son of one of these old families, to his father's chagrin and his grandfather's fury, is now an executive in the local branch of a national corporation. The leading family doctor has two sons, one of whom now takes up the practice; the other—who is soon to marry the daughter of the second largest factory—will probably be the next district attorney. So it has traditionally been, and so it is today in the small towns of America.

Class consciousness is not equally characteristic of all levels of American society: it is most apparent in the upper class. Among the underlying population everywhere in America there is much confusion and blurring of the lines of demarcation, of the status value of clothing and houses, of the ways of money-making and of money-spending. The people of the lower and middle classes are of course differentiated by the values, things, and experiences to which differing amounts of income lead, but often they are aware neither of these values nor of their class bases.

Those of the upper strata, on the other hand, if only because they are fewer in number, are able with much more ease to know more about one another, to maintain among themselves a common tradition, and thus to be conscious of their own kind. They have the money and the time required to uphold their common standards. A propertied class, they are also a more or less distinct set of people who, mingling with one another, form compact circles with common claims to recognition as the leading families of their cities.

1

Examining the small city, both the novelist and the sociologist have felt most clearly the drama of the old and the new upper classes. The struggle for status which they have observed going on in these towns may be seen on a historic scale in the modern course of the whole of Western Society; for centuries the parvenues and snobs of new upper classes have stood in tension with the 'old guard.' There are, of course, regional variations but across the country the small-town rich are surprisingly standardized. In these cities today, two types of upper classes prevail, one composed of rentier and socially older families, the other of newer families which, economically and socially, are of a more entrepreneurial type. Members of these two top classes understand the several distinctions between them, although each has its own particular view of them.[1]

It should not be supposed that the old upper class is necessarily 'higher' than the new, or that the new is simply a *nouveau riche*, struggling to drape new-won wealth in the prestige garments worn so easily by the old. The new upper class has a style of life of its own, and although its members—especially the women —borrow considerably from the old upper-class style, they also— especially the men—debunk that style in the name of their own values and aspirations. In many ways, these two upper sets compete for prestige and their competition involves some mutual deflation of claims for merit.

The old upper-class person feels that his prestige originates in time itself. 'Somewhere in the past,' he seems to say, 'my Original Ancestor rose up to become the Founder Of This Local Family Line and now His Blood flows in my veins. I am what My Family has been, and My Family has always been among the very best people.' In New England and in the South, more families than in other regions are acutely conscious of family lines and old residence, and more resistant to the social ascendancy of the newly rich and the newly arrived. There is perhaps a stronger and more embracing sense of family, which, especially in the South, comes to include long faithful servants as well as grandchildren. The sense of kinship may be extended even to those who, although not related by marriage or blood, are considered as 'cousins' or 'aunts' because they 'grew up with mother.' Old upper-class families thus tend to form an endogenous cousinhood, whose clan piety and sense of kinship lead to a reverence for the past and often to a cultivated interest in the history of the region in which the clan has for so long played such an honorable role.

To speak of 'old families' is of course to speak of 'wealthy old families,' but in the status world of the old upper class, ready money and property are simply assumed—and then played down: 'Of course, you have to have enough of this world's goods to stand the cost of keeping up, of entertaining and for church donations . . . but social standing is more than money.' The men and women of the old upper class generally consider money in a negative way— as something in which the new upper-class people are too closely interested. 'I'm sorry to say that our larger industrialists are increasingly money-conscious,' they say, and in saying it, they have in mind the older generation of industrialists who are now retired, generally on real-estate holdings; these rich men and their women folk, the old upper class believes, were and are more interested in 'community and social' qualifications than in mere money.

One major theme in old upper-class discussions of smaller business people is that they made a great deal of money during the late war, but that socially they aren't to be allowed to count. Another theme concerns the less respectable ways in which the money of the newly moneyed people has been earned. They mention pin-ball concessionaires, tavern keepers, and people in the trucking lines. And, having patronized them, they are quite aware of the wartime black markets.

The continuance of the old-family line as the basis of prestige is challenged by the ripsnorting style as well as the money of the new upper classes, which World War II expanded and enriched, and made socially bold. Their style, the old upper classes feel, is replacing the older, quieter one. Underlying this status tension, there is often a tendency of decline in the economic basis of many old upper-class families, which, in many towns, is mainly real estate. Yet the old upper class still generally has its firm hold on local financial institutions: in the market centers of Georgia and Nebraska, the trading and manufacturing towns of Vermont and California—the old upper-class banker is usually the lord of his community's domain, lending prestige to the businessmen with whom he associates, naming The Church by merely belonging to it. Thus embodying salvation, social standing and financial soundness, he is accepted by others at his own shrewd and able valuation.

In the South the tension between old and new upper classes is often more dramatic than in other regions, for here old families have been based on land ownership and the agricultural economy. The synthesis of new wealth with older status, which of course has been under way since the Civil War, has been accelerated since the slump and World War II. The old southern aristocracy, in fictional image and in researched fact, is indeed often in a sorry state of decline. If it does not join the rising class based on industry and trade, it will surely die out, for when given sufficient time if status does not remain wealthy it crumbles into ignored eccentricity. Without sufficient money, quiet dignity and self-satisfied withdrawal comes to seem mere decay and even decadence.

The emphasis upon family descent, coupled with withdrawal, tends to enhance the status of older people, especially of those older women who become dowager judges of the conduct of the young. Such a situation is not conducive to the marriage of old upper-class daughters to sons of a new but up-and-coming class of wealth. Yet the industrialization of the smaller cities steadily breaks up old status formations and leads to new ones: the rise of the enriched industrialist and tradesman inevitably leads to the decline of the land-owning aristocracy. In the South, as well as elsewhere, the larger requirements of capital for agricultural endeavor on sufficient scale, as well as favorable taxation and subsidy for 'farmers,' lead to new upper-class formations on the land as in the city.

The new and the old upper classes thus stand in the smaller cities eyeing one another with considerable tension, with some disdain, and with begrudging admiration. The upper-class man sees the old as having a prestige which he would like to have, but also as an old fogy blocking important business and political traffic and as a provincial, bound to the local set-up, without the vision to get up and go. The old upper-class man, in turn, eyes the new and thinks of him as too money-conscious, as having made money and as grabbing for more, but as not having acquired the social background or the style of cultured life befitting his financial rank, and as not really being interested in the civic life of the city, except in so far as he might use it for personal and alien ends.

When they come up against the prestige of the old upper class on business and on civic and political issues, the new upper-class men often translate that prestige into 'old age,' which is associated in their minds with the quiet, 'old-fashioned' manner, the slower civic tempo, and the dragging political views of the old upper class. They feel that the old upper-class people do not *use* their prestige to make money in the manner of the new upper class. They do not understand old prestige as something to be enjoyed; they see it in its political and economic relevance: when they do not have it, it is something standing in their way.*

* The woman of the new upper class has a somewhat different image: she often sees the prestige of the old upper class as something 'cultural' to appreciate. She often attempts to give to the old status an 'educational' meaning: this is especially true among those younger women of the station-wagon set whose husbands are professional men and who are themselves from a 'good college.' Having education themselves, and the time and money with which to organize cultural community affairs, the new upper-class women have more respect for the 'cultural' component of the old upper-class style than do their men. In thus acknowledging the social superiority of the older class, new upper-class women stress those of its themes which are available to them also. But such women form today the most reliable cash-in area for the status claims of

2

That the social and economic split of the upper classes is also a political split is not yet fully apparent in all localities, but it is a fact that has tended to become national since World War II.

Local upper classes—new and old, seen and unseen, active and passive—make up the social backbone of the Republican party. Members of the old upper class, however, do not seem as strident or as active politically in the postwar scene as do many of the new. Perhaps it is because they do not feel able, as Allison Davis and others have suggested of the old southern upper classes, 'to lessen the social distance between themselves and the voters.' Of course, everywhere their social position 'is clearly recognized by the officials. They are free from many of the minor legal restrictions, are almost never arrested for drunkenness or for minor traffic violations, are seldom called for jury duty, and usually receive any favors they request.'[2] They are, it is true, very much concerned with tax rates and property assessments, but these concerns, being fully shared by the new upper classes, are well served without the personal intervention of the old.

The new upper class often practices those noisy political emotions and status frustrations which, on a national scale and in extreme form, have been so readily observable in The Investigators. The key to these political emotions, in the Congress as in the local society, lies in the status psychology of the *nouveau riche*.* Such newly enriched classes—ranging from Texas multi-millionaires to petty Illinois war profiteers who have since consolidated their holdings—feel that they are somehow held down by the status pretensions of older wealth and older families. The suddenly $30,000-a-year insurance salesmen who drive the 260 hp cars and guiltily buy vulgar diamond rings for their wives; the suddenly $60,000-a-year businessmen who put in 50-foot swimming pools and do not know how to act toward their new servants—they feel

the old upper classes in the small towns. Toward the middle classes, in general, such women snobbishly assert: 'They might be interested in cultural things but they would not have the opportunities or background or education. They could take advantage of the lecture series, but they don't have the background for heading it.'

* See below, FOURTEEN: The Conservative Mood.

that they have achieved something and yet are not thought to be good enough to possess it fully. There are men in Texas today whose names are strictly local, but who have more money than many nationally prominent families of the East. But *they* are not often nationally prominent, and even when they are, it is not in just the same way.

Such feelings exist, on a smaller scale, in virtually every smaller city and town. They are not always articulated, and certainly they have not become the bases of any real political movement. But they lie back of the wide and deep gratification at beholding men of established prestige 'told off,' observing the general reprimanded by the upstart, hearing the parvenu familiarly, even insultingly, call the old wealthy by their first names in public controversy.

The political aim of the petty right formed among the new upper classes of the small cities is the destruction of the legislative achievements of the New and Fair Deals. Moreover, the rise of labor unions in many of these cities during the war, with more labor leaders clamoring to be on local civic boards; the increased security of the wage workers who during the war cashed larger weekly checks in stores and banks and crowded the sidewalks on Saturday; the big new automobiles of the small people—all these class changes of the last two decades psychologically threaten the new upper cass by reducing their own feelings of significance, their own sense of a fit order of prestige.

The old upper classes are also made less socially secure by such goings on in the street, in the stores, and in the bank; but after all, they reason: 'These people do not really touch us. All they have is money.' The newly rich, however, being less socially firm than the old, do feel themselves to be of lesser worth as they see others also rise in the economic worlds of the small cities.

Local society is a structure of power as well as a hierarchy of status; at its top there is a set of cliques or 'crowds' whose members judge and decide the important community issues, as well as many larger issues of state and nation in which 'the community' is involved.[3] Usually, although by no means always, these cliques are composed of old upper-class people; they include the larger businessmen and those who control the banks who usually also have connections with the major real-estate holders. Informally organized, these cliques are often each centered in the several economic functions: there is an industrial, a retailing, a banking clique. The cliques overlap, and there are usually some men who, moving from one to another, co-ordinate viewpoints and decisions. There are also the lawyers and administrators of the solid rentier families, who, by the power of proxy and by the many contacts between old and new wealth they embody, tie together and focus in decision the power of money, of credit, of organization.

Immediately below such cliques are the hustlers, largely of new upper-class status, who carry out the decisions and programs of the top—sometimes anticipating them and always trying to do so. Here are the 'operations' men—the vice-presidents of the banks, successful small businessmen, the ranking public officials, contractors, and executives of local industries. This number two level shades off into the third string men—the heads of civic agencies, organization officials, the pettier civic leaders, newspaper men, and, finally, into the fourth order of the power hierarchy—the rank and file of the professional and business strata, the ministers, the leading teachers, social workers, personnel directors.

On almost any given topic of interest or decision, some top clique, or even some one key man, becomes strategic to the decision at hand and to the informal co-ordination of its support among the important cliques. Now it is the man who is the clique's liaison with the state governor; now it is the bankers' clique; now it is the man who is well liked by the rank and file of both Rotary Club and Chamber of Commerce, both Community Chest and Bar Association.

Power does not reside in these middle-level organizations; key decisions are not made by their membership. Top men belong to them, but are only infrequently active in them. As associations, they help put into effect the policy-line worked out by the higher circles of power; they are training grounds in which younger hustlers of the top prove themselves; and sometimes, especially in the smaller cities, they are recruiting grounds for new members of the top.

'We would not go to the "associations," as you call them—that is, not right away,' one powerful man of a sizable city in the mid-South told Professor Floyd Hunter. 'A lot of those associations, if you mean by associations the Chamber of Commerce or the Community Council, sit around and discuss "goals" and "ideals." I don't know what a lot of those things mean. I'll be frank with you, I do not get onto a lot of those committees. A lot of the others in town do, but I don't ... Charles Homer is the biggest man in our crowd ... When he gets an idea, others will get the idea ... recently he got the idea that Regional City should be the national headquarters for an International Trade Council. He called in some of us [the inner crowd], and he talked briefly about his idea. He did not talk much. We do not engage in loose talk about the "ideals" of the situation and all that other stuff. We get right down to the problem, that is, how to get this Council. We all think it is a good idea right around the circle. There are six of us in the meeting ... All of us are assigned tasks to carry out. Moster is to draw up the papers of incorporation. He is the lawyer. I have a group of friends that I will carry along. Everyone else has a group of friends he will do the same with. These fellows are what you might call followers.

'We decide we need to raise $65,000 to put this thing over. We could raise that amount within our own crowd, but eventually this thing is going to be a community proposition, so we decide to bring the other crowds in on the deal. We decide to have a meeting at the Grandview Club with select members of other crowds ... When we meet at the Club at dinner with the other crowds, Mr. Homer makes a brief talk; again, he does not need to talk long. He ends his talk by saying he believes in his proposition enough that he is willing to put $10,000 of his own money into it for the first year. He sits down. You can see some of the other crowds getting their heads together, and the Growers Bank crowd, not to be outdone, offers a like amount plus a guarantee that they will go along with the project for three years. Others throw in $5,000 to $10,000 until—I'd say within thirty or forty minutes—we have pledges of the money we need. In three hours the whole thing is settled, including the time for eating!

'There is one detail I left out, and it is an important one. We went into that meeting with a board of directors picked. The constitution was all written, and the man who was to head the council as executive was named ... a third-string man, a fellow who will take advice ... The public doesn't know anything about the project until it reaches the stage I've been talking about. After the

matter is financially sound, then we go to the newspapers and say
there is a proposal for consideration. Of course, it is not news to a
lot of people by then, but the Chamber committees and other civic
organizations are brought in on the idea. They all think it's a good
idea. They help to get the Council located and established. That's
about all there is to it.'[4]

3

The status drama of the old and the new upper class; the class
structure that underpins that drama; the power system of the
higher cliques—these now form the rather standard, if somewhat
intricate, pattern of the upper levels of local society. But we could
not understand that pattern or what is happening to it, were we to
forget that all these cities are very much part of a national system
of status and power and wealth. Despite the loyal rhetoric practiced by many Congressional spokesmen, no local society is in
truth a sovereign locality. During the past century, local society
has become part of a national economy; its status and power hierarchies have come to be subordinate parts of the larger hierarchies of the nation. Even as early as the decades after the Civil
War, persons of local eminence were becoming—merely local.[5]
Men whose sphere of active decision and public acclaim was regional and national in scope were rising into view. Today, to remain merely local is to fail; it is to be overshadowed by the
wealth, the power, and the status of nationally important men. To
succeed is to leave local society behind—although certification by
it may be needed in order to be selected for national cliques.

All truly old ways in America are, of course, rural. Yet the value
of rural origin and of rural residences is sometimes ambiguous.
On the one hand, there is the tradition of the town against the hayseed, of the big city against the small-town hick, and in many
smaller cities, some prestige is achieved by those who, unlike the
lower, working classes, have been in the city for all of one generation. On the other hand, men who have achieved eminence often
boast of the solidity of their rural origin; which may be due to the
Jeffersonian ethos which holds rural virtues to be higher than the
ways of the city, or to the desire to show how very far one has
come.

If, in public life, the farm is often a good place to have come from, in social life, it is always a good place to own and to visit. Both small-city and big-city upper classes now quite typically own and visit their 'places in the country.' In part, all this, which even in the Middle West began as far back as the eighteen-nineties, is a way by which the merely rich attempt to anchor themselves in what is old and esteemed, of proving with cash and loving care and sometimes with inconvenience, their reverence for the past. So in the South there is the exactly restored Old Plantation Mansion, in Texas and California the huge cattle spread or the manicured fruit ranch, in Iowa the model farm with its purebred stock and magnificent barns. There is also the motive of buying the farm as an investment and as a tax evasion, as well as, of course, the pleasure of such a seasonable residence and hobby.

For the small town and the surrounding countryside, these facts mean that local status arrangements can no longer be strictly local. Small town and countryside are already pretty well consolidated, for wealthy farmers, especially upon retiring, often move into the small city, and wealthy urban families have bought much country land. In one middle-western community, Mr. Hollingshead has reported, some twenty-five families of pioneer ancestry have accumulated more than sixty per cent of the surrounding one hundred sixty square miles of rich agricultural land.[6] Such concentration has been strengthened by marriages between rural and urban upper-class families. Locally, any 'rural aristocracy' that may prevail is already centered in at least the small city; rural upper classes and the local society of smaller cities are in close contact, often in fact, belonging to the same higher cousinhood.

In addition to the farms owned by city families and the town-centered activities and residences of rural families, there is the increased seaçonal change of residence among both rural and small-town upper classes. The women and children of the rural upper classes go to 'the lake' for the summer period, and the men for long week ends, even as New York families do the same in the winters in Florida. The democratization of the seasonable vacation to coast, mountain, or island now extends to local upper classes of small cities and rural district, where thirty years ago it was more confined to metropolitan upper classes.

The connections of small town with countryside, and the cen-

tering of the status worlds of both upon the larger city, are most
dramatically revealed when into the country surrounding a small
town there moves a set of gentlemen farmers. These seasonal
residents are involved in the conduct and values of the larger cities
in which they live; they know nothing and often care less for local
claims to eminence. With their country estates, they come to occupy the top rung of what used to be called the farm ladder,
although they know little or nothing of the lower rungs of that
ladder. In one middle-western township studied by Evon Vogt,
such urban groups own half the land.[7] They do not seek connections with local society and often do not even welcome its advances, but they are passing on these country estates to their children and now even to their grandchildren.

The members of local society, rural and urban, can attempt to
follow one of two courses: they can withdraw and try to debunk
the immoral ways of the newcomers, or they can attempt to join
them, in which case they too will come to focus their social ways
of life upon the metropolitan area. But whichever course they
elect, they soon come to know, often with bitterness, that the new
upper class as well as the local upper-middle classes, among whom
they once cashed in their claims for status, are watching them
with close attention and sometimes with amusement. What was
once a little principality, a seemingly self-sufficient world of status, is becoming an occasionally used satellite of the big-city upper
class.

What has been happening in and to local society is its consolidation with the surrounding rural area, and its gradual incorporation in a national system of power and status. Muncie, Indiana, is
now much closer to Indianapolis and Chicago than it was fifty
years ago; and the upper classes of Muncie travel farther and
travel more frequently than do the local middle and lower classes.
There are few small towns today whose upper classes, both new
and old, are not likely to visit a near-by large city at least every
month or so. Such travel is now a standard operation of the business, educational, and social life of the small-city rich. They have
more friends at a distance and more frequent relations with them.
The world of the local upper-class person is simply larger than it

was in 1900 and larger than the worlds of the middle and lower classes today.

It is to the metropolitan upper classes that the local society of the smaller cities looks; its newer members with open admiration, its older, with less open admiration. What good is it to show a horse or a dog in a small city of 100,000 population, even if you could, when you know that *The* Show will be in New York next fall? More seriously, what prestige is there in a $50,000 local deal, however financially convenient, when you know that in Chicago, only 175 miles away, men are turning over $500,000? The very broadening of their status area makes the small-town woman and man unsatisfied to make big splashes in such little ponds, makes them yearn for the lakes of big city prestige, if not for truly national repute. Accordingly, to the extent that local society maintains its position, even locally, it comes to mingle with and to identify itself with a more metropolitan crowd and to talk more easily of eastern schools and New York night clubs.

There is one point of difference between the old and the new upper classes in the smaller cities that is of great concern to the old, for it causes the new to be a less ready and less reliable cash-in area for the status claims of the old. The old upper class, after all, is old only in relation to the new and hence needs the new in order to feel that all is right in its little world of status. But the new, as well as many of the old, know well that this local society is now only local.

The men and women of the old upper class understand their station to be well within their own city. They may go to Florida or California in the winter, but they go always as visitors, not as explorers of new ways or as makers of new business contacts. They feel their place to be in their own city and they tend to think of this city as containing all the principles necessary for ranking all people everywhere. The new upper class, on the other hand, tends to esteem local people in terms of the number and types of contacts they have with places and people outside the city—which the true old upper-class person often excludes as 'outsiders.' Moreover, many articulate members of the middle and lower classes look up to the new upper class because of such 'outside' contacts which, in a decisive way, are the very opposite of 'old family residence.' Old family residence is a criterion that is community-cen-

tered; outside contacts center in the big city or even in the national
scene.*

4

Today 'outside contacts' often center in one very specific and
galling reminder of national status and power which exists right
in the local city: During the last thirty years, and especially with
the business expansions of World War II, the national corporation
has come into many of these smaller cities. Its arrival has upset
the old economic status balances within the local upper classes;
for, with its local branch, there have come the executives from
the big city, who tend to dwarf and to ignore local society.[8]

Prestige is, of course, achieved by 'getting in with' and imitating
those who possess power as well as prestige. Nowadays such social
standing as the local upper classes, in particular the new upper

---

* More aggressive than the old, the new upper-class criterion for the
really top people is not only that they are rich but that they are 'going
places' and have connections with others who are 'going places' in an
even bigger way than they. In one typical small city, the heroes of the
new upper class were described to me as 'Boys with a lot of dynamite . . .
They're in there together going places and doing everything that's good
for [the city]. They operate nationally, see, and that's very important in
their outlook. They're not very active in strictly local affairs, but they
are active men. They have active investments all over, not money just
lying around doing nothing.' Stories of old families that have fallen and
of active new families that have risen illustrate to the new upper class
the 'workings of democracy' and the possibility of 'anybody with the
energy and brains' getting ahead. Such stories serve to justify their own
position and style, and enable them to draw upon the national flow of
official myths concerning the inevitable success of those who know how
to work smartly. The old upper classes do not tell such stories, at least
not to strangers, for among them prestige is a positive thing in itself,
somehow inherent in their way of life, and indeed, their very being.
But to the new upper-class man, prestige seems something that he himself does not truly possess, but could very well use in his business and
social advancement; he tends to see the social position of the old upper
class as an instrument for the 'selling' of a project or the making of more
money. 'You can't get anything done in this town without them [the old
upper class]. The handles on those names are very important . . .
Look, if you and I go out on a project in this town, or any other town
we've got to have names with handles. Investors, proprietors, and so on,
they just hold back until we do that. Otherwise if we had the finest
project in the world, it would be born dead.'

classes, may secure, is increasingly obtained through association
with the leading officials of the great absentee-owned corporations, through following their style of living, through moving
to their suburbs outside the city's limits, attending their social
functions. Since the status world of the corporation group does not
characteristically center in the local city, local society tends to
drift away from civic prestige, looking upon it as 'local stuff.'

In the eyes of the new upper class, the old social leaders of the
city come gradually to be displaced by the corporation group. The
local upper classes struggle to be invited to the affairs of the new
leaders, and even to marry their children into their circles. One of
the most obvious symptoms of the drift is the definite movement
of the local upper-class families into the exclusive suburbs built
largely by the corporation managers. The new upper class tends
to imitate and to mingle with the corporation group; the 'bright
young men' of all educated classes tend to leave the small city and
to make their careers within the corporate world. The local world
of the old upper class is simply by-passed.

Such developments are often more important to women than
to men. Women are frequently more active in social and civic
matters—particularly in those relating to education, health, and
charities—if for no other reason than that they have more time for
them. They center their social life in the local cities because 'it is
the thing to do,' and it is the thing to do only if those with top prestige do it. Local women, however, gain little or no social standing
among the corporate elite by participating in local affairs, since
the executives' wives, corporation- and city-centered, do not concern themselves with local society, nor even with such important
local matters as education; for they send their own children to
private schools or, on lower executive levels, to their own public
schools in their own suburbs, distinct and separate from the city's.
A typical local woman could work herself to the bone on civic matters and never be noticed or accepted by the executives' wives.
But if it became known that by some chance she happened to be
well acquainted with a metropolitan celebrity, she might well be
'in.'

Local women often participate in local and civic affairs in order
to help their husband's business, but the terms of the executive's
success lie within his national corporation. The corporate officials

have very few business dealings with strictly local businessmen. They deal with distant individuals of other corporations who buy the plant's products or sell it materials and parts. Even when the executive does undertake some deal with a local businessman, no social contact is required—unless it is part of the corporation's 'good-will' policy. So it is quite unnecessary for the executive's wife to participate in local society: the power of the corporation's name will readily provide him with all the contacts in the smaller city that he will ever require.

5

Perhaps there was a time—before the Civil War—when local societies composed the only society there was in America. It is still true, of course, that every small city is a local hierarchy of status and that at the top of each there is still a local elite of power and wealth and esteem. But one cannot now study the upper groups in even a great number of smaller communities and then—as many American sociologists are prone to do—generalize the results to the nation, as the American System.[9] Some members of the higher circles of the nation do live in small towns—although that is not usual. Moreover, where they happen to maintain a house means little; their area of operation is nation-wide. The upper social classes of all the small towns of America cannot merely be added up to form a national upper class; their power cliques cannot merely be added up to form the national power elite. In each locality there *is* an upper set of families, and in each, with certain regional variations, they are quite similar. But the national structure of classes is not a mere enumeration of equally important local units. The class and status and power systems of local societies are not equally weighted; they are not autonomous. Like the economic and political systems of the nation, the prestige and the power systems are no longer made up of decentralized little hierarchies, each having only thin and distant connections, if any at all, with the others. The kinds of relations that exist between the countryside and the town, the town and the big city, and between the various big cities, form a structure that is now national in scope. Moreover, certain forces, which by their very nature are not rooted in any one town or city, now modify, by direct as well

as indirect lines of control, the local hierarchies of status and
power and wealth that prevail in each of them.

It is to the cities of the Social Register and the celebrity, to the
seats of the corporate power, to the national centers of political
and military decision, that local society now looks—even though
some of its older members will not always admit that these cities
and corporations and powers exist socially. The strivings of the
new upper class and the example of the managerial elite of the
national corporation cause local societies everywhere to become
satellites of status and class and power systems that extend beyond their local horizon. What town in New England is socially
comparable with Boston? What local industry is economically
comparable with General Motors? What local political chief with
the political directorate of the nation?

3

Metropolitan 400

THE little cities look to the big cities, but where do the big cities look? America is a nation with no truly national city, no Paris, no Rome, no London, no city which is at once the social center, the political capital, and the financial hub. Local societies of small town and large city have had no historic court which, once and for all and officially, could certify the elect. The political capital of the country is not the status capital, nor even in any real sense an important segment of Society; the political career does not parallel the social climb. New York, not Washington, has become the financial capital. What a difference it might have made if from the beginning Boston and Washington and New York had been combined into one great social, political, and financial capital of the nation! Then, Mrs. John Jay's set ('Dinner and Supper List for 1787 and 1788'), in which men of high family, great wealth, and decisive power mingled, might, as part of the national census, have been kept intact and up-to-date.[1]

And yet despite the lack of official and metropolitan unity, today—seventeen decades later—there does flourish in the big cities of America a recognizable upper social class, which seems in many ways to be quite compact. In Boston and in New York, in Philadelphia and in Baltimore and in San Francisco, there exists a solid core of older, wealthy families surrounded by looser circles of newer, wealthy families. This older core, which in New York was once said—by Mrs. Astor's Ward McAllister—to number Four Hundred, has made several bids to be The Society of America, and perhaps, once upon a time, it almost succeeded. Today, in so

far as it tries to base itself on pride of family descent, its chances
to be truly national are subject to great risks. There is little doubt,
however, that among the metropolitan 400's, as well as among
their small-town counterparts, there is an accumulation of advantages in which objective opportunity and psychological readiness
interact to create and to maintain for each generation the world
of the upper social classes. These classes, in each of the big cities,
look first of all to one another.

1

Before the Civil War the big-city upper classes were compact
and stable. At least social chroniclers, looking back, say that they
were. 'Society,' Mrs. John King Van Rensselaer wrote, grew 'from
within rather than from without . . . The foreign elements absorbed were negligible. The social circle widened, generation by
generation, through the abundant contributions made by each
family to posterity . . . There was a boundary as solid and as
difficult to ignore as the Chinese Wall.' Family lineage ran back to
the formation of the colonies and the only divisions among upper-
class groups 'were those of the church; Presbyterians, Dutch Re-
formed and Episcopalians formed fairly definite sections of a compact organization.'[2]

In each locality and region, nineteenth-century wealth created
its own industrial hierarchy of local families. Up the Hudson, there
were patroons, proud of their origins, and in Virginia, the planters.
In every New England town, there were Puritan shipowners and
early industrialists, and in St. Louis, fashionable descendants of
French Creoles living off real estate. In Denver, Colorado, there
were wealthy gold and silver miners. And in New York City, as
Dixon Wecter has put it, there was 'a class made up of coupon-
clippers, sportsmen living off their fathers' accumulation, and a
stratum like the Astors and Vanderbilts trying to renounce their
commercial origins as quickly as possible.'[3]

The richest people could be regarded as a distinct caste, their
fortunes as permanent, their families as honorably old. As long as
they kept their wealth and no newer and bigger wealth threat-
ened it, there was no reason to distinguish status by family lineage
and status by wealth.[4] The stability of the older upper classes
rested rather securely upon the coincidence of old family and

great wealth. For the push, the wealth, the power of new upper classes was contained by the old, who, while remaining distinct and unthreatened, could occasionally admit new members.

In the decades following the Civil War, the old upper classes of the older cities were overwhelmed by the new wealth. 'All at once,' Mrs. Van Rensselaer thought, Society 'was assailed from every side by persons who sought to climb boldly over the walls of social exclusiveness.' Moreover, from overseas the immigrants came, like southerners, and later westerners, to make their fortunes in the city. 'Others who had made theirs elsewhere, journeyed to New York to spend them on pleasure and social recognition.'⁵

From the eighteen-seventies until the nineteen-twenties, the struggle of old family with new money occurred on a grandiose national scale. Those families that were old because they had become wealthy prior to the Civil War attempted to close up their ranks against the post-Civil War rich. They failed primarily because the new wealth was so enormous compared with the old that it simply could not be resisted. Moreover, the newly wealthy could not be contained in any locality. Like the broadening national territory, new wealth and power—in family and now in corporate form as well—grew to national size and scope. The city, the county, the state could not contain this socially powerful wealth. Everywhere, its possessors invaded the fine old families of metropolitan society.

All families would seem to be rather 'old,' but not all of them have possessed wealth for at least two but preferably three or four generations. The formula for 'old families' in America is money plus inclination plus time. After all, there have only been some six or seven generations in the whole of United States history. For every old family there must have been a time when someone was of that family but it was not 'old.' Accordingly, in America, it is almost as great a thing to be an ancestor as to have an ancestor.

It must not be supposed that the pedigreed families do not and have not admitted unregistered families to their social circles, especially after the unregistered have captured their banking firms. It is only that those whose ancestors bought their way into slightly

older families only two or three generations ago now push hard to
keep out those who would follow suit. This game of the old rich
and the parvenu began with the beginning of the national history,
and continues today in the small town as in the metropolitan center. The one firm rule of the game is that, given persistent inclination, any family can win out on whatever level its money permits.
Money—sheer, naked, vulgar money—has with few exceptions
won its possessors entrance anywhere and everywhere into American society.

From the point of view of status, which always tries to base itself
on family descent, this means that the walls are always crumbling;
from the more general standpoint of an upper social class of more
than local recognition, it means that top level is always being reno-
vated. It also means that, no matter what its pretensions, the
American upper class is merely an enriched bourgeoisie, and that,
no matter how powerful its members may be, they cannot invent
an aristocratic past where one did not exist. One careful genealo-
gist has asserted that at the beginning of this century, there were
'not ten families occupying conspicuous social positions' in either
the moneyed set or the old-family set of New York 'whose pro-
genitors' names appeared on Mrs. John Jay's dinner list.'[6]

In America, the prideful attempt to gain status by virtue of family descent has been an uneasy practice never touching more than
a very small fraction of the population. With their real and invented ancestors, the 'well-born' and the 'high-born' have attempted
to elaborate pedigrees and, on the basis of their consciousness of
these pedigrees, to keep their distance from the 'low-born.' But
they have attempted this with an underlying population which, in
an utterly vulgar way, seemed to glory in being low-born, and
which was too ready with too many jokes about the breeding of
horses to make such pretensions easy or widespread.

There has been too much movement—of family residence and
between occupations, in the lifetime of an individual and between the generations—for feeling of family line to take root. Even
when such feeling does strengthen the claims of the upper classes,
it is without avail unless it is honored by the underlying strata.
Americans are not very conscious of family lines; they are not
the sort of underlying population which would readily cash in

claims for prestige on the basis of family descent. It is only when a social structure does not essentially change in the course of generations, only when occupation and wealth and station tend to become hereditary, that such pride and prejudice, and with them, such servility and sense of inferiority, can become stable bases of a prestige system.

The establishment of a pedigreed society, based on the prestige of family line, was possible, for a brief period, despite the absence of a feudal past and the presence of mobility, because of the *immigrant* situation. It was precisely during the decades when the flow of the new immigration into the big cities was largest that metropolitan Society was at its American peak. In such Yankee ghettoes, claims for status by descent were most successful, not so much among the population at large as among those who claimed some descent and wanted more. Such claims were and are involved in the status hierarchy of nationality groups.

But there came a time when the lowly immigrant no longer served this purpose: the flow of immigration was stopped, and in a little while everyone in North America became—or soon would become—a native-born American of native-born parents.

Even while the supply of immigrants was huge and their number in the big cities outnumbered those of native parentage, liberal sentiments of nationalism were becoming too strong to be shaped by the barriers of strict descent. 'The Americanization of the Immigrant'—as an organized movement, as an ideology, and as a fact—made loyalties to one ideological version of the nation more important than Anglo-Saxon descent. The view of the nation as a glorious melting pot of races and nations—carried by middle classes and intelligentsia—came to prevail over the Anglo-Saxon views of those concerned with 'racial' descent and with the pedigreed, registered society. Besides, each of these national groups— from the Irish to the Puerto Rican—has slowly won local political power.

The attempt to create a pedigreed society has gone on among an upper class whose component localities competed: the eastern seaboard was settled first; so those who remained there have been local families longer than the families of more recently populated regions. Yet there are locally eminent families who have been locally eminent in many small New England towns for as long as any Boston family; there are small-town southern families whose claims for continuity of cousinhood could not be outdone by the most fanatic Boston Brahmin; and there are early California families who, within their own strongly felt framework of time, feel older and better established than any New York family might be. The localities competed economically as well. The mining families and the railroad families and the real-estate families—in each industry, in each locality and region, as we have said, big wealth created its own hierarchy of local families.

The pedigree is a firm and stable basis of prestige when the class structure is firm and stable. Only then can all sorts of conventions and patterns of etiquette take root and flower in firm economic ground. When economic change is swift and mobility decisive, then the moneyed class as such will surely assert itself; status pretensions will collapse and time-honored prejudices will be swept away. From the standpoint of class, a dollar is a dollar, but from the standpoint of a pedigreed society, two identical sums of money—the one received from four generations of inherited trusts, the other from a real kill on the market last week—are very different sums. And yet, what is one to do when the new money becomes simply enormous? What is Mrs. Astor (the pedigreed lady of Knickerbocker origin married to old, real-estate wealth) going to do about Mrs. Vanderbilt (of the vulgar railroad money and the more vulgar grandfather-in-law) in 1870? Mrs. Astor is going to lose: in 1883 she leaves her calling card at Mrs. Vanderbilt's door, and accepts an invitation to Mrs. Vanderbilt's fancy-dress ball.[7] With that sort of thing happening, you cannot run a real pedigreed status show. Always in America, as perhaps elsewhere, society based on descent has been either by-passed or bought-out by the new and vulgar rich.*

* But not only the fast-moving mechanics of class upset the show. Almost anything fast moving does. For the conventions of a style of life are important to the prestige of local society, and only where class and status relations are stable can conventions be stabilized. If conventions are truly rigid, then dress becomes 'costume,' and conventions become 'traditions.' High prestige of ancestors, of old age, of old wealth, of antiques, of 'seniority' of residence, and membership and of old ways of doing anything and everything—they go together and together make up the status conventions of a fixed circle in a stable society.

When social change is swift, prestige tends to go to the young and the beautiful, even if they are the damned; to the merely different and

Here, in the social context of the self-made man, the parvenu claimed status. He claimed it *as* a self-made man rather than despite it. In each generation some family-made men and women have looked down upon him as an intruder, a *nouveau riche*, as an outsider in every way. But in each following generation—or the one following that—he has been admitted to the upper social classes of the duly pedigreed families.

2

The status struggle in America is not something that occurred at a given time and was then done with. The attempt of the old rich to remain exclusively prominent by virtue of family pedigree has been a continual attempt, which always fails and always succeeds. It fails because in each generation new additions are made; it succeeds because at all times an upper social class is making the fight. A stable upper class with a really fixed membership does not exist; but an upper social class does exist. Change in the membership of a class, no matter how rapid, does not destroy the class. Not the identical individual or families, but the same type prevails within it.

There have been numerous attempts to fix this type by drawing the line in a more or less formal way. Even before the Civil War, when new wealth was not as pushing as it later became, some social arbiter seemed to be needed by worried hostesses confronted with social decisions. For two generations before 1850, New York Society depended upon the services of one Isaac Brown, sexton of Grace Church, who, we are told by Dixon Wecter, had a 'faultless memory for names, pedigrees, and gossip.' He was quite ready to tell hostesses about to issue invitations who was in mourning,

---

to the 'novel,' even if they are the vulgar. Costumes then become 'old-fashioned,' and what matters, above all, is to be 'fashionable.' The appearance value of one's house, and even of one's manners and one's self, become subject to fashion. There is, in short, an appreciation of the new for its own sake: that which is new is prestigeful. In such a situation, money more easily decides who can keep up with such a dynamic and steeply graded pattern of consumption differences in dresses, cars, houses, sports, hobbies, clubs. It is, of course, to such a situation as this, and not to a stabilized leisure class, that Veblen directed his phrases: 'ostentatious consumption' and 'conspicuous waste.' For America, and for the second generation of the period of which he wrote, he was generally correct.

who had gone bankrupt, who had friends visiting them, who were the new arrivals in town and in Society.' He would preside at the doorstep at parties, and some observers claimed that he 'possessed a list of "dancing young men" for the benefit of newly arrived party-givers.'[8]

The extravagant wealth of the post-Civil War period called for a more articulate means of determining the elect, and Ward McAllister, for a time, established himself as selector. In order that 'society might be given that solidity needed to resist invasion of the flashiest profiteers,' McAllister wished to undertake the needed mixture of old families with position but without fashion, and the ' "swells" who had to entertain and be smart in order to win their way.' He is said to have taken his task very seriously, giving over 'his days and nights to study of heraldry, books of court etiquette, genealogy, and cookery . . .' In the winter of 1872–3, he organized the Patriarchs, 'a committee of twenty-five men "who had the right to create and lead Society" by inviting to each ball four ladies and five gentlemen on their individual responsibility, which McAllister stressed as a sacred trust.' The original patriarchs were old-family New Yorkers of at least four generations, which, in McAllister's American generosity, he thought 'make as good and true a gentleman as forty.'[9]

During the 'eighties, McAllister had been dropping comments to newspaper men that there were really 'only about 400 people in fashionable New York Society. If you go outside that number you strike people who are either not at ease in a ballroom or else make other people not at ease.'[10] In 1892, when both the exclusiveness of the Patriarchs and the popularity of Ward McAllister were beginning seriously to decline, he published his list of '400,' which in fact contained about 300 names. It was simply the roll-call of the Patriarch Balls, the inner circle of pre-Civil War New York families, embellished by unattached daughters and sons who liked to dance, and a select few of the new rich whom McAllister deemed fit for admittance. Only nine out of a list of the ninety richest men of the day[11] appear on his list.

The attention given McAllister's list of the '400,' and his subsequent retirement from high society, reflect the precarious situation of the old upper classes he tried to consolidate. Not only in New York, but in other cities as well, all sorts of attempts have

been made to preserve the 'old-guard' from the social entrée of
new wealth. McAllister's demise symbolizes the failure of all these
attempts. The only sensible thing that could be done was to admit
the new wealth, or at least selected members of it. This, the most
successful attempt, *The Social Register*, has done.

In the gilded age of the 1880's, a New York bachelor who had
inherited 'a small life-income and a sound though inconspicuous
social standing,' decided to publish 'a list of the Best People from
which advertising was wisely excluded but which merchants
might buy.'[12] *The Social Register* presented a judicious combination of the old with the new, and, with the hearty support of
friends among such New York clubs as Calumet and Union, became an immediate success. The first *Social Register* of New York
contained some 881 families; in due course, lists were published
for other cities, and the business of compiling and publishing such
lists became incorporated as The Social Register Association. During the 'twenties, social registers were being issued for twenty-
one cities, but nine of these were later dropped 'for lack of interest.' By 1928, twelve volumes were being printed in the autumn of
each year, and ever since then there have been Social Registers
for New York and Boston (since 1890), Philadelphia (1890),
Baltimore (1892), Chicago (1893), Washington (1900), St.
Louis (1903), Buffalo (1903), Pittsburgh (1904), San Francisco
(1906), Cleveland (1910), and Cincinnati (1910).[13]

The Registers list the 'socially elect' together with addresses,
children, schools, telephone numbers, and clubs. Supplements
appear in December and January, and a summer edition is published each June. The Association advises the reader to purchase
an index containing all the names in all the Registers, this being
useful in so far as there are many intermarriages among families
from the various cities and changes of address from one city to
another.

The Social Register describes the people eligible for its listing as 'those families who by descent or by social standing or from
other qualifications are naturally included in the best society of
any particular city or cities.' The exact criteria for admission, however, are hard to discern perhaps because, as Wecter has asserted,
'an efficient impersonality, detachment, and air of secret inquisi-
tion surround *The Social Register*. A certain anonymity is essen-

tial to its continued success and prestige.'[14] Today, the Social Register Association, with headquarters in New York, seems to be run by a Miss Bertha Eastmond, secretary of the Association's founder from the early days. She judges all the names, some to be added, some to be rejected as unworthy, some to be considered in the future. In this work, she may call upon the counsel of certain social advisers, and each city for which there is a Register has a personal representative who keeps track of current names, addresses, and telephone numbers.

Who are included in the some 38,000 conjugal family units now listed,[15] and why are they included? Anyone residing in any of the twelve chosen cities may apply for inclusion, although the recommendations of several listed families must be obtained as well as a list of club memberships. But money alone, or family alone, or even both together do not seem to guarantee immediate admittance or final retention. In a rather arbitrary manner, people of old-family are sometimes dropped; second generations of new wealth which try to get in are often not successful. To say, however, that birth and wealth are not sufficient is not to say that they, along with proper conduct, are not necessary.

Moderately successful corporation executives, once they set their minds to it, have been known to get into the Register, but the point should not be overstressed. In particular, it ought to be made historically specific: the thirty-year span 1890–1920 was the major period for entrance into the registered circle. Since the first decade of the twentieth century, in fact, the rate of admission of new families into the Social Register—at least in one major city, Philadelphia—has steadily declined: during the first decade of this century, there was a 68 per cent increase, by the decade of the 'thirties, the rate of increase was down to 6 per cent.[16]

Those who are dropped from *The Social Register* are often so well known that much is made of their being dropped; the 'arbitrary' character of the Register is then used to ridicule its social meaning. Actually, Dixon Wecter has concluded, 'unfavorable publicity seems as near as one can come to the reason for banishment, but this again is applied with more intuition than logic . . . It is safe to say that anyone who keeps out of [the newspaper's] columns—whatever his private life may be, or clandestine rumors may report—will not fall foul of *The Social Register*.'[17]

With all the seemingly arbitrary selection and rejection, and with all the snobbery and anguish that surrounds and even characterizes it, *The Social Register* is a serious listing that does mean something. It is an attempt, under quite trying circumstances, to close out of the truly proper circles the merely *nouveau riche* and those with mere notoriety, to certify and consolidate these proper circles of wealth, and to keep the chosen circles proper and thus presumably worthy of being chosen. After all, it is the only list of registered families that Americans have, and it is the nearest thing to an official status center that this country, with no aristocratic past, no court society, no truly capital city, possesses. In any individual case, admission may be unpredictable or even arbitrary, but as a group, the people in *The Social Register* have been chosen for their money, their family, and their style of life. Accordingly, the names contained in these twelve magic volumes do stand for a certain type of person.

3

In each of the chosen metropolitan areas of the nation, there is an upper social class whose members were born into families which have been registered since the *Social Register* began. This registered social class, as well as newly registered and unregistered classes in other big cities, is composed of groups of ancient families who for two or three or four generations have been prominent and wealthy. They are set apart from the rest of the community by their manner of origin, appearance, and conduct.

They live in one or more exclusive and expensive residential areas in fine old houses in which many of them were born, or in elaborately simple modern ones which they have constructed. In these houses, old or new, there are the correct furnishings and the cherished equipage. Their clothing, even when it is apparently casual and undoubtedly old, is somehow different in cut and hang from the clothes of other men and women. The things they buy are quietly expensive and they use them in an inconspicuous way. They belong to clubs and organizations to which only others like themselves are admitted, and they take quite seriously their appearances in these associations.

They have relatives and friends in common, but more than that, they have in common experiences of a carefully selected and family-controlled sort. They have attended the same or similar private and exclusive schools, preferably one of the Episcopal boarding schools of New England. Their men have been to Harvard, Yale, Princeton, or if local pride could not be overcome, to a locally esteemed college to which their families have contributed. And now they frequent the clubs of these schools, as well as leading clubs in their own city, and as often as not, also a club or two in other metropolitan centers.

Their names are not in the chattering, gossiping columns or even the society columns of their local newspapers; many of them, proper Bostonians and proper San Franciscans that they are, would be genuinely embarrassed among their own kind were their names so taken in vain—cheap publicity and cafe-society scandal are for newer families of more strident and gaudy style, not for the old social classes. For those established at the top are 'proud'; those not yet established are merely conceited. The proud really do not care what others below them think of them; the conceited depend on flattery and are easily cheated by it, for they are not aware of the dependence of their ideas of self upon others.*

* A word about Thorstein Veblen's *The Theory of the Leisure Class* (1899) which—fortunately—is still read, not because his criticism of the American upper class is still adequate, but because his style makes it plausible, even when the criticism is not taken seriously. What he wrote remains strong with the truth, even though his facts do not cover the scenes and the characters that have emerged in our own time. It remains strong because we could not see the newer features of our own time had he not written what and as he did. Which is one meaning of the fact that his biases are the most fruitful that have appeared in the literature of American social protest. But all critics are mortal; and Veblen's theory is in general no longer an adequate account of the American system of prestige.

The Theory of the Leisure Class, is not *the* theory of *the* leisure class. It is *a* theory of a particular element of the upper classes in one period of the history of one nation. It is an account of the status struggle between new and old wealth and, in particular, it is an examination of the *nouveau riche,* so much in evidence in Veblen's formative time, the America of the latter half of the nineteenth century, of the Vanderbilts, Goulds, and Harrimans, of Saratoga Springs and Newport, of the glitter and the gold.

It is an analysis of an upper class which is climbing socially by translating its money into symbols of status, but doing so in a status situation in which the symbols are ambiguous. Moreover, the audience for the Veblenian drama is not traditional, nor the actors firmly set in an in-

Within and between the various cliques which they form, members of these proud families form close friendships and strong loy-

---

herited social structure, as in feudalism. Accordingly, consumption patterns are the only means of competing for status honor. Veblen does not analyze societies with an old nobility or a court society where the courtier was a successful style of life.

In depicting the higher style of American life, Veblen—like the actors of whom he writes—seems to confuse aristocratic and bourgeois traits. At one or two points, he does so explicitly: 'The aristocratic and the bourgeois virtues—that is to say the destructive and pecuniary traits—should be found chiefly among the upper classes . . .'[18] One has only to examine the taste of the small businessmen to know that this is certainly not true.

'Conspicuous consumption,' as Veblen knew, is not confined to the upper classes. But today I should say that it prevails *especially* among one element of the new upper classes—the *nouveau riche* of the new corporate privileges—the men on expense accounts, and those enjoying other corporate prerogatives—and with even more grievous effects on the standard and style of life of the professional celebrities of stage and screen, radio and TV. And, of course, among recent crops of more old-fashioned *nouveau riche* dramatized by the 'Texas millionaires.'

In the middle of the twentieth century, as at the end of the nineteenth which Veblen observed, there *are* fantastic goings-on: 'Tenor Mario Lanza now owns an outsize, custom-built white Cadillac with a gold-plated dashboard . . . Restaurateur Mike Romanoff ships his silk and pongee shirts air express to Sulka's in Manhattan for proper laundering . . . Construction Tycoon Hal Hayes . . . has a built-in bar in his Cadillac plus faucets for Scotch, bourbon, champagne and beer in his home. . . .'[19] But in established local society, the men and women of the fourth and fifth generation are quietly expensive and expensively quiet; they are, in fact, often deliberately inconspicuous in their consumption: with unpretentious farm houses and summer retreats, they often live quite simply, and certainly without any ostentatious display of vulgar opulence.

The terms of Veblen's theory are not adequate to describe the established upper classes of today. Moreover—as we shall see in FOUR, Veblen's work, as a theory of the American status system, does not take into adequate account the rise of the instituted elite or of the world of the celebrity. He could not, of course, have been expected in the eighteen-nineties to see the meaning for a truly national status system of 'the professional celebrities,' who have arisen as part of the national media of mass communication and entertainment, or anticipate the development of national glamour, whereby the debutante is replaced by the movie star, and the local society lady by the military and political and economic managers—'the power elite'—whom many now celebrate as their proper chieftains.

alties. They are served at one another's dinners and attend one another's balls. They take the quietly elegant weddings, the somber funerals, the gay coming-out parties with seriousness and restraint. The social appearances they seem to like best are often informal, although among them codes of dress and manner, the sensibility of what is correct and what is not done, govern the informal and the natural as well as the formal.

Their sense of civic service does not seem to take direct political form, but causes them gladly to lead the charitable, educational, and cultural institutions of their city. Their wealth is such—probably several millions on the average—that they do not usually have to use the principal; if they do not wish to work, they probably do not have to. Yet their men—especially the more substantial older men—generally do work and sometimes quite diligently. They make up the business aristocracy of their city, especially the financial and legal aristocracy. The true gentleman—in the eastern cities, and increasingly across the nation—is usually a banker or a lawyer, which is convenient, for those who possess a fortune are in need of trusted, wise, and sober men to preserve its integrity. They are the directors and the presidents of the major banks, and they are the senior partners and investment counselors of the leading law firms of their cities.

Almost everywhere in America, the metropolitan upper classes have in common, more or less, race, religion, and nativity. Even if they are not of long family descent, they are uniformly of longer American origin than the underlying population. There are, of course, exceptions, some of them important exceptions. In various cities, Italian and Jewish and Irish Catholic families—having become wealthy and powerful—have risen high in status. But however important, these are still exceptions: the model of the upper *social* classes is still 'pure' by race, by ethnic group, by national extraction. In each city, they tend to be Protestant; moreover Protestants of class-church denominations, Episcopalian mainly, or Unitarian, or Presbyterian.

In many cities—New York for example—there are several rather than one metropolitan 400. This fact, however, does not mean that the big-city upper classes do not exist, but rather that in such cities the status stucture is more elaborate than in those with more unified societies. That there are social feuds between competing status centers does not destroy the status hierarchy.

The family of higher status may belong to an exclusive country club where sporting activities and social events occur, but this pattern is not of decisive importance to the upper levels, for 'country clubs' have spread downward into the middle and even into the lower-middle classes. In smaller cities, membership in the best country club is often the significant organizational mark of the upper groups; but this is not so in the metropolitan status market. It is the gentleman's club, an exclusive male organization, that is socially most important.

Gentlemen belong to the metropolitan man's club, and the men of the upper-class stature usually belong to such clubs in more than one city; clubs for both sexes, such as country clubs, are usually local. Among the out-of-town clubs to which the old upper-class man belongs are those of Harvard and Princeton and Yale, but the world of the urban clubs extends well beyond those anchored in the better schools. It is not unusual for gentlemen to belong to three or four or even more. These clubs of the various cities are truly exclusive in the sense that they are not widely known to the middle and lower classes in general. They are above those better-known arenas where upper-class status is more widely recognized. They are of and by and for the upper circles, and no other. But they are known and visited by the upper circles of more than one city.*

To the outsider, the club to which the upper class man or woman belongs is a badge of certification of his status; to the insider, the club provides a more intimate or clan-like set of exclusive groupings which places and characterizes a man. Their core of membership is usually families which successfully claim status by descent. From intimate association with such men, newer members borrow status, and in turn, the accomplishments of the newer entrants help shore up the status of the club as a going concern.

Membership in the right clubs assumes great social importance when the merely rich push and shove at the boundaries of society, for then the line tends to become vague, and club membership clearly defines exclusiveness. And yet the metropolitan clubs are important rungs in the social ladder for would-be members of the top status levels: they are status elevators for the new into the old upper classes; for men, and their sons, can be gradually advanced

* Even in 1933, some fifty New Yorkers maintained their full-rate dues in Boston's Somerset Club.[20]

from one club to the next, and so, if successful, into the inner citadel of the most exclusive. They are also important in the business
life within and between the metropolitan circles: to many men of
these circles, it seems convenient and somehow fitting to come to
important decisions within the exclusive club. 'The private club,'
one national magazine for executives recently put it, is becoming 'the businessman's castle.'[21]

The metropolitan upper classes, as wealthy classes having control of each locality's key financial and legal institutions, thereby
have business and legal relations with one another. For the economy of the city, especially of a metropolitan area, is not confined
to the city. To the extent that the economy is national and big-
city centered, and to the extent that the upper classes control its
key places of big-city decision—the upper classes of each city are
related to those of other cities. In the rich if gloomy quiet of a Boston club and also in the rich and brisk chrome of a Houston club—
to belong is to be accepted. It is also to be in easy, informal touch
with those who are socially acceptable, and so to be in a better
position to make a deal over a luncheon table. The gentlemen's
club is at once an important center of the financial and business
network of decision and an essential center for certifying the socially fit. In it all the traits that make up the old upper classes seem
to coincide: the old family and the proper marriage and the correct residence and the right church and the right schools—and the
power of the key decision. The 'leading men' in each city belong
to such clubs, and when the leading men of other cities visit them,
they are very likely to be seen at lunch in Boston's Somerset or
Union, Philadelphia's Racquet or Philadelphia Club, San Francisco's Pacific Union, or New York's Knickerbocker, Links, Brook,
or Racquet and Tennis.[22]

4

The upper-class style of life is pretty much the same—although
there are regional variations—in each of the big cities of the nation. The houses and clothing, the types of social occasions the
metropolitan 400 care about, tend to be homogeneous. The Brooks
Brothers suit-and-shirt is not extensively advertised nationally
and the store has only four branches outside New York City, but it
is well-known in every major city of the nation, and in no key city

do the 'representatives' of Brooks Brothers feel themselves to be strangers.[23] There are other such externals that are specific and common to the proper upper-class style, yet, after all, anyone with the money and the inclination can learn to be uncomfortable in anything but a Brooks Brothers suit. The style of life of the old upper social classes across the nation goes deeper than such things.

The one deep experience that distinguishes the social rich from the merely rich and those below is their schooling, and with it, all the associations, the sense and sensibility, to which this educational routine leads throughout their lives.

The daughter of an old upper-class New York family, for example, is usually under the care of nurse and mother until she is four years of age, after which she is under the daily care of a governess who often speaks French as well as English. When she is six or seven, she goes to a private day school, perhaps Miss Chapin's or Brearley. She is often driven to and from school by the family chauffeur and in the afternoons, after school, she is in the general care of the governess, who now spends most of her time with the younger children. When she is about fourteen she goes to boarding school, perhaps to St. Timothy's in Maryland or Miss Porter's or Westover in Connecticut. Then she may attend Finch Junior College of New York City and thus be 'finished,' or if she is to attend college proper, she will be enrolled, along with many plain middle-class girls, in Bryn Mawr or Vassar or Wellesley or Smith or Bennington. She will marry soon after finishing school or college, and presumably begin to guide her own children through the same educational sequence.*

The boy of this family, while under seven years of age, will follow a similar pattern. Then he too will go to day school, and, at a rather earlier age than the girls, to boarding school, although for boys it will be called prep school: St. Mark's or St. Paul's, Choate or

---

* 'The daughter of the industrial leader, of the great professional man must thrive in a complex civilization which places little premium upon its women's homelier virtues: meekness and modesty, earnestness and Godliness. Yet such a man must, according to the *mores* of his kind, send his daughter to one of a handful of institutions whose codes rest upon these foundations . . . Of the 1,200-odd private schools for girls in this country, curiously enough only a score or more really matter . . . so ephemeral are the things which make one school and mar another that intangible indeed are the distinctions.'[24]

Groton, Andover or Lawrenceville, Phillips Exeter or Hotchkiss.[25] Then he will go to Princeton or Harvard, Yale or Dartmouth. As likely as not, he will finish with a law school attached to one of these colleges.

Each stage of this education is important to the formation of the upper-class man or woman; it is an educational sequence that is common to the upper classes in all the leading cities of the nation. There is, in fact, a strong tendency for children from all these cities to attend one of the more fashionable boarding or prep schools in New England, in which students from two dozen or so states, as well as from foreign countries, may be readily found. As claims for status based on family descent become increasingly difficult to realize, the proper school transcends the family pedigree in social importance. Accordingly, if one had to choose one clue to the national unity of the upper social classes in America today, it would best be the really exclusive boarding school for girls and prep school for boys.

Many educators of the private school world feel that economic shifts bring to the top people whose children have had no proper family background and tone, and that the private school is a prime institution in preparing them to live at the top of the nation in a manner befitting upper-class men and women. And whether the headmasters know it or not, it seems to be a fact that like the hierarchy of clubs for the fathers—but in more important and deeper ways—the private schools do perform the task of selecting and training newer members of a national upper stratum, as well as upholding the higher standards among the children of families who have long been at the top. It is in 'the next generation,' in the private school, that the tensions between new and old upper classes are relaxed and even resolved. And it is by means of these schools more than by any other single agency that the older and the newer families—when their time is due—become members of a self-conscious upper class.

As a selection and training place of the upper classes, both old and new, the private school is a unifying influence, a force for the nationalization of the upper classes. The less important the pedigreed family becomes in the careful transmission of moral and cultural traits, the more important the private school. The school—rather than the upper-class family—is the most important agency for transmitting the traditions of the upper social classes, and regulating the admission of new wealth and talent. It is the characterizing point in the upper-class experience. In the top fifteen or twenty such schools, if anywhere, one finds a prime organizing center of the national upper social classes. For in these private schools for adolescents, the religious and family and educational tasks of the upper social classes are fused, and in them the major tasks of upholding such standards as prevail in these classes are centered.*

These schools are self-supporting and autonomous in policy, and the most proper of them are non-profit institutions. They are not 'church schools' in that they are not governed by religious bodies, but they do require students to attend religious services, and although not sectarian, they are permeated by religiously inspired principles. The statement of the founders of Groton, still used today, includes this fundamental aim: 'Every endeavor will be made to cultivate manly, Christian character, having regard to moral and physical as well as intellectual development. The Headmaster of the School will be a clergyman of the Protestant Episcopal Church.'[27]

'The vitals of a prep-school are not located in the curriculum. They are located in a dozen other places, some of them queer places indeed: in the relations between boys and faculty; in who the boys are and where they come from; in a Gothic chapel or a shiny new gymnasium; in the type of building the boys live in and the sort of thing they do after supper; and, above all in the headmaster.'[28] There is a kind of implicit ideal for the school to be an organized extension of the family, but a large family in which the proper children from Boston and Philadelphia and New York to-

* 'These schools for boys,' the editors of *Fortune* have written, 'are conspicuous far out of proportion to the numbers enrolled in them. More than seven million boys and girls in the U.S. now (1944) receive secondary education, 460,000 of whom are in private schools. Of this number more than 360,000 were in Catholic schools (1941 figures, latest available) and more than 10,000 in military schools, whose special purposes are obvious. Of the remainder, girls' schools, whose job is also relatively well defined, accounted for almost 30,000 more. Forty thousand odd were in co-educational schools, largely day schools. Some 20,-000 were in the schools for boys, the group that particularly desires self-justification.'[26]

gether learn the proper style of conduct. This family ideal is strengthened by the common religious practices of the school, which tend to be Episcopalian; by the tendency for given upper-class families to send all their sons to the same schools that the father, or even grandfather, attended; and by the donations as well as the social and sentimental activities of the alumni associations. The underlying purpose of the Choate School, for example, is to prove that family and school may be effectively combined, so that a boy while gaining the benefits that school provides—in particular 'spiritual leadership' and 'association with boys of purpose'—will retain the intimate influences that ought to characterize a proper home.

Daily life in the exclusive schools is usually quite simple, even Spartan; within its atmosphere of snobbish simplicity, there is a democracy of status. Everyone follows more or less the same routine, and there are no opportunities for officially approved inclinations for ostentatious display or snobbery.[29]

These schools are not usually oriented to any obvious practical end. It is true that the boys' schools are invariably preparatory for college; while those for girls offer one curriculum for college preparation, and one terminal course for girls contemplating earlier marriage. But the middle-class ethos of competitiveness is generally lacking. One should, the school seems to say, compare one's work and activity not with the boy or girl next to you, but with what you and your teacher believe is your own best. Besides, if you are too interested, you become conspicuous.

Certainly competition for status among students is held to a minimum: where allowances are permitted, they are usually fixed at modest levels, and the tendency is for boys to have no spending money at all; the wearing of school blazers by boys, or a uniform jumper or blouse, skirt and sweater by girls, is not, as it is usually interpreted by outsiders, so much upper-class swash as it is an attempt to defeat displays of haberdashery within the exclusive group. And girls, however rich, are not usually allowed to own their own horses.

The elders of the school community are those older children in the higher Forms, and they become the models aspired to by the younger children. For young boys, up to eight and nine, there are carefully chosen Housemothers; between twelve and thirteen, they are weaned from women and have exclusively male teachers, although the wives of instructors often live with their husbands in apartments within the boys' dormitories and continue a virtual kinship role with them. Care is taken that the self-image of the child not be slapped down, as it might by an insecure parent, and that manners at table as elsewhere be imbibed from the general atmosphere rather than from authoritarian and forbidding figures.

Then one will always know what to do, even if one is sometimes puzzled. One will react appropriately upon meeting the man who is too carefully groomed and above all, the man who tries too hard to please, for one knows that that is not necessary if one is 'the right sort of person.' There will be the manner of simplicity and the easy dignity that can arise only out of an inner certainty that one's being is a definitely established fact of one's world, from which one cannot be excluded, ignored, snubbed, or paid off. And, in due course, as a young broker, banker, executive, one will *feel* smooth and handsome, with the easy bonhomie, the look of superior amusement, and all the useful friendships; one will have just the proper touch of deference toward the older men, even if they *are* members of your own club, and just the right degree of intelligence and enthusiasms—but not too much of either, for one's style is, after all, a realization of the motto of one's schooling: nothing in excess.[30]

Harvard or Yale or Princeton is not enough. It is the really exclusive prep school that counts, for that determines which of the 'two Harvards' one attends. The clubs and cliques of college are usually composed of carry-overs of association and name made in the lower levels at the proper schools; one's friends at Harvard are friends made at prep school. That is why in the upper social classes, it does not by itself mean much merely to have a degree from an Ivy League college. That is assumed: the point is not Harvard, but which Harvard? By Harvard, one means Porcellian, Fly, or A.D.: by Yale, one means Zeta Psi or Fence or Delta Kappa Epsilon; by Princeton, Cottage, Tiger, Cap and Gown, or Ivy.[31] It is the prestige of a properly certified secondary education followed by a proper club in a proper Ivy League college that is the standard admission ticket to the world of urban clubs and parties in any major city of the nation. To the prestige of the voice and manner, constructed in such schools, local loyalties bow, for that experience is a major clue to the nation-wide upper class that is homogeneous and self-conscious.

Among those who are being educated in similar ways, the school naturally leads to marriage. The prep schools for boys are usually within a convenient range of boarding schools for girls of similar age, and several times a year the students from each are thrown together for chaperoned occasions. There are, in addition, the sisters of the other boys and the brothers of the other girls. And for those attending the more exclusive boys' and girls' colleges, there are formally arranged visits and parties—in short, dating patterns—established between them. On the college level, the exclusive schools become components of a broadened marriage market, which brings into dating relation the children of the upper social classes of the nation.

5

The rich who became rich before the Civil War also became the founders of most old American families, and those who have become rich since then have joined them. The metropolitan upper class which they have formed has not been and is not now a pedigreed society with a fixed membership, but for all of that, it has become a nationally recognized upper social class with many homogeneous features and a strong sense of unity. If new families are added to it, they are always wealthy families, and new or old, their sons and daughters attend the same types of exclusive schools and tend to marry one another. They belong to the same associations at the same set of Ivy League colleges, and they remain in social and business touch by means of the big-city network of metropolitan clubs. In each of the nation's leading cities, they recognize one another, if not strictly as peers, as people with much in common. In one another's biographies they recognize the experiences they have had in common; in their financial positions of brokerage firm, bank, and corporation, they recognize the interests they would all serve. To the extent that business becomes truly national, the economic roles of the upper classes become similar and even interchangeable; to the extent that politics becomes truly national, the political opinion and activity of the upper classes become consolidated. All those forces that transform a confederation of localities and a scatter of companies into a corporate nation, also make for the coinciding interests and functions and unity of the metropolitan 400.   .

The upper social classes have come to include a variety of members concerned with power in its several contexts, and these concerns are shared among the members of the clubs, the cousinhoods, the firms, the law offices. They are topics of conversation around the dinner table, where family members and club associates experience the range of great issues in a quite informal context. Having grown up together, trusting one another implicitly, their personal intimacy comes to include a respect for the specialized concerns of each member as a top man, a policy-maker in his own particular area of power and decision.

They spread into various commanding circles of the institutions of power. One promising son enters upon a high governmental career—perhaps the State Department; his first cousin is in due course elevated to a high executive place in the headquarters of a corporation; his uncle has already ascended to naval command; and a brother of the first cousin is about to become the president of a leading college. And, of course, there is the family law firm, whose partners keep in close touch with outlying members and with the problems they face.

Accordingly, in the inner circles of the upper classes, the most impersonal problems of the largest and most important institutions are fused with the sentiments and worries of small, closed, intimate groups. This is one very important meaning of the upper-class family and of the upper-class school: 'background' is one way in which, on the basis of intimate association, the activities of an upper class may be tacitly co-ordinated. It is also important because in such circles, adolescent boys and girls are exposed to the table conversations of decision-makers, and thus have bred into them the informal skills and pretensions of decision-makers; in short, they imbibe what is called 'judgment.' Without conscious effort, they absorb the aspiration to be—if not the conviction that they are—The Ones Who Decide.

Within and between the upper-class families as well as their firms and offices, there are the schoolboy friendships and the prep schools and the college clubs, and later the key social and political clubs. And, in all these houses and organizations, there are the men who will later—or at the time of meeting—operate in the diverse higher circles of modern society.

The exclusive schools and clubs and resorts of the upper social classes are not exclusive merely because their members are snobs. Such locales and associations have a real part in building the upper-class character, and more than that, the connections to which they naturally lead help to link one higher circle with another.

So the distinguished law student, after prep school and Harvard, is 'clerk' to a Supreme Court judge, then a corporation lawyer, then in the diplomatic service, then in the law firm again. In each of these spheres, he meets and knows men of his own kind, and, as a kind of continuum, there are the old family friends and the schoolboy chums, the dinners at the club, and each year of his life the summer resorts. In each of these circles in which he moves, he acquires and exercises a confidence in his own ability to judge, to decide, and in this confidence he is supported by his ready access to the experience and sensibility of those who are his social peers and who act with decision in each of the important institutions and areas of public life. One does not turn one's back on a man whose presence is accepted in such circles, even under most trying circumstances. All over the top of the nation, he is 'in,' his appearance, a certificate of social position; his voice and manner, a badge of proper training; his associates, proof at once of their acceptance and of his stereotyped discernment.

4

The Celebrities

ALL those who succeed in America—no matter what their circle
of origin or their sphere of action—are likely to become involved
in the world of the celebrity. This world, which is now the American forum of public honor, has not been built from below, as a
slow and steady linking of local societies and metropolitan 400's.
It has been created from above. Based upon nation-wide hierarchies of power and wealth, it is expressed by nation-wide means
of mass communication. As these hierarchies and these media
have come to overlay American society, new types of prestigeful
men and women have come to compete with, to supplement, and
even to displace the society lady and the man of pedigreed
wealth.

With the incorporation of the economy, the ascendancy of the
military establishment, and the centralization of the enlarged
state, there have arisen the national elite, who, in occupying the
command posts of the big hierarchies, have taken the spotlight of
publicity and become subjects of the intensive build-up. At the
same time, with the elaboration of the national means of mass
communication, the professional celebrities of the entertainment
world have come fully and continuously into the national view.
As personalities of national glamour, they are at the focal point of
all the means of entertainment and publicity. Both the metropolitan 400 and the institutional elite must now compete with and
borrow prestige from these professionals in the world of the celebrity.

But what are the celebrities? The celebrities are The Names

that need no further identification. Those who know them so far
exceed those of whom they know as to require no exact computa-
tion. Wherever the celebrities go, they are recognized, and moreover, recognized with some excitement and awe. Whatever they
do has publicity value. More or less continuously, over a period of
time, they are the material for the media of communication and
entertainment. And, when that time ends—as it must—and the celebrity still lives—as he may—from time to time it may be asked,
'Remember him?' That is what celebrity means.

1

In cafe society, the major inhabitants of the world of the celebrity—the institutional elite, the metropolitan socialite, and the
professional entertainer—mingle, publicly cashing in one another's claims for prestige. It is upon cafe society that all the spotlights
of publicity often coincide, spreading the glamour found there to
wider publics. For in cafe society national glamour has become a
hard fact of well-established business routines.

Cafe society exists in the restaurants and night clubs of New
York City—from Fiftieth to Sixtieth streets, between Third Avenue and Sixth. Maury Paul (the original 'Cholly Knickerbocker')
seems to have invented the phrase in 1919 to indicate a small
group of people who mingled in public but would not be likely
to visit in one another's homes. By 1937, when *Fortune* magazine
printed an incisive report on cafe society,[1] the professional celebrities of erotic beauty and transient talent were well-planted at
the key tables, along with such charter members of the old upper
classes as John Hay ('Jock') Whitney.

Cafe society is above all founded upon publicity. Its members
often seem to live for the exhibitionist mention of their doings and
relations by social chroniclers and gossip columnists. Beginning as
professional party-givers or as journalists, these chroniclers, along
with headwaiters, have come to be professional celebrators and
have shaped the world of celebrity as others know it. Maury Paul
in 1937 was still commenting upon the accredited metropolitan
400, although he covered their livelier aspects. His successor, today's 'Cholly Knickerbocker,' one Igor Cassini, is not so limited.
The world he writes about is more glossy than accredited and certainly is not bound by *The Social Register*. Around such names as

Stork Club, columnists of tabloid and television have co-operated to fashion an aura of glamour seldom equaled in volume by the majesty of other courts.[2]

Perhaps it began in the 'twenties when socialites became really bored with Newport, and began to look to Broadway, then to Hollywood, for livelier playmates and wittier companions. Then, the speakeasy became a crossroads of Society and Broadway and Hollywood. 'Its Ward McAllister was the bootlegger; its visiting list was Dun & Bradstreet's; its Mrs. Astor could come from across the railroad tracks if only she came via Hollywood . . .' 'Prohibition,' write the editors of *Fortune*, 'helped pull it out of private houses and respectable hotels into speakeasies in search first of a drink and then of adventure; the automobile and radio industries gave it some new millionaires; rising real estate values drove Society out of its old brownstone houses into apartments and reconciled it to standardized mass entertainment parallel with new standardized mass housing; and if short skirts at first raised its eyebrows, Greenwich Village lowered its sex standard.'[3]

Five decades before, John L. Sullivan could not be recognized by Mrs. Astor's Ward McAllister; but Gene Tunney was welcomed by cafe society. And in 1924, what was the 400 to do, when the Prince of Wales seemed to prefer the jazz palace to the quiet homes of the proper families?[4] Cafe society rather than Newport frequently became the social target of new millionaires. And the new upper classes of the time—much of their wealth derived from the entertainment industries—seemed to press less upon the old upper classes than upon cafe society, in which they found ready entrée.

Nowadays, cafe society often seems to be the top of such American Society as is on national view. For, if its inhabitants do not have dinner rights in a few exclusive homes, they are instantly recognizable from their photographs. Cafe society's publicity has replaced the 400's family-line, printer's ink has replaced blueblood, and a sort of talent in which the energy of hoped-for success, rather than the assurance of background or the manners of inherited wealth, is the key to the big entrance. In the world of the celebrity, the hierarchy of publicity has replaced the hierarchy of descent and even of great wealth. Not the gentleman's club, but the night club, not Newport in the afternoon but Manhattan at night; not the old family but the celebrity. By 1937, according to *Fortune*'s listings, about one-third of the cafe society 'social list' was not in *The Social Register;*[5] today the proportion is probably less than that.

The professional celebrity, male and female, is the crowning result of the star system of a society that makes a fetish of competition. In America, this system is carried to the point where a man who can knock a small white ball into a series of holes in the ground with more efficiency and skill than anyone else thereby gains social access to the President of the United States. It is carried to the point where a chattering radio and television entertainer becomes the hunting chum of leading industrial executives, cabinet members, and the higher military. It does not seem to matter what the man is the very best at; so long as he has won out in competition over all others, he is celebrated. Then, a second feature of the star system begins to work: all the stars of any other sphere of endeavor or position are drawn toward the new star and he toward them. The success, the champion, accordingly, is one who mingles freely with other champions to populate the world of the celebrity.

This world is at once the pinnacle of the prestige system and a big-scale business. As a business, the networks of mass communication, publicity, and entertainment are not only the means whereby celebrities are celebrated; they also select and create celebrities for a profit. One type of celebrity, accordingly, is a professional at it, earning sizeable income not only from working in, but virtually living on, the mass media of communication and distraction.

The movie stars and the Broadway actress, the crooners and the TV clowns, are celebrities because of what they do on and to these media. They are celebrated because they are displayed as celebrities. If they are not thus celebrated, in due time—often very short—they lose their jobs. In them, the panic for status has become a professional craving: their very image of self is dependent upon publicity, and they need increasing doses of it. Often they seem to have celebrity and nothing else. Rather than being celebrated because they occupy positions of prestige, they occupy positions of prestige because they are celebrated. The basis of the celebration—in a strange and intricate way—is at once personal and synthetic: it is their Talent—which seems to mean their appearance value and their skill combined into what is known as A Personality. Their very importance makes them seem charming people, and they are celebrated all the time: they seem to live a sort of gay, high life, and others, by curiously watching them live it, celebrate them as well as their celebrated way of life.

The existence and the activities of these professional celebrities long ago overshadowed the social antics of the 400, and their competition for national attention has modified the character and the conduct of those who bear great institutional prestige. In part, they have stolen the show, for that is their business; in part, they have been given the show by the upper classes who have withdrawn and who have other business to accomplish.

The star of the silver screen has displaced the golden debutante, to the point where the latter, in New York or Boston or even Baltimore, is happy indeed to mingle in cafe society with these truly national queens. There is no doubt that it is enormously more important to one's prestige to have one's picture on the cover of a truly big national magazine than in the society column of any newspaper in America or even ten of them. And there is no doubt who gets on the cover of such magazines. The top spot for young ladies is probably *Life:* during the decade of the 'forties, no debutante from any city got there as a debutante, but no less than 178 movie queens, professional models, and the like were there displayed.

More serious public figures too, must now compete for attention and acclaim with the professionals of the mass media. On provincial levels, politicians play in hillbilly bands; on national levels, they are carefully groomed and coached for the TV camera, and, like other performers, the more important of them are subject to review by entertainment critics:

'Last night's "information talk" by President Eisenhower,' Jack Gould of *The New York Times* reported on 6 April 1954, 'was much his most successful television appearance . . . The President and his television consultant, Robert Montgomery, apparently found a "format" that enabled General Eisenhower to achieve relaxation and immeasurably greater freedom of movement. The result was the attainment of television's most desired quality—naturalness . . . As the program began the President was shown

sitting on the edge of a desk, his arms folded and a quiet smile
on his lips. To his right—and the viewer's left—was seen the flag.
Then casually and conversationally he began speaking. The same
mood and tone were sustained for the next half hour . . . In past
appearances when he used prompters, the President's eyes never
quite hit the camera; he always was looking just a hair to the left
or to the right. But last night his eyes were dead on the lens and
the viewer had a sense of being spoken to directly . . . As he neared
the end of his talk and wanted to employ added emphasis, the
General alternately knotted his hands or tapped the fingers of one
on the palm of the other. Because they were intuitive his actions
had the stamp of reality . . . The contents of General Eisenhower's
informal talk admittedly were not too earthshaking . . .'[6]

It is quite proper that 'The New 400' should be listed by the
gossip columnist who, in the world of the celebrity, has replaced
the well-bred man-about-town and the social hostess—the self-
conscious social arbiters who once lent stability to the metropolitan 400. In charge of the publicity, these new arbiters are not the
obvious satellites of any of those about whom they write and talk.
They are quite ready to tell us who belongs to 'The New 400,'
as well as to identify them with 'our magnificent accomplishments as a nation.' In 1953, Igor Loiewski Cassini—who became
'Cholly Knickerbocker' during the nineteen-forties—published a
list of 399 names which he believed to represent the 'aristocracy
of achievement in this country.'[7] These, he holds, are people who
are 'loyal' Americans, leaders in their field of work, men of 'excellent character,' men of 'culture and taste,' whole men having harmonious qualities as well as humility. Any such list, Cassini asserts, would change from year to year, since it is leadership and
humility that get them in and their children won't make it unless
they 'have also bequeathed all the talents that have made them
leaders.'

All of which is more or less complicated nonsense. Actually,
Cassini's list is a rather arbitrary selection from among the three
types of people continuously, or on occasion, caught up in the
world of celebrity:

I. There are the professional celebrities—making up some 30
per cent of the list—names of the entertainment industries,
champions of sport, art, journalism, and commentating. The larg-

est sub-group among these are straight entertainers, although a handful of them could as well be considered 'businessmen' of the entertaining world.

II. There are the metropolitan 400—but only some 12 per cent of them—people of family lineage and property. Some of these seem merely to have been born into such families, but the majority combine old families with active business positions.

III. Well over half of 'The New 400'—58 per cent—are simply people who occupy key positions in the major institutional hierarchies: most of these are government and business officials, although many are involved in both domains. There is also a small scattering (7% of the whole) of scientists, medical men, educators, religionists, and labor leaders.[8]

2

As a social grouping, the metropolitan 400 has been supplemented and displaced, but as individuals and as cliques, they have become part of the national system of prestige. That system does not now center in the several metropolitan 400's. For if, as we have said, the 400's of various cities can find no one city to which to look, in all cities, large and small, they can all look to the nationally celebrated, and those among them with the inclination and the money can join the world of the celebrity.

What many local observers assume to be the decline of the big-city upper classes is, in fact, the decline of the metropolitan 400 as the most emphatic public bearer of prestige.[9] If members of the 400 do not become part of this national system, they must withdraw into quiet local islands, living in another dimension than that of industrial and political power. Those who would now claim prestige in America must join the world of the celebrity or fade from the national scene.

The metropolitan 400 reached its peak of publicized prestige as the top of the national system of prestige about the turn of the century. In the 'eighties and 'nineties, the older families had contended with newer families of wealth, but by World War I these newer families had gotten in. Today, the new wealthy of the post-Civil War period are among the established upper classes of various big cities all over the country. But, during the 'twenties and 'thirties, as we have seen, the new and more glamorous contenders for prestige came to overshadow the metropolitan 400's, which thus had to contend not only with new upper classes, but the celebrities of the entertainment world as well. Even before the 'twenties, complaints and reminiscences by members of the 400 began frequently to be heard.[10] But all this is by no means to say that there is no longer a metropolitan 400. In fact, one feature of cafe society has remained 'the celebrated socialites' as well as 'the society-minded celebrities' who inhabit it. The prestige of the metropolitan 400 within cafe society is revealed by the fact that many people of older society and wealth could gain entrée but do not care to do so.[11] But it is also true that the old certainty of position is no longer so firm among those who 'do not care' to enter the ranks of the new celebrated.

The metropolitan 400 has not declined at the same rate in all the major cities. The center of its decline, and its replacement in public view by cafe society, has been New York City, and generally in the Middle West, which apes the East. In Philadelphia and in the South, its decline has proceeded more slowly. 'Society' is quite diverse: 'In Atlanta, "the club you belong to counts"; in Washington "anyone 'official' is society"; in Detroit it is "who you are in the auto industry"; in Miami "it's simply your Dun & Bradstreet rating." In Los Angeles the new society is intertwined with the movie colony. "One thing that's forced us to change," explains the *Los Angeles Examiner's* Society Editor Lynn Spencer, "is that now when Eastern socialites come West, they're more interested in seeing our movie stars than in meeting our own Western Society." '[12]

In New York, the old Knickerbocker Society has virtually withdrawn from the ostensible social scene; but, in Chicago it was still possible in 1954 for some two hundred pedigreed socialites, all supposedly with firm dinner rights, to know that Mrs. Chauncey McCormick—who serves impeccable dinners on gold plate and Lowestoft china—was Queen of the Society which they formed.[13]

The main drift in status, however, is clearly revealed by the parade of women who have been given American acclaim:[14]

1. The type of woman known as The Salon Lady—who passes before us in the pages of Proust—has never been known in America. The salon lady was the status representative of the household she commanded; as hostess, she judged who was and who was not to be admitted socially to it. If she gave birth to children, private

tutors, not she, educated them. And in her salon, where courtiers jousted with one another intellectually for her attention, the value and the fact of monogamous virtue frequently broke down. Eroticism became a sort of competitive sport in which women and men conquered one another in ways that were intriguing and exciting.

Apart from stray figures like Mabel Dodge of lower Fifth Avenue and Taos, New Mexico, there have not been women who ran genuine salons in the sense that salons were run as artistic and intellectual centers in Europe. The drawing rooms of the most famous American society ladies have been more often peopled by bores than by dilettantish intellectuals. They have, of course, contained a 'few dandies in the sense known to Savile Row and the boulevards of Paris,' but their *forte*, as Dixon Wecter put it, has most usually been the mimicry of personalities and their 'fame in repartee' has often rested 'upon the affinity between stammering and drollery.'[15] The dominant type of 'Society' man in America between the Civil War and World War I was rather the dancing man —the cotillion leader; and accordingly, discussion, let alone the type heard in the salon, has not played a noticeable part in the life of the American society lady.

The society lady, who held the balls and arranged the advantageous marriage for her daughter, was queen for only a relatively short period and only among a rather small public. The fashionable lady may have longed for publicity, but as a fashionable lady she did not have much of a chance to get it. By the 'twenties, when the mass media began their work with serious consequences, the society lady knew that her brief national time was over.

II. The leading figure of metropolitan 400 during the 'twenties and 'thirties was the debutante. Traditionally, the debut was for the purpose of introducing a young girl of high family to an exclusive marriage market, and hence perpetuating the set of upper families as an exclusive circle. In 1938, about 1,000 debuts were made, at an average cost of $8,000 each; but they could not really compete as spectacles with Hollywood. As a status model the debutante declined, not only because of the competition of the more entertaining glamour girls of the fashion industry and cafe society but because by the middle 'thirties the metropolitan 400, as based on family lineage, had so diminished in social exclusiveness that the debutante had no Society into which to make her debut. Or, at least, it did not seem a well-enough defined Society. By 1938, the editors of *Fortune* were noting that the vanishing of polite society left 'the debutante all dressed up with no place to go.'[16]

Some debutantes of the 'thirties tried to compete with Hollywood. They hired press agents who saw to it that their pictures were in the newspapers and articles about them were printed in the national magazines. The 'trick,' Elsa Maxwell has said, was 'to look so bizarre and so extreme that the truck drivers gasp but the ever-present cameraman will be bound to flash a bulb.'[17] As 'glamorous members of the younger set,' interested in charities and horse-racing, their faces—with complexions 'as translucent as alabaster'—appeared, endorsing soap in the women's magazines.[18] Grade-A debutantes not only frequented midtown East Side bars, but also worked as mannequins and even as salesgirls in exclusive shops. But their very use by advertising media and fashion industry revealed the ambiguity of their 'social distinction.'

Perhaps the extravagant private ball and the publicity that attended the debut of Brenda Frazier signified both the height of the debutante as a publicized American woman and the demise of the debutante's monopoly on glamour. Today the debutante is frequently not 'introduced to society' at private parties at her parent's sumptuous home; she comes out along with ninety-nine other girls at a large subscription dance in a hotel.[19] The assembly line of interlocking subscription dances is not so automatic 'that it will produce a debutante no matter who is put into it . . . There are ten committees guarding the approaches to the debut in New York, though a girl need not pass muster with more than five . . .'[20] To these subscription dances are attached most of the social secretaries, who keep lists of sub-debs and debutantes and eligible boys and arrange coming-out parties. Business magazines advise executives as to when and how to arrange for their daughter's debut, even if they are not listed in *The Social Register*. If the executive goes about it right, he is assured, his daughter 'can be considered as successfully launched socially as if she were a blueblood.'[21]

There are still private debuts, but the mass debuts now predominate, and probably will so long as 'society as a well-organized, clearly defined group' does not exist after the debutante year. Yet the year of the debut is still of social importance, no matter how standardized, since 'everything's got to be crammed into that short period because after that it disintegrates.'[22]

In so far as the more socially prominent modern debutante makes her debut into anything that will give her celebrity she makes it into cafe society. And, in so far as she is celebrated widely, she must compete with the other glamorous occupants of cafe society. The professional institutions of Conover and Powers, Mona Gardner reported in 1946, 'have raised modeling to such a glamour pinnacle that eligible men would far rather have a Powers or Conover girl on the arm, or in the home, than one of the bluebloods.'[23]

III. In cafe society today there are still the crew-cut young men from Yale and the debutante, but now there are also the heavy expense-account executives and The All-American Girl.[24] In any New York night club on a big night at the time of the two-o'clock show her current model can be found: with the doll face and the swank body starved down for the camera, a rather thin, ganted girl with the wan smile, the bored gaze, and often the slightly opened mouth, over which the tongue occasionally slides to insure the highlights. She seems, in fact, always to be practicing for those high, nervous moments when the lens is actually there. The terms of her competition are quite clear: her professional stance is the stance of the woman for whom a haughty kind of unconquerable eroticism has become a way of life. It is the expensive look of an expensive woman who feels herself to be expensive. She has the look of a girl who knows her fate rests quite fully—even exclusively—upon the effect of her look upon a certain type of man.

This is the queen—the all-American girl—who, whether she be debutante or fashion model or professional entertainer, sets the images of appearance and conduct which are imitated down the national hierarchy of glamour, to the girls carefully trained and selected for the commercial display of erotic promise, as well as to the young housewife in the kitchen. While the public, by its imitation, openly supports her image as a piece of very fancy sex, it is duly shocked when disclosures are occasionally made revealing the commercial fulfillment of this promise. But how could it be otherwise? The model's money does not add up to much. But the men she meets have money, and her tastes quickly become expensive. The men she meets control careers, and she wants a career.

She is of, but not solidly in, the world of breakfasts at noon and the long lunch. The all-American girl sits at the top of cafe society, and cafe society, we must remember, is a profitable set of businesses, supported by executives on expense accounts. And so the imitators of the queen sometimes become expense-account girls.[25] No 'New American Woman' of Theodore Dreiser's era knew as well as the all-American girl knows that 'the wages of sin might easily be success.'

The public is quite used to the idea of vice, but it likes to think it involves only idle rich boys and poor country girls. The men involved in the vice of cafe society, however, are by no means boys; they are not idle; they need not personally be rich; and they are not interested in poor or innocent or country girls. The women involved are not exactly girls; they may have come from smaller cities, but they are now very much big city; they are not innocent, and they are not exactly poor. One easily forgets that the underside of the glamour of cafe society is simply a service trade in vice. Those engaged in it—the procurers, the prostitutes, the customers, who buy and sell assorted varieties of erotical service—are often known to their associates as quite respectable. And the all-American girl, as a photographed image and as a person, is often a valued and indispensable helpmate to the great American salesman.

Among those whom Americans honor none is so ubiquitous as the young girl. It is as if Americans had undertaken to paint a continuing national portrait of the girl as Queen. Everywhere one looks there is this glossy little animal, sometimes quite young and sometimes a little older, but always imagined, always pictured, as The Girl. She sells beer and she sells books, cigarettes, and clothes; every night she is on the TV screen, and every week on every other page of the magazines, and at the movies too, there she is.

3

We have noted that since Mrs. John Jay's eighteenth-century dinner list, the political, military, and economic elite have not neatly coincided with those of superior social status. This is clearly reflected in the Society of Washington, D.C., today. In so far as there is a metropolitan 400 in Washington, it is merely one element in the social life of the Capitol, and is, in fact, overshadowed and out-ranked by official Society, especially by the Embassy Row along Massachusetts Avenue. Yet not all officials take Society seriously, and some avoid it altogether; moreover, key officials, regardless of social qualifications, must be invited, and, given the facts of politics, the turnover rate is high.[26]

If cafe society and all that it represents has invaded and distracted New York Society, the ascendancy of politics and the fact of political turnover have made Society difficult to maintain in Washington. There is nothing that could be called cafe society in Washington; the key affairs are in private houses or in official residences, and most elaborately in the embassies with their titled attachés. In fact, there is no really firm line-up of Society in Washington, composed as it is of public officials and politicians, of familied hostesses and wealthy climbers, of widows with know-how and ambassadors with unofficial messages to impart.

Yet prestige is the shadow of money and power. Where these are, there it is. Like the national market for soap or automobiles and the enlarged arena of federal power, the national cash-in area for prestige has grown, slowly being consolidated into a truly national system. Since the men of the higher political, economic, and military circles are an elite of money and power, they accumulate a prestige that is considerably above the ordinary; all of them have publicity value and some of them are downright eminent; increasingly, by virtue of their position and by means of conscious public relations, they strive to make their names notable, their actions acceptable, their policies popular. And in all this, they tend to become national celebrities.

Members of the power elite are celebrated because of the positions they occupy and the decisions they command. They are celebrities because they have prestige, and they have prestige because they are thought to have power or wealth. It is true that they, too, must enter the world of publicity, become material for the mass media, but they are sought as material almost irrespective of what they do on and to these media.

The prestige of the Congressmen, John Galbraith has remarked,[27] is graded by the number of votes he controls and by the committees he is on. The official's importance is set by the number of people working under him. The prestige of the businessman is measured less by his wealth or his income—although, of course, these are important—than by the size of his business. He borrows his prestige from the power of his company as measured by its size, and from his own position in its hierarchy. A small businessman making a million a year is not so important and does not have the national prestige enjoyed by the head of a major corporation who is making only two hundred thousand. In the military ranks, of course, all this is made formal and rigid.

At the turn of the century, the nationalization of status meant that there were rising elite groups with which local upper classes in every town and city of the nation had to compare themselves, and that when they did so, they came to realize that only locally were they at the top. Now, fifty years later, it means that, and much more. For what separates that age from ours is the rise of mass communication, the prime means of acclaim and even a creator of those acclaimed. From the coincidence of the mass media and the big organization there has emerged the prestige of the national elite. These national means of mass communication have been the channels through which those at the top could reach the underlying population. Heavy publicity, the technique of the build-up, and the avaricious demand of the media for continuous copy have placed a spotlight upon these people such as no higher circles of any nation in world history have ever had upon them.

The big institutions are in themselves graded worlds of prestige. They are stratified by level of office, with each level carrying its appropriate prestige. They constitute a hierarchy of people who by training and position defer to those above them, and come in time to respect their commanders who have such enormous power over them. No one can have such an organized deference group below him, and possess such powers of command as it provides, without also acquiring prestige among those who are directly of the big institution itself.

Instead of servants, there is the row of private secretaries; instead of the fine old house, the paneled office; instead of the private car, the company's limousine, the agency's chauffeur, the Air Force's motor pool. Frequently, of course, there are both the fine old house and the paneled office. Yet the prestige of the elite is, in the first instance, a prestige of the office they command rather than of the families to which they belong.

The position held in the national corporation has become a major basis for status claims. The corporation is now the organized power center of the propertied classes; the owning and managerial elites of the big-city upper class, as well as the members of local society, now tend to look to the corporation in claiming and in assigning prestige to one another, and from it they derive many of the status privileges they enjoy.* Inside the corporation and outside it among other corporate worlds as well as in the country at large, they gain the prestige of their positions.

As the national state becomes enlarged, the men who occupy the command posts within it are transformed from 'merely dirty politicians' into statesmen and administrators of note. Of course, it is true that the status pretenses of politicians have to be held carefully in curb: high political figures, even when it goes against their status grain, have had to learn to be folksy, and, from the standpoint of more ceremonial codes, vulgar in their tone of speech and style of life. Yet as the power of political institutions becomes greater, the men at the top become celebrities in a national system of prestige that cannot very well be resisted.

As military men have become more powerful during the wars and during the war-like interludes between, they too have joined the new national prestige scheme. They, as well as policemen, derive such importance as they have from the simple fact that violence is the final support of power and the final resort of those who would contest it. Only when revolution or crime threaten to disturb domestic order does the police captain, and only when diplomacy and war threaten international order, do the generals and admirals, come to be recognized for what at all times they are: indispensable elements of the order of power that prevails within and between the national states of the world.

A nation becomes a great power only on one condition: that its military establishment and resources are such that it could really threaten decisive warfare. In the rank order of states a nation must fight a great war successfully in order to be truly great. The effective force of what an ambassador says is a rather direct reflection of how mighty the general, how large and effective the fighting force standing back of him, is supposed to be. Military power determines the political standing of nations, and to the ex-

* See SEVEN: The Corporate Rich.

tent that nationalism is honored, to that extent generals and admirals share decisively in the system of national honor.

The public prestige of these various institutions varies, and accordingly the prestige of their elites. The prestige of public office and military position, for example, is higher in times of war, when business executives become dollar-a-year men and railroad colonels, and all groups rally behind the militant state at war. But when business-as-usual prevails, when businessmen leave government to others, public office and military status have often been vilified, as the prestige of public employment is deflated in favor of big business.

During the 'twenties the president of General Electric apparently was considered too valuable a man to be president of the United States;* and, even during the 'thirties, members of the mere cabinet of the United States were not always to be placed on an equal footing with members of very rich families.** Yet this

* '. . . In his inside circle of business and legal associates,' Ida Tarbell has noted of Owen D. Young, 'while everyone agrees that he would make a "great president," there is a feeling that he is too valuable a public servant where he is, to be, as one man put it to me, "spoiled by the presidency" . . . He has other admirers that intimate as much: Will Rogers who wants to keep him "to point to with pride"; Dr. Nicholas Murray Butler, who in introducing him in the fall of 1930 at a complimentary dinner said: "Our guest of honor is a public servant, although he holds no office. Whether the public servant receives office or not is accidental, and if this public servant by accident does assume office, as likely as not it is apt to reduce a great deal of the public servant's public service." '[28]

Mr. Young stated in his own economic metaphysics in 1931: 'A certain amount of horseplay seems to be required as stage effect for the functioning of democratic government. The world has learned that it can afford a certain amount of horseplay in politics. It is awakening to the realization that it cannot have horseplay in economics . . . Charming as politics may be at times on the stage, she is often petulant and petty in the dressing rooms . . . Nothing is clearer, from the experiences of the last ten years, than the necessity of keeping our economic machinery and especially our finance free from the domination and control of politics.'[29]

** Thus Harold Ickes writes concerning a 'state visit from the heads of one political entity to those of another political entity': 'Only a few chosen souls were asked to sit on the porch where the King and Queen spent most of their time, and apparently Jim Farley was the only mem-

lack of esteem for political office when compared with high corporate position has been changing and will change more—as the several elites come closer together within the state, and all of them learn better how to avail themselves of the means of publicity well within their powers to buy, command, or otherwise use. Those whose power or wealth exceeds their reputation will all the more readily become engaged in the means of publicity. More and more they play to the microphone and the lens as well as the news conference.[31]

4

Those who are familiar with the humanities, we should recall, often shy at the word 'prestige'; they know that in its origins it means dazzling the eye with conjuring tricks. Prestige, it is often held, is a mysterious force. 'Whatever has been a ruling power in the world,' Gustave Le Bon once remarked, 'whether it be ideas or men, has in the main enforced its authority by means of that irresistible force expressed by the word "prestige" . . . Prestige in reality is a sort of domination exercised on our mind by an individual, a work, or an idea . . .' This domination 'paralyzes our critical faculty' and fills us with 'astonishment and respect . . .'[32]

Mr. Gladstone much preferred 'honor' to 'prestige.' But, of course, as Harold Nicolson has noted,[33] the meaning of prestige varies in the several countries of the western world.* Moreover, men of power do not want to believe that prestige is merely some-

---

ber of the Cabinet, aside from the Hulls, who was considered worthy of inclusion among the elect. But J. P. Morgan was there and John D. Rockefeller, Jr., and Mrs. Cornelius Vanderbilt, etc. The rest of the members of the Cabinet milled about with the common herd down on the lawn, some fifteen hundred of them, and at not too frequent intervals the King and Queen would graciously go down among the herd bowing here and there and being introduced to some of the more select.'[30]

* In France 'prestige' carries an emotional association of fraudulence, of the art of illusion, or at least of something adventitious. In Italy, too, the word is often used to mean something 'dazzling, deceptive or legendary.' And in Germany, where it is a definitely foreign word, it corresponds to the German *Anshen* or 'esteem'; or to *der Nimbus,* which is close to our 'glamour'; or it is a variant of 'national honor,' with the hysterical obstinacy everywhere associated with such phrases.

thing nice that is given to the powerful. They want their prestige
to imply that other people are prepared to believe in their power
'without that power having either to be demonstrated or exercised.' But still this conception is neither complete nor satisfactory. In fact, it is a conception of prestige very convenient for the
already powerful—for those who would maintain it cheaply, without having to use power. And, of course, it is convenient for such
people to believe that their repute is based on amiable virtues
rather than past power.

Yet it is true that the power of guns or of money is not all
there is to prestige. Some reputation must be mixed with power
in order to create prestige. An elite cannot *acquire* prestige
without power; it cannot *retain* prestige without reputation. Its
past power and success builds a reputation, on which it can coast
for a while. But it is no longer possible for the power of an elite
based on reputation alone to be maintained against reputation
that is based on power.

If the prestige of elite circles contains a large element of moral
reputation, they can keep it even if they lose considerable power;
if they have prestige with but little reputation, their prestige can
be destroyed by even a temporary and relative decline of power.
Perhaps that is what has happened to the local societies and metropolitan 400's of the United States.

In his theory of American prestige, Thorstein Veblen, being
more interested in psychological gratification, tended to overlook
the social function of much of what he described. But prestige is
not merely social nonsense that gratifies the individual ego: it
serves, first of all, a unifying function. Many of the social phenomena with which Veblen had so much fun—in fact most 'status
behavior'—serve to mediate between the elite of various hierarchies and regions. The locales of status are the meeting places for
various elites of decision, and leisure activities are one way of se-
curing co-ordination between various sections and elements of the
upper class.

Like high families and exclusive schools, status activities also
provide a marriage market, the functions of which go well beyond
the gratifications of displayed elegance, of brown orchids and
white satin: they serve to keep a propertied class intact and un-

scattered; by monopoly of sons and daughters, anchoring the class in the legalities of blood lines.

'Snobbish' exclusiveness secures privacy to those who can afford it. To exclude others enables the high and mighty to set up and to maintain a series of private worlds in which they can and do discuss issues in which they train their young informally for the decision-making temper. In this way they blend impersonal decision-making with informal sensitivities, and so shape the character structure of an elite.

There is another function—today the most important—of prestige and of status conduct. Prestige buttresses power, turning it into authority, and protecting it from social challenge. 'Prestige lost by want of success,' Le Bon has remarked, 'disappears in a brief space of time. It can also be worn away, but more slowly, by being subjected to discussion . . . From the moment prestige is called in question it ceases to be prestige. The gods and men who have kept their prestige for long have never tolerated discussion. For the crowd to admire, it must be kept at a distance.'[34]

'Power for power's sake' is psychologically based on prestige gratification. But Veblen laughed so hard and so consistently at the servants and the dogs and the women and the sports of the elite that he failed to see that their military, economic, and political activity is not at all funny. In short, he did not succeed in relating a view of their power over armies and factories to what he believed, quite rightly, to be their funny business. He was, in my view, not quite serious enough about status because he did not see its full and intricate importance to power. He saw 'the kept classes' and 'the underlying population,' but in his time, he could not really understand the prestige of the power elite.[35]

The heart of Veblen's conception of prestige, and even some of its terms, were set forth by John Adams in the late eighteenth century.[36] But to know that John Adams anticipated much of Veblen's idea is in no way to deprecate Veblen, for is not his theory essentially an extended piece of worldly wisdom, long known and perhaps often stated, but stated by Veblen in magnificent form and at a time when it could take hold of a literate public? Adams, however, went farther than Veblen in at least two respects: He was shrewder psychologically—and more complicated; among his comments we also come upon certain passages in which he

tries to connect status phenomena, conceived as the realities of
social and personal life, with the political sphere, conceived, as
his generation was wont, as a problem of constitution building.
Adams understands the status system of a nation in a way that
Veblen does not, as politically relevant, and in this we had better
listen to John Adams:

'A death bed, it is said, shows the emptiness of titles. That may
be. But does it not equally show the futility of riches, power, liberty, and all earthly things? . . . Shall it be inferred from this, that
fame, liberty, property and life, shall be always despised and neglected? Shall laws and government, which regulate sublunary
things be neglected, because they appear baubles at the hour of
death?

' . . . The rewards . . . in this life, are *esteem* and *admiration* of
others—the punishments are *neglect* and *contempt*—nor may anyone imagine that these are not as real as the others. The desire of
the esteem of others is as real a want of nature as hunger—and
the neglect and contempt of the world as severe a pain, as the
gout or stone . . . It is a principal end of government to regulate
this passion, which in its turn becomes a principal means of government. It is the only adequate instrument of order and subordination in society, and alone commands effectual obedience to
laws, since without it neither human reason, nor standing armies,
would ever produce that great effect. Every personal quality, and
every blessing of fortune, is cherished in proportion to its capacity
of gratifying this universal affection for the esteem, the sympathy,
admiration and congratulations of the public . . .

'Opportunity will generally excite ambition to aspire; and if
even an improbable case should happen of an exception to this
rule, danger will always be suspected and apprehended, in such
circumstances, from such causes. We may soon see, that a form of
government, in which every passion has an adequate counter-
poise, can alone secure the public from the dangers and mischiefs,
of such rivalries, jealousies, envies and hatreds.'

Just what does Veblen's theory of status have to say about the
operations of the political economy? The metropolitan 400—about
which Veblen wrote—did not become the center of a national system of prestige. The professional celebrities of the mass media are

without power of any stable sort and are in fact ephemeral figures among those we celebrate.

Yet there is an elite demand for some sort of organization of enduring and stable prestige, which Veblen's analysis misses. It is a 'need' quite consciously and quite deeply felt by the elite of wealth and especially the elite of power in the United States today.

During the nineteenth century neither the political nor the military elite were able to establish themselves firmly at the head or even near the head of a national system of prestige. John Adams's suggestions, which leaned in that direction, were not taken up.[37] Other forces and not any official system of distinction and honor have given such order as it has had to the American polity. The economic elite—for this very reason it is uniquely significant—rose to economic power in such a way as to upset repeated attempts to found national status on enduring family lines.

But in the last thirty years, there have been signs of a status merger among the economic, political, and military elite. As an elite of power, they have begun to seek, as powerful men everywhere have always sought, to buttress their power with the mantle of authoritative status. They have begun to consolidate their new status privileges—popularized in terms of the expense account but rooted deeply in their corporate way of life. As they come more fully to realize their position in the cultural world of nations, will they be content with the clowns and the queens—the professional celebrities—as the world representatives of their American nation?

Horatio Alger dies hard, but in due course will not those Americans who are celebrated come to coincide more clearly with those who are the most powerful among them? The rituals of democratic leadership are firmly expected, but in due course will not snobbery become official and the underlying population startled into its appropriate grade and rank? To believe otherwise, it might seem, is to reject all that is relevant in human history. But on the other hand, the liberal rhetoric—as a cloak for actual power—and the professional celebrity—as a status distraction—do permit the power elite conveniently to keep out of the limelight. It is by no means certain, just at this historical juncture, that they are not quite content to rest uncelebrated.

5

In the meantime, the American celebrities include the trivial as well as the grim. Behind all The Names are the images displayed in tabloid and on movie screen, over radio and television —and sometimes not displayed but just imagined. For now all of the higher types are seen by those lower down as celebrities. In the world of the celebrities, seen through the magnifying glass of the mass media, men and women now form a kaleidoscope of highly distracting images:

In downtown New York, on a short street with a graveyard at one end and a river at the other, the rich are getting out of company limousines. On the flattened top of an Arkansas hill, the grandson of a late mogul is creating a ranch with the enthusiasm of a schoolboy.[38] Behind a mahogany table in the caucus room of the United States Senate, seven senators lean toward the television lenses. In Texas an oil man, it is said, is taking out two hundred thousand dollars a day.[39] Somewhere in Maryland people in red coats are riding to hounds; in a Park Avenue apartment, a coal miner's daughter, having lived in the married state for twenty months, has just decided to accept a five-and-one-half million dollar settlement.[40] At Kelly Field, the General walks carelessly between rows of painfully rigid men; on Fifty-Seventh Street, expensive women inspect the taut manikins. Between Las Vegas and Los Angeles, an American-born Countess is found dead in her railway compartment, lying full-length in a long mink coat alongside a quarter of a million dollars worth of jewelry.[41] Seated in Boston, a board of directors orders three industrial plants moved, without employees, to Nashville. And in Washington, D.C., a sober politician, surrounded by high military aides and scientific advisers, orders a team of American airmen to fly toward Hiroshima.

In Switzerland are those who never know winter except as the chosen occasion for sport, on southern islands those who never sweat in the sun except at their February leisure. All over the world, like lords of creation, are those who, by travel, command the seasons and, by many houses, the very landscape they will see each morning or afternoon they are awakened. Here is the old whiskey and the new vice; the blonde girl with the moist mouth, always ready to go around the world; the silver Mercedes climbing the mountain bend, going where it wants to go for so long as it wants to stay. From Washington, D.C., and Dallas, Texas, it is reported that 103 women have each paid $300 for a gold lipstick. On a yacht, with its crew of ten, somewhere off the Keys, a man of distinction lies on his bed and worries about the report from his New York office that the agents of the Bureau of Internal Revenue are busy again.

Here are the officials at the big desks with the four telephones, the ambassadors in the lounge-rooms, talking earnestly but somehow lightly. Here are the men who motor in from the airport with a secret service man beside the chauffeur, motorcycled outriders on either flank, and another tailing a block behind. Here are the people whose circumstances make them independent of the good will of others, never waiting for anyone but always waited upon. Here are the Very Important Persons who during the wars come and go, doubled up in the General's jeep. Here are those who have ascended to office, who have been elevated to distinguished employments. By the sound of their voices, it is evident that they have been trained, carefully yet casually, to be somebody.

Here are the names and faces and voices that are always before you, in the newspapers and on the radio, in the newsreels and on the television screen; and also the names and faces you do not know about, not even from a distance, but who really run things, or so informed sources say, but you could never prove it. Here are the somebodies who are held to be worthy of notice: now they are news, later they will be history. Here are the men who own a firm of lawyers and four accountants. Here are the men who have the inside track. Here are all the expensive commodities, to which the rich seem appendages. Here is the money talking in its husky, silky voice of cash, power, celebrity.

5

The Very Rich

MANY Americans now feel that the great American fortunes are
something that were made before World War I, or at least that they
were broken up for good by the crash of 1929. Except perhaps in
Texas, it is felt, there are no very rich anymore, and, even if there
are, they are simply elderly inheritors about to die, leaving their
millions to tax collectors and favorite charities. Once upon a time
in America there were the fabulously rich; now that time is past
and everyone is only middle class.

Such notions are not quite accurate. As a machine for producing
millionaires, American capitalism is in better shape than such unsound pessimism would indicate. The fabulously rich, as well as
the mere millionaires, are still very much among us; moreover,
since the organization of the United States for World War II, new
types of 'rich men' with new types of power and prerogative have
joined their ranks. Together they form the corporate rich of America, whose wealth and power is today comparable with those of
any stratum, anywhere or anytime in world history.

1

It is somewhat amusing to observe how the scholarly world has
changed its views of the big-business circles of which the very rich
are a part. When the great moguls were first discovered in print,
the muckrakers of journalism had their counterparts in the academic journals and books; during the 'thirties, The Robber Barons
clawed and bit their way to infamy, as Gustavus Myers's neglected work became a Modern Library best-seller and Matthew
Josephson and Ferdinand Lundberg were the men to quote. Just

now, with the conservative postwar trend, the robber barons are being transformed into the industrial statesmen. The great corporations, full of publicity consciousness, are having their scholarly histories written, and the colorful image of the great mogul is becoming the image of a constructive economic hero from whose great achievement all have benefited and from whose character the corporate executive borrows his right to rule and his good, solid, justified feelings about doing so. It is as if the historians could not hold in their heads a hundred-year stretch of history but saw all of it carefully through the political lens of each and every administration.

Two general explanations for the fact of the very rich—now and in the past—are widely available. The first, of muckraker origin, was best stated by Gustavus Myers, whose work is a gigantic gloss in pedantic detail upon Balzac's assertion that behind every great fortune there lies a crime. The robber barons, as the tycoons of the post-Civil-War era came to be called, descended upon the investing public much as a swarm of women might descend into a bargain basement on Saturday morning. They exploited national resources, waged economic wars among themselves, entered into combinations, made private capital out of the public domain, and used any and every method to achieve their ends. They made agreements with railroads for rebates; they purchased newspapers and bought editors; they killed off competing and independent businesses, and employed lawyers of skill and statesmen of repute to sustain their rights and secure their privileges. There *is* something demonic about these lords of creation; it is not merely rhetoric to call them robber barons. Perhaps there is no straightforward economic way to accumulate $100 million for private use; although, of course, along the way the unstraightforward ways can be delegated and the appropriator's hands kept clean. If all the big money is not easy money, all the easy money that is safe is big. It is better, so the image runs, to take one dime from each of ten million people at the point of a corporation than $100,000 from each of ten banks at the point of a gun. It is also safer.

Such harsh images of the big rich have been frequently challenged, not so much on the grounds of any error in the facts advanced, as on the grounds that they result from estimations from

the point of view of legality, morality, and personality, and that
the more appropriate view would consider the economic function that the propertied moguls have performed in their time and
place. According to this view, which has been most ably summed
up by Joseph Schumpeter, the propertied giants are seen as men
who stand at the focal points of the 'perennial gale of innovations'
that sweeps through the heyday of capitalism. By their personal
acumen and supernormal effort, they create and combine private
enterprises in which are embodied new technical and financial
techniques or new uses for old ones. These techniques and the
social forms they have assumed are the very motors of the capitalist advance, and the great moguls who create and command
them are the pace-setters of the capitalist motion itself. In this
way, Schumpeter combines a theory of capitalist progress with a
theory of social stratification to explain, and indeed to celebrate,
the 'creative destruction' of the great entrepreneurs.[1]

These contrasting images—of the robber and of the innovator
—are not necessarily contradictory: much of both could be true,
for they differ mainly in the context in which those who hold them
choose to view the accumulators of great fortune. Myers is more
interested in legal conditions and violations, and in the more bru-
tal psychological traits of the men; Schumpeter is more interested
in their role in the technological and economic mechanics of various phases of capitalism, although he, too, is rather free and easy
with his moral evaluations, believing that only men of superior
acumen and energy in each generation are lifted to the top by the
mechanics they are assumed to create and to focus.

The problem of the very rich is one example of the larger problem of how individual men are related to institutions, and, in turn,
of how both particular institutions and individual men are related
to the social structure in which they perform their roles. Although
men sometimes shape institutions, institutions always select and
form men. In any given period, we must balance the weight of the
character or will or intelligence of individual men with the objective institutional structure which allows them to exercise these
traits.

It is not possible to solve such problems by referring anecdotally
either to the guile or the sagacity, the dogmatism or the determination, the native intelligence or the magical luck, the fanaticism

or the superhuman energy of the very rich as individuals. These are but differing vocabularies, carrying different moral judgments, with which the activities of the accumulators may be described. Neither the ruthlessness and illegality, with which Gustavus Myers tends to rest content, nor the far-sighted, industrial statesmanship, with which many historians now seem happier, are *explanations*—they are merely accusation or apology. That is why modern social psychologists are not content to explain the rise of any social and economic stratum by moral reference to the personal traits of its members.

The more useful key, and one which rests easier within the modern mind, is provided by more objective circumstances. We must understand the objective structure of opportunities as well as the personal traits which allow and encourage given men to exploit these objective opportunities which economic history provides them. Now, it is perfectly obvious that the personal traits required for rising and for holding one's place among waterfront gangsters will be different from those required for success among peaceful sheepherders. Within American capitalism, it is equally obvious that different qualities were required for men who would rise in 1870 than for men who would rise eight decades later. It seems therefore rather beside the point to seek the key to the very rich in the secret springs of their personalities and mannerisms.

Moreover, explanations of the rich as a social fact by reference to their personal traits as individuals are usually tautological. The test of 'ability,' for example, in a society in which money is a sovereign value is widely taken to be money-making: 'If you are so smart, why aren't you rich?' And since the criterion of ability is the making of money, of course ability is graded according to wealth and the very rich have the greatest ability. But if that is so, then ability cannot be used in explanation of the rich; to use the acquisition of wealth as a sign of ability and then to use ability as an explanation of wealth is merely to play with two words for the same fact: the existence of the very rich.

The shape of the economy at the time of Carnegie's adolescence was more important to his chances than the fact that he had a practical mother. No matter how 'ruthless' Commodore Vanderbilt might have been, he would have accomplished little in appropriating railroads had the political system not been utterly corrup-

tible. And suppose the Sherman Act had been enforced in such
a way as to break up the legal buttress of the great corporation.[2]
Where would the very rich in America—no matter what their psychological traits—now be? To understand the very rich in America, it is more important to understand the geographical distribution of oil and the structure of taxation than the psychological traits
of Haroldson L. Hunt; more important to understand the legal
framework of American capitalism and the corruptibility of its
agents than the early childhood of John D. Rockefeller; more important to understand the technological progression of the capitalist mechanism than the boundless energy of Henry Ford, more
important to understand the effects of war upon the need for oil
and the tax loophole of depletion than Sid Richardson's un-
doubted sagacity; more important to understand the rise of a system of national distribution and of the mass market than the fru-
gality of F. W. Woolworth. Perhaps J. P. Morgan did as a child
have very severe feelings of inadequacy, perhaps his father did
believe that he would not amount to anything; perhaps this did
effect in him an inordinate drive for power for power's sake. But
all this would be quite irrelevant had he been living in a peasant
village in India in 1890. If we would understand the very rich we
must first understand the economic and political structure of the
nation in which they become the very rich.

It requires many types of men and vast quantities of national
endowment to run capitalism as a productive apparatus and a
money-making machine. No type of man could have accumulated
the big fortunes had there not been certain conditions of economic, material, and political sort. The great American fortunes are
aspects of a particular kind of industrialization which has gone
on in a particular country. This kind of industrialization, involving
very private enterprise, has made it possible for men to occupy
such strategic positions that they can dominate the fabulous
means of man's production; link the powers of science and labor;
control man's relation to nature—and make millions out of it. It is
not hindsight that makes us sure of this; we can easily predict it of
nations not yet industrialized, and we can confirm it by observing
other ways of industrialization.

The industrialization of Soviet Russia has now revealed clearly to the world that it is possible to carry through a rapidly advancing industrialization without the services of a private stratum of multimillionaires. That the Soviet Union has done so at the cost of political freedom does not alter the *fact* of the industrialization. The private corporation—and its attendant multimillionaire accumulations—is only one way, not the only way, to industrialize a nation. But in America it has been the way in which a vast rural continent has been turned into a great industrial grid. And it has been a way that has involved and allowed the great accumulators to appropriate their fortunes from the industrial process.

The opportunities to appropriate great fortunes out of the industrialization of America have included many facts and forces which were not and could not be contingent upon what manner of men the very rich have been, or upon anything they have done or did not do.

The basic facts of the case are rather simple. Here was a continental domain full of untapped natural resources. Into it there migrated millions of people. As the population steadily increased, the value of the land continuously rose. As the population increased, it formed at once a growing market for produce and goods and a growing labor supply. Since the agricultural sector of the population was growing, the industrialist did not have to depend upon his own laborers in factory and mine for his market.

Such facts of population and resources do not of themselves lead to great accumulations. For that, a compliant political authority is needed. It is not necessary to retail anecdotes about the legal illegalities and the plainer illegalities which the very rich of each of our three generations have successfully practiced, for they are well known. It is not possible to judge quantitatively the effects of these practices upon the accumulations of great fortunes, for we lack the necessary information. The general facts, however, are clear: the very rich have used existing laws, they have circumvented and violated existing laws, and they have had laws created and enforced for their direct benefit.

The state guaranteed the right of private property; it made legal the existence of the corporation, and by further laws, interpretations of laws, and lack of reinforcement made possible its elaboration. Accordingly, the very rich could use the device of the corporation to juggle many ventures at once and to speculate with other people's money. As the 'trust' was outlawed, the holding company law made it legal by other means for one corporation to own stock in another. Soon 'the formation and financing of holding companies offered the easiest way to get rich quickly that had ever legally existed in the United States.'[3] In the later years of higher taxes, a combination of 'tax write-offs' and capital gains has helped the accumulation of private fortunes before they have been incorporated.

Many modern theories of industrial development stress technological developments, but the number of inventors among the very rich is so small as to be unappreciable. It is, as a matter of fact, not the far-seeing inventor or the captain of industry but the general of finance who becomes one of the very rich. That is one of the errors in Schumpeter's idea of the 'gale of innovations': he systematically confuses technological gain with financial manipulation. What is needed, as Frederick Lewis Allen once remarked, is 'not specialized knowledge, but persuasive salesmanship, coupled with the ability to command the millions and the investment-sales machinery of a large banking house, and to command also the services of astute corporation lawyers and stock-market operators.'[4]

In understanding the private appropriations of the very rich, we must also bear in mind that the private industrial development of the United States has been much underwritten by outright gifts out of the people's domain. State, local, and federal governments have given land free to railroads, paid for the cost of shipbuilding, for the transportation of important mail. Much more free land has been given to businesses than to small, independent homesteaders. Coal and iron have been legally determined not to be covered by the 'mineral' rights held by the government on the land it leased. The government has subsidized private industry by maintaining high tariff rates, and if the taxpayers of the United States had not paid, out of their own labor, for a paved road system, Henry Ford's astuteness and thrift would not have enabled him to become a billionaire out of the automobile industry.[5]

In capitalistic economies, wars have led to many opportunities for the private appropriation of fortune and power. But the complex facts of World War II make previous appropriations seem puny indeed. Between 1940 and 1944, some $175 billion worth of prime supply contracts—the key to control of the nation's means of production—were given to private corporations. A full two-thirds of this went to the top one hundred corporations—in fact, almost one-third went to ten private corporations. These companies then made money by selling what they had produced to the government. They were granted priorities and allotments for materials and parts; they decided how much of these were to be passed down to sub-contractors, as well as who and how many sub-contractors there should be. They were allowed to expand their own facilities under extremely favorable amortization (20 per cent a year) and tax privileges. Instead of the normal twenty or thirty years, they could write off the cost in five. These were also generally the same corporations which operated most of the government-owned facilities, and obtained the most favorable options to 'buy' them after the war.

It had cost some $40 billion to build all the manufacturing facilities existing in the United States in 1939. By 1945, an additional $26 billion worth of high-quality new plant and equipment had been added—two thirds of it paid for directly from government funds. Some 20 of this $26 billion worth was usable for producing peacetime products. If to the $40 billion existing, we add this $20 billion, we have a $60 billion productive plan usable in the post-war period. The top 250 corporations owned in 1939 about 65 per cent of the facilities then existing, operated during the war 79 per cent of all new privately operated facilities built with government money, and held 78 per cent of all active prime war supply contracts as of September 1944.[6] No wonder that in World War II, little fortunes became big and many new little ones were created.

2

Before the Civil War, only a handful of wealthy men, notably Astor and Vanderbilt, were multimillionaires on a truly American scale. Few of the great fortunes exceeded $1,000,000; in fact, George Washington, who in 1799 left an estate valued at $530,000, was judged to be one of the richest Americans of his time. By the 1840's, in New York City and all of Massachusetts, there were only thirty-nine millionaires. The word 'millionaire,' in fact, was coined only in 1843, when, upon the death of Peter Lorillard (snuff, banking, real estate), the newspapers needed a term to denote great affluence.[7]

After the Civil War, these men of earlier wealth were to be recognized as Family Founders, the social shadow of their earlier wealth was to affect the status struggle within the metropolitan 400, and in due course their fortunes were to become part of the higher corporate world of the American economy. But the first really great American fortunes were developed during the economic transformation of the Civil War era, and out of the decisive corruptions that seem to be part of all American wars. A rural, commercial capitalism was then transformed into an industrial economy, within the legal framework of the tariff, the National Banking Act of 1863 and, in 1868, the Fourteenth Amendment, which by later interpretations sanctified the corporate revolution. During this shift in political framework and economic base, the first generation of the very rich came to possess units of wealth that dwarfed any that had previously been appropriated. Not only were the peaks of the money pyramid higher, but the base of the upper levels was apparently broader. By 1892, one survey revealed the existence of at least 4,046 American millionaires.[8]

In our own era of slump and war, there is debate about the number and the security—and even the very existence—of great American fortunes. But about the latter nineteenth century all historians seem agreed: between the Civil War and World War I, great captains of enormous wealth rose speedily to pre-eminence.

We shall take this generation, which came to full maturity in the 'nineties, as the first generation of the very rich. But we shall use it merely as a bench mark for the two following generations, the second coming to maturity about 1925, and the third, in the middle years of the twentieth century. Moreover, we shall not study merely the six or seven best-known men upon whom textbook historians and anecdotal biographers have based their criticisms and their adulations. For each of these last three generations, we have gathered information about the richest ninety or so individuals. In all, our study of these three lists enables us to expand our view of the American rich to include 275 American men and women, each of whom has possessed a minimum of about $30 million.[9]*

* See this footnote for a statement of the procedures used in selecting the very rich.

Among the very rich one can find men born poor and men born rich, men who were—and are—as flamboyant in their exercise of the power of money as they were in accumulating it, and others as miserly in their lives as harsh in their acquisitions. Here is John D. Rockefeller—the pious son of a Baptist peddler—who created literally scores of multimillionaire descendents. But here is Henry O. Havemeyer whose grandfather left him three million, and Henrietta Green who as a child was taught to study the financial pages of the paper and died at age eighty-two leaving 100 million. And we must not forget George F. Baker, Jr., a Harvard graduate and inheritor of the presidency of the First National Bank of New York, who bathed and shaved and dressed each morning on his speed cruiser coming into Wall Street from Long Island, and who, in 1929, with six other bankers, mobilized a quarter of a billion dollars in a futile effort to stabilize the crash.[10]

The big rich are not all of the past nor are they all from Texas. It is true that five of the richest *ten* among us today are of the Texas crop, but of the 90 richest men and women of 1950 of whom we have adequate knowledge, only 10 per cent are Texans.

Popular literature now offers many glimpses of fabulously rich individuals in various postures—august and ridiculous; of various origins—humble and elevated; of different styles of life—gay, sad, lonely, convivial. But what do all these glimpses mean? Some started poor, some were born rich—but which is the *typical* fact? And what are the keys to their success? To find out we must go beyond the six or seven tycoons in each generation about whom social historians and biographers have provided endless anecdotes. We must study a large enough number of individuals to feel that we have a representative group.

The 275 people about whom we have gathered information represent the bulk of those individuals who are known to historians, biographers, and journalists as the richest people living in the United States since the Civil War—the 90 richest of 1900, the 95 of 1925, and the 90 of 1950. Only by examining such groups are we able to ask and to answer, with some accuracy, the deceptively simple questions that interest us about the origins and careers of the very rich.

At the top of the 1900 group is John D. Rockerfeller with his billion dollars; at the top in 1925 is Henry Ford I with his billion;

and, in 1950, it is reported (although it is not so certain as in other periods) that H. L. Hunt is worth 'one or two billions.' The fortune of another Texan, Hugh Roy Cullen, has also been reputed of late to come to a billion.[11] These three or four men are probably the richest of the rich Americans; they are the only billionaires of which financial biographers are fairly certain.*

3

In none of the latest three generations has a majority of the very rich been composed of men who have risen.

During the course of American history since the Civil War, the proportion of the very rich whose fathers worked as small farmers or storekeepers, as white-collar employees or wage workers has steadily decreased. Only 9 per cent of the very rich of our own time originated in lower-class families—in families with only enough money to provide essential needs and sometimes minor comforts.

The history of the middle-class contribution to the very rich is a fairly stable one: in the 1900 generation, it provided two out of ten; in 1925, three; and in 1950 again two. But the upper-class and the lower-class contributions have quite steadily reversed themselves. Even in the famous nineteenth-century generation, which scholarly historians usually discuss with the anectocal de-

* The same amount of money of course has had different value at different periods. But we have not allowed this fact to modify our listings. We are *not* here interested in the question of whether $15 million in 1900 was worth $30 or $40 million in 1950 values. Our sole interest is in *the* richest at each of these periods, regardless of how rich that may be compared with the rich of other periods, or compared with the income and property of the population at large. The wealth of each generation, accordingly, is presented here in the dollar value of the time each generation reached the mature age of about 60.

Because of the unknown factor of inflation, it is necessary to use extreme caution in interpreting such facts as the following: of the 1950 generation, including billionaire Hunt, some six people are estimated to own more than $300 million, compared with no more than three such people in 1900 or 1925. Farther down the pyramid from these exalted levels, the distribution according to size of fortune is rather similar in each of the three generations. Roughly, about 20 per cent of each group are in the 100 million or more bracket; the remaining being rather equally divided between the $50–99 million and the $30–49 million levels.

tails of the self-making myth, as many of the very rich derived from the upper class (39 per cent) as from the lower. Still, it is a fact that in that generation, 39 per cent of the very rich were sons of lower-class people. In the 1925 generation, the proportion had shrunk to 12 per cent, and by 1950, as we have seen, to 9 per cent. The upper classes, on the other hand, contributed 56 per cent in 1925; and in 1950, 68 per cent.

The reality and the trend are clearly the upper-class recruitment of the truly upper class of propertied wealth. Wealth not only tends to perpetuate itself, but as we shall see, tends also to monopolize new opportunities for getting 'great wealth.' Seven out of ten of the very rich among us today were born into distinctly upper-class homes, two out of ten on the level of middle-class comfort, and only one in lower-class milieu.

Occupationally, 'upper class' among these very rich has meant the big businessman. At no time has the entire business stratum in America, big and little, been greater than 8 or 9 per cent of the working population at large; but in these three generations of the very rich as a whole, seven out of ten of the fathers have been urban entrepreneurs; one has been a professional man, one has been a farmer, and one has been a white-collar employee or wage worker. Across the generations these proportions have been quite stable. The very rich—of 1900 as of 1950—have come out of the entrepreneurial strata; and, as we shall see, in a rather curious way, on their higher levels, many of them have continued to be active in an 'entrepreneurial' manner.

About 10 per cent of those who have possessed the great American fortunes have been born in foreign lands, although only 6 per cent grew up outside the United States, immigrating after they were adult. Of the late nineteenth-century generation which reached full maturity by 1900, of course, more were foreign-born than in 1950. About 13 per cent of the 1900 rich were foreign-born, compared with about 24 per cent of the adult male U.S. population who were at that time foreign-born. By 1950, only 2 per cent of the very rich were foreign-born (compared with 7 per cent of the white 1950 population).[12]

The eastern seaboard has, of course, been the historical locale of the very rich: in all, some eight out of ten of those who grew up in America have done so in this region. There were as many from the East in 1925 (82 per cent) as in 1900 (80 per cent). By 1950, however, the proportions from the East—as among the population in the country as a whole—had dropped (to 68 per cent), a direct result of the emergence of the southwestern multimillionaires, who make up some 10 per cent of the very rich of 1950, compared with only about 1 per cent in 1900 and in 1925. The proportions who grew up in the Chicago-Detroit-Cleveland area have remained rather constant over the three historical epochs, 16 per cent in 1900 to 19 per cent in 1950.

The very rich come from the cities, especially from the larger cities of the East. Even in 1900, a full 65 per cent of the general American population lived in rural areas,[13] and many more than that had grown up on the farm; but only 25 per cent of the very rich of 1900 came from rural areas. And, since 1925 more than six out of ten of the very rich have grown up in metropolitan areas.

American-born, city-bred, eastern-originated, the very rich have been from families of higher class status, and, like other members of the new and old upper classes of local society and metropolitan 400, they have been Protestants. Moreover, about half have been Episcopalians, and a fourth, Presbyterians.[14]

With such facts before us, we would expect, and we do find, that the very rich have always been more highly educated than the common run of the population: even in 1900, 31 per cent of the very rich had graduated from college; by 1925, 57 per cent had done so; and by 1950, 68 per cent of the holders of great American fortunes were college graduates. That educational advantages are generally a result of family advantages is made clear by the fact that within each generation those from higher class levels are better educated than those from lower—in 1900, 46 per cent of those of upper-class levels, but only 17 per cent of those from lower, had graduated from college. But, by the third generation considered here—the very rich of 1950—the difference in the amount of education according to class origin decreased: 60 per cent of the very rich who had originated on lower or middle-class levels graduated from college, compared with 71 per cent of those from the upper classes.

Half of all those among the very rich who attended any college attended those of The Ivy League; in fact, almost a third went either to Harvard or to Yale, the rest being scattered among Princeton, Columbia, Cornell, Dartmouth, and Pennsylvania. An additional 10 per cent attended other famous eastern colleges, such as Amherst, Brown, Lafayette, Williams, Bowdoin, and another 10 per cent were students at one of a handful of well-known technical schools. The remaining 30 per cent went to colleges and universities scattered all over the United States.

The preponderance of Ivy League colleges is, of course, a direct result of the higher class origin of the very rich: as the proportions of very rich from the upper classes increases, so do the proportions who attend the Ivy League schools. Of those who were college educated, 37 per cent of the 1900 generation, 47 per cent of 1925, and 60 per cent of 1950 very rich attended such schools.

Back in 1900, when only 39 per cent of the very rich were children of upper-class parents, 88 per cent of those originating in such upper-class families are known to have inherited fortunes of a half a million dollars or more—usually much more. By 1950, some 93 per cent of the very rich from the upper classes were inheritors. It is frequently said that taxes now make it impossible for the very rich to leave outright a fortune of $90 or $100 million to their children, and this is, in a simple legal sense, true. Yet, the 1950 very rich are very much a continuation of the very rich of 1925; in fact, more of a continuation than those of 1925 were of the 1900 generation. While 56 per cent of the very rich of 1925 originated in the upper classes, only 33 per cent had relatives among the very rich of 1900. But 68 per cent of the 1950 very rich originated in the upper classes and 62 per cent had relatives among the very rich of the earlier generations.

Moreover, by the middle years of the twentieth century, it is, in some ways easier to transfer position and power to one's children than it was in 1900 or 1925, for then the lines of power and position were not so elaborately organized, buttressed, and entrenched in well-established circles, and the transfer of power and position seemed to be firmly assured only by means of huge personal fortunes. Among the very rich of 1950, however, there are many ways, as we shall have occasion to see, to pass on to children strategic positions in the apparatus of appropriation that constitutes the higher corporate level of American free, private enterprise.

4

The very rich in America are not dominantly an idle rich and never have been. The proportions among them that are rentiers and not much else, have, of course, increased significantly: in 1900, some 14 per cent; in 1925, some 17 per cent; and by 1950, 26 per cent. By virtue of how they spend their time, about one-fourth of the very richest people can now be called members of a leisure class.

Yet neither the idea of the very rich as miserly coupon clippers nor as flamboyant playboys is the representative fact. The idle miser as well as the busy spendthrift are represented among the very rich of America, but, in the history of the great American fortunes, the misers have not all been *mere* coupon clippers; they have usually 'worked' in some way to increase the value of the coupons they would have to clip—or at least pretended to do so while having others to manage for them.* And the spendthrifts

* The supposed shamefulness of labor, on which many of Veblen's conceptions of the upper classes rest, does not square very well with the Puritan work ethic so characteristic of much of American life, including many upper-class elements. I suppose that in his book on the leisure class, Veblen is speaking only of upper, not middle, classes—certainly he is not writing of wealthy Puritan middle classes. He did not want to call what the higher businessman does 'work,' much less productive work. The very term, leisure class, became for him synonymous with upper class, but there has been and there is a *working* upper class—in fact, a class of prodigiously active men. That Veblen did not approve of their work, and in fact refused to give it that term—work being one of his positive words—is irrelevant. Moreover, in this case it obscures and distorts our understanding of the upper classes as a social formation. Yet for Veblen fully to have admitted this simple fact would have destroyed (or forced the much greater sophistication of) his whole perspective and indeed one of the chief moral bases of his criticism.

From one rather formal viewpoint, it should be noted that Veblen was a profoundly conservative critic of America: he wholeheartedly accepted one of the few unambiguous, all-American values: the value of efficiency, of utility, of pragmatic simplicity. His criticism of institutions and the personnel of American society was based without exception on his belief that they did not adequately fulfill this American value. If he was, as I believe, a Socratic figure, he was in his own way as American as Socrates in his was Athenian. As a critic, Veblen was effective precisely because he used the American value of efficiency to criticize

have not all been merely that: some have gambled a million and often come up with two or three more; for their spendthrift activities have often been in the realm of appropriative speculation.

The men among the idle rich of 1900 were either third- or fourth-generation Astors or third-generation Vanderbilts: on their estates they relaxed with their horses, or on beaches with their yachts offshore, while their wives played often frantic and always expensive social games. By 1925, there were only a few more rentiers among the very rich but many more of them were women. They lived as expensively as did those of 1900, but now they were more scattered over the United States and they were given less publicity in the emerging world of the celebrity. Having beyond any doubt 'arrived' socially, these very rich women often became engaged by 'the arts' instead of 'society,' or busily pretended to be.[15] And in fact, some of them were spending more time in philanthropy than in social amusements or personal splendor, a fact that was in part due to the sober, Puritan beliefs of John D. Rockefeller from whose accumulations much of their money derived.

In the 1950 generation, both the proportion of rentiers (which we have seen to be 26 per cent) and the proportions of women among them (70 per cent) have increased, but they do not seem to form any one social type. There are the modern playgirls—Doris Duke and Barbara Hutton now expertly and expensively trying to conserve their youth; but there are also those who live, as did Mrs. Anita McCormick Blaine, an active life of spending money and time on philanthropy and education, taking little active part in social affairs. And there was Hetty Sylvia H. Green Wilks, the modern version of the miserly coupon clipper, who, as a child, had spent her summers 'in a barred and shuttered house and had to

American reality. He merely took this value seriously and used it with devastatingly systematic rigor. It was a strange perspective for an American critic in the nineteenth century, or in our own. One looked down from Mont St. Michel, like Henry Adams, or across from England, like Henry James. With Veblen perhaps the whole character of American social criticism shifted. The figure of the last-generation American faded and the figure of the first-generation American—the Norwegian immigrant's son, the New York Jew teaching English literature in a midwestern university, the southerner come north to crash New York—was installed as the genuine, if no longer 100-per-cent-American, critic.

go to bed at 7:30 p.m. for no lights burned in the Green house after that hour.'[16]

The history of the very rich in America is, in the main, a patri-archal history: men have always held from 80 to 90 per cent of great American fortunes. The increase, over the generations, in the proportions of the very rich who are recruited from inheritors of great wealth has not meant that all the rich have become 'idle.' We have seen that 62 per cent of the very rich of 1950 were born into families connected with earlier generations of very rich; but that only 26 per cent of the 1950 very rich are in their life-ways an idle rich. And many of the very rich who have inherited their wealth have spent their lives working to keep it or to increase it. The game that has interested them most has been the game of the big money.

Yet some 26 per cent of the very rich of today are rentiers and more or less economically idle; and another 39 per cent occupy high positions in firms owned or controlled by their families.[17] The rentiers and the family-managers thus account for 65 per cent of the very rich of our time. What of the 35 per cent remaining who *rose* to very rich status?

5

If many of those who were born into the very rich have spent their lives working, it is obvious that those who rose into it from middle and lower class levels are not likely to have been idle. The rise into the very rich stratum seems to involve an economic career which has two pivotal features: the big jump and the ac-cumulation of advantages.

I. No man, to my knowledge has ever entered the ranks of the great American fortunes merely by saving a surplus from his salary or wages. In one way or another, he has to come into command of a strategic position which allows him the chance to appropriate big money, and usually he has to have available a considerable sum of money in order to be able to parlay it into really big wealth. He may work and slowly accumulate up to this big jump, but at some point he must find himself in a position to take up the main chance for which he has been on the lookout. On a salary of two or three hundred thousand a year, even forgetting taxes, and living like a miser in a board shack, it has been mathematically impossible to save up a great American fortune.*

ii. Once he has made the big jump, once he has negotiated the main chance, the man who is rising gets involved in the accumulation of advantages, which is merely another way of saying that to him that hath shall be given. To parlay considerable money into the truly big money, he must be in a position to benefit from the accumulation advantages. The more he has, and the more strategic his economic position, the greater and the surer are his chances to gain more. The more he has, the greater his credit—his opportunities to use other people's money—and hence the less risk he need take in order to accumulate more. There comes a point in the accumulation of advantages, in fact, when the risk is no risk, but is as sure as the tax yield of the government itself.

The accumulation of advantages at the very top parallels the vicious cycle of poverty at the very bottom. For the cycle of advantages includes psychological readiness as well as objective opportunities: just as the limitations of lower class and status position produce a lack of interest and a lack of self-confidence, so do objective opportunities of class and status produce interest in advancement and self-confidence. The confident feeling that one can of course get what one desires tends to arise out of and to feed back into the objective opportunities to do so. Energetic aspiration lives off a series of successes; and continual, petty failure cuts the nerve of the will to succeed.[19]

---

* If you started at 20 years of age and worked until you were 50 or so, saving $200,000 a year, you would still have, at a rate of 5 per cent compound interest, only $14 million, less than half of the lower limits we have taken for the great American fortunes.

But if you had bought only $9,900 worth of General Motors stock in 1913, and, rather than use your judgment, had gone into a coma—allowing the proceeds to pile up in General Motors—then, in 1953, you would have about $7 million.

And, if you had not even exercised the judgment of choosing General Motors, but merely put $10,000 into each of the total of 480 stocks listed in 1913—a total investment of about $1 million—and then gone into a coma until 1953, you would have come out worth $10 million and have received in dividends and rights another $10 million. The increase in value would have amounted to about 899 per cent, the dividend return at 999 per cent. Once you have the million, advantages would accumulate—even for a man in a coma.[18]

Most of the 1950 very rich who are related to the very rich of earlier generations have been born with the big jump already made for them and the accumulation of advantages already firmly in operation. The 39 per cent of the very rich of 1900 who originated from the upper classes inherited the big jump; and a few of them, notably the Vanderbilts and Astors, also inherited the positions involving the accumulation of advantages. J. P. Morgan's father left him $5 million and set him up as a partner in a banking firm connected with financial concerns in both Europe and America. That was his big jump. But the accumulation of advantages came later when, in his capacity as financier and broker, J. P. Morgan could lend other people's money to promote the sale of stocks and bonds in new companies, or the consolidation of existing companies, and receive as his commission enough stock to eventually enable his firm to control the new corporation.[20]

After experience and profit in a lumber business, with his millionaire father's financial support, Andrew Mellon went into his father's bank and expanded it to national scale. He then became involved in the accumulation of advantages by lending the bank's money to young businesses—particularly in 1888, when the owners of patents for the refining of aluminum sold a share of their Pittsburgh Reduction Company to the Mellons in return for $250,000 which they used to construct a mill. Andrew saw to it that this aluminum company remained a monopoly, and that the Mellons came out the controlling power.[21]

No man, to my knowledge, has ever entered the ranks of the great American fortunes merely by a slow bureaucratic crawl up the corporate hierarchies. 'Many of the top executives in some of our largest corporations,' Benjamin F. Fairless, Chairman of the Board of U. S. Steel, said in 1953, 'have spent a lifetime in the field of industrial management without ever having been able to accumulate as much as a million dollars. And I know that to be fact because I happen to be one of them myself.'[22] That statement is not true in the sense that the heads of the larger corporations do not typically become millionaires: they do. But it is true in the sense that they do not become millionaires because they are 'experts' in the field of industrial management; and it is true in that it is not by industry but by finance, not by management but by promotion and speculation that they typically become enriched. Those who have risen into the very rich have been economic politicians and members of important cliques who have been in positions permitting them to appropriate for personal uses out of the accumulation of advantages.

Very few of those who have risen to great wealth have spent the major portions of their working lives steadily advancing from one position to another within and between the corporate hierarchies. Such a long crawl was made by only 6 per cent of the very rich in 1900, and 14 per cent in 1950. But even these, who apparently did move slowly up the corporate hierarchy, seem rarely to have made the grade because of talents in business management. More often such talents as they possessed were the talents of the lawyer or—very infrequently—those of the industrial inventor.

The long crawl comes to a pay-off only if it is transformed into an accumulation of advantages; this transformation is often a result of a merger of companies. Usually such a merger takes place when the companies are relatively small and often it is cemented by marriage—as when the du Ponts bought out Laflin and Rand, their largest competitor, and Charles Copeland—assistant to the president of Laflin and Rand—became assistant treasurer of du Pont and married Luisa D'Anbelot du Pont.[23]

The slow movement through a sequence of corporate positions may also mean that one has accumulated enough inside information and enough friendship to be able, with less risk or with no risk, to speculate in the promotion or manipulation of securities. That is why the generation of 1925 contains the largest proportions of the very rich making the long crawl; then the market was open for such profits and the rules of speculation were not so difficult as they were later to become.

Whatever type of venture it is that enables the rich man to parlay his stake into a great appropriation, at one point or another the 'bureaucratic' men have usually been as much 'entrepreneurs' as were the classic founders of fortunes after the Civil War. Many of them, in fact—like Charles W. Nash[24]—broke out on their own to found their own companies. Once the crawl was made, many of these men, especially of the 1925 set, took on all the gambling spirit and even some of the magnificence usually associated with the robber barons of the late nineteenth century.

The economic careers of the very rich are neither 'entrepreneurial' nor 'bureaucratic.' Moreover, among them, many of those who take on the management of their families' firms are just as 'entrepreneurial' or as 'bureaucratic' as those who have not enjoyed such inheritance. 'Entrepreneur' and 'bureaucrat' are middle-class words with middle-class associations and they cannot be stretched to contain the career junctures of the higher economic life in America.

The misleading term 'entrepreneur' does not have the same meaning when applied to small businessmen as it does when applied to those men who have come to possess the great American fortunes. The sober bourgeois founding of a business, the gradual expanding of this business under careful guidance until it becomes a great American corporation is not an adequate picture of the fortune founders at the higher levels.

The entrepreneur, in the classic image, was supposed to have taken a risk, not only with his money but with his very career; but once the founder of a business has made the big jump he does not usually take serious risks as he comes to enjoy the accumulation of advantages that lead him into great fortune. If there is any risk, someone else is usually taking it. Of late, that someone else, as during World War II and in the Dixon-Yates attempt, has been the government of the United States. If a middle-class businessman is in debt for $50,000, he may well be in trouble. But if a man manages to get into debt for $2 million, his creditors, if they can, may well find it convenient to produce chances for his making money in order to repay them.[25]

The robber barons of the late nineteenth century usually founded or organized companies which became springboards for the financial accumulations that placed them among the very rich. In fact, 55 per cent of the very rich of 1900 made the first step to great fortune by the big jump of promoting or organizing their own companies. By 1925, however, and again in 1950, only 22 per cent of the very rich made such a jump.

Very rarely have the men of any of these generations become very rich merely by the energetic tutelage of one big firm. The accumulation of advantages has usually required the merging of other businesses with the first one founded—a financial operation —until a large 'trust' is formed. The manipulation of securities and fast legal footwork are the major keys to the success of such higher entrepreneurs. For by such manipulation and footwork they attained positions involved in the accumulation of advantages.

The major economic fact about the very rich is the fact of the accumulation of advantages: those who have great wealth are in a dozen strategic positions to make it yield further wealth. Sixty-five per cent of the very richest people in America today are involved in enterprises which their families have passed on to them or are simply living as rentiers on the huge returns from such properties. The remaining 35 per cent are playing the higher economic game more actively, if no more daringly, than those who used to be called entrepreneurs but who in later day capitalism are more accurately called the economic politicians of the corporate world.

There are several ways to become rich. By the middle of the twentieth century in the United States, it has become increasingly difficult to earn and to keep enough money so as to accumulate your way to the top. Marriage involving money is at all times a delicate matter, and when it involves big money, it is often inconvenient and sometimes insecure. Stealing, if you do not already have much money, is a perilous undertaking. If you are really gambling for money, and do so long enough, your capital will, in the end, balance out; if the game is fixed, you are really earning it or stealing it, or both, depending on which side of the table you sit. It is not usual, and it never has been the dominant fact, to create a great American fortune merely by nursing a little business into a big one. It is not usual and never has been the dominant fact carefully to accumulate your way to the top in a slow, bureaucratic crawl. It is difficult to climb to the top, and many who try fall by the way. It is easier and much safer to be born there.

6

In earlier generations the main chance, usually with other people's money, was the key; in later generations the accumulation of corporate advantages, based on grandfathers' and father's

position, replaces the main chance. Over the last three generations, the trend is quite unmistakable: today, only 9 per cent of
the very rich came from the bottom; only 23 per cent are of middle-class origin; 68 per cent came from the upper classes.

The incorporation of the United States economy occurred on
a continent abundantly supplied with natural resources, rapidly
peopled by migrants, within a legal and political framework willing and able to permit private men to do the job. They did it. And
in fulfilling their historical task of organizing for profit the industrialization and the incorporation, they acquired for their private
use the great American fortunes. Within the private corporate system, they became the very rich.

In realizing the power of property and in acquiring instruments for its protection, the very rich have become involved, and
now they are deeply entrenched, in the higher corporate world
of the twentieth-century American economy. Not great fortunes,
but great corporations are the important units of wealth, to which
individuals of property are variously attached. The corporation
is the source of wealth, and the basis of the continued power and
privilege of wealth. All the men and the families of great wealth
are now identified with large corporations in which their property
is seated.

Economically, as we have seen, neither the inheritors nor the
accumulators have become an idle rich class of leisurely and cultivated persons. There are such among them, but almost three-
fourths of the very rich of our day have continued to be more or
less, and in one way or another, economically active. Their economic activities are, of course, corporation activities: promoting
and managing, directing and speculating.

Moreover, as the propertied family has entered the corporate
economy, it has been joined in the corporate world by the managers of these properties, who, as we shall presently see, are not
themselves exactly unpropertied, and who, in fact, are not an entirely distinct economic species from the very rich. The organizing
center of the propertied classes has, of course, shifted to include
other powers than those held by the big propertied families. The
property system, of which rich men form so key a part, has been
strengthened by its managerial reorganization, and it has been
supplemented by the executive stratum, within and between the

great corporations, which works energetically for the common interests of the corporate rich.

Socially, the men and women of the great American fortunes have taken their places as leaders of the several metropolitan 400's. Of the ninety members of the 1900 very rich, only nine were included in Ward McAllister's 1892 list, but roughly half of the families in our 1900 listing have descendants who in 1940 were listed in the Social Registers of Philadelphia, Boston, Chicago, or New York. The very rich are leading members of the metropolitan 400. They belong to its clubs, and many of them, and almost all of their children, went to Groton and then to Harvard, or to other such schools. Twelve of the fifteen sons (who lived to be of college age) of the ten men out of the 1900 very rich whom Frederick Lewis Allen selected as the leading financiers of 1905, went to either Harvard or Yale; the other three to Amherst, Brown, and Columbia.[26]

The very rich do not reign alone on top of visible and simple hierarchies. But that they have been supplemented by agents and by hierarchies in the corporate structure of the economy and of the state does not mean that they have been displaced. Economically and socially, the very rich have not declined. After the crash and after the New Deal, the very rich have had to operate with skilled, legal technicians (both in and out of governments) whose services are essential in the fields of taxes and government regulations, corporate reorganization and merger, war contracts and public relations. They have also adopted every conceivable type of protective coloration for the essentially irresponsible nature of their power, creating the image of the small-town boy who made good, the 'industrial statesman,' the great inventor who 'provides jobs,' but who, withal, remains just an average guy.

What has happened is that the very rich are not so visible as they once seemed, to observers of the muckraker age, for example—who provided the last really public view of the top of American society. The absence of systematic information and the distraction of 'human-interest' trivia tend to make us suppose that they do not really matter and even that they do not really exist. But they are still very much among us—even though many are hidden, as it were, in the impersonal organizations in which their power, their wealth, and their privileges are anchored.

6

The Chief Executives

MANY of those who are disposed to celebrate the American economy rest their case upon a curious jumble of notions about the chief executives of the big corporations. Within the free, private, enterprising system, it is said, there has arisen a set of executives who are quite distinct from the 'crude old-fashioned entrepreneurs' out for themselves in the ruthless ways of a capitalism now long dead. These executives, who have risen to the top, have come to be responsible trustees, impartial umpires, and expert brokers for a plurality of economic interests, including those of all the millions of small property holders who hold stock in the great American enterprises, but also the wage workers and the consumers who benefit from the great flow of goods and services.

These executives, it is held, are responsible for the refrigerator in the kitchen and the automobile in the garage—as well as all the planes and bombs that now guard Americans from instant peril. All of them, or nearly all, have come up from the bottom of the ladder; they are either farm boys who have now made good in the big city, or poor immigrants who have come to America and now enjoy the dream of success it allows. Full of the know-how that made America great; efficient, straightforward, honest, the chief executives, it is often said, ought really to be allowed to run the government, for if only such men were in charge there would be no waste, no corruption, no infiltration. Dirty politics, in short, would become clean business.

On a slightly higher level of sophistication, however, rather unpleasant things are said about the executives. After all, they are powerful men, rather new men of power, but upon what basis does their power rest? They are not the owners of the corporate properties, and yet they run the corporate show. If their interests are quite distinct from the interests of the rightful owners, just what are those interests? Have not these chief executives carried through a silent revolution, a managerial revolution from the top, and has not their revolution transformed the very meaning of property? Are not, in short, the old expropriators now expropriated by their salaried managers? Maybe the chief executives are trustees for a variety of economic interests, but what are the checks upon how fair and well they perform their trusts? And was it not the state, subject to the control of a free electorate, that was to be the responsible trustee, the impartial umpire, the expert broker of conflicting interests and contending powers?

Both the pleasantries and the unpleasantries about the executives are generally wrong and equally jumbled. The pleasantries are often mere kindergarten chatter for economic illiterates; the unpleasantries often rest on some very fast inferences from a few simple facts about the scale, the organization, and the meaning of private property in America. For in the agreeable as well as the disagreeable notions about the higher economic circles, one simple fact is often overlooked: the chief executives and the very rich are *not* two distinct and clearly segregated groups. They are both very much mixed up in the corporate world of property and privilege, and to understand either we must understand something of the upper levels of their corporate world.

1

The corporations are the organized centers of the private property system: the chief executives are the organizers of that system. As economic men, they are at once creatures and creators of the corporate revolution, which, in brief, has transformed property from a tool of the workman into an elaborate instrument by which his work is controlled and a profit extracted from it. The small entrepreneur is no longer the key to the economic life of America; and in many economic sectors where small producers and distributors do still exist they strive mightily—as indeed they must if they are not to be extinguished—to have trade associations or governments act for them as corporations act for big industry and finance.[1]

Americans like to think of themselves as the most individualistic people in the world, but among them the impersonal corporation has proceeded the farthest and now reaches into every area and detail of daily life. Less than two-tenths of 1 per cent of all the manufacturing and mining companies in the United States now employ half of all the people working in these basic industries.[2] The story of the American economy since the Civil War is thus the story of the creation and consolidation of this corporate world of centralized property.

I. In the development of each major industrial line, competition between many small firms tends to be most frequent at the industry's beginning. There is then a jockeying and maneuvering which, in due course, results in consolidation and merger. Out of the youthful competition, there emerges the Big Five, or the Big Three, as the case may be: a small set of firms which shares what there is to share of the industry's profits, and which dominates the decisions made by and for the industry. 'The power exercised by a few large firms,' John K. Galbraith has remarked, 'is different only in degree and precision of its exercise from that of the single-firm monopoly.'[3] If they compete with one another they do so less in terms of price than in terms of 'product development,' advertising, and packaging.[4] No single firm among them decides, but neither is the decision made impersonally by a competitive, autonomous market. There is simply too much at stake for that sort of slipshod method to be the going rule. Decisions become, explicitly or implicitly, the decisions of committees; the Big Three or Four, one way or another, are in on the major decisions that are rendered. In this there need be no explicit conspiracy, and certainly none that is provable. What is important is that each big producer makes his decisions on the basis of his impression of the reactions of the other big producers.

II. In the process of corporate consolidation many owning entrepreneurs and even salaried managers become too narrow; they cannot detach themselves from their own particular company. Managers with less personal feelings for any one firm come gradually to displace such men narrowed by their own experience and interests. On the higher levels, those in command of great corporations must be able to broaden their views in order to become industrial spokesmen rather than merely heads of one or the other of the great firms in the industry. In short, they must be able to move from one company's policy and interests to those of the industry. There is one more step which some of them take: They move from the industrial point of interest and outlook to the interests and outlook of the class of all big corporate property as a whole.

The transitions from company to industry and from industry to class are aided by the fact that corporate ownership is, in a limited way, scattered. The very fact of the spread of ownership among the very rich and the chief executives of the great corporations makes for a unity of the property class, since the control of many corporations by means of various legal devices has excluded the smaller but not the larger propertied interests.[5] The 'scatter' of sizeable property is within a quite small circle; the executives and owners who are in and of and for this propertied class cannot merely push the narrow interests of each property; their interests become engaged by the whole corporate class.

III. The six and a half million people who owned stock in publicly held corporations in 1952 made up less than 7 per cent of all adults in the population.[6] But that is not the whole story; in fact, by itself, it is misleading. What is important is, first, what types of people own any stock? And second, how concentrated is the value of the stock they own?

First of all: 45 per cent of the executives, 26 per cent of all professional persons, and 19 per cent of all supervisory officials hold stock. But only 0.2 per cent of the unskilled workers, 1.4 per cent of the semi-skilled workers, and 4.4 per cent of foremen and skilled workers hold stock.[7] Some 98.6 per cent of all workers in manufacturing own no stock whatsoever.

Second, in 1952, only 1.6 million (25 per cent) of the 6.5 million people who held any stock received as much as $10,000 per year from any and all sources. We do not know how much of that $10,000 came from dividends, but there is reason to believe that the average proportion was not great.[8] In 1949, some 165,000—about one-tenth of 1 per cent of all U.S. adults—received 42 per cent of *all* the corporate dividends going to individuals. The minimum income of these people for that year was $30,000.[9] The idea of a really wide distribution of economic ownership is a cultivated illusion: at the very most, 0.2 or 0.3 per cent of the adult population own the bulk, the pay-off shares, of the corporate world.

iv. The top corporations are not a set of splendidly isolated giants. They have been knit together by explicit associations, within their respective industries and regions and in supra-associations such as the NAM. These associations organize a unity among the managerial elite and other members of the corporate rich. They translate narrow economic powers into industry-wide and class-wide powers; and they use these powers, first, on the economic front, for example with reference to labor and its organizations; and, second, on the political front, for example in their large role in the political sphere. And they infuse into the ranks of smaller businessmen the views of big business.

When such associations appear to be unwieldy, containing conflicting lines of argument, cliques have emerged within them which have attempted to steer their programs and lend direction to their policies.[10] In the higher circles of business and its associations, there has long been a tension, for example, between the 'old guard' of practical conservatives and the 'business liberals,' or sophisticated conservatives.[11] What the old guard represents is the outlook, if not always the intelligent interests, of the more narrow economic concerns. What the business liberals represent is the outlook and the interests of the newer propertied class as a whole. They are 'sophisticated' because they are more flexible in adjusting to such political facts of life as the New Deal and big labor, because they have taken over and used the dominant liberal rhetoric for their own purposes, and because they have, in general, attempted to get on top of, or even slightly ahead of, the trend of these developments, rather than to fight it as practical conservatives are wont to do.

v. The growth and interconnections of the corporations, in short, have meant the rise of a more sophisticated executive elite which now possesses a certain autonomy from any specific property interest. Its power is the power of property, but that property is not always or even usually of one coherent and narrow type. It is, in operating fact, class-wide property.

Would it not, after all, be quite strange if, in a country so de-

voted to private property and where so much of it is now piled
up, and in an atmosphere which in the last fifty years has often
been quite hostile, where men of economic means also possess, we
are continually told, the greatest administrative and managerial
ability in the world—would it not be strange if they did *not* consolidate themselves, but merely drifted along, doing the best they
could, merely responding to day-to-day attacks upon them?

vi. Such consolidation of the corporate world is underlined by
the fact that within it there is an elaborate network of interlocking directorships. 'Interlocking Directorate' is no mere phrase: it
points to a solid feature of the facts of business life, and to a sociological anchor of the community of interest, the unification of outlook and policy, that prevails among the propertied class. Any
detailed analysis of any major piece of business comes upon this
fact, especially when the business involves politics. As a minimum inference, it must be said that such arrangements permit
an interchange of views in a convenient and more or less formal
way among those who share the interests of the corporate rich.
In fact, if there were not such overlapping directorships, we
should suspect the existence of less formal, although quite adequate, channels of contact. For the statistics of interlocking directorates do not form a clean index to the unity of the corporate
world or the co-ordination of its policy: there can be and there is
co-ordinated policy without interlocking directors, as well as interlocking directors without co-ordinated policy.[12]

vii. Most of the thirty-odd billion dollar corporations of today
began in the nineteenth century. Their growth was made possible
not only by machine technology but by the now primitive office instruments of typewriters, calculators, telephones, and rapid printing, and, of course, the transportation grid. Now the technique of
electronic communication and control of information is becoming
such that further centralization is entirely possible. Closed-circuit
television and the electronic calculator put control of an enormous array of production units—no matter now decentralized
such technical units may be—under the control of the man in the
front office. The intricately specialized apparatus of the corporation will inevitably be more easily held together and controlled.

The trend within the corporate world is toward larger financial
units tied into intricate management networks far more central-

ized than is the case today. Productivity has and will increase fabulously, especially when automation makes it possible to interlock several machines in such a way as to eliminate the need for much of the human control at the point of production that is now required. That means that the corporate executives will not need to manage huge organizations of people; rather, in *Business Week's* words, they will be 'operating great mechanical organizations using fewer and fewer people.'[13]

All this has not been and is not now inevitable; certainly the enormous size of the modern corporation cannot be explained as due to increased efficiency; many specialists regard the size now typical of the giants as already in excess of the requirements of efficiency. In truth, the relationship of corporate size to efficiency is quite unknown; moreover, the scale of the modern corporation is usually due more to financial and managerial amalgamations than to technical efficiency.* But inevitable or not, the fact is that today the great American corporations seem more like states within states than simply private businesses. The economy of America has been largely incorporated, and within their incorporation the corporate chiefs have captured the technological innovation, accumulated the existing great fortunes as well as much lesser, scattered wealth, and capitalized the future. Within the financial and political boundaries of the corporation, the industrial revolution itself has been concentrated. Corporations command raw materials, and the patents on inventions with which to turn them into finished products. They command the most expensive, and therefore what must be the finest, legal minds in the world, to invent and to refine their defenses and their strategies. They employ man as producer and they make that which he buys as consumer. They clothe him and feed him and invest his money. They make that with which he fights the wars and they finance the ballyhoo of advertisement and the ob-

---

* 'At the very least,' John M. Blair of the Federal Trade Commission has contended, 'the widely-held assumption that the ownership and control of plural production units by single corporate enterprises contributes to efficiency would seem to rest upon an overwhelming absence of supportable facts. The only noticeable gain achieved by these large corporations is in the purchase of materials, which undoubtedly results more from their superior buying power than any technological or managerial efficiency.'[14]

scurantist bunk of public relations that surround him during the wars and between them.

Their private decisions, responsibly made in the interests of the feudal-like world of private property and income, determine the size and shape of the national economy, the level of employment, the purchasing power of the consumer, the prices that are advertised, the investments that are channeled. Not 'Wall Street financiers' or bankers, but large owners and executives in their self-financing corporations hold the keys of economic power. Not the politicians of the visible government, but the chief executives who sit in the political directorate, by fact and by proxy, hold the power and the means of defending the privileges of their corporate world. If they do not reign, they do govern at many of the vital points of everyday life in America, and no powers effectively and consistently countervail against them, nor have they as corporate-made men developed any effectively restraining conscience.*

* Neither the search for a new equilibrium of countervailing power conducted by the economist, John K. Galbraith, nor the search for a restraining corporate conscience, conducted by the legal theorist, A. A. Berle, Jr., is convincing. Both are concerned to show the restraints upon the acknowledged powers of the corporation: Galbraith finding it from without, in a new version of the equilibrium theory; Berle, from within, in an odd view of the conscience of the powerful.

1. Many exceptions must be noted to any equilibrium that may prevail among the new giants. Some industries are integrated from the source of supply to the ultimate consumer; and in some industries, such as residential construction, the individual contractor is squeezed between strong craft unions and strong suppliers, rather than balancing with them. Moreover, as is recognized by Mr. Galbraith himself, 'countervailing power' does not work in periods of inflation, for then the corporation's resistance to wage demands is reduced, and it is easy to pass on the increased costs to the consumer, whose demands, in turn, are so strong that the retailer is pressed to satisfy them, and thus cannot wield his power against the corporate producer. In such times, the big units, far from being held in countervailance, become a 'coalition against the public.' The big power blocs gang up on the consumer, rather than benefit him by countervailing against one another. It also would seem that market power does not exactly 'generate' countervailing power: with the exception of railroading, strong unions did not develop in strong industries, until government backed them up in the 'thirties. Nor do chain stores prosper in countervailance to automobiles or petroleum but rather in the relatively unconcentrated field of food suppliers. The

2

The corporate world is only two or three generations old, yet even in this short time, it has selected and created certain types of men who have risen with it and within it. What manner of men are they? We are not here interested in the bulk of the corporate managers, nor in any average executive—if such a conception is meaningful and revealing. We are interested in the very top men of the corporate world—top according to the criteria which they themselves use in grading one another: the controlling positions they occupy.

The chief executives are the men who occupy the top two or three command posts in each of those hundred or so corporations which, measured by sales and capital, are the largest. If, in any one year we list these leading corporations, in all industrial lines,

---

new equilibrium, in short, is not self-regulating. To know that power does not automatically 'beget' its countervailing power, one has only to think of farm laborers and white-collar employees. But the weaker unit, Mr. Galbraith urges, *ought* to organize an opposition; then perhaps it will be able to get the aid of government, and government *should* support the weaker side of any imbalance. Thus weakness, as well as strength, is to lead to countervailing power, and *the theory of the big equilibrium becomes less a theory of the going fact than a suggested guideline to public policy,* a moral proposal for strategic action. Moreover, it is assumed that the government is less an integral element of the balance than an umpire biased toward shoring up those with weak market power. When the conceptions of the big balance are laid alongside the qualifications and exceptions which must be made, they do not seem so compelling as the bold initial statement of 'countervailing power.' Like the 'competition' among little entrepreneurs, which it is designed to replace, 'countervailing power' among the big blocs is more ideological hope than factual description, more dogma than realism.[15]

11. As for Mr. Berle's search for a corporate conscience, see the remainder of this chapter for an account of the men who have presumably developed it. In a money-economy, expediency may follow the longer or the shorter run. Their inclination for longer-run profits, for a stable take, in an economy integrated with political institutions and shored up by military purchases, requires that corporations become more political; and today they are, of course, as much political as economic institutions. As political institutions, they are of course totalitarian and dictatorial, although externally, they display much public relation and liberal rhetoric of defense. Mr. Berle, in brief, mistakes expedient public relations for a 'corporate soul.'[16]

and from their top levels select the presidents and the chairmen of their boards, we shall have listed the chief executives. We have six or seven careful studies of such executives, covering the period of the last century.[17]

Are the top executives of the big corporations a distinct breed of men, or are they merely a miscellaneous collection of Americans? Are they what Balzac would have called a genuine social type? Or do they represent a cross-section of Americans who happen to be successful? The top executives of the big companies are not, and never have been, a miscellaneous collection of Americans; they are a quite uniform social type which has had exceptional advantages of origin and training, and they do not fit many of the stereotypes that prevail about them.

The top executives of 1950 are not country boys who have made good in the city: whereas 60 per cent of the population about the time of their birth, in 1890, lived in rural areas, only 35 per cent of the 1950 executives were born in rural communities. And this was even more true in 'the good old days': even in 1870, only half of the executives were farm born, compared with 93 per cent of the 1820 population.

They are not immigrants, poor or rich, or even the sons of immigrants who have made good in America. The families of about half of the 1950 executives settled in America before the revolution—which is not a much different proportion than among the population at large, and which of course represents a decline from the 1870 executives, of whom 86 per cent were of colonial families. Yet only 8 per cent of the post-Civil-War executives have been foreign-born—and only 6 per cent of the 1950 set, less than half the 15 per cent foreign-born among the representative population at the time of their birth. The proportion of sons of the foreign-born—of the second generation—has increased, especially in the newer industries of distribution and mass entertainment and communication; but it still remains below the representative level. Over three-quarters of the 1950 executives are American-born of American-born fathers.

The business executives are predominately Protestant and more likely, in comparison with the proportions of the population at large, to be Episcopalians or Presbyterians than Baptists or Methodists. The Jews and Catholics among them are fewer than among the population at large.

These urban, white, Protestant Americans were born into families of the upper and upper-middle classes. Their fathers were mainly entrepreneurs: 57 per cent are sons of businessmen; 14 per cent, of professional men; 15 per cent, of farmers. Only 12 per cent are sons of wage workers or of lower white-collar employees. This entrepreneurial origin more emphatically sets the executives off as a group apart when we remember that at the time of their start in life—around 1900—only 8 per cent of all the men at work in America were businessmen, only 3 per cent were professional men. Some 25 per cent were then 'farmers'—an ambiguous term—and almost 60 per cent, five times greater a proportion than among the executives, were in wage or salary work.

Moreover, apart from a decline in farm boys, the executives of the entire post-Civil-War era are substantially similar in occupational origin. At any period, over 60 per cent—usually closer to 70 —of American executives have been from the business and professional classes; and never more than 10 or 12 per cent from the wage worker or lower white-collar employee level. In fact, only 8 per cent of the paternal grandfathers of the 1950 executives were wage or office workers, while 57 per cent of the male population were. Of these grandfathers, 54 per cent were business or professional, at a time when no more than 9 per cent of the male population was; 33 per cent of the grandfathers were farmers or planters, roughly the same as the general male population.

For at least two generations now, the families of the top executives of the big American corporations have, as a group, been far removed from wage work and the lower white-collar ranks. In fact, their families are in a substantial proportion citizens of good repute in the local societies of America. And only 2½ per cent of the top executives who were under 50 years of age in 1952 (the newest crop) come up from the ranks of wage-worker families.[18]

Back in 1870, not more than 1 or 2 per cent of adult American men had graduated from college, but about one-third of the 1870 executives had. Among today's executives, nine times as great a proportion (60 per cent) are college graduates as among the comparable white males between 45 and 55 years of age (7 per cent). Moreover, almost half of them have had formal educational training beyond college, 15 per cent in law, 15 per cent in engineering, and about the same proportion in miscellaneous courses and schools.[19]

The typical executives, today as in the past, were born with a big advantage: they managed to have fathers on at least upper middle-class levels of occupation and income; they are Protestant, white, and American-born. These factors of origin led directly to their second big advantage: they are well educated in the formal sense of college and post-college schooling. That such facts of origin were keys to their educational advantages is clear from the simple fact that among them—as among any group we might study—those with the highest origins have had the best chances for formal education.

The salaries of the executives vary somewhat by the industry they are in, but in 1950 the top 900 executives averaged about $70,000 a year; the chief executive officers among them, about $100,000.[20] But salaries are not typically their only source of income. In the briefcases of virtually every major executive there is a portfolio ready for additional stock certificates. There are many places of secure anchorage in the corporate world,* but the most secure is the position of the owner of big pieces of corporate property. In the big corporation the fact that the executives do not own the property they manage means that by their decisions they do not risk their own property. When the profits are high they continue to receive high salaries and bonuses. When they don't go so well, their salaries often continue quite high even though their bonuses drop. The bulk of executives today, in addition to salary payments, received bonuses, either in stock or cash, and often in installments over a period of years.[21] In 1952, among the highest paid executives were Crawford Greenewalt, President of E. I. du Pont de Nemours and Co., with $153,290 in salary and $350,000 in bonuses; Harlow Curtice, then one of four executive vice-presidents of General Motors, received $151,200 in salary and $370,000 in bonuses; Eugene G. Grace, President of Bethlehem Steel Corp., received $150,000 as salary and $306,652 in bonuses. Charles E. Wilson, with his much-publicized salary and stockholdings, was the highest paid executive in American industry: $201,000 in sal-

* See below, SEVEN: The Corporate Rich.

ary and $380,000 in bonuses, plus an unknown amount in dividends.[22]

The executives do not constitute a 'leisure class,'[23] but they are not without the higher comforts. By the time they are fifty or sixty years of age, most chief executives have impressive houses, usually in the country, but not too far from 'their cities.' Whether they also have places in town depends somewhat on the city—they are more likely to in New York or Boston than in Los Angeles. Now they are receiving large incomes, from their salaries as well as from dividends which may amount to as much or more. And so at about this point they branch out in a variety of ways. Many acquire sizable farms and go in for raising fancy livestock. Wilson, of Detroit and Washington, has Ayrshire cattle on his Michigan farm and plans to experiment with a new breed on his Louisiana plantation.[24] Cyrus Eaton has short-horn cattle. Mr. Eisenhower, in his smaller way, now emulates his models with Aberdeen-Angus. The executives are definitely numerous among the three or four thousand people who own boats of over 65 feet or 15 ton displacement. They may even ride to hounds, and moreover, like Mr. George Humphrey, wear pink coats while doing so. The leisure of many chief executives is taken up by country places and a good deal of hunting. Some fly by private plane to the Canadian woods, others have private cabanas at Miami or Hobe Sound.

It is not characteristic of American executives to read books, except books on 'management' and mysteries; 'The majority of top executives almost never read drama, great fiction, the philosophers, the poets. Those who do venture into this area . . . are definitely sports of the executive type, looked upon by their colleagues with mingled awe and incredulity.'[25] Executive circles do not overlap very much with those of artistic or literary interest. Among them are those who resent reading a report or a letter longer than one page, such avoidance of words being rather general. They seem somehow suspicious of long-winded speeches, except when they are the speakers, and they do not, of course, have the time. They are very much of the age of the 'briefing,' of the digest, of the two-paragraph memo. Such reading as they do, they often delegate to others, who clip and summarize for them. They are talkers and listeners rather than readers or writers. They pick up much of what they know at the conference table and from friends in other fields.

3

If we attempt to draw blueprints of the external careers of the executives, we find several more or less distinct types:

I. Entrepreneurs, by definition, start or organize a business with their own or with others' funds, and as the business grows so does their stature as executives. Less educated than other executives, this type tends to begin working at an earlier age and to have worked in several companies. According to the careful tally of Miss Suzanne I. Keller, a grand total of 6 per cent of the top corporation executives in 1950 America have followed such an entrepreneurial route to the top.

II. Some executives have been placed in companies owned by their fathers or other relatives and have subsequently inherited their positions. These men tend to begin work later in their lives than other types, and frequently never work in companies other than the one in which they eventually come to the top. In these companies, however, they often work for considerable periods before assuming the key posts of command. Some 11 per cent of the 1950 executives are such family-managers.

III. Another 13 per cent did not begin in business at all, but as professional men, primarily lawyers. Their work in their profession leads—usually after professional success—to their becoming corporation presidents or board chairmen. As the incorporation of the economy got under way, William Miller has noted, corporations felt the need, on the one hand, to get in touch with lawyers in public office and, on the other, 'to have growing recourse to private legal advice in the making of day to day business decisions. The demand for such advice, indeed, became so great that the best paid metropolitan lawyers almost without exception after 1900 made business counseling the focus of their work, at the expense of traditional advocacy; and many lawyers yielded to the blandishments of the corporations to become house counsel and even regular business executives themselves.'[26] Today, the success of the corporation depends to a considerable extent upon minimizing its tax burden, maximizing its speculative projects through mergers, controlling government regulatory bodies, influencing state and national legislatures. Accordingly, the lawyer is becoming a pivotal figure in the giant corporation.

iv. These three types of careers—entrepreneurial, family, and professional—have been followed by about one-third of the top 1950 executives. The external career-line of the remaining 68 per cent is a series of moves, over a long period of time, within and between the various levels and circles of the corporate business world

Two generations ago, 36 per cent of the executives—as compared with only 6 per cent today—were entrepreneurial; 32 per cent were family-managers, as against 11· per cent today; there were about the same proportion then of professional men, 14 per cent, as now, 13 per cent. Steadily and swiftly—from 18 per cent in 1870 to 68 per cent in 1950—the career of the business executive has become a movement within and between the corporate hierarchies.

If we examine the careers of 900 top 1950 executives—the largest group of contemporary executives whose careers have been studied—we find that the bulk of them began their work for large companies, and that about one-third of them have never worked for any other company than the one they now head. The greater number worked for one or two other companies, and over 20 per cent worked for three or four. So there is typically some criss-crossing of corporate boundaries in their climb. Even so, their average age when they were hired by their present company was about twenty-nine.

About a third, as one might expect on the basis of their origin and education, started in their present company as executives. Well over a third—in fact 44 per cent—started in various 'departments.' That leaves about 24 per cent who started as clerks or laborers. We must, however, be careful about interpreting such figures. Low jobs in themselves do not mean anything, especially when one considers the backgrounds and higher educations of these executives. The taking of a clerical or, much better, a labor job for awhile 'to learn the business' is often a sort of ritual for some families and some companies. At any rate, more of the *chief* executives started on the executive level; more of the younger men started in the more specialized departments. For example, over one-third of those under 50 had a position in 'sales' just before their top jobs.[27]

Those are the outside facts of the executive's career. But the outside facts, no matter how added up, are not inside facts. There is the bureaucratic crawl and there is the entrepreneurial leap. But there is also the deal of the fixer, the coup of the promoter, the maneuver of the clique. Words like entrepreneur and bureaucrat are no more adequate to convey the realities of the higher corporate career than of the appropriation of great fortunes. They are, as we have noted in connection with the very rich, middle-class words, and retain the limitations of middle-class perspectives.

'Entrepreneur' suggests the picture of a man with all the risks of life about him, soberly founding an enterprise and carefully nurturing its growth into a great company. In 1950, a far more accurate picture of the 'entrepreneurial' activity of the corporate elite is the setting up of a financial deal which merges one set of files with another. The chief executives of today do less building up of new organizations than carrying on of established ones. And, as Robert A. Gordon has indicated, they are less creative, restless, dynamic individuals than professional co-ordinators of decisions, 'approving decisions that flow up . . . from . . . subordinates, but doing less and less initiation.'[28]

It is usual in studies of business executives to term such a career, 'bureaucratic,' but, strictly speaking, this is not correct. The bureaucratic career, properly defined, does not mean merely a climb up, from one level to the next, of a hierarchy of offices. It does involve that, but more importantly, it means the setting up of strict and unilateral qualifications for each office occupied. Usually these qualifications involve both specified formal training and qualifying examinations. The bureaucratic career also means that men work for salaried advancement without any expectation of coming to own even a part of the enterprise, of personally appropriating a portion of the accumulated property of the enterprise, by bonuses or stock options or lavish pension and insurance plans.*

Just as the word 'entrepreneur,' as used to refer to the career of the very rich of today, is often misleading, so the word 'bureaucratic,' as used to refer to corporation executives on the higher levels, is misleading. Both the advancement of the chief executives and the accumulations of the very rich, on the higher levels,

---

* For more on the bureaucratic career, see below ELEVEN: The Theory of Balance.

are definitely mixed up in a 'political' world of corporate cliques. To advance within and between private corporate hierarchies means to be chosen for advancement by your superiors—administrative and financial—and there are no strict, impersonal rules of qualifications or seniority known to all concerned in this process.

On the higher levels of the corporate world, careers are neither 'bureaucratic' nor 'entrepreneurial;' they are a composite of pay-offs, involving speculators, men with great American fortunes, and executives in jobs with chances to make money. The owners alone can no longer say with William H. Vanderbilt in 1882, 'The public be Damned.' Neither can the professional executives alone. Together—as a set of corporate cliques—they can say what they want, although today they are usually too wise in the ways of public relations to say it, and besides they do not need to say it.

4

There is, of course, no one type of corporate hierarchy, but one general feature of the corporate world does seem to prevail quite widely. It involves a Number One stratum at the top whose members as individuals—and increasingly as committees—advise and counsel and receive reports from a Number Two stratum of operating managers.[29]

It is of the Number One stratum that the very rich and the chief executives are a part. The Number Two men are individually responsible for given units, plants, departments. They stand between the active working hierarchies and the directing top to which they are responsible. And in their monthly and yearly reports to the top executives, one simple set of questions is foremost: Did we make money: If so, how much? If not, why not?

Decision-making by individual executives at the top is slowly being replaced by the worried-over efforts of committees, who judge ideas tossed before them, usually from below the top levels. The technical men, for example, may negotiate for months with the salesmen over a tubeless tire before the chief executives descend to operation-level conferences.[30] Theirs is not the idea nor even the decision, but The Judgment. On the top levels this judgment usually has to do with the spending of money to make more money and the getting of others to do the work involved. The 'running' of a large business consists essentially of getting somebody to make something which somebody else will sell to somebody else for more than it costs. John L. McCaffrey, the chief executive of International Harvester, recently said, '. . . he [a business presi·dent] seldom lies awake very long thinking about finances or law suits or sales or production or engineering or accounting problems . . . When he approaches such problems the president can bring to bear on them all the energy and the trained judgment and past experience of his whole organization.' And he goes on to say what top executives do think about at night: 'the biggest trouble with industry is that it is full of human beings.'

The human beings on the middle levels are mainly special-ists. 'We sit at our desks all day,' this chief executive continues, 'while around us whiz and gyrate a vast number of special activi-ties, some of which we only dimly understand. And for each of these activities, there is a specialist . . . All of them, no doubt, are good to have. All seem to be necessary. All are useful on frequent occasions. But it has reached the point where the greatest task of the president is to understand enough of all these specialties so that when a problem comes up he can assign the right team of ex-perts to work on it . . . How can he maintain the interest of and get full advantage from the specialists who are too specialized to pro-mote? On the one hand, the company absolutely requires the skills of the specialists in order to carry on its complicated opera-tions. On the other hand, he has to get future top management from somewhere. And that somewhere has to be largely within the existing company, if he is to have any management morale at all . . . we live in a complicated world—a world that has spiritual and moral problems even greater than its economic and technical problems. If the kind of business system we now have is to survive, it must be staffed by men who can deal with problems of both kinds.'[31]

It is below the top levels, it is where the management hierar-chies are specialized and varied by industrial line and adminis-trative contour, that the more 'bureaucratic' types of executives and technicians live their corporate lives. And it is below the top levels,in the domain of the Number Two men, that responsibility is lodged. The Number One stratum is often too high to be blamed and has too many others below it to take the blame. Besides, if it is the top, who is in a position to fix the blame upon its members?

It is something like the 'line' and 'staff' division invented by the army. The top is staff; the Number Two is line, and thus operational. Every bright army officer knows that to make decisions without responsibility, you get on the staff.[32]

On the middle levels, specialization is required. But the operating specialist will not rise; only the 'broadened' man will rise. What does that mean? It means, for one thing, that the specialist is below the level on which men are wholly alerted to profit. The 'broadened' man is the man who, no matter what he may be doing, is able clearly to see the way to maximize the profit for the corporation as a whole, in the long as well as in the short run. The man who rises to the top is the broadened man whose 'specialty' coincides with the aims of the corporation, which is the maximizing of profit. As he is judged to have realized this aim, he rises within the corporate world. Financial expediency is the chief element of corporate decision, and generally, the higher the executive, the more he devotes his attention to the financial aspect of the going concern.[33]

Moreover, the closer to the corporate top the executive gets, the more important are the big-propertied cliques and political influence in the making of his corporate career. This fact, as well as the considerations for co-optation that prevail, is nicely revealed in a letter that Mr. Lammot du Pont wrote in 1945 in response to a suggestion from a General Motors executive that General George C. Marshall be appointed to the board of directors. Mr. du Pont discussed the proposal: 'My reasons for not favoring his membership on the board are: First his age [The General was then 65]; second, his lack of stockholdings, and third, his lack of experience in industrial business affairs.' Mr. Alfred P. Sloan, chairman of General Motors, in considering the matter, generally concurred, but added: 'I thought General Marshall might do us some good, when he retires, following his present assignment—assuming he continues to live in Washington; recognizing the position he holds in the community and among the government people and the acquaintances he has—and he became familiar with our thinking and what we are trying to do, it might offset the general negative attitude toward big business, of which we are a symbol and a profitable business, as well. It seems to me that might be some reason,

and in that event the matter of age would not be particularly consequential.'

In considering other appointments, Mr. Sloan wrote to W. S.
Carpenter, a large owner of du Pont and General Motors: 'George
Whitney [G. M. director and chairman of J. P. Morgan & Co.] belongs to the board of directors of quite a number of industrial organizations. He gets around a lot because he lives in New York
where many contacts are easily and continuously made. Mr.
Douglas [Lewis W. Douglas, a G. M. board member, chairman of
the Mutual Life Insurance Company, former Ambassador to
Great Britain] is, in a way, quite a public character. He seems
to spend a great deal of time in other things. It seems to me that
such people do bring into our councils a broader atmosphere than
is contributed by the "du Pont directors" and the General Motors
directors.'[34]

Or examine a late case of corporate machination that involved
the several types of economic men prevailing in higher corporate
circles. Robert R. Young—financial promoter and speculator—recently decided to displace William White, chief executive of the
New York Central Railroad and a lifetime career executive in railroad operation.* Young won—but did it really matter? Success in

* Over a luncheon table Young offered White the title of 'chief operating officer' and stock options—'an opportunity to buy Central stock at a
fixed price and without any obligation to pay for it unless it went up.'
White refused, announcing that if Young moved in he would give up
his contract: $120,000-per-year salary until retirement at 65; a $75,000-
a-year consultant fee for the next five years; then a $40,000-a-year
pension for life.

Immediately White hired, out of Central's funds, a public relations
firm at $50,000 a year plus expenses, turned over the $125 million advertising budget of the Central to the coming fight, and engaged a professional proxy solicitor from Wall Street. From Palm Beach, Young
began maneuvering cliques among the rich and among friends with
contacts to get control of blocks of the property. His side came to include three important members of the very rich—Allen P. Kirby of the
Woolworth fortune; and two men each worth over $300 million: Clint
Murchison, with whom Young had previously done business, and Sid
Richardson, whose ranch Young had visited. The deal shaped up in
such a way that a block of 800,000 shares at $26 a share ($20.8 million
worth) was secured. Of course, the multimillionaires did not have to
put up the cash: They borrowed it—mainly from the Allegheny Corporation, which Young is presumably able to treat as his personal property

the corporate world does not follow the pattern it follows in the novel, *Executive Suite*, in which the technologically inclined young man, just like William Holden, wins by making a sincere speech about corporate responsibility. Besides the favors of two friends, each a leading member of the very rich, Mr. Young's income, over the past seventeen years—most of it from capital gains —is reported to be well in excess of $10 million. His yearly income is well over a million, his wife's, half a million—and they manage to keep, after taxes, some 75 per cent of it.[37] But then, no fiction known to us begins to grasp the realities of the corporate world today.

5

When successful executives think back upon their own careers, they very often emphasize what they always call 'an element of luck.' Now what is that? We are told that Mr. George Humphrey makes it a point to have 'lucky men' work with him. What this means, translated out of the magical language of luck, is that there is an accumulation of corporate success. If you are successful, that shows that you are lucky, and if you are lucky, you are chosen by those up the line, and thus you get chances to be more successful. Time and time again, in close-ups of the executive career, we ob-

---

and .07 per cent of which he personally owns. And they borrowed it in such a way as to cover all risk except 200,000 shares. They were on the scheduled new board of directors. Young had 800,000 voting shares.

Chase National Bank, a Rockefeller bank, had had the trusteeship of these shares and now had sold them to Murchison and Richardson. John J. McCloy, the Bank's board chairman, arranged for White to meet Richardson and Murchison, who flew up the next day to New York City. The Texans, who now owned 12½ per cent of the New York Central, attempted to arrange a compromise. They failed, and a fight for the votes of the more scattered owners began.[35]

Young's side spent $305,000. (Later the New York Central repaid it, thus footing the bills of both the winners and the losers.) One hundred solicitors for White from coast to coast were reaching stockholders, as well as several hundred volunteer employees of the railroad. Young also engaged a professional proxy solicitation firm; he also had the services of Diebold, Inc., a firm manufacturing office furniture which Murchison owned—250 of its salesmen were hired to solicit proxies. If Young won, the office furniture for New York Central might henceforth be made by Diebold.[36]

serve how men in the same circles choose one another. For example, Mr. Humphrey was on an advisory committee to the Commerce Department. There he meets Mr. Paul Hoffman. Later, when Mr. Hoffman heads ECA, he pulls in Mr. Humphrey to run an advisory committee on German industry. There General Clay notices him. General Clay naturally knows General Eisenhower, so when General Eisenhower goes up, General Clay recommends Mr. Humphrey to his close friend, President Eisenhower.[38]

There is another item that ties in with the network of friends which people call 'luck': the social life of the corporation. It is a reasonable assumption that part of the executive career is spent 'politic-ing.' Like any politician, especially when he is at or near the top of his hierarchy, the successful executive tries to win friends and to make alliances, and he spends, one suspects, a good deal of time guessing about the cliques he thinks oppose him. He makes power-plays, and these seem part of the career of the managerial elite.

To make the corporation self-perpetuating, the chief executives feel that they must perpetuate themselves, or men like themselves —future men not only trained but also indoctrinated. This is what is meant when it was truly said recently of a man high in the world's largest oil company that he 'is really as much a product of the company as are the two million barrels of oil products it makes every day.' As future executives move upward and toward the center, they become members of a set of cliques, which they often confusedly refer to as a team. They must listen. They must weigh opinions. They must not make snap judgments. They must fit into the business team and the social clique. In so far as the career is truly corporate, one advances by serving the corporation, which means by serving those who are in charge of it and who judge what its interests are.[39]

The executive career is almost entirely a career within the corporate world, less than one out of ten of the top men over the last three generations having entered *top* position from independent professional or from outside hierarchies. Moreover, it is increasingly a career within one company: back in 1870, more than six out of ten executives gained the top rung from outside the corporation; by 1950, almost seven out of ten did so from within the company.[40] First you are a vice-president, then you are president

You must be known well, you must be well liked, you must be an insider.

Success in the higher corporate world is obviously determined by the standards of selection that prevail and the personal application of these standards by the men who are already at the top. In the corporate world, one is drawn upward by the appraisals of one's superiors. Most chief executives take much pride in their ability 'to judge men'; but what are the standards by which they judge? The standards that prevail are not clear-cut and objective; they seem quite intangible, they are often quite subjective, and they are often perceived by those below as ambiguous. The professors of 'business psychology' have been busy inventing more opaque terms, and searching for 'executive traits,' but most of this 'research' is irrelevant nonsense, as can readily be seen by examining the criteria that prevail, the personal and social characteristics of the successes, and their corporate style of life.

On the lower and middle levels of management, objective criteria having to do with skillful performance of occupational duties do often prevail. It is even possible to set up rules of advancement and to make them known in a regular bureaucratic manner. Under such conditions, skill and energy do often pay off without what one may call the corporate character having to be developed. But once a man of the lower ranks becomes a candidate for higher corporate position, the sound judgment, the broadened view, and other less tangible traits of the corporate character are required. 'Character,' *Fortune* magazine observers have remarked, even how the man looks as an executive, became more important than technical ability.[41]

One often hears that practical experience is what counts, but this is very short-sighted, for those on top control the chances to have practical experience of the sort that would be counted for the higher tasks of sound judgment and careful maneuver. This fact is often hidden by reference to an abstract, transferrable quality called 'managerial ability,' but many of those who have been up close to the higher circles (but not of them) have been led to suspect that there probably is no such thing. Moreover, even if there were such a generalized ability, only the uninformed would think that it was what was needed in high policy office, or that one should go to the trouble of recruiting $200,000-a-year men for such work. For that you hire a $20,000-a-year man, or better still, you employ a management counseling firm, which is what the $200,000-a-year men do. Part of their 'managerial ability' consists precisely in knowing their own inabilities and where to find someone with the requisite ability and the money to pay for it. In the meantime, the most accurate single definition of ability—a many-sided word—is: usefulness to those above, to those in control of one's advancement.

When one reads the speeches and reports of executives about the type of man that is required, one cannot avoid this simple conclusion: he must 'fit in' with those already at the top. This means that he must meet the expectations of his superiors and peers; that in personal manner and political view, in social ways and business style, he must be like those who are already in, and upon whose judgments his own success rests. If it is to count in the corporate career, talent, no matter how defined, must be discovered by one's talented superiors. It is in the nature of the morality of corporate accomplishment that those at the top do not and cannot admire that which they do not and cannot understand.

When it is asked of the top corporate men: 'But didn't they have to have *something* to get up there?' The answer is, 'Yes, they did.' By definition, they had 'what it takes.' The real question accordingly is: what does it take? And the only answer one can find anywhere is: the sound judgment, as gauged by the men of sound judgment who select them. The fit survive, and fitness means, not formal competence—there probably is no such thing for top executive positions—but conformity with the criteria of those who have already succeeded. To be compatible with the top men is to act like them, to look like them, to think like them: to be of and for them—or at least to display oneself to them in such a way as to create that impression. This, in fact, is what is meant by 'creating'— a well-chosen word—'a good impression.' This is what is meant— and nothing else—by being a 'sound man,' as sound as a dollar.

Since success depends upon personal or a clique choice, its criteria tend to be ambiguous. Accordingly, those on the lower edge of the top stratum have ample motive and opportunity to study carefully those above them as models, and to observe critically and with no little anxiety those who are still their peers. Now they are above the approval of technical ability and formal competence, business experience and ordinary middle-class respectability. That is assumed. Now they are in the intangible, ambiguous world of the higher and inner circles, with whose members they must come into a special relation of mutual confidence. Not bureau-cratic rules of seniority or objective examinations, but the con-fidence of the inner circle that one is of them and for them, is a prerequisite for joining them.[42]

Of the many that are called to the corporate management, only a few are chosen. Those chosen are picked, not so much for strictly personal characteristics—which many of them cannot really be said to possess—as for qualities judged useful to 'the team.' On this team, the prideful grace of individuality is not at a premium.

Those who have started from on high have from their begin-nings been formed by sound men and trained for soundness. They do not have to think of having to appear as sound men. They just are sound men; indeed, they embody the standards of soundness. Those who have had low beginnings must think all the harder be-fore taking a risk of being thought unsound. As they succeed, they must train themselves for success; and, as they are formed by it, they too come to embody it, perhaps more rotundly than those of the always-high career. Thus, high or low origin, each in its own way, operates to select and to form the sound men with well-bal-anced judgment.

It is the criteria of selection, it is the power to conform with and to use these criteria that are important in understanding the chief executives—not merely the statistics of origin. It is the structure of the corporate career and its inner psychological results that form the men at the top, not merely the external sequence of their career.

So speak in the rich, round voice and do not confuse your supe-riors with details. Know where to draw the line. Execute the cere-mony of forming a judgment. Delay recognizing the choice you have already made, so as to make the truism sound like the deeply pondered notion. Speak like the quiet competent man of affairs and never personally say No. Hire the No-man as well as the Yes-man. Be the tolerant Maybe-man and they will cluster around you, filled with hopefulness. Practice softening the facts into the optimistic, practical, forward-looking, cordial, brisk view. Speak to the well-blunted point. Have weight; be stable: caricature what you are supposed to be but never become aware of it much less amused by it. And never let your brains show.

6

The criteria for executive advancement that prevail are revealingly displayed in the great corporations' recruitment and training programs, which reflect rather clearly the criteria and judgments prevailing among those who have already succeeded. Among today's chief executives there is much worry about tomorrow's executive elite, and there are many attempts to take inventory of the younger men of the corporation who might develop in ten years or so; to hire psychologists to measure talent and potential talent; for companies to band together and set up classes for their younger executives, and indeed to employ leading universities which arrange distinct schools and curricula for the managers of tomorrow; in short, to make the selection of a managerial elite a staff function of the big company.

Perhaps half of the large corporations now have such programs.[43] They send selected men to selected colleges and business schools for special courses, Harvard Business School being a favorite. They set up their own schools and courses, often including their own top executives as lecturers. They scout leading colleges for promising graduates, and arrange tours of rotating duty for men selected as potential 'comers.' Some corporations, in fact, at times seem less like businesses than vast schools for future executives.

By such devices, the fraternity of the chosen have attempted to meet the need for executives brought about by the corporate expansion of the 'forties and 'fifties. This expansion occurred after the scarce job market of the 'thirties, when companies could pick and choose executives from among the experienced. During the war there was no time for such programs, which, on top of the slump, made for a decade-and-a-half gap in executive supply. Behind the deliberate recruiting and training programs there is also the uneasy feeling among the top cliques that the second-level executives are not as broad-gauge as they themselves: their programs are designed to meet the felt need for perpetuation of the corporate hierarchy.

So the corporations conduct their raids among the college seniors, like college fraternities among the freshmen. The colleges, in turn, have more and more provided courses thought to be helpful to the corporate career. It is reliably reported that the college boys are 'ready to be what the corporation wants them to be . . . They are looking hard for cues.'[44] Such 'alertness and receptivity may well be a more important characteristic of the modern manager than the type of education he received. Luck obviously plays a part in the rise of any top executives, and they seem to manage to meet luck better than halfway.'[45]

The cues are readily available: As corporation trainees, the future executives are detached from a central pool and slated for permanent jobs, 'only after they have been given a strong indoctrination in what is sometimes called the "management view." The indoctrination may last as long as two years and occasionally as long as seven.' Each year, for example, General Electric takes unto itself over 1,000 college graduates and exposes them for at least 45 months, usually much longer, to a faculty of 250 full-time General Electric employees. Many people are watching them, even their peers contribute to the judging, for which, it is said, the trainee is grateful, for thus he will not be overlooked. Training in 'Human Relations' pervades the broad-gauge program. 'Never say anything controversial,' 'You can always get anybody to do what you wish,' are themes of the 'effective presentation' course worked up by the Sales Training Department of the knowledgable corporation.

In this human-relations type of training, the effort is to get people to feel differently as well as to think differently about their human problems. The sensibilities and loyalties and character, not merely the skills, of the trainee must be developed in such a way as to transform the American boy into the American executive. His very success will be an insulation of mind against the ordinary problems and values of non-corporate people. Like all well-designed indoctrination courses, the social life of the trainee is built into the program: to get ahead one must get along, with one's peers and with one's superiors. All belong to the same fraternity; all of one's 'social needs can be filled within the company orbit.' To find his executive slot in this orbit, the trainee must 'take advantage of the many contacts that rotation from place to place affords.' This too is company policy: 'If you're smart,' says one smart trainee, 'as soon as you know your way around you start telephoning.'[46]

There are many arguments pro and con about training programs for executives, but the Crown-Prince type of program *is* a central argument among the top executives of big corporations. Nine out of ten young men, even today, do not graduate from college—they are excluded from such executive training schools, although most of them will work for corporations. What effects do such programs have among those who have been called to the corporation but are not among those chosen as Crown Princes? Yet there must be some way to inflate the self-images of the future executives in order that they may take up the reins with the proper mood and in the proper manner and with the sound judgment required.

The majority view of one small but significant sample of executives is that the man who knows 'the technique of managing, not the content of what is managed,' the man who knows 'how to elicit participative consultation . . . how to conduct problem-solving meetings . . .' will be the top executive of the future.* He will be a team player without unorthodox ideas, with leadership rather than drive. Or, as *Fortune* summarizes the argument: 'Their point goes something like this: We do need new ideas, a questioning of accepted ways. But the leader hires people to do this for him. For this reason, then, the creative qualities once associated with the line are now qualities best put in staff slots. The top executive's job, to paraphrase, is not to look ahead himself, but to check the excesses of the people who do look ahead. He is not part of the basic creative engine; he is the governor.' Or, as one executive put it: 'We used to look primarily for brilliance . . . Now that much abused word "character" has become very important. We don't care if you're a Phi Beta Kappa or a Tau Beta Phi. We want a well-rounded person who can handle well-rounded people.'[48] Such a man does not invent ideas himself; he is a broker for well-rounded ideas: the decisions are made by the well-rounded group.

Lest all this be thought merely a whimsical fad, not truly reflecting the ideological desert and anxiety of the executive world, con-

---

* Of 98 top executives and personnel planners recently asked to choose between the executive 'primarily concerned with human relations' and 'the man with strong personal convictions . . . not shy about making unorthodox decisions,' some 63 were willing to make the choice: 40 said the human relations man, 23 the man of conviction.[47]

sider sympathetically the style of conduct and the ideology of
Owen D. Young—late president of General Electric—who serves
well as the American prototype of modern man as executive. In
the early twentieth century, we are told by Miss Ida Tarbell, the
typical industrial leader was a domineering individual, offensive
in his belief that business was essentially a private endeavor. But
not Owen Young. During World War I and the 'twenties, he
changed all that. To him, the corporation was a public institution,
and its leaders, although not of course elected by the public, were
responsible trustees. 'A big business in Owen D. Young's mind is
not . . . a private business . . . it is an institution.'

So he worked with people outside his own company, worked on
an industry-wide basis, and laughed at 'the fear that co-operation of any kind might be construed as conspiracy.' In fact, he
came to feel trade associations, in the corporate age, performed
one role that once 'the church,' in a time of small businesses in a
local county, performed: the role of moral restrainer, the keeper
of 'proper business practices.' During the war, he became a kind
of 'general liaison officer between the company and various [gov-
ernment] boards, a kind of general counsel,' a prototype of the
many executives whose co-operation with one another during the
wars set the shape of peacetime co-operation as well.

His interest in the properties he managed could not have been
more personal had he owned them himself. Of one company he
helped develop, he wrote to a friend: 'We have worked and
played with it together so much that I feel sure it is not boasting
to say that no one knows the strength and weakness—the good and
bad side of this property better than you and I. In fact I doubt
if there were ever such a great property which was known so
well . . .'

His face was always 'friendly and approachable' and his smile,
one colleague said, 'his smile alone is worth a million dollars.' Of
his decision, it was said, 'it was not logical document . . . It was
something his colleagues felt was intuitive rather than reasoned
—a conclusion born of his pondering, and though you might by
rule and figures prove him wrong, you knew he was right!'[49]

7

The Corporate Rich

SIXTY glittering, clannish families do not run the American economy, nor has there occurred any silent revolution of managers who have expropriated the powers and privileges of such families. The truth that is in both these characterizations is less adequately expressed as 'America's Sixty Families' or 'The Managerial Revolution,' than as the managerial reorganization of the propertied classes into the more or less unified stratum of the corporate rich.[1]

As families and as individuals, the very rich are still very much a part of the higher economic life of America; so are the chief executives of the major corporations. What has happened, I believe, is the reorganization of the propertied class, along with those of higher salary, into a new corporate world of privilege and prerogative. What is significant about this managerial reorganization of the propertied class is that by means of it the narrow industrial and profit interests of specific firms and industries and families have been translated into the broader economic and political interests of a more genuinely class type. Now the corporate seats of the rich contain all the powers and privileges inherent in the institutions of private property.

The recent social history of American capitalism does not reveal any distinct break in the continuity of the higher capitalist class. There are, to be sure, accessions in each generation, and there is an unknown turnover rate; the proportions of given types of men differ from one epoch to the next. But over the last half a century, in the economy as in the political order, there has been a remarkable continuity of interests, vested in the types of higher economic men who guard and advance them. The main drift of the

upper classes, composed of several consistent trends, points un-
ambiguously to the continuation of a world that is quite congenial
to the continuation of the corporate rich. For in this stratum are
now anchored the ultimate powers of big property whether they
rest legally upon ownership or upon managerial control.

The old-fashioned rich were simply the propertied classes, organized on a family basis and seated in a locality, usually a big
city. The corporate rich, in addition to such people, include those
whose high 'incomes' include the privileges and prerogatives that
have come to be features of high executive position. The corporate
rich thus includes members of the big-city rich of the metropolitan
400, of the national rich who possess the great American fortunes,
as well as chief executives of the major corporations. The propertied class, in the age of corporate property, has become a corporate rich, and in becoming corporate has consolidated its power
and drawn to its defense new men of more executive and more
political stance. Its members have become self-conscious in terms
of the corporate world they represent. As men of status they have
secured their privileges and prerogatives in the most stable private institutions of American society. They are a corporate rich
because they depend directly, as well as indirectly, for their
money, their privileges, their securities, their advantages, their
powers on the world of the big corporations. All the old-fashioned
rich are now more or less of the corporate rich, and the newer types
of privileged men are there with them. In fact, no one can become
rich or stay rich in America today without becoming involved, in
one way or another, in the world of the corporate rich.

1

During the 'forties and 'fifties, the national shape of the income
distribution became less a pyramid with a flat base than a fat diamond with a bulging middle. Taking into account price changes
and tax increases, proportionately more families in 1929 than in
1951 (from 65 to 46 per cent) received family incomes of less than
$3,000; fewer then than now received between $3,000 and $7,500
(from 29 to 47 per cent); but about the same proportions (6 and
7 per cent) in both 1929 and 1951 received $7,500 or more.*[2]

* This shift—which of course is even more decisive as between say
1936 and 1951—is generally due to several economic facts:[3] (1) There

Many economic forces at work during the war, and the war-preparations boom that has followed it, have made some people on the very bottom levels rise into what used to be the middle-range income levels, and some of those who used to be in the middle-range of income levels became upper-middle or upper. The changed distribution of real income has thus affected the middle and lower levels of the population, with which, of course, we are not here directly concerned. Our interest is in the higher levels; and the forces at work on the income structure have not changed the decisive facts of the big money.

At the very top of the mid-century American economy, there are some 120 people who each year receive a million dollars or more. Just below them, another 379 people appropriate between a half a million and a million. Some 1,383 people get from $250,000 to $499,999. And below all these, there is the broader base of 11,490 people who receive from $100,000 to $249,999.

Altogether, then, in 1949, there were 13,822 people who declared incomes of $100,000 or more to the tax collector.[5] Let us draw the line of the openly declared corporate rich at that level: $100,000 a year and up. It is not an entirely arbitrary figure. For there is one fact about the fat diamond that remains true regardless of how many people are on each of its levels: on the middle and higher levels especially, the greater the yearly income, the greater the proportion of it from property, and the smaller the

has been rather full employment—which during the war and its aftermath brought virtually all who wanted to work into the income-receiving classes. (2) There has been a great doubling up of income within families. In 1951, less than 16 per cent of the families at each of the two extremes, under $2,000 and over $15,000, consisted of families in which the wife also worked; but in the income range of $3,000 to $9,999, the proportion of working wives increased progressively with family income from 16 to 38 per cent.[4] (3) During the 'twenties and 'thirties, large proportions of the very poor were farmers, but now fewer people are farmers and for those on the farm a prosperity has been backed up by various kinds of government subsidy. (4) Union pressure—which since the late 'thirties has forced a constant increase in wages. (5) Welfare programs of the government coming out of the 'thirties have put a floor under incomes—by wage minimums, social security for aged, and pensions for the unemployed and disabled veterans. (6) Underneath the whole prosperity of the 'forties and 'fifties, of course, is the structural fact of the war economy.

proportion from salaries, entrepreneurial withdrawal, or wages. The rich of the higher incomes, in short, are still of the propertied class. The lower incomes derive from wages.*

One hundred thousand dollars a year is the income level on which property enters the income picture in a major way: two-thirds (67 per cent) of the money received by the 13,702 people in the declared $100,000 and up to $999,999 bracket comes from property—from dividends, capital gains, estates, and trusts. The remaining one-third is split between chief executives and top entrepreneurs.

The higher you go into these upper reaches, the more does property count, and the less does income for services performed. Thus 94 per cent of the money of the 120 people receiving a million dollars or more in 1949 came from property, 5 per cent from entrepreneurial profits, 1 per cent from salaries. Among these 120 people, there was considerable variation in the type of property from which their money came.[6] But, regardless of the legal arrangements involved, those with big incomes receive it overwhelmingly from corporate property. That is the first reason that all the rich are now corporate rich, and that is the key economic difference between the rich and the more than 99 per cent of the population who are well below the $100,000 income level.

In these tax-declared high-income classes, people come and go; every year the exact number of people varies. In 1929, when taxes were not so high as to make it so dangerous as now to declare high incomes, there were about 1,000 more such declarations than in 1949—a total of 14,816 declared incomes of $100,000 or more. In 1948 there were 16,280; in 1939 only 2,921.[7] But on the highest levels there remains throughout the years a hard core of the very wealthy. Four-fifths of the 75 people who appropriated one million

---

* Some 86 per cent of the money received by people paying taxes on less than $10,000 in 1949 came from *salaries and wages;* 9 per cent, from business or partnership prcfits; only 5 per cent from property owned.

As a proportion of money received, *entrepreneurial withdrawals* bulk largest among those receiving from $10,000 to $99,999 per year— 34 per cent of the income gotten by people on this income level is business profits; 41 per cent, salaries and wages; and 23 per cent from property. (Two per cent is 'miscellaneous income,' annuities or pensions.)

dollars or more in 1924, for example, got one million or more in at least one other year between 1917 and 1936. The chances are good that those who make it in one year will make it in another year or two.* Farther down the pyramid, only 3 or 4 per cent of the population during the decade after World War II have held as much as $10,000 in liquid assets.[9]

2

Since virtually all statistics of income are based on declarations to tax collectors, they do not fully reveal the 'income' differences between the corporate rich and other Americans. In fact, one major difference has to do with privileges that are deliberately created for the exclusion of 'income' from tax records. These privileges are so pervasive that we find it hard to take seriously the great publicity given to the 'income revolution,' which is said to have taken place over the last twenty years. A change, as we have just reported, has taken place in the total income distribution of the United States; but we do not find it very convincing to judge from declared income tax records that the share the rich receive of all the wealth in the country has decreased.[10]

* Such figures are, of course, only crude indications of the meaning of the big money, as they do not take into account the element of inflation. The number of corporate rich for any given year, as well as the number of million-dollar incomes, is related to the tax rate and to the profit level of the corporate world. Periods of low taxes and high profits are periods in which the declared million-dollar incomes flourish: in the ideal year of 1929, 513 people, estates, or trusts, told the government they had received incomes of one million or more. The average of these million-dollar incomes was $2.36 million, and after taxes the average million-dollar man had 1.99 million left. In the slump year of 1932, there were still 20 people who reported incomes of one million or more; by 1939, when three-fourths of all the families in the United States had incomes of less than $2,000 a year, there were 45 such million-dollar incomes reported. With the war, however, the number of million-dollar incomes increased as did the general level of income. In 1949 when both profits and taxes were high, the average income of the 120 people who told the government they had received one million or more was 2.13 million; after taxes they were left with $910,000. In 1919, however, when taxes and profits were high although profits were falling a bit, only 65 people earned one million or more, averaging 2.3 million before taxes, but only $825,000 after taxes.[8]

Tax rates being high, the corporate rich are quite nimble in figuring out ways to get income, or the things and experiences that income provides, in such a way as to escape taxation. The manner in which the corporate rich pay their taxes is more flexible and provides more opportunities for shrewd interpretations of the law than is true for the middle and lower classes. People of higher income figure their own tax deductions, or more usually have them figured by the experts they hire. Perhaps those whose income derives from property or from entrepreneurial and professional practice are as honest—or as dishonest—as poorer people on wages and salary, but they are also economically bolder, they have greater opportunities and greater skill, and, even more importantly, they have access to the very best skills available for such matters: accomplished lawyers and skillful accountants who specialize in taxation as a science and a game. In the nature of the case, it would be impossible to prove with exactitude, but it is difficult not to believe that as a general rule the higher the income and the more varied its sources, the greater the likelihood of the shrewd tax return. Much declared money is tricked, legally and illegally, from the tax collector; much illegal money is simply not declared.

Perhaps the most important tax loophole in retaining current income is the long-term capital gain. When a military man writes a best-seller or has it written for him, when a businessman sells his farm or a dozen pigs, when an executive sells his stock—the profit received is not considered as income but as capital gain, which means that the profit to the individual after taxes is approximately twice what it would have been if that same amount of money had been received as a salary or a dividend. Individuals claiming long-term capital gains pay taxes on only 50 per cent of that gain. The half that is taxed is taxed at a progressive rate applicable to a person's total income; but the maximum tax on such gains is 52 per cent. This means that at no time can the tax paid on these capital gains be more than 26 per cent of the total gain received; and it will be smaller if the total income, including the gain, leaves the individual in a lower income tax bracket. But when the flow of money is turned around the other way, a capital *loss* of over $1,000 (those under $1,000 may be deducted from ordinary income) can be spread backward or forward in a five-year span to offset capital gains.

Aside from capital gains, the most profitable tax loophole is perhaps the 'depletion allowance' on oil and gas wells and mineral deposits. From 5 to 27½ per cent of the gross income received on an oil well, but not exceeding 50 per cent of the net income from the property, is tax-free each year. Moreover, all the costs of drilling and developing an oil well can be deducted as they occur—instead of being capitalized and depreciated over the years of the well's productive life.[11] The important point of privilege has less to do with the percentage allowed than with the continuation of the device long after the property is fully depreciated.

Those with enough money to play around may also off-set taxes by placing money in tax-free municipal bonds; they may split their income among various family members so that the taxes paid are at a lower rate than the combined income would have required. The rich cannot give away to friends or relatives more than a lifetime total of $30,000 plus $3,000 each year without paying a gift tax; although, in the name of both husband and wife, a couple can give twice that amount. The rich man can also make a tax-deductible gift (up to 20 per cent of yearly income that is given to recognized charities is not taxed as income) that will provide him security for the rest of his life. He can donate to a named charity the principal of a fund, but continue to receive the income from it.* He thus makes an immediate deduction on his income tax return; and he cuts that part of his estate that is subject to inheritance taxes.[13]

There are other techniques that help the rich preserve their money after they are dead in spite of high estate taxes. For example, it is possible to set up a trust for a grandchild, and stipulate that the *child* receive the income from the trust as long as he is alive, although the property legally belongs to the grandchild. It is

* For example, a man can give $10,000 worth of stock to a theological seminary, which—because of tax savings—actually costs him only $4,268.49. In ten years, let us assume, the stock increases in market value to $16,369.49, and the man receives $6,629 in income payments which is 50 per cent more than the cost of his gift. When the man dies, of course, the seminary will own the stock and receive its earnings.[12]

only at the death of the child (instead of both the original owner *and* the child) that an estate tax is paid.

A family trust saves taxes—both current income tax and estate tax levied upon death—for income of the trust fund is taxed separately. In addition, the trust provides the property holder with continuous professional management, eliminates the worries of responsibility, keeps the property intact in one manageable sum, builds the strongest possible legal safeguards to property, and, in effect, enables the owner to continue to control his property after he is dead.°

There are many kinds of trusts, and the law is rather complicated and strict in their application; but in one type of short-term trust 'what you do is Indian-give ownership of property to a trustee—and actually give away its income—for some set period (of more than 10 years). Then if the trust meets all other requirements, you're clear of tax on that income.'[15]

Twenty-five years ago, there were no more than 250 foundations in the entire United States; today there are thousands. Generally, a foundation is defined as 'any autonomous, non-profit legal entity that is set up to "serve the welfare of mankind." It administers wealth that is transferred to it through tax-free gifts or bequests.' Actually, the setting up of foundations has often become a convenient way of avoiding taxes, 'operating as private banks for their donors; not infrequently, the "mankind" they have served turned out to be a few indigent relatives.' The Revenue Act of

---

° 'Take the case of a married man,' a magazine for executives carefully explains, 'who has a taxable income of $30,000, including a $1,000 return on a $25,000 investment. After taxes, that $1,000 of income is worth only $450. Accumulating it each year for 10 years at compound interest of 4 per cent would produce, at the most, a fund of about $5,650 for his family. But suppose the man transfers the $25,000 investment to a short-term trust. If the arrangement meets certain requirements, the trust will pay a tax of about $200 on each $1,000 of income, leaving $800. In 10 years, that could build up to about $9,600—a gain of 70 per cent over what could have been accumulated without a trust . . . [This is not allowed in all states.] At the termination of the trust, the man would get back his $25,000, plus unrealized appreciation. The accumulated income would go to the trust beneficiary, someone within his family in a light tax status.'[14]

1950 tried 'to plug up some of the bigger loopholes' but 'dubious foundations still have an advantage—the tax collector has a hard time getting information about them . . . revenue men complain they haven't time or manpower to check more than a tiny fraction of the reports already filed by foundations. They have to steer largely by instinct in deciding which ones to investigate,' and even the 1950 law does not require that all pertinent data concerning them be furnished to the government.

In recent years, more businesses have been creating foundations, thus making a bid for local and national good will, while encouraging research in their own industries. The corporation so engaged does not have to pay taxes on the 5 per cent of its profits that it yearly gives to its foundation. Very rich families also can keep control of their business after a death in the family by giving large shares of the company stock to a foundation (Ford is unusual in this respect only in the magnitude of the sums involved). The size of the inheritance tax, which might otherwise force a sale of stock to outsiders in order to pay the taxes, is reduced. 'If a man's chief concern is to raise a tax-free umbrella over part of his income and to give some jobs to needy retainers,' an alert business magazine advises its executive readers, 'he should by all means set up his own foundation, no matter how small. Then he may even prefer to have the overhead eat up all the income.'[16]

For virtually every law taxing big money, there is a way those with big money can avoid it or minimize it. But such legal and illegal maneuvers are only part of the income privileges of the corporate rich: working hand-in-hand with the rules and regulations of the government, the corporations find ways directly to supplement the income of the executive rich. These various forms of feathering the nest now make it possible for executive members of the corporate rich to live richly on seemingly moderate incomes, while paying taxes lower than the law seemingly intends as fair and just. Among such privileged arrangements are following:

Under the deferred pay contract, the corporation signs up for a given salary for a number of years, and further agrees to pay an annual retainer after retirement as long as the executive doesn't go to work for any competing firm. The executive's loyalty is thus linked to the company, and he is able to spread his income into the years when lower earnings will result in reduced taxes. One Chrysler executive, for example, recently signed a contract yielding him $300,000 a year for the next five years, then $75,000 a year for the rest of his life. A recently retired Chairman of U. S. Steel's Board, who was receiving a $211,000 salary, now gets $14,000 a year as his pension, plus $55,000 a year in 'deferred pay.'[17]

The classic case of deferred payment is perhaps the one worked out for a famous entertainer, who was in a position to demand $500,000 a year for 3 years. 'Instead, he arranged to take $50,000 a year for the next 30 years. No one seriously expects him to be active in show business when he is approaching 80, but by spreading out his income and keeping it in lower tax brackets he was able to cut the total income tax he will have to pay by nearly $600,000, according to one estimate.'[18] Such fabulous arrangements are not limited to the world of show business, even though there they may be more publicized: Even the most respected and staid companies are now in many instances taking care of their key people by such means.

Executives are given restricted options to buy stock at or below current market value. This keeps the executive with the company; for he is able to pick up the option only after a specified period of time such as a year, or he may only be able to use it to buy limited quantities of stock over a longer period of time—say five years.[19] To the executive as riskless entrepreneur, at the time he picks up his option, there comes an immediate profit (the difference between the option price previously set and the market value of the stock at the time when he buys it). Most of the profit he makes if he later sells the stock is not considered taxable income by an obliging government: it is taxed at the lower capital gains rate. Nothing prevents him from borrowing money to pick up his option, and then selling the stock in six months at the higher market value. For example, in 1954, the president of an aircraft company was given—in salary, bonus, and pension credits—about $150,000, but after taxes he took home only about $75,000. However, if he wished to sell the 10,000 shares of stock he had bought on his company's option plan several months before, he could, after paying all taxes due, have also taken home $594,375.[20] About one out of six companies listed on the New York Stock Exchange gave stock options to executives within a year or so after the 1950 tax law made them attractive as capital gains. Since then, the practice has spread.[21]

3

The corporate rich are a propertied rich, but big property is not all that they possess; the corporate rich are able to accumulate and to retain high incomes, but high incomes are not all they accumulate for keeps. In addition to big property and high income, they enjoy the corporate privileges that are part of the newer status system of the incorporated economy of the United States. These status privileges of the corporate rich are now standard practices, essential, even though shifting, features of business-as-usual, part of the going pay-off for success. Criticism of them does not arouse indignation on the part of anyone in a position voluntarily to do anything about them, and much less about the corporate system in which they are firmly anchored.

None of these privileges are revealed by examination of the yearly income or the property holding. They are, one might say, fringe benefits of the higher circles. The 'fringe benefits' which lower salaried and wage earners have been given—primarily private pension and welfare plans, social security and unemployment insurance—have risen from 1.1 per cent of the national payroll in 1929 to 5.9 per cent in 1953.[22] It is not possible to calculate with suitable precision the 'fringe benefits' taken by the riskless entrepreneurs of the big corporations, but it is now certain that they have become quite central to the higher emoluments. It is because of them that the corporate rich may be considered, in a decisive way, to be members of a directly privileged class. The corporations from which their property and incomes derive are also the seats of the privileges and prerogatives. The great variety of these privileges substantially increases their standard of consumption, buttresses their financial position against the ups and downs of the economic system, lends shape to their whole style of living, and lifts them into a security as great as that of the corporate economy itself. Designed to increase the wealth and the security of the rich in a manner that avoids the payment of taxes, they also strengthen their loyalties to the corporations.[23]

Among the accoutrements that often go with the big executive job but are never reported to tax collectors are such fringe benefits as these: free medical care, payments of club fees, company lawyers and accountants available for tax, financial and legal advice, facilities for entertaining customers, private recreation areas —golf courses, swimming pools, gymnasiums—scholarship funds for children of executives, company automobiles, and dining rooms for executive use.[24] By 1955, some 37 per cent of all the Cadillac registrations in Manhattan, and 20 per cent in Philadelphia, were in company names.[25] 'A company dedicated to keeping its officers happy,' one reliable observer recently noted, 'can with all propriety have a company airplane for business trips and a yacht and a hunting-fishing lodge in the north woods to entertain its biggest customers.* It can also arrange to hold its conventions in Miami in midwinter. The effect, as far as company executives go, is to provide wonderful travel and vacation facilities without cost. The company officers go south in the winter and north by summer; take along enough work or enough customers to justify the trip, and proceed to have a very pleasant time of it . . . At home the executives can also ride around in company-owned and chauffeured automobiles. Naturally the company is happy to pay their dues at the best available country club, for the purposes of entertaining customers on the golf course, and at the best town club, for intimate lunches and dinners.' [27] You name it and you can find it. And it is increasing: it is free to the executive, and deductible as an ordinary business expense by the corporation.

These higher emoluments may also extend to lavish gifts of wonderful toys for adults, like automobiles and fur coats, and conveniences like deep freezes for the purchasing agents and business contacts not directly employed by the company. All this has been widely publicized and decried in the political field,** but, as

* Businessmen now fly nearly four million hours a year in private planes—more than all scheduled, commercial airlines put together.[26]

** For example: 'Over the past two years more than 300 Congressmen have taken trips abroad at a cost to the U.S. taxpayer estimated unofficially at over $3,500,000. Many of the junkets were unquestionably useful and legitimate fact-finding tours and inspections. Others unquestionably represented some fancy free-loading. Last week the House of Representatives Rules Committee served notice that the lid was on junkets.

any business executive of stature well knows, such gifts of business friendship are standard practice within and especially between big firms.

Back in 1910, for example, White Sulphur Springs in the hills of West Virginia was on the same social circuit as Bar Harbor and Newport. In 1954, the Chesapeake and Ohio Railroad, which owns the Greenbrier resort hotel in White Sulphur Springs, invited as guests top level executives who are, in fact or potentially, important shippers and who feel honored to be invited. In 1948, the C & O paid for everything, but the response was so great from the business, social, and political celebrities who accepted the invitation that they now come on their own expense accounts. The resort operates year-round but the Spring Festival is the big social-business event.[29]

In Florida, there is now being constructed an entire resort town, with an average population of 3,000, which will be rented to executives and their guests on a year-round basis. The companies involved can either sublet it to their employees or write off the cost as a business-expense deduction during the times it is used for entertaining customers, holding conventions or important conferences.[30]

The Continental Motors Corporation operates duck-hunting expeditions at Lost Island, Arkansas. Assuming that the golf, cocktail, dinner, and night club routine is 'old-hat' to any executive by the time he is big enough to be an important customer, Continental set up a 'customer relations program' which has been going some fifteen years. Such 'lodge-type' selling retreats are concentrated in the primary goods industries, where the big sales are made, president to president,. rather than in consumer goods. Everyone on the hunt is 'a president or a vice-president, or maybe a general or an admiral.' In the same vicinity, at least three other corporations also operate exclusive duck-hunting clubs. Top employees as well as clients are usually among the guests at such duck, deer, and trout facilities.[31]

'The Committee, which must approve all investigating authority, said it planned to approve free foreign travel only for members of the Foreign Affairs, Armed Services, and Insular Affairs Committees. Around Congress the gag last week,' *The New York Times* concluded, 'was that it would be tough to muster the usual quorum in Paris this summer.'[28]

More widely recognized, but still not seriously studied is the wide-ranging and far-reaching fact of the expense account. No one knows, and there is no way to find out for sure, just how much of high living and exciting entertainment is made possible for the new privileged classes solely because of the expense account. 'The vice-president of one firm,' economist Richard A. Girard recently reported, 'is assigned a flat $20,000 each year to cover any entertaining he may decide to do. His contract specifies that he does not have to account for the money.'[32] Tax officials play a continual game with members of the corporate rich over expense-account deductions but generally insist that each case is unique—which means there are no set rules and the revenue agent has wide responsibility.

'Theatre people estimate that thirty to forty per cent of the New York theatre audience is an expense-account audience, and that this is the percentage between life and death.'[33] Moreover, 'in cities like New York, Washington and Chicago,' one investigator feels it 'safe to say that at any given moment well over half of all the people in the best hotels, the best nightclubs and the best restaurants are charging the bill as an expense account item to their companies, which in turn are charging it to the government in the form of tax deductions'—and goes on to assert what is well known: 'There is something about an expense account that brings out the latent rascality, rapacity and mendacity in even the otherwise most honorable man. Expense account forms have long been known affectionately by their fond possessors as "swindle sheets." Filling out an expense account itemization has been regarded as a kind of contest of wits with the company auditor, in which it is perfectly justifiable to use the most outrageous half-truths, little white lies and outright fantasies, anything at all which the auditor, regardless of how outraged he might be, cannot absolutely prove to be false.'[34]

We have by no means reported all of the privileges of the corporate rich, confining ourselves mainly to legally and officially sanctioned types. Many of the new privileges—especially the higher emoluments—have long been known and are quite accepted by heads of state and by higher officials of public office. The governor is given 'the governor's mansion' in which to live rent free; the president, with $50,000 a year tax-free expenses, also has his White House, which contains his serviced living quarters as well as offices of administration. But what has happened, as the corporation has become the anchor point for the privileges that go with great wealth, is that such higher emoluments have become normal among the private rich as they have become transformed into the corporate rich. When, in their happier moods, corporation executives speak lovingly of their corporations as One Big Family, one can understand that in a very real sense they are asserting a sociological truth about the class structure of American society. For the powers and privileges of property, shared among the corporate rich, are now collective, and the individual has such privileges most securely only in so far as he is part of the corporate world.

4

America has *not* become a country where individual pleasures and powers are bounded by small incomes and high taxes. There are incomes high enough to remain high despite the taxes and there are many ways of escaping and minimizing taxes. There is maintained in America, and there is being created and maintained every year, a stratum of the corporate rich, many of whose members possess far more money than they can personally spend with any convenience. For many of them, the prices of things are simply irrelevant. They never have to look at the right hand column of a menu; they never have to take orders from anybody, they never have to do really disagreeable things except as a self-imposed task; they never have to face alternatives hedged in by considerations of cost. They never *have* to do anything. They are, according to all appearances, free.

But are they really free?

The answer is Yes, within the terms of their society, they are really free.

But does not the possession of money somehow limit them?

The answer is No, it does not.

But are not those just the hurried answers, are there not more considered, deeper-going answers?

What kind of deeper-going answers? And what does freedom

mean? Whatever else it may mean, freedom means that you have
the power to do what you want to do, when you want to do it, and
how you want to do it. And in American society the power to do
what you want, when you want, how you want, requires money.
Money provides power and power provides freedom.

But are there no limits on all this?

Of course there are limits to the power of money, and the free-
doms based on that power. And there are also psychological traps
for the rich, as among misers and spendthrifts on all levels, which
distort their capacity for freedom.

The miser enjoys the possession of money as such. The spendthrift enjoys the spending of money as such. Neither—in the pure
type—can look upon money as a means to free and various ends of
life, whatever they may be. The miser's pleasure is in the potentiality of his spending power, so he draws back from the actual
spending. He is a tense man, afraid of losing the potentiality and
so never realizing it. His security and his power are embodied in
his hoard, and in fearing to lose it, he fears loss of his very self. He
is not merely a stingy man, nor necessarily a merely avaricious
man. He is an impotent voyeur of the economic system, one for
whom the possession of money for its own sake, and not as a means
to any further end, has become the end of life. He cannot complete the economic act. And money, which to most economic
men is a means, becomes to the miser a despotic end.

The spendthrift, on the other hand, is a man for whom the act
of spending is itself a source of pleasure. He does not feel happy
on a spending spree because of his expected ease or pleasure from
the goods acquired. The act of senseless spending is in itself his
pleasure and reward. And in this act the spendthrift advertises his
unconcern with mere money. He consumes conspicuously to show
that he is above pecuniary considerations, thus revealing how
highly he values them.

No doubt both of these oddities of the money system are available among the American rich today, but they are not typical.
For most members of the corporate rich money remains a gratifying medium of exchange—a pure and unadulterated means to
an enormous variety of concrete ends. For most of them, money is
valued for what it will purchase in comfort and fun, status and

alcoholism, security and power and experience, freedom and boredom.

On the bottom level of the money system one never has enough money, which is the key link in the hand-to-mouth way of existence. One is, in a sense, below the money system—never having enough money to be firmly a part of it.

On the middle levels, the money system often seems an endless treadmill. One never gets enough; $8,000 this year seems to place one in no better straits than did $6,000 the last. There are suspicions among people on such levels, that were they to make $15,000, they would still be on the treadmill, trapped in the money system.

But above a certain point in the scale of wealth, there is a qualitative break: the rich come to know that they have so much that they simply do not have to think about money at all: it is only they who have truly won the money game; they are above the struggle. It is not too much to say that in a pecuniary society, only then are men in a position to be free. Acquisition as a form of experience and all that it demands no longer need to be a chain. They can be above the money system, above the scramble on the treadmill: for them it is no longer true that the more they have, the harder it seems to make ends meet. That is the way we define the rich as personal consumers.

For the very poor, the ends of necessity never meet. For the middle classes there are always new ends, if not of necessity, of status. For the very rich, the ends have never been separated, and within the limits of the common human species, they are today as free as any Americans.

The idea that the millionaire finds nothing but a sad, empty place at the top of this society; the idea that the rich do not know what to do with their money; the idea that the successful become filled up with futility, and that those born successful are poor and little as well as rich—the idea, in short, of the disconsolateness of the rich—is, in the main, merely a way by which those who are not rich reconcile themselves to the fact. Wealth in America is directly gratifying and directly leads to many further gratifications.

To be truly rich is to possess the means of realizing in big ways one's little whims and fantasies and sicknesses. 'Wealth has great privileges,' Balzac once remarked, 'and the most enviable of them all is the power of carrying out thoughts and feelings to the uttermost; of quickening sensibility by fulfilling its myriad caprices.'[35] The rich, like other men, are perhaps more simply human than otherwise. But their toys are bigger; they have more of them; they have more of them all at once. *

As for the happiness of the rich, that is a matter that can be neither proved nor disproved. Still, we must remember that the American rich are the winners within a society in which money and money-values are the supreme stakes. If the rich are not happy it is because none of us are happy. Moreover, to believe that they are unhappy would probably be un-American. For if they are not happy, then the very terms of success in America, the very aspirations of all sound men, lead to ashes rather than fruit.

Even if everyone in America, being human, were miserable, that would be not reason to believe that the rich were *more* miserable. And if everyone is happy, surely that is no reason to believe that the rich are excluded from the general American bliss. If those who win the game for which the entire society seems designed are not 'happy,' are then those who lose the happy ones? Must we believe that only those who live within, but not of, the American society can be happy? Were it calamitous to lose, and horrible to win, then the game of success would indeed be a sad game, doubly so in that it is a game everyone in and of the American culture cannot avoid playing. For to withdraw is of course objectively to lose, and to lose objectively, although subjectively to believe one has not lost—that borders on insanity. We simply must believe that the American rich are happy, else our confidence in the whole endeavor might be shaken. For of all the possible values of human society, one and one only is truly sovereign, truly universal, truly sound, truly and completely acceptable goal of man in America. That goal is money, and let there be no sour grapes about it from the losers.

* One of the propositions with which Howard Hughes has been associated was the purchase of RKO from Floyd Odlum for almost nine million dollars. 'I needed it like I needed small pox!' When asked to account for this move, Hughes seriously answers, '. . . the only reason I bought RKO from Floyd Odlum was because I enjoyed the many flights down to his ranch in Indio [California] while we discussed the details of the purchase.'[36]

'He is king . . .' one of Balzac's characters proclaims, 'he can do what he chooses; he is above everything, as all rich men are. To him, henceforth, the expression: "All Frenchmen are equal before the law," is the lie inscribed at the head of a charter. He will not obey the laws, the laws will obey him. There is no scaffold, no headsman, for millionaires!'

'Yes, there is,' replied Raphael, 'they are their own headsmen!'

'Another prejudice,' cried the banker.[37]

5

The newer privileges of the corporate rich have to do with the power of money in the sphere of consumption and personal experience. But the power of money, the prerogatives of economic position, the social and political weight of corporate property, is by no means limited to the sphere of accumulation and consumption, corporate or personal. In fact, from the standpoint of the American elite, of which the corporate rich are only one segment, the power over consumer goods is not nearly so important as the institutional powers of wealth.

1. The Constitution is the sovereign political contract of the United States. By its fourteenth amendment it gives due legal sanction to the corporations, now the seat of the corporate rich, managed by the executives among them. Within the political framework of the nation, this corporate elite constitutes a set of governing groups, a hierarchy developed and run from the economic top down. The chief executives are now at the head of the corporate world, which in turn is a world of economic sovereignty within the nation's politically sovereign area. In them is vested the economic initiative, and they know it and they feel it to be their prerogative. As chiefs of the industrial manorialism, they have looked reluctantly to the federal government's social responsibility for the welfare of the underlying population. They view workers and distributors and suppliers of their corporate systems as subordinate members of their world, and they view themselves as individuals of the American individualistic sort who have reached the top.

They run the privately incorporated economy. It cannot be said that the government has interfered much during the last decade, for in virtually every case of regulation that we examine the regulating agency has tended to become a corporate outpost.[38] To control the productive facilities is to control not only things but the men who, not owning property, are drawn to it in order to work. It is to constrain and to manage their life at work in the factory, on the railroad, in the office. It is to determine the shape of the labor market, or to fight over that shape with union or government. It is to make decisions in the name of the enterprise as to how much to produce of what and when and how to produce it and how much to charge for it.

II. Money allows the economic power of its possessor to be translated directly into political party causes. In the eighteen-nineties, Mark Hanna raised money from among the rich for political use out of the fright caused by William Jennings Bryan and the Populist 'nightmare'; and many of the very rich have been unofficial advisers to politicians. Mellons, Pews, and du Ponts have long been campaign contributors of note, and, in the post-World War II period, the Texas millionaires have contributed sizable amounts of money in campaigns across the nation. They have helped McCarthy in Wisconsin, Jenner in Indiana, Butler and Beall in Maryland. In 1952, for example, one oil tycoon (Hugh Roy Cullen) made thirty-one contributions of from $500 to $5,000 each (totaling at least $53,000), and his two sons-in-law helped out (at least $19,750 more) ten Congressional candidates. It is said that the Texas multimillionaires now use their money in the politics of at least thirty states. Murchison has contributed to political candidates outside Texas since 1938, although he got no publicity until 1950, when he and his wife, at Joseph McCarthy's request, contributed $10,000 to defeat Senator Tydings of Maryland, and in 1952 sent money to beat McCarthy's Connecticut foe, Senator William Benton.[39]

In 1952, 'the six top Republican and Democratic political committees received 55 per cent of their total receipts [this includes only those receipts of groups that spent money in two or more states] in 2,407 contributions of $1,000 or more.'* Such figures

* Heading the list of contributions to the Republican party were the Rockefellers ($94,000), the du Ponts ($74,175), the Pews ($65,100), the Mellons($54,000), the Weirs ($21,000), the Whitneys ($19,000), the Vanderbilts ($19,000), the Goelets ($16,800), the Milbanks ($16,-

are absolute minimums since many contributions can be made by
family members of different names, not easily recognized by the
reporters.

III. But it is not so much by direct campaign contributions that
the wealthy exert political power. And it is not so much the very
rich as the corporate executives—the corporate reorganizers of the
big propertied class—who have translated the power of property
into political use. As the corporate world has become more intricately involved in the political order, these executives have become
intimately associated with the politicians, and especially with the
key 'politicians' who form the political directorate of the United
States government.

The nineteenth-century economic man, we are accustomed to
believe, was a shrewd 'specialist' in bargaining and haggling. But
the growth of the great corporation and the increased intervention of government into the economic realm have selected and
formed and privileged economic men who are less hagglers and
bargainers on any market than professional executives and adroit
economic politicians. For today the successful economic man,
either as propertied manager or manager of property, must influence or control those positions in the state in which decisions of
consequence to his corporate activities are made. This trend in
economic men is, of course, facilitated by war, which thus creates
the need to continue corporate activities with political as well as
the economic means. War is of course the health of the corporate
economy; during war the political economy tends to become more
unified, and moreover, political legitimations of the most unques-
tionable sort—national security itself—are gained for corporate
economic activities.

'Before World War I, businessmen fought each other; after the
war they combined to present a united front against consumers.'[41]
During World War II they served on innumerable advisory committees in the prosecution of the war. They were also brought into
the military apparatus more permanently by the awarding to

---

500), and Henry R. Luce ($13,000). Heading the list of contributions
to the Democratic party were the Wade Thompsons of Nashville ($22,-
000), the Kennedys ($20,000), Albert M. Greenfield of Philadelphia
($16,000), Matthew H. McCloskey of Pennsylvania ($10,000), and the
Marshall Fields ($10,000).[40]

many businessmen of commissions in the reserve officer corps.*
All this has been going on for a long time and is rather well
known, but in the Eisenhower administration the corporate executives publicly assumed the key posts of the executive branch of
the government. Where before the more silent power and the
ample contract was there, now there was also the loud voice.

Is there need for very subtle analysis of such matters when the
Secretary of the Interior, Douglas McKay, blurted out to his friends
in the Chamber of Commerce, on 29 April 1953, 'We're here in
the saddle as an Administration representing business and industry?'[43] Or when Secretary of Defense Wilson asserted the identity
of interests between the United States of America and the General Motors Corporation? Such incidents may be political blun-
ders—or would be, were there an opposition party—but are they not
as well revelations of deeply held convictions and intentions?

There are executives who are as afraid of such political identification as 'non-partisan' labor leaders are of third parties. For a
long time the corporate rich had been in training as an opposition
group; the brighter ones then came to feel vaguely that they might
be on the spot. Before Eisenhower, such power as they wielded
could more easily be politically irresponsible. After Eisenhower
that is not so easy. If things go wrong, will not they—and with
them business—be blamed?

But John Knox Jessup, chairman of the editorial board of *Fortune*, feels that the corporation can supplant the archaic system

* A survey of the backgrounds of dollar-a-year men in Washington
during World War II shows that what industry loaned the government
was, except for a very few men, its financial experts, not men experienced in production: '. . . the salesmen and purchasing agents in WPB
are under Ferdinand Eberstadt, former Wall Street investment banker.
The alibi that these men have special qualifications for their jobs took a
terrific beating when WPB within the past month found it necessary to
put . . . through a special training course to teach them the funda-
mentals of industrial production . . . And that brings us to the dollar-
a-year men who padded WPB's payrolls with their companies' salesmen
and purchasing agents. The dollar-a-year boys were supposed to be industry's loan of its top-management experts and financial experts to the
government to help run a winning war. Now top management in industry is made up of two types of men . . . production experts and
financial experts . . . Its production experts industry kept for its own
business.'[42]

of states as a framework for self-government—and thus fill the vacuum of the middle levels of power. For, as chief of the corporate commonwealth, the manager has the political job of keeping all his constituents reasonably happy. Mr. Jessup argues that the balances of economic and political domains have already broken down: 'Any President who wants to run a prosperous country depends on the corporation at least as much as—probably more than—the corporation depends on him. His dependence is not unlike that of King John on the landed barons of Runnymede, where Magna Carta was born.'[44]

In general, however, the ideology of the executives, as members of the corporate rich, is conservatism without any ideology. They are conservative, if for no other reason than that they feel themselves to be a sort of fraternity of the successful. They are without ideology because they feel themselves to be 'practical' men. They do not think up problems; they respond to alternatives presented to them, and such ideology as they have must be inferred from such responses as they make.

During the last three decades, since the First World War in fact, the distinction between the political and the economic man has been diminishing; although the corporation managers have, in the past, distrusted one of their own who stays too long in the political arena. They like to come and go, for then they are not responsible. Yet more and more of the corporate executives have entered government directly; and the result has been a virtually new political economy at the apex of which we find those who represent the corporate rich.*

The questions which these obvious facts of the political power of the corporate rich raise have to do not so much with the personal integrity of the men involved, and certainly not so much with their personal gains in wealth, prestige, and power. These are important questions which we shall discuss when we note the general prevalence of the higher immorality and the structure of the power elite as a whole. But the important political question is whether or not these facts can be added up to proof of a structural connection between the corporate rich and what we shall call the political directorate.

* See below, TWELVE: The Power Elite, for a fuller discussion of the political role of the executives.

Have the very rich and the top executives, the upper classes of local society and of the metropolitan 400, the strategic cliques of the corporate world, actually occupied many positions of power within the formal political system? They have, of course, made raids upon the government, they have gained privileges within it. But have they been and are they now active politically? Contrary to official legend, scholarly myth, and popular folklore, the answer to that question is a complicated but a quite definite Yes.

We should, however, be quite mistaken to believe that the political apparatus is merely an extension of the corporate world, or that it has been taken over by the representatives of the corporate rich. The American government is not, in any simple way nor as a structural fact, a committee of 'the ruling class.' It is a network of 'committees,' and other men from other hierarchies besides the corporate rich sit in these committees. Of these, the professional politician himself is the most complicated, but the high military, the warlords of Washington, are the newest.

8

The Warlords

During the eighteenth century, observers of the historic scene began to notice a remarkable trend in the division of power at the top of modern society: Civilians, coming into authority, were able to control men of military violence, whose power, being hedged in and neutralized, declined. At various times and places, of course, military men had been the servants of civilian decision, but this trend—which reached its climax in the nineteenth century and lasted until World War I—seemed then, and still seems, remarkable simply because it had never before happened on such a scale or never before seemed so firmly grounded.

In the twentieth century, among the industrialized nations of the world, the great, brief, precarious fact of civilian dominance began to falter; and now—after the long peace from the Napoleonic era to World War I—the old march of world history once more asserts itself. All over the world, the warlord is returning. All over the world, reality is defined in his terms. And in America, too, into the political vacuum the warlords have marched. Alongside the corporate executives and the politicians, the generals and admirals—those uneasy cousins within the American elite—have gained and have been given increased power to make and to influence decisions of the gravest consequence.

1

All politics is a struggle for power; the ultimate kind of power is violence. Why, then, is not military dictatorship the normal and usual form of government? For the greater part of human history, men have, in fact, lived under the sword, and in any serious disturbance of human affairs, real or imagined, societies do tend to revert to military rule. Even nowadays, we often overlook these more or less common facts of world history because we inherit certain values which, during the eighteenth and nineteenth centuries, have flourished under a regime of civilian authority. Even if the ultimate form of power is coercion by violence, all power contests within and between nations of our tradition have not reached the ultimate point. Our theories of government have assumed and our constitution has led to institutions in which violence has been minimized and subjected to efficient checks in the balance of civilian dominance. During the long peace of the modern west, history has been referred more to the politician, to the rich and to the lawyer than to the general, the bandit, and the admiral. But how did that peace come about? How did civilians rather than men of violence become dominant?

In his discusion of the military, Gaetano Mosca[1] makes an assumption which we do not share, but which does not disturb our acceptance of his general line of reasoning. He assumes that, in any society, there is a sort of quota of men who when appropriately provoked will resort to violence. If, says Mosca, we give such men genius and the historical opportunity, we will get a Napoleon; if we give them a great ideal, we will get a Garibaldi; if we give them a chance, and nothing else, we will get a Mussolini or, we may add, in a business civilization, a gangster.

But, says Mosca, if you give such a man a job in a certain kind of social hierarchy, you will get a professional soldier and often civilians can control him.

Of course, there have been bases of internal peace other than the professional standing army. There has been 'God's peace' imposed by a priesthood, and the 'King's Peace' imposed in medieval Europe against those who felt that their honor and power depended upon the sword. But the big fact about peace in modern, or even in world history, is—as one might expect—an ambiguous fact: it is that peace has been due to the centralization and monopoly of violence by the national state, but that the existence of a world now organized into some eighty-one such national states is also the prime condition of modern war.

Before the national state, men of violence could and did frequently resort to violence on a local scale, and feudalism in Europe as well as in the Orient was in many ways a local rule by men of violence. Before the national state centralized and monopolized the means of violence, power tended continually to re-create itself in small, scattered centers, and rule by local gangs was often a going fact of the pre-national history of mankind. But the highwayman of Spain became—under Ferdinand and Isabella who were building a nation—a man of the crown, and in due course a conquistador and in due course again, a soldier of the queen. The man of local violence came, in short, to be a member of a national standing army beholden to the civilian head of the state.

Now what kind of remarkable institution is this standing army that it can channel the combative tendencies of men of violence so that they come under civilian authority, and in fact adopt among themselves such obedience as their very code of honor? For if the standing army, in the modern nation, has come to monopolize violence, to become strong enough to dominate society, why has it not done so? Why, instead, has it quite frequently tapered up to and accepted the civilian authority of the civilian head of the state? Why do armies subordinate themselves? What are the secrets of the standing army?

There are no secrets, there are several quite open mechanisms which have been at work wherever standing armies are under civilian control. First of all, these armies have been 'aristocratic' kinds of institutions. Whenever, as in the early Bolshevik enthusiasm, attempts have been made to do away with this character, they have failed. There is maintained in the national standing army an absolute distinction between officers and men; and the officer group has generally been recruited from among the ruling strata of the civilian population or from those who sympathize with their interests; accordingly, the balance of forces *within* the ruling strata has been reflected within the standing army. And finally, there have developed in this standing army, or in many of them, certain gratifications which even men of violence often want: the security of a job, but more, the calculable glory of living according to a rigid code of honor.

'Is it to be supposed,' John Adams asked in the late eighteenth century, 'that the regular standing armies of Europe, engage in the service, from pure motives of patriotism? Are their officers men of contemplation and devotion, who expect their reward in a future life? Is it from a sense of moral, or religious duty that they risk their lives, and reconcile themselves to wounds? Instances of all these kinds may be found. But if any one supposes that all, or the greater part of these heroes, are actuated by such principles, he will only prove that he is unacquainted with them. Can their pay be considered as an adequate encouragement? This, which is no more than a very simple and moderate subsistence, would never be a temptation to renounce the chances of fortune in other pursuits, together with the pleasures of domestic life, and submit to this most difficult and dangerous employment. No, it is the consideration and the chances of laurels, which they acquire by the service.

'The soldier compares himself with his fellows, and contends for promotion to be a Corporal: the Corporals vie with each other to be Sergeants: the Sergeants will mount breaches to be Ensigns: and thus every man in an army is constantly aspiring to be something higher, as every citizen in the commonwealth is constantly struggling for a better rank, that he may draw the observation of more eyes.'[2]

Prestige to the point of honor, and all that this involves, has, as it were, been the pay-off for the military's renunciation of political power. This renunciation has gone quite far: it has been incorporated in the military code of honor. Inside their often trim bureaucracy, where everything seems under neat control, army officers have felt that 'politics' is a dirty, uncertain, and ungentlemanly kind of game; and in terms of their status code, they have often felt that politicians were unqualified creatures inhabiting an uncertain world.

The status mechanisms of the standing army have not always worked to the end of civilian dominance, and there is nothing inevitable about their working to that end. We know, for example, that the curse of the nations of the Spanish world has been the fact that whenever army officers have gotten a foothold in the councils of state, they have tried to dominate them, and that when they have no foothold in those councils, they may march upon the capital.

2

All of these reflections, having to do with world trends and world facts, bear in an especially acute way on the situation of the American military establishment and its higher echelons of generals and admirals. Like other nations, the United States was born in violence, but it was born at a time when warfare did not seem to be a dominating feature of human society. And it was born in a place which could not easily be reached by the machines of war, was not easily open to the devastation of war, not subject to the anxiety of those who live in military neighborhoods. In the time and place of its earlier period, the United States was well situated to erect and to maintain a civilian government, and to hold well subordinated such militarist ambition as might prevail.

A young country whose nationalist revolution was fought against mercenary soldiers, employed by the British and quartered in American homes, would not be likely to love professional soldiers. Being a wide, open land surrounded by weak neighbors, Indians and wide oceans, the sovereign United States for the long decades of the nineteenth century did not have to carry the burden of a permanent and large military overhead. Moreover, from the time of the Monroe Doctrine until it was applied to Britain in the later part of the nineteenth century, the British fleet, in order to protect British markets in the western hemisphere, stood between the United States and the continental states of Europe. Even after World War I, until the rise of Nazi Germany, the America that had become creditor to the bankrupt nations of Europe had little military threat to fear.[3] All this has also meant that, as in the islands of Britain, a navy rather than an army was historically the prime military instrument; and navies have much less influence upon national social structures than armies often have, for they are not very useful as a means of repressing popular revolt. Generals and admirals, accordingly, did not play much of a role in political affairs and civilian dominance was firmly set.

A country whose people have been most centrally preoccupied by the individual acquisition of wealth would not be expected to favor subsidizing an organized body of men who, economically speaking, are parasitical. A country whose middle class cherished

freedom and personal initiative would not be likely to esteem disciplined soldiers who all too often seemed to be tyrannically used
in the support of less free governments. Economic forces and
political climate, therefore, have historically favored the civilian
devaluation of the military as an at-times necessary evil but always
a burden.

The Constitution of the United States was constructed in fear
of a powerful military establishment. The President, a civilian,
was declared commander-in-chief of all the armed forces, and
during war, of the state militia's as well. Only Congress could declare war, or vote funds for military use—and for only two years at
a time. The individual states maintained their own militia, separate and apart from the national establishment. There was no pro-
vision for a flow of advice from military to civilian chiefs. If there
were provisions for violence in the constitution, they were reluc-
tant provisions, and the agents of violence were held to a strictly
instrumental role.

After the revolutionary generation, the upper classes were not
of a military stamp; the American elite did not systematically
include among its members high-ranking military figures; it developed no firm tradition of military service; prestige was not rendered to military servants. The ascendancy of economic over military men in the sphere of 'honor' was made quite apparent when,
during the Civil War, as indeed up to World War I, the hiring of
a substitute for the draft was not looked down upon. Military men,
accordingly, on their often isolated posts along the old internal
frontier, did not enter the higher circles of the nation.

No matter what hardships, and they were often severe, were
encountered by those who crossed the hemisphere and no matter
how military their expeditions and communities—and in many
ways they were for considerable periods definitely camps of war—
still those who headed the nation were not stamped with the military mind and the military outlook.

And yet, considering the whole of United States history, we are
confronted with a rather curious situation: we are told that we
have never been and are not a militarist nation, that in fact we
distrust the military experience, yet we note that the Revolution
led to the ascendancy of General Washington to the Presidency,

and that there were bids among certain rejected officers, in the Order of Cincinnati, to form a military council and install a militarist king. Then too, frontier battling and skirmishes had something to do with the political success of Generals Jackson, Harrison, and Taylor in the Mexican War. And there was also the Civil War, which was long and bloody and split American society across the middle, leaving scars that still remain much in evidence. Civilian authority, on both sides, remained in control through it and after it, but it did lead to the ascendancy of General Grant to the Presidency, which became a convenient front for economic interests. All the Presidents from Grant through McKinley, with the exceptions of Cleveland and Arthur, were Civil War officers, although only Grant was a professional. And again, with the little Spanish-American War, we note that the roughest, toughest of them all—perhaps because he was not a professional—Theodore Roosevelt—emerged in due course in the White House. In fact, about half of the thirty-three men who have been President of the United States have had military experience of some sort; six have been career officers; nine have been generals.

From Shays' Rebellion to the Korean War there has been no period of any length without official violence. Since 1776, in fact, the United States has engaged in seven foreign wars, a four-year Civil War, a century of running battles and skirmishes with Indians, and intermittent displays of violence in China, and in subjugating the Caribbean and parts of Central America.* All of these occurrences may have been generally regarded as nuisances interferring with the more important business at hand, but, at the very least, it must be said that violence as a means and even as a value is just a little bit ambiguous in American life and culture.

* In 1935, the editors of *Fortune* wrote: "It is generally supposed that the American military ideal is peace. But unfortunately for this highschool classic, the U.S. Army, since 1776, has filched more square miles of the earth by sheer military conquest than any army in the world, except only that of Great Britain. And as between Great Britain and the U.S. it has been a close race, Britain having conquered something over 3,500,000 square miles since that date, and the U.S. (if one includes wresting the Louisiana Purchase from the Indians) something over 3,100,000. The English-speaking people have done themselves proud in this regard.'4

The clue to this ambiguity lies in this fact: historically, there
has been plenty of violence, but a great deal of it has been directly
performed by 'the people.' Military force has been decentralized in
state militia almost to a feudal point. Military institutions, with few
exceptions, have paralleled the scattered means of economic
production and the confederate means of political power. Unlike
the Cossacks of the Eurasian Steppes, the technical and numerical
superiority of the American frontiersman who confronted the
American Indian made it unnecessary for a true warrior stratum
and a large, disciplined administration of violence to emerge. Virtually every man was a rifleman: given the technical level of the
warfare, the means of violence remained decentralized. That
simple fact is of the greatest consequence for civilian dominance
as well as for the democratic institutions and ethos of earlier times
in America.

Historically, democracy in America has been underpinned
by the militia system of armed citizens at a time when the rifle was
the key weapon and one man meant one rifle as well as one vote.
Schoolbook historians, accordingly, have not been prone to think
about changes in American military institutions and weapons systems as causes of political and economic changes. They bring out
military forces for an Indian skirmish and a distant war, and then
they tuck them away again. And perhaps the historians are right.
But the first armies in Europe based on universal conscription, it
ought to be remembered, were revolutionary armies. Other countries armed their populations reluctantly; Metternich at the Congress of Vienna urged the abolition of mass conscription; Prussia adopted it only after her professional army suffered defeats
without it; the Tzars, only after the Crimean war; and Austria,
only after Bismarck's recruits defeated Franz Josef's troops.[5]

The introduction of mass conscript armies in Europe involved
the extension of other 'rights' to the conscripts in an effort to
strengthen their loyalties. In Prussia, and later in Germany, this
was a quite deliberate policy. The abolishment of serfdom and
later the development of social-security plans accompanied the
establishment of mass conscription. Although the correspondence
is not exact, it seems clear that to extend the right to bear arms to
the population at large has involved the extension of other rights
as well. But in the United States, the right to bear arms was not *ex-*

tended by an arms-bearing stratum to an unarmed population: the population bore arms from the beginning.

Up to World War I, military activities did not involve the discipline of permanent military training, nor a monopoly of the tools of violence by the federal government, nor the professional soldier at the top of a large and permanent military establishment. Between the Civil War and the Spanish-American War, the army averaged about 25,000 men, organized on a regimental basis, with regiments and companies largely scattered on posts along the internal frontier and farther west. Through the Spanish-American War, the United States Army was militia-organized, which meant decentralized and with an unprofessional officer corps open to much local influence.

The small regular army was supplemented by state militias formed into The US Volunteers, the commanders of these troops being appointed by the governors of the states. In this quite unprofessional situation, regular army men could be and often were jumped to generalship in The Volunteers. Politics—which is also to say civilian control—reigned supreme. At any given time, there were few generals, and the rank of colonel was often even the West Pointer's height of aspiration.

3

Around the old army general of the late nineteenth century, in his neatly disheveled blue uniform, there hang wisps of gun smoke from the Civil War. In the Civil War he had distinguished himself, and between that war and the Spanish-American fracas he had fought Indians in a most adventurous way. The dash of the cavalry has rubbed off on him—even if at times making him something of a dashing imbecile (Remember Custer and the Little Big Horn!). He lives something of the hardy life which Theodore Roosevelt esteemed. He often wears a mustache, and sometimes a beard, and usually he has a certain unshaven look. Grant had worn a private's uniform with unshined buttons and ancient boots and the manner carried on. This old army man has fought up-close: it was not until World War I that an official effort was made 'to conserve trained personnel'; many generals and dozens of colonels were killed in Civil War battles or afterward in Indian skirmishes.

He did not earn the respect of his men by logistical planning in the Pentagon; he earned it by better shooting, harder riding, faster improvisation when in trouble.

The typical general of 1900[6] was of an old American family and of British ancestry. He was born about 1840 in the northeastern section of the United States and probably grew up either there or in the north central section, in a rural area or perhaps a small town. His father was a professional man, and the chances are fairly good that his father had political connections—which may or may not have aided him in his career. It took him a little more than thirty-eight years to become a major-general from the time he entered the army or West Point. When he came into top command, he was about sixty years old. If he was religious, he probably attended the Episcopal church. He married, sometimes twice, and his father-in-law, also a professional, might also have had some political connections. While in the service, he did not belong to a political party; but after retirement, he may have dabbled a bit in Republican politics. It is as unlikely that he wrote anything as that someone wrote very much about him. Officially, he had to retire at sixty-two; and he died, on the average, at the age of seventy-seven.

Only a third of these old army generals had been to West Point and only four others had completed college; the old army did not go to school. But we must remember that many southerners—who had been West Pointers and who had predominated in the old federal army—had gone home to fight in the Confederate army. Sometimes the army general of 1900 had been commissioned during the Civil War, sometimes he had come up through the volunteers of the state militia, sometimes he had personally recruited enough men and then he was a colonel. After he was in the regular army, his promotion was largely by seniority, which was greatly speeded up during wars, as during his jump from colonelcy during the Spanish-American War. At least half of the old army generals had higher connections with generals and politicians. General Leonard Wood, for example, who was a medical captain in 1891, became White House physician, and later, under his friends, Theodore Roosevelt and William Howard Taft, ended up in 1900 as Chief of Staff.

Only three of the top three-dozen army men ever went into

business—and two of these were non-regulars. Local merchants in frontier towns often loved this old army; for it fought Indians and cattle thieves and the army post meant money for the local economy. And in larger towns, the army was at times authorized to break strikes. Small boys also loved it.

Between the Civil War and the naval expansion under Theodore Roosevelt, the army was more in the public eye and its claims for status were cashed in by the lower classes. But the navy was more like a gentleman's club, which occasionally went on exploring and rescuing expeditions, and the prestige of the navy was among the upper classes. This explains, and is in part explained by, the higher level of origin and more professional training of its officer corps.

Apart from the British inheritance of sea power, there was the prestige of Admiral Mahan's theory, linking the greatness of the nation to her sea power, and falling easily upon the ears of Navy Undersecretary Theodore Roosevelt. The higher prestige of the navy, coming to a wider public during the Spanish-American War, has been due to the fact that the skills of the naval officer were more mysterious to laymen than those of the army—few civilians would dare try to command a ship, but many might a brigade. Since there was not, as in the army, a volunteer system—there was the prestige of skill augmented by the prestige of a formal, specialized education at Annapolis. There was also the fact of heavy capital investment, represented by the ships in the naval officer's command. And finally, there was the absolute authority that The Master of a ship exercises—especially in view of the sea tradition of contempt for the deckhand, which, applied to the enlisted sailors, lifted the officers high indeed.

The typical admiral of 1900 was born about 1842 of colonial stock and British ancestry. His father had a professional practice of one kind or another; but more important, he was of the upper levels of the northeastern seaboard, more likely than not of an urban center. The future admiral had the academy education plus two years on a receiving ship. He was only fourteen years old when he entered the navy; and if he was religious, he was definitely Protestant. Some forty-three years after he was accepted at the Academy he became a rear admiral. He was then fifty-eight years old. He had married within his own class level. He probably wrote one book, but chances were less that someone wrote a book about him; he may, however, have received an honorary degree after the war of 1898; and he retired from the navy at sixty-two years of age. He had held the rank of rear admiral for only three years; and he died ten years after compulsory retirement at the average age of seventy-two.

Even in 1900, the top of the navy was strictly Annapolis, and gentlemanly too. Recruited from higher class levels than the army, residing more in the East, having had better preparatory training and then the Academy, the admiral had also served in the Civil War, after which he slowly rose by avoiding innovation, in personal life or in military duties. Given the meticulous crawl of his career, it was important that he be commissioned early and live long, in order to reach admiralcy before compulsory retirement at sixty-two. It usually took some twenty-five years to become a captain. 'Officers spent so long a time in the lower subordinate grades that they never learned to think for themselves. They usually reached command ranks so late that they had lost their youth and ambition and had learned only to obey, not to command ...'*

From one-third to one-half of the duty of the top officers was spent at sea, occurring of course mainly while of lower rank. About half of the top thirty-five naval men had returned at one time or another to Annapolis as instructors or officials. And some took postgraduate work there. But the key to the bureaucratic snafu that has often characterized the navy is that as the ships and the guns and the logistics became more technically complicated, the men who ran them acquired rank less by technical specialty than by seniority. Accordingly, the skipper became somewhat alienated from his ship and had to take responsibility for matters which he did not altogether understand. The bureau heads, who ran the

* 'In December 1906, the age of the youngest captain in the American Navy was 55 and the average time spent in that grade was 4.5 years; in Great Britain the youngest captain was 35 and the average time spent in that grade was 11.2 years.' The figures for France, Germany, and Japan are similar to the British. 'The same situation was true of the flag officers. In the United States they usually averaged only 1.5 years in that rank before retirement,' but in Great Britain, France, Germany, and Japan, between 6 and 14 years.[7]

navy, had access to the Secretary, and were often thick with Congressmen. But despite the prominent connections, only one ad-admiral of this period went into business, and only two went into (local) politics.

Such, in brief, was the civilian controlled military establishment of the United States in the later nineteenth century, with its half-professionalized high officer corps, whose members were not in any important sense of the American elite of businessmen and politicians. But this is not the later nineteenth century, and most of the historical factors which then shaped the military roles within the nation no longer exert the slightest influence on the shape of the higher echelons of America.

4

In the middle of the twentieth century, the influence of such peaceful and civilian values as exist in the United States—and with them the effective distrust and subordination of professional military men—must be balanced by the unprecedented situation which the American elite now defines as the situation of the nation:

I. For the first time, the American elite, as well as effective sections of the underlying population, begin to realize what it means to live in a military neighborhood, what it means to be technically open to catastrophic attack upon the national domain. Perhaps they also realize how very easy a military time the United States as a nation has had, given its geographical isolation, its enlarging and pacified domestic market, its natural resources needed for industrialization, and requiring military operations only against a technologically primitive population. All that is now history: the United States is now as much a military neighbor of the Soviet Union—or even more so—as Germany has been of France in previous centuries.

II. This is brought home, immediately and dramatically, by the more careful estimates, now publicly available, of the physical effects of the latest weapons system. One saturation attack, it is not unreasonable to suppose, would result in some 50 million casualties, or nearly one-third of the population.[8] That the United States could immediately retaliate with comparable effects upon the enemy does not, of course, lessen those upon her own domain and population.

Such technical possibilities may be taken in a political and an industrial way, or in their strictly military meaning. The American elite in charge of that decision have taken them primarily in their military meaning. The terms in which they have defined international reality are predominantly military. As a result, in the higher circles there has been a replacement of diplomacy in any historically recognized sense by calculations of war potential and the military seriousness of war threats.

Moreover, the new weaponry has been developed as a 'first line of defense.' Unlike poison gas and bacteria, it has not been considered as a reserve against its use by the enemy, but as the major offensive weapon. And such grand strategy as has been made public has been officially based upon the assumption that such weapons will be used during the first days of general war. Indeed, that is now the common assumption.

III. These definitions of reality and proposed orientations to it have led to a further feature of America's international posture: for the first time in American history, men in authority are talking about an 'emergency' without a foreseeable end. During modern times, and especially in the United States, men had come to look upon history as a peaceful continuum interrupted by war. But now, the American elite does not have any real image of peace —other than as an uneasy interlude existing precariously by virtue of the balance of mutual fright. The only seriously accepted plan for 'peace' is the fully loaded pistol. In short, war or a high state of war preparedness is felt to be the normal and seemingly permanent condition of the United States.

IV. The final new feature we would mention of the United States situation, as now officially defined, is even more significant. For the first time in their history, the American elite find themselves confronting a possible war which they admit among themselves and even in public, that none of the combatants would *win*. They have no image of what 'victory' might mean, and they have no idea of any road to victory. Certainly the generals have no idea. In Korea, for example, it became quite clear that the stalemate was produced by 'a paralysis of will' on the political level. Lieutenant-Colonel Melvin B. Voorhees reports the following from an interview with General James Van Fleet: 'Reporter: "General, what is our goal?" Van Fleet: "I don't know. The answer must come from higher authority." Reporter: "How may we know, General, when and if we achieve victory?" Van Fleet: "I don't know, except that somebody higher up will have to tell us." ' 'That,' commented a *Time* editoralist, 'sums up the last two years of the Korean war.'[9] In previous times, leaders of nations in preparing for war had theories of victory, terms of surrender, and some of them at least were confident of the military means of imposing them. By World War II, the United States war aims had become quite vague in any political or economic sense, but there *were* strategic plans for victory by violent means. But now there is no literature of victory. Given the means of violence that now exist, 'massive re-taliation' is neither a war plan nor an image of victory, but merely a violent diplomatic—which is to say political—gesture and a recognition that all-out war between two nations has now become the means of their mutual destruction. The position amounts to this: with war all nations may fall, so in their mutual fright of war, they survive. Peace is a mutual fright, a balance of armed fear.

I am not concerned, at this point, to debate any of the defini-tions of reality that play into the national position or the policies of the United States. Yet given these features of the world situa-tion as it is officially defined today, we ought to realize that ortho-dox military strategy and military expertise of all types have be-come irrelevant and misleading in all decisions about world affairs that might lead to peace. Clearly all the decisive problems, fore-most among them, the problems of war and peace, now become in a more complete sense than ever before, political problems. Whether NATO has ten or thirty divisions is, from a military standpoint, as irrelevant as whether Germany is or is not to be rearmed. In the light of the now established facts concerning the effect of all-out bombing, such questions have ceased to be mili-tary issues of the slightest importance. They are political ques-tions concerning the ability of the United States to line up the nations of Europe.

But: given the military definition of reality that prevails among the men with the power of decision, the rise of the generals and the admirals into the higher circles of the American elite becomes completely understandable and legitimate, completely realistic and desirable. For this new international position of the United States, and the new international context itself—both as defined by the elite—have made for a change in their focus of attention. The rise to enlarged command and increased status of the warlords of Washington is but the most obvious sign of this broadening of attention. Decisions of the greatest consequence have become largely international. If it is too much to say that, for many of the elite, domestic politics have become important mainly as ways of retaining power at home in order to exert abroad the power of the national establtshment, surely it is true that domestic decisions in virtually all areas of life are increasingly justified by, if not made with, close reference to the dangers and opportunities abroad.

At the same time, it is not strange that there has been civilian alarm in high places over the increased power of the warlords. This alarm would be more responsible if it led to effective challenge of the military definition of reality in favor of political and economic and human images of world affairs. But then, it is easier to be alarmed over warlords, who, of course, are both a cause and a result of the definitions of reality that prevail.

5

As the American means of violence have been enlarged and centralized, they have come to include an enormously complicated bureaucratic structure, reaching to the rimlands of Asia and well into the peninsula of Europe with its instruments of perception, and into the heart of Eurasia with its strategic air force. Such changes in the institutions and reach of the means of violence could not but make equally significant changes in the men of violence: the United States warlords.

The most dramatic symbol of the scale and shape of the new military edifice is the Pentagon.[10] This concrete and limestone maze contains the organized brain of the American means of violence. The world's largest office building, the United States Capitol would fit neatly into any one of its five segments. Three football fields would reach only the length of one of its five outer walls. Its seventeen and a half miles of corridor, 40,000-phone switchboards, fifteen miles of pneumatic tubing, 2,100 intercoms, connect with one another and with the world, the 31,300 Pentagonians. Prowled by 170 security officers, served by 1,000 men and women, it has four full-time workers doing nothing but replacing light bulbs, and another four watching the master panel which synchronizes its 4,000 clocks. Underneath its river entrance are five handball courts and four bowling alleys. It produces ten tons of non-classified waste paper a day, which is sold for about $80,000 a year. It produces three nation-wide programs a week in its radio-TV studio. Its communication system permits four-party conversations between people as far apart as Washington, Tokyo, Berlin, and London.

This office building, in this intricate architectural and human maze, is the everyday milieu of the modern warlords. And no Indian fighters are to be found among them.

At the head of the military bureaucracy, below the President of the United States and the Secretary of Defense, whom he appoints, and his assistants, there sits, behind office walls of sheet steel, a military board of directors—the Joint Chiefs of Staff. Immediately below the Joint Chiefs there is a higher circle of generals and admirals which presides over the elaborate and far-flung land, sea, and air forces, as well as the economic and political liaisons held necessary to maintain them, and over the publicity machines.

Since Pearl Harbor, in a series of laws and directives, a serious attempt has been made to unify the several branches of the service. Easier civilian control would result from such unity; but it has not been altogether successful. The high navy especially, has often felt neglected; and each of the services has, on occasion, gone to Congress over the head of its Secretary—the air force at one time even winning its point against the opposition of the Secretary. In 1949, the Hoover Commission reported that the military establishment lacked central authority and adequate budgetary routines; that it was not a 'team,' and that the link between scientific research and strategic plans was weak. 'The lack of central authority in the direction of the national military establishment, the rigid statutory structure established under the act, and divided responsibility have resulted in a failure to assert clear civilian control over the armed forces.'[11]

At the very top, among civilians and military, there have been, since World War II, sweeping changes of personnel—although the types of men have not decisively changed.[12] As Secretary, there has been a politician, a broker, a general, a banker, a corporation executive. Directly confronting such men, sit the four highest military who are 'all military.'* From the military's standpoint, perhaps the ideal civilian at the top would be a front to Congress but a willing tool of military decision. But this is not always the type that prevails. Recently, for example, the Secretary of the Navy moved an admiral out of a top job for reasons of 'policy differences.'[14] There is undoubtedly tension, the men on either side being, like all men, to some degree prisoners of their pasts.

There are, of course, cliques among the high military, variously related to one another and variously related to given civilian policies and cliques. These become apparent when hidden tensions become open controversies—as at the time of MacArthur's dismissal from his Eastern command. At that time there was, in addition to the MacArthur school of Asia First, already declining in influence, the Marshall-set who gave priority to Europe. There was also the Eisenhower-Smith group, which had great influence but did not run the army; and there was the dominant group who did run it, the Bradley-Collins team.[15]** And there is the rather standard split between those who feel that the need of the services is for 'truly professional armed forces' commanded by 'combat line offi-

* The chairman of the Joint Chiefs of Staff, Admiral Arthur W. Radford, is the son of a civil engineer; the Chief of Naval Operations, Admiral Robert B. Carney, is the son of a navy commander; the Army Chief of Staff, General Matthew B. Ridgway, is the son of a regular army officer; and the Chief of Staff of the Air Force, General Nathan F. Twining, has two brothers who are Annapolis men.[13]

** The Joint Chiefs of Staff appointed in 1953, for example, have all held major commands in the Pacific, and there was some feeling upon their appointment that they were more Asia-minded than the more European-minded Bradley, Collins, Vandenberg, and Fechteler they replaced. All of them were also reported to favor the tactical side of air warfare as over the strategic—at least they were not pure and simple 'big-bomb' men. Admiral Radford, in fact, as commander-in-chief of the Pacific fleet led the 'revolt of the admirals' against the B-36 in the budget controversy of 1949.[16]

cers' and those who are happier about the rise of the new 'specialists' and staff men.[17]

As the military increase in power, more tense cliques will
probably develop among them, despite 'unification'—which is, of
course, by no means completed. When the military are a minority
fighting for survival, they are more likely to hang together than
when they are dominant members of the power elite, for then it
is no question of survival but of expansion.

In the early twentieth century, the militia system had been centralized; and now the weapons systems have developed to the
point where rifles are mere toys. The arming of the citizen is now
within a disciplined organization under firmly centralized control,
and the means of suppressing illegitimate violence have increased. As a result, those outside the military ruling circles are
helpless militarily. Yet, at the same time, virtually the entire population is involved in war, as soldiers or as civilians—which means
that they are disciplined in a hierarchy at whose head there sit
the warlords of Washington.

6

The nearest the modern general or admiral comes to a small-
arms encounter of any sort is at a duck hunt in the company of
corporation executives at the retreat of Continental Motors, Inc.
One insurance company, in fact, 'has been insuring officers for a
decade and a half, went through World War II . . . and survived
. . . during the Korean War, the mortality rate of officer policyhold-
ers serving in the battle zone was below the average for industry
as a whole.'[18] As a further fact, Brigadier General S. L. A. Marshall's studies have revealed that in any given action of World War
II, probably no more than 25 per cent of the soldiers who were in a
position to fire their weapons at the enemy actually pulled the
trigger.[19]

The general and the admiral are more professionalized executives than inherited images of fighting men would suggest. Two-
thirds of the top generals of 1950[20] graduated from The Point (all
of the admirals, both in 1900 and 1950, graduated from the Naval
Academy); most saw service in World War I, and most of them
lived through the general anti-militarist peace of the 'twenties and
'thirties, begging for appropriations, denying the merchants-of-

death charges. Above them all towered the spit-and-polish image of Pershing.

During the interwar years nothing really happened in their professional lives. It was in some ways as if a doctor were passing his life without seeing any patients, for the military were not called upon really to exercise their professional skill. But they had the services. Perhaps that is the clue to their development in such periods: in them there is intensified the desire, too deeply rooted to examine, to conform to type, to be indistinguishable, not to reveal loss of composure to inferiors, and above all, not to presume the right to upset the arrangements of the chain of command. It was important that those above them could not find anything against them; and, at home and abroad, the life of the professional military went on in their own little colonies, quite insulated from the economic and political life of the nation. In the civilian distrust that prevailed, the military were supposed to 'stay out of politics,' and most of them seemed glad to do so.

The military life of the interwar officer revolved around his rank. Through the rank of colonel, promotion was by seniority, and standing before the officer was 'the hump'—a concentration of four or five thousand officers, most of them commissioned during World War I. As a result of this hump, it took a man 'twenty-two years to climb from the junior captain to the senior captain.' He could 'scarcely hope to top the grade of captain before reaching his fifties.'[21]

The social life of the interwar officer also revolved around his rank. Toward the world of civilians, as well as among their unappreciated selves, there was intense consciousness of rank. General George C. Marshall's wife, remembering this period, recalls an officer's wife remarking, 'At a tea such as this one you always ask the highest-ranking officer's wife to pour coffee, not tea [because] coffee outranks tea.' She also remembers the life of the colonel in the slump when—as she elsewhere notes—the army was so pressed for funds that target practice was curtailed: 'Our quarters at Fort Moultrie were not a home, but a hotel. The house had been built by the Coast Artillery in its balmy days, but now the place was in bad repair. It had 42 French doors leading out on the lower and top verandas, which extended around three sides of the house.' And when Marshall became a general: 'In front of the cottage stood a beautiful new Packard car—to replace our little Ford. So he had one thrill out of his generalcy, for a Packard in those times of depression was indeed a marvelous thrill. I was quite overcome with joy.'[22]

Another colonel's lady remembers the rank order among wives: 'When someone suggested that a committee be selected to buy the books, the doctor's wife, who knew my weakness, murmured my name, but the colonel's wife appointed the three highest ranking ladies present.' And she too remembers the life abroad among higher military personnel: 'In China our domestic staff had consisted of five . . . The pay freeze [during the slump] which cut out these automatic increases hurt more junior than senior officers. No general was affected by it, and only one admiral. Seventy-five per cent of the loss, in the army, was stood by lieutenants, captains, warrant officers and nurses.'[23] It was in these interwar days that second-lieutenant Eisenhower met Mamie Doud, whose father was prosperous enough to retire to leisure in Denver at the age of thirty-six and, with his family, winter in San Antonio.

It is reported, as of 1953, that 'a typical career officer at age forty-five or fifty may accumulate as much as $50,000 of insurance over the years.'[25] And of the interwar naval officer's life, it has been said: 'The summer cruises were exciting, and the gold stripes and extra privileges of upper-class life made you begin to feel like somebody after all. And you . . . learned good manners, and visited your roommate's home in Philadelphia one Christmas holiday and got your first taste of the social pampering in store for personable young navy men . . . you listened to so many lectures admonishing you *not* to consider yourself superior to a civilian that you found yourself feeling that you really *were* a cut above, but that it would be improper to show that you thought so.'[26]

Yet it has not generally been true in the United States that, as Veblen would have it, since 'war is honorable, warlike prowess is honorific.'[27] Nor has it been true that military officers have generally derived from, or become, members of Veblen's leisure class.*

---

* 'While it is a fact that our army officers are better paid than any others in the world,' it was authoritatively stated in 1903, 'yet the pursuit of the profession of arms offers to our men no pecuniary inducement. If they do not possess outside sources of income, they are expected to live within their pay; sixty per cent, or more, have no income

It is more true of the navy than of the army—the air force is too
new for such developments. On the whole, the high officers of the
army and navy have been men of the upper-middle rather than
truly higher or definitely lower classes. Only a very small percentage of them are of working-class origin. They have been the sons
of professional men, of businessmen, of farmers, of public officials, and of military men. They are overwhelmingly Protestant,
mainly Episcopalians or Presbyterians. Few have served in the
ranks.[29]

And for almost all of them of today, World War II is the pivotal
event. It is the pivot of the modern military career and of the
political and military and social climate in which that career is
being enacted. Younger men among the top today saw combat
duty in leading regiments or divisions, and older men, rapidly advanced in the great expansion, rose to the top headquarters at
home and abroad.

7

Social origins and early backgrounds are less important to the
character of the professional military man than to any other high
social type. The training of the future admiral or general begins early and is thus deeply set, and the military world which he
enters is so all-encompassing that his way of life is firmly centered
within it. To the extent that these conditions exist, whether he is
the son of a carpenter or a millionaire is that much less important.

The point should not, of course, be pushed too far. Although the
military is the most bureaucratic of all types within the American
elite, it is not absolutely bureaucratic, and, as in all bureaucracies,
on its higher levels it becomes less so than on its lower and middle.
Nevertheless, when we examine the military career, one fact appears to be so central that we need not go far beyond it. That fact
is that for most of their careers, the admirals and the generals have
followed a quite uniform and pre-arranged pattern. Once we
know the ground rules and the pivotal junctures of this standard-

beyond their pay [40 per cent did] . . . Most prized of all the details,
probably, is that of military attaché at one of the United States legations
abroad . . . Officers who accept such posts generally have outside incomes of their own or such as are derived through their family connections.'[28]

ized career, we already know as much as we can find out from the detailed statistics of a multitude of careers.

The military world selects and forms those who become a professional part of it. The harsh initiation at The Point or The Academy—and on lower levels of the military service, in basic training—reveals the attempt to break up early civilian values and sensibilities in order the more easily to implant a character structure as totally new as possible.

It is this attempt to break up the earlier acquired sensibilities that lies back of the 'breaking' of the recruit and the assignment to him of very low status in the military world. He must be made to lose much of his old identity in order that he can then become aware of his very self in the terms of his military role. He must be isolated from his old civilian life in order that he will come eagerly to place the highest value on successful conformity with military reality, on deep acceptance of the military outlook, and on proud realization of success within its hierarchy and in its terms. His very self-esteem becomes quite thoroughly dependent upon the appraisals he receives from his peers and his superiors in the chain of command. His military role, and the world of which it is a part, is presented to him as one of the higher circles of the nation. There is a strong emphasis upon the whole range of social etiquette, and, in various formal and informal ways, he is encouraged to date girls of higher rather than of lower status. He is made to feel that he is entering upon an important sector of the higher circles of the nation, and, accordingly, his conception of himself as a self-confident man becomes based upon his conception of himself as a loyal member of an ascendant organization. The only 'educational' routine in America that compares with the military is that of the metropolitan 400's private schools, and they do not altogether measure up to the military way.[39]

West Point and Annapolis are the beginning points of the warlords, and, although many other sources of recruitment and ways of training have had to be used in the emergencies of expansion, they are still the training grounds of the elite of the armed forces.[31] Most of the top generals and all of the admirals of today are of West Point or of The Academy, and they definitely feel it. In fact, if no such caste feeling existed among them, these character-se-

lecting and character-forming institutions would have to be called
failures.

The caste feeling of the military is an essential feature of the
truly professional officer corps which, since the Spanish-American War, has replaced the old decentralized, and somewhat locally political, militia system. 'The objective is the fleet,' naval
Captain L. M. Nulton has written, 'the doctrine is responsibility,
and the problem is the formation of military character.'³² Of the
period when most present-day admirals were at Annapolis, it was
asserted by Commander Earle: 'The discipline of the Naval Academy well illustrates the principle that in every community discipline means simply organized living. It is the condition of living
right because without right living, civilization cannot exist. Persons who will not live right must be compelled to do so, and upon
such misguided individuals there must be placed restraints. To
these alone is discipline ever harsh or a form of punishment. Surely
this is just as it should be. The world would be better if such individuals were made to feel the tyranical, unyielding, and hard-
nailed fist in order to drive them from an organization to which
they have not right to belong.'*

The military world bears decisively upon its inhabitants because it selects its recruits carefully and breaks up their previously
acquired values; it isolates them from civilian society and it stand-
ardises their career and deportment throughout their lives.
Within this career, a rotation of assignment makes for similarity
of skills and sensibilities. And, within the military world, a higher
position is not merely a job or even the climax of a career; it is clearly a total way of life which is developed under an all-encompassing system of discipline. Absorbed by the bureaucratic hierarchies
in which he lives, and from which he derives his very character
and image of self, the military man is often submerged in it, or as a
possible civilian, even sunk by it. As a social creature, he has
until quite recently been generally isolated from other areas of
American life; and as an intellectual product of a closed educa-

* He adds: 'On Sundays there is compulsory attendance at church . . .
(which helps) him to realize that he is not merely an individual but is a
member of an organization even in his devotions, as is evidenced by the
prayer for his brothers in the fleet, by one for his fellow members in the
Academy, both of which he hears every Sunday morning . . .'³³

tional system, with his experience itself controlled by a code and a sequence of jobs, he has been shaped into a highly uniform type.

More than any other creatures of the higher circles, modern warlords, on or above the two-star rank, resemble one another, internally and externally. Externally, as John P. Marquand has observed,[34] their uniforms often seem to include their facial mask, and certainly its typical expressions. There is the resolute mouth and usually the steady eye, and always the tendency to expressionlessness; there is the erect posture, the square shoulders, and the regulated cadence of the walk. They do not amble; they stride. Internally, to the extent that the whole system of life-training has been successful, they are also reliably similar in reaction and in outlook. They have, it is said, 'the military mind,' which is no idle phrase: it points to the product of a specialized bureaucratic training; it points to the results of a system of formal selection and common experiences and friendships and activities —all enclosed within similar routines. It also points to the fact of discipline—which means instant and stereotyped obedience within the chain of command. The military mind also indicates the sharing of a common outlook, the basis of which is the metaphysical definition of reality as essentially military reality. Even within the military realm, this mind distrusts 'theorists,' if only because they tend to be different: bureaucratic thinking is orderly and concrete thinking.

The fact that they have succeeded in climbing the military hierarchy, which they honor more than any other, lends self-assurance to the successful warlords.The protections that surround their top positions make them even more assured and confident. If they should lose confidence in themselves what else would there be for them to lose? Within a limited area of life, they are often quite competent, but to them, in their disciplined loyalty, this area is often the only area of life that is truly worthwhile. They are inside an apparatus of prerogative and graded privilege in which they have been economically secure and unworried. Although not usually rich, they have never faced the perils of earning a living in the same way that lower and middle-class persons have. The orderly ranks of their chain of command, as we have seen, are carried over into their social life: such striving for status as they have known has been within an unambiguous and well-organized hierarchy of status, in which each knows his place and remains within it.

In this military world, debate is no more at a premium than persuasion: one obeys and one commands, and matters, even unimportant matters, are not to be decided by voting. Life in the military world accordingly influences the military mind's outlook on other institutions as well as on its own. The warlord often sees economic institutions as means for military production and the huge corporation as a sort of ill-run military establishment. In his world, wages are fixed, unions impossible to conceive. He sees political institutions as often corrupt and usually inefficient obstacles, full of undisciplined and cantankerous creatures. And is he very unhappy to hear of civilians and politicians making fools of themselves?

It is men with minds and outlooks formed by such conditions who in postwar America have come to occupy positions of great decision. It cannot be said—as we shall presently make clear—that they have necessarily sought these new positions; much of their increased stature has come to them by virtue of a default on the part of civilian political men. But perhaps it can be said, as C. S. Forester has remarked in a similar connection, that men without lively imagination are needed to execute policies without imagination devised by an elite without imagination.[35] But it must also be said that to Tolstoy's conception of the general at war—as confidence builder pretending by his manner that he knows what the confusion of battle is all about—we must add the image of the general as the administrator of the men and machines which now make up the greatly enlarged means of violence.

In contrast with the inter-war careers and activities, the warlord of post-World War II who is slated for the top will have spent a crucial tour of duty in the Pentagon, where on the middle and lower ranks each man has a superior looking over his shoulder, and where, at the top, civilians and military look over one another's shoulders. The army's lieutenant colonel or the navy's commander in his thirties will probably make his jump, if at all, in or quite near the Pentagon. Here, as a cog in an intricate machine, he may come into the view of those who count, here he may be picked up for staff position and later be given the forward-looking command. So, in an earlier day, was Pershing impressed by George C. Marshall; so Nimitz was impressed by Forrest Sherman; Hap Arnold was impressed by Lauris Norstad; Eisenhower by Gruenther; Gruenther by Schuyler.

What will the future warlord do in the Pentagon, where there seem more admirals than ensigns, more generals than second lieutenants? He will not command men, or even for quite a while a secretary. He will read reports and brief them as inter-office memos; he will route papers with colored tags—red for urgent, green for rush-rush, yellow for expedite. He will serve on one of the 232 committees. He will prepare information and opinion for those who make decisions, carefully guarding his superior's Yes. He will try to become known as a 'comer,' and, even as in the corporate world, somebody's bright young man. And, as in all bureaucratic mazes, he will try to live by the book ('Standard Operating Procedure') but know just how far to stretch its letter in order to be an expediter, an operator, who on lower levels can procure another secretary for his office-unit, and on higher levels, another air wing. It is the activities of the warlords on still higher levels that we must now examine.

9

The Military Ascendancy

SINCE Pearl Harbor those who command the enlarged means of American violence have come to possess considerable autonomy, as well as great influence, among their political and economic colleagues. Some professional soldiers have stepped out of their military roles into other high realms of American life. Others, while remaining soldiers, have influenced by advice, information, and judgment the decisions of men powerful in economic and political matters, as well as in educational and scientific endeavors. In and out of uniform, generals and admirals have attempted to sway the opinions of the underlying population, lending the weight of their authority, openly as well as behind closed doors, to controversial policies.

In many of these controversies, the warlords have gotten their way; in others, they have blocked actions and decisions which they did not favor. In some decisions, they have shared heavily; in others they have joined issue and lost. But they are now more powerful than they have ever been in the history of the American elite; they have now more means of exercising power in many areas of American life which were previously civilian domains; they now have more connections; and they are now operating in a nation whose elite and whose underlying population have accepted what can only be called a military definition of reality. Historically, the warlords have been only uneasy, poor relations within the American elite; now they are first cousins; soon they may become elder brothers.

1

Although the generals and admirals have increasingly become
involved in political and economic decisions, they have not shed
the effects of the military training which has moulded their characters and outlook. Yet on the higher levels of their new careers
the terms of their success have changed. Examining them closely
today, one comes to see that some are not so different from corporation executives as one had first supposed, and that others
seem more like politicians of a curious sort than like traditional
images of the military.

It has been said that a military man, acting as Secretary of Defense for example, might be more civilian in effect than a civilian who, knowing little of military affairs and personnel, is easily
hoodwinked by the generals and admirals who surround him. It
might also be felt that the military man in politics does not have
a strong-willed, new and decisive line of policy, and even that, in
a civilian political world, the general becomes aimless and, in his
lack of know-how and purpose, even weak.[1]

On the other hand, we must not forget the self-confidence that
is instilled by the military training and career: those who are successful in military careers very often gain thereby a confidence
which they readily carry over into economic and political realms.
Like other men, they are of course open to the advice and moral
support of old friends who, in the historical isolation of the military
career, are predominantly military. Whatever the case may be
with individuals, as a coherent group of men the military is probably the most competent now concerned with national policy; no
other group has had the training in co-ordinated economic, political, and military affairs; no other group has had the continuous
experience in the making of decisions; no other group so readily
'internalizes' the skills of other groups nor so readily engages their
skills on its own behalf; no other group has such steady access to
world-wide information. Moreover, the military definitions of political and economic reality that now generally prevail among the
most civilian of politicians cannot be said to weaken the confidence of the warlords, their will to make policy, or their capacity
to do so within the higher circles.

The 'politicalization' of the high military that has been going on over the last fifteen years is a rather intricate process: As members of a professional officer corps, some military men develop a vested interest—personal, institutional, ideological—in the enlargement of all things military. As bureaucrats, some are zealous to enlarge their own particular domains. As men of power, some develop quite arrogant, and others quite shrewd, drives to influence, enjoying as a high value the exercise of power. But by no means are all military men prompted by such motives.* As a type of man, the professional military are not inherently out for political power, or, at least, one need not rest the case upon any such imputation of motive. For even if they are not desirous of political power, power essentially political in nature may be and has been thrust upon them by civilian default; they have been much used—willingly or not—by civilians for political purposes.

From the standpoint of the party politician, a well-trained general or admiral is an excellent legitimator of policies, for his careful use often makes it possible to lift the policy 'above politics,' which is to say above political debate and into the realm of administration, where, as statesman Dulles said in support of General Eisenhower for President, there are needed men with the capacity for 'making grave decisions.'[3]

From the standpoint of the political administrator, military men are often believed useful because they constitute a pool of men trained in executive skills but not openly identified with any private interests. The absence of a genuine Civil Service'** which selects and trains and encourages career men, makes it all the more tempting to draw upon the military.

Politicians thus default upon their proper job of debating policy, hiding behind a supposed military expertise; and political administrators default upon their proper job of creating a real

---

* 'It is drummed into every military manager in the course of his not-inconsiderable education, from the day he enters West Point to the day death makes him eligible for an Arlington burial with honors, that he is to back away from anything resembling a political decision, and that he is to stay well on his side of anything that resembles a line separating his responsibility from civilian authority. Admiral Leahy has written, "I was so completely lacking in political campaigning experience as to be unable to formulate any opinion. Whereupon the President (F.D.R.) said to me in jest, 'Bill, politically you belong in the Middle Ages.' " '[2]

** See below, TEN: The Political Directorate.

civilian career service. Out of both these civilian defaults, the professional military gain ascendancy. It is for such reasons, more than any other, that the military elite—whose members are presumably neither politically appointed nor politically responsible—have been drawn into the higher political decisions.

Once they enter the political arena—willingly, reluctantly, or even unknowingly—they are of course criticized; they become politically controversial and, like any other political actors, they are open to attack. Even when they are not explicitly in politics, the military are attacked politically. In the American context of civilian distrust, the military has always been a handy target of political abuse. But the matter now goes farther than that. In 1953, Senator McCarthy, as Hanson Baldwin put it, 'tried to assume command of the Army and stormed at officers with long and faithful service because they . . . obeyed the orders of their legitimate superiors.'[4] Thus he entered, without benefit of induction, the chain of command. The warlord sees how such attacks have virtually destroyed the public respect and the internal morale of the State Department, and he is afraid that his organization, too, will be hollowed out. Moreover, since he holds power to affect economic affairs, having a majority cut of the budget, he is open to attack by new civilian administrative heads who lean on him but also kick him around, as well as by political demagogues who are out to exploit his 'errors' or invent 'errors' for him to commit.

As politics get into the army, the army gets into politics. The military has been and is being made political, on the one hand, by civilian default, and on the other, by civilian criticism of military decisions.

Not always being aware of just what is happening, believing in their mask of 'military expert,' and being used to command, the military often react to criticism in a rather rigid way. In the army book, there is no Standard Operating Procedure for fighting a Senator. There seem only two ways out: One way, especially if there is a war on, is a field command and obeying orders rigidly without political question. In other words, go soldierly and withdraw, be aloof and stiff in your dignity. The other way is to go all out politically, by the classic ways of forming alliances with political figures, and, given their executive position, maybe some new ways too. For, so long as they remain officers, they cannot very well go explicitly and openly political in the party sense—although some have done so. But, in the main, they will necessarily work carefully and behind the scenes—they will, in short, be open to membership, with other military men, with corporation executives, and with members of the political directorate and of the Congress, to form or to join pro-military cliques on the higher levels.

One must also remember that, by virtue of their training and experience, the professional military believe firmly in the military definition of world reality, and that, accordingly, given the new and enormous means of violence and the nervous default of civilian diplomacy, they are genuinely frightened for their country. Those with the most conviction and, in their terms, ability, will be frustrated by retreat into the role of the strictly apolitical technician of violence. Besides, many are too high up and already too deeply involved for soldierly withdrawal.

It is in terms of this situation that we must understand the political ways of the warlords, and the higher influence military men have now come to exert within the power elite of America. Military men are supposed to be the mere instruments of political men, but the problems they confront increasingly require political decisions. To treat such political decisions as 'military necessities' is of course to surrender civilian responsibility, if not decision, to the military elite. But if the military metaphysics, to which the civilian elite now clings, are accepted, then by definition warfare is the only reality, that is to say, the necessity, of our time.

2

As the United States has become a great world power, the military establishment has expanded, and members of its higher echelons have moved directly into diplomatic and political circles. General Mark Clark, for example, who has probably had more political experience while on active duty than any other American warlord, 'believes in what he calls the "buddy system"—a political man and a military man working together,' of which he has said: 'In the past, many American generals were inclined to say of politics: "To hell with it, let's talk politics later." But you can't do it this way any more.'[5]

In 1942, General Clark dealt with Darlan and Giraud in North Africa; then he commanded the Eighth Army in Italy; then he was occupation commander for Austria; and, in 1952, he became US Commander in newly sovereign Japan, as well as head of the US Far East Command and UN Commander in Korea. General George C. Marshall, after being the President's personal representative to China, became Secretary of State (1947–49), then Secretary of Defense (1950–51). Vice Admiral Alan G. Kirk was Ambassador to Belgium in the late 'forties and then to Russia. In 1947, the Assistant Secretary of State for occupied areas was Major General John H. Hildring who dealt 'directly with the military commanders who control the execution of policy in Germany, Austria, Japan and Korea';[6] Brigadier General Frank T. Hines was Ambassador to Panama; and General Walter Bedell Smith was Ambassador to Russia. General Smith later became the head of the Central Intelligence Agency (1950–53), then Under Secretary of State (1953–54). As occupation commander in Germany, there was General Lucius D. Clay; of Japan, General MacArthur. And no diplomat, but a former Army Chief of Staff, General J. Lawton Collins, went to troubled Indo-China in 1954 'to restore some order' in an area which he said 'had essential political and economic importance for Southeast Asia and the free world.'[7]

Moreover, while still in uniform as well as out of it, high-ranking officers have engaged in policy debate. General Omar Bradley, one of the most articulate deniers of undue military influence in civilian decisions, has appeared before Congressional committees, as well as before broader publics, in support of policies involving economic and political as well as strictly military issues. General Marshall, for example, has submitted arguments against the Wagner-Taft resolution which favored increased immigration to Palestine and its further development as a Jewish homeland.[8] With Generals Bradley, Vandenberg, and Collins, as well as Admiral Sherman, General Marshall has also defended before Congressional committees the Truman administration against Republican attack upon its Far-Eastern policy, and the ousting of General MacArthur from his Far-Eastern command.

General Bradley has made numerous speeches which in their context were readily interpreted, by Senator Taft and Hanson Baldwin among others, as relevant to the political issues of the 1952 Presidential elections. 'This speech,' wrote Hanson Bald-

win, 'helped put General Bradley and the Joint Chiefs of Staff
into the political hustings where they have no business to be.'[9]
Senator Taft, who accused the Joint Chiefs of Staff of being
under the control of the political administration and of echoing
their policies rather than rendering merely expert advice, was
himself supported by General Albert Wedemeyer, as well as by
General MacArthur. Another general, Bonner Fellers, was on the
Republican National Committee.

In the 1952 election, in direct violation of U.S. Army Regulation
600-10, General MacArthur, in public speeches, attacked the policies of the duly elected administration, delivered the keynote address at the Republican convention, and made it clear that he was
open to the Presidential nomination. But another general, Eisenhower, also not retired, was successfully supported for this role.
Both of these generals, as well as what might be considered their
political policies, were supported by other military men. There is
no doubt about it: there are now Republican and Democratic generals. There are also, as we now know well, officers who are for or
against individual Senators—such as McCarthy—and who in their
military positions lean one way or the other to reveal it or to hide
it.

In 1954, a notable array of the high military—headed by retired
Lt. General George E. Stratemeyer with retired Rear Admiral
John G. Crommelin as Chief of Staff—offered their names in an
effort to rally ten million signatures for a McCarthy petition.[10]
This occurred in the context of the military ascendancy at a time
when the words of Old Soldier MacArthur had not faded: 'We of
the military shall always do what we are told to do. But if this nation is to survive, we must trust the soldier once our statesmen fail
to preserve the peace.' (1953)—'I find in existence a new and
heretofore unknown and dangerous concept that the members of
our armed forces owe primary allegiance and loyalty to those who
temporarily exercise the authority of the Executive Branch of government rather than to the country and its Constitution which
they are sworn to defend. No proposition could be more dangerous.' (1951)[11]

But more important perhaps than the straightforward assumption of political roles, the private advice, or the public speeches, is

a more complex type of military influence: high military men have become accepted by other members of the political and economic elite, as well as by broad sectors of the public, as authorities on issues that go well beyond what has historically been considered the proper domain of the military.

Since the early 'forties, the traditional Congressional hostility toward the military has been transformed into something of a 'friendly and trusting' subservience. No witness—except of course J. Edgar Hoover—is treated with more deference by Senators than the high military. 'Both in what it did and in what it refused to do,' we read in an official government account, 'the wartime Congress co-operated consistently and almost unquestioningly with the suggestions and the requests from the Chief of Staff.'[12] And in the coalition strategy, while the President and the Prime Minister 'decided,' theirs were choices approved by the military and made from among alternatives organized and presented by the military.

According to the Constitution, the Congress is supposed to be in charge of the support and governing of the armed might of the nation. During times of peace, prior to World War II, professional politicians in the Congress did argue the details of military life with the military, and made decisions for them, debating strategy and even determining tactics. During World War II, Congressmen 'voted' for such items as the Manhattan Project without having the slightest idea of its presence in the military budget, and when—by rumor—Senator Truman suspected that something big was going on, a word from the Secretary of War was enough to make him drop all inquiry. In the postwar period, the simple fact is that the Congress has had no opportunity to get real information on military matters, much less the skill and time to evaluate it. Behind their 'security' and their 'authority' as experts, the political role of the high military in decisions of basic political and economic relevance has become greatly enlarged. And again, it has been enlarged as much or more because of civilian political default—perhaps necessarily, given the organization and personnel of Congress—than by any military usurpation.[13]

3

No area of decision has been more influenced by the warlords and by their military metaphysics than that of foreign policy and international relations. In these zones, the military ascendancy has coincided with other forces that have been making for the downfall of civilian diplomacy as an art, and of the civilian diplomatic service as an organized group of competent people. The military ascendancy and the downfall of diplomacy have occurred precisely when, for the first time in United States history, international issues are truly at the center of the most important national decisions and increasingly relevant to virtually all decisions of consequence. With the elite's acceptance of military definitions of world reality, the professional diplomat, as we have known him or as we might imagine him, has simply lost any effective voice in the higher circles.

Once war was considered the business of soldiers, international relations the concern of diplomats. But now that war has become seemingly total and seemingly permanent, the free sport of kings has become the forced and internecine business of people, and diplomatic codes of honor between nations have collapsed. Peace is no longer serious; only war is serious. Every man and every nation is either friend or foe, and the idea of enmity becomes mechanical, massive, and without genuine passion. When virtually all negotiation aimed at peaceful agreement is likely to be seen as 'appeasement,' if not treason, the active role of the diplomat becomes meaningless; for diplomacy becomes merely a prelude to war or an interlude between wars, and in such a context the diplomat is replaced by the warlord.

Three sets of facts about American diplomacy and American diplomats are relevant to the understanding of what has been happening: the relative weakness of the professional diplomatic service; its further weakening by 'investigation' and 'security' measures; and the ascendancy among those in charge of it of the military metaphysics.

1. Only in those settings in which subtle nuances of social life and political intention blend, can 'diplomacy'—which is at once a political function and a social art—be performed. Such an art has seemed to require those social graces usually acquired by persons of upper-class education and style of life. And the career diplomat has, in fact, been representative of the wealthier classes.*

---

* This has been secured by the policy of paying the diplomats such low salaries that they could not exist in a foreign post without private

But up to 1930, a *career* in the foreign service had not led to the ambassadorial ranks.** Of the eighty-six men who served as American ambassadors between 1893 and 1930, only about one-fourth of them had held positions in the foreign service prior to their appointment as ambassadors. 'The British Ambassador,' D. A. Hartman has pointed out, 'represents the final stage of a definite career in the Foreign Service, while the American ambassadorship is scarcely more than a belated episode in the life of a businessman, politician, or lawyer.'[16]

During the long Democratic tenure something like a career service, based upon upper-class recruitment, had been developed. Of the thirty-two ambassadors and top ministers of 1942, almost half were graduates of private preparatory schools frequented by the children of the metropolitan 400; and of the top one hundred and eighteen officers in the Foreign Service, fifty-one were Harvard, Princeton or Yale.[17]

When the Republicans assumed office in 1953, there were 1,305 Foreign Service officers (out of a total State Department of 19,405) serving the seventy-two diplomatic missions and one hundred ninety-eight consular offices of the United States.[18] Forty of the

income. Given the social obligations of the diplomatic life, it is almost impossible to live on an ambassadorial salary in any of the major capitals of the world. It was estimated in the early 'forties that it cost an ambassador at an important post from $75,000 to $100,000 a year to entertain in a manner befitting his station; the highest official salary of an ambassador is only $25,000.[14]

** None of the 18 top ambassadors of 1899 could be termed 'careermen' in the sense that they had spent most of their adult lives working in the Foreign Service. Ten of them had never held a diplomatic post before becoming ambassadors; and another six had been in diplomatic service for not longer than nine years before 1899. Only two had started in the diplomatic service longer than a decade before: Oscar S. Straus, Ambassador to Turkey, and Andrew D. White, Ambassador to Germany. Most of these ambassadors seem to have acquired their appointments as a reward for party faithfulness: eleven had been active in politics, about half of these in conjunction with legal careers. There was one professor and one journalist; and the remaining five men were businessmen, often again in conjunction with a law career. As a group the ambassadors of 1899 came from comfortable families, often of great wealth, were educated in the best schools of America and Europe—six of them graduating from Ivy League schools—and had held important positions in business or politics.[15]

seventy-two chiefs of United States missions abroad had been career diplomats 'whose appointments to particular posts may have been by the President but whose tenure in the foreign service is unaffected by the change in administration.'[19] There were two alternatives open to the career men—they could retire, or they could resign from their posts and become available for other assignments under the new administration.

By this time it would seem that a foreign-service career leading up to an ambassadorship had become more firmly entrenched, since nineteen of the top twenty-five ambassadors appointed by President Eisenhower were career men. But it might also be said that by 1953 it was no longer an 'honor' to a prominent businessman, lawyer, or politician to be appointed as the ambassador to the generally small countries in which almost all of these career men served.[20] However, later in his administration, President Eisenhower began to appoint unsuccessful politicians and political helpmates to the smaller countries hitherto reserved for career men. Thus in Madrid, John D. Lodge—defeated for governor of Connecticut—replaced the veteran diplomat James C. Dunn. In Libya, John L. Tappin—ski expert and chief of a division of 'Citizens for Eisenhower'—replaced career-man Henry S. Villard.[21] In the more coveted diplomatic posts, representing America were millionaire bankers; members, relatives, and advisers of the very rich; high corporate lawyers; the husbands of heiresses.

II. Even before the change of administration, the morale and competence of the career service had been severely weakened by investigation and dismissal of personnel. Then Senator McCarthy's associate, Scott McLeod, moved from the FBI to the head of both security and personnel in the Department of State. Mr. McLeod, who 'believes that "security" is a basic criterion of diplomacy,' has remarked that after checking all other qualifications, he asks himself: 'How would I like him to be behind a tree with me in a gunfight? You get pretty high standards if you think along such lines. And that's the way I like to think in these investigations.'[22] There were many men who 'wouldn't fit behind a tree' with policeman McLeod, and among many Foreign Service officers who still held their positions 'the impression grew that it wasn't safe to report the truth to Washington about any foreign situation when the truth didn't jibe with the preconceived notions of the people in Washington.'*²³

Following a long list of men already dismissed for reasons of 'loyalty,' in the fall of 1954, a career diplomat of twenty-three years service, John Paton Davies, was dismissed not on the grounds of loyalty, but because of 'lack of judgment, discretion and reliability'; his opinions on China policy ten years previously not jibing with the current administration policy.²⁵ The comments on this case by career men expressed their state of mind. A recent member of the Policy Planning Staff of the State Department wrote: 'One hopes that the American public will see at last that the word "security" has become a euphemism. It covers the primitive political drive of the last five years to eliminate intellectual and moral distinction from the Government service, and to staff the Government instead with political good fellows who cannot be suspected of superiority. Under the reorganized Foreign Service, for example, educational standards for admission are being avowedly lowered. It is as if the mediocrity of the mindless has become the ideal.'²⁶ George Kennan, a veteran diplomat and a distinguished student of foreign affairs, has advised a class of students at Princeton not to choose the foreign service as a career. In other words: 'the morale of the State Department is so broken that its finest men flee from it, and advise others to flee.'²⁷

III. For years of course the military attachés have been at their foreign posts, where they are supposedly the Ambassador's aides as well as a link in an intelligence service; but 'many of them, in the post-war years, have viewed the Foreign Service and State

---

* This was not, of course, an entirely new feature of the Foreign Service. For instance: 'The basic burden of the reporting of the China Service in the critical years was that, in the inevitable clash between the Chinese Communists and Chiang Kai-shek, Chiang would be the loser. This correctness in judgment has resulted, however, not in honor either collectively or individually to the China Service. China has gone Communist. In some fashion the men of the China Service were held responsible. The China Service, therefore, no longer exists. Of the twenty-two officers who joined it before the beginning of World War II, there were in 1952 only two still used by the State Department in Washington . . . Most of the rest were still serving the American government, but not . . . where their intimate knowledge of a China with whom we were desperately at war in Korea might be useful.'²⁴

Department with ill-disguised contempt and made themselves virtually independent of the Ambassadors under whom they should work.'*

The problem, however, goes well beyond such relatively low-order tension. The military, as we have seen, have become ambassadors as well as special envoys. In many of the major international decisions, the professional diplomats have simply been by-passed, and matters decided by cliques of the high military and political personnel. In the defense agreements signed by the United States and Spain in September of 1953, as in the disposition in 1945 and 1946 of the western Pacific islands captured from the Japanese, the military has set policy of diplomatic relevance without or against the advice of the diplomats.[29] The Japanese peace treaty was not arranged by diplomats but by generals; a peace treaty with Germany has not been made: there have only been alliances and agreements between armies. At Panmunjom, the end of the Korean war was 'negotiated' not by a diplomat but by a General in open collar and without necktie. 'The American services,' writes the London *Economist*, 'have successfully implanted the idea that there are such things as purely military factors and that questions which involve them cannot be adequately assessed by a civilian. British theory and experience denies both these propositions . . .'[30]

So Admiral Radford, who has told a Congressional Commit-

---

* In April 1954, the army prohibited officers abroad from keeping diaries, after the world discovered that Major General Grow, military attaché to Moscow, had kept a diary in which he advocated war against the Soviet Union, expressed his distaste for the ambassador and his dislike for his contacts. While visiting Frankfurt, Germany, he left the diary in a hotel room, from which it was promptly stolen, photographed, and returned. The Soviet Union made propaganda. The general, clearly an unfortunate type for intelligence work, is perhaps less to be blamed than the 'spoils system' of the army intelligence system by which he was placed in Moscow. General Grow is not lonely in his incompetence. The most important attaché post in the postwar period was filled by a general—Iron Mike O'Daniel—whose two-fisted fighting style often seemed his only recommendation. Two attachés in eastern Europe after the war 'were notorious, one for his convivial habits, the other for selling on the black market some excess clothing he had bought.' Another general—head of G2 during the war, was recalled from London for investigation of black-market charges.[28]

tee that Red China had to be destroyed even if it required a fifty-year war, argued, as chairman of the Joint Chiefs of Staff, for the use of 500 planes to drop tactical A-bombs on Vietminh troops before the fall of Dienbienphu. If China openly came into the picture, we are unofficially told, Peking was to be given atomic treatment.[31] This political situation was defined by him as military, and as such argued for with a voice as loud as those of his civilian bosses, the Secretary of Defense and the Secretary of State. In August 1954, General Mark Clark publicly stated that Russia should be ejected from the United Nations, and diplomatic relations with her broken off. General Eisenhower, then President, disagreed with his intimate friend, but the President's word did not stop General James A. Van Fleet from publicly subscribing to General Clark's views.[32] Not that it was too important an issue, for the UN has regularly been by-passed in important decisions and conclaves. The UN did not organize the Geneva conference; the UN did not consider the United States action in Guatemala.[33] The by-passing of the UN in the most important East-West conflicts and its general political weakening is one aspect of the downfall of diplomacy in the postwar period. The other aspect is the military ascendancy, as personnel and as metaphysics.

In America, diplomacy has never been successfully cultivated as a learned art by trained and capable professionals, and those who have taken it up have not been able to look forward to obtaining the top diplomatic posts available, for these have been largely bestowed according to the dictates of politics and business. Such professional diplomatic corps as the United States has possessed, along with the chances to build up such a corps in the future, have been sabotaged by recent investigation and dismissal. And, in the meantime, the military has been and is moving into the higher councils of diplomacy.

4

The military establishment has, of course, long been economically relevant. The Corps of Engineers—historically the elite of the West Pointers—has in peacetime controlled rivers and harbor construction. Local economic, as well as Congressional, interests have not been unaware of the pork-barrel possibilities, nor of the chance to have The Corps disapprove of the Reclamation Bureau's plans for multiple-purpose development of river valleys. 'Actually'—we are told by Arthur Maass in his discussion of 'the lobby that can't be licked'—'up to about 1925, the Corps disbursed 12 per cent of the total ordinary expeditures of the government.'[34]

But now the economic relevance of the military establishment is on a qualitatively different scale.* The national budget has increased, and within it the percentage spent by and for the military. Since just before World War II, the percentage has never gone below about 30 per cent, and it has averaged over 50 per cent, of the entire government budget. In fact, two out of every three dollars in the budget announced in 1955 was marked for military security.[36] And as the role of government in the economy has increased, so has the role of the military in the government.

We should constantly keep in mind how recent the military ascendancy is. During World War I the military entered the higher economic and political circles only temporarily, for the 'emergency'; it was not until World War II that they intervened in a truly decisive way. Given the nature of modern warfare, they had to do so whether they wanted to or not, just as they had to invite men of economic power into the military. For unless the military sat in on corporate decisions, they could not be sure that their programs would be carried out; and unless the corporation chieftains knew something of the war plans, they could not plan war production. Thus, generals advised corporation presidents and corporation presidents advised generals. 'My first act on becoming Chief of Ordnance of June 1, 1942,' Lt. General Levin H. Campbell, Jr., has said, 'was to establish a personal advisory staff consisting of four outstanding business and industrial leaders who were thoroughly familiar with all phases of mass production.'[37]

During World War II, the merger of the corporate economy and the military bureaucracy came into its present-day significance. The very *scale* of the 'services of supply' could not but be economically decisive: The Services of Supply, *Fortune* remarked in 1942, 'might . . . be likened to a holding company of no mean

* Between 1789 and 1917, the U.S. government spent about 29½ billion dollars; but in the single fiscal year of 1952, the military alone was allotted 40 billion. In 1913, the cost per capita of the military establishment was $2.25; in 1952, it was almost $250.[35]

proportions. In fact—charged with spending this year some $32 billion, or 42 per cent of all that the U.S. will spend for war—it makes U.S. Steel look like a fly-by-night, the A.T. and T. like a country-hotel switchboard, Jesse Jones's RFC or any other government agency like a small-town boondoggle. In all of Washington, indeed, there is scarcely a door—from Harry Hopkins's Munitions Assignments Board on down—in which [General] Somervell or his lieutenants have not come to beg, to borrow, or to steal.'[38] The very *organization* of the economics of war made for the coincidence of interest and the political mingling among economic and military chiefs: 'The Chief of Ordnance has an advisory staff composed of Bernard M. Baruch, Lewis H. Brown of Johns-Manville Corp., K. T. Keller of Chrysler Corp., and Benjamin F. Fairless of United States Steel Corp. Ordnance contracts are placed by four main branches . . . Each branch director . . . [is] assisted by an advisory industrial group, composed of representatives of the major producers of weapons in which the branch deals.'[39]

The military establishment and the corporations were of course formally under the control of civilian politicians. As managers of the largest corporate body in America, 'the military had a board of directors . . . the President, the service Secretaries, the men on the military-affairs committees of Congress. Yet many of the men on the board, i.e., the Congressmen, can really do little more than express general confidence, or the lack of it, in the management. Even the most influential directors, the President and the Secretary of Defense, can usually argue with the management only as laymen arguing with professionals—a significantly different relationship from that of board and management in industry.'[40]

The coming together of the corporations and the military was most dramatically revealed in their agreement upon the timing and the rules of 'reconversion.' The military might lose power; the corporations would no longer produce under the prime contracts they held; reconversion, if not handled carefully, could easily disturb the patterns of monopoly prevailing before war production began. The generals and the dollar-a-year executives saw to it that this did not happen.[41]

After World War II, military demands continued to shape and to pace the corporate economy. It is accordingly not surprising that during the last decade, many generals and admirals, instead of merely retiring, have become members of boards of directors.*

It is difficult to avoid the inference that the warlords, in their trade of fame for fortune, are found useful by the corporate executives more because of whom they know in the military and what they know of its rules and ways than because of what they know of finance and industry proper. Given the major contracts that are made by the military with private corporations, we can readily understand why business journalists openly state: 'McNarney knows Convair's best customer, The Pentagon, as few others do— a fact well known to his friend, Floyd Odlum, Convair chairman.' And 'in business circles the word has gone out: Get yourself a general. What branch of the government spends the most money? The military. Who, even more than a five-percenter, is an expert

* General Lucius D. Clay, who commanded troops in Germany, then entered the political realm as occupation commander, is now the board chairman of the Continental Can Company. General James H. Doolittle, head of the 8th Air Force shortly before Japan's surrender, is now a vice-president of Shell Oil. General Omar N. Bradley, who commanded the 12th Army group before Berlin, going on to high staff position, then became the board chairman of Bulova Research Laboratories; in February 1955, Chairman Bradley allowed his name to be used—'General of the Army Omar N. Bradley'—on a full-page advertisement in support, on grounds of military necessity, of the new tariff imposed on Swiss watch movements. General Douglas MacArthur, political general in Japan and Korea is now chairman of the board at Remington Rand, Inc. General Albert C. Wedemeyer, commander of U.S. forces in the China theater, is now a vice-president of AVCO Corporation. Admiral Ben Moreell is now chairman of Jones & Laughlin Steel Corp. General Jacob Evers is now technical adviser to Fairchild Aircraft Corp. General Ira Eaker is vice-president of Hughes Tool Co. General Brehon Somervell, once in charge of army procurement, became, before his death in 1955, chairman and president of Koppers Co. Admiral Alan G. Kirk, after serving as Ambassador to Russia, became chairman of the board and chief executive officer of Mercast, Inc., which specializes in high-precision metallurgy. General Leslie R. Groves, head of the Manhattan Project, is now a vice-president of Remington Rand in charge of advanced research; General E. R. Quesada, of the H-Bomb test, is a vice-president of Lockheed Aircraft Corporation; General Walter Bedell Smith is now vice-chairman of American Machine and Foundry Company's board of directors; Army Chief of Staff General Matthew B. Ridgway, having apparently turned down the command of Kaiser's automotive invasion of Argentina, became chairman of the board of the Mellon Institute of Industrial Research.[42]

on red tape? A general or an admiral. So make him Chairman of the Board.'[43]

The increased personnel traffic that goes on between the military and the corporate realms, however, is more important as one clue to a structural fact about the United States than as an expeditious means of handling war contracts. Back of this shift at the top, and behind the increased military budget upon which it rests, there lies the great structural shift of modern American capitalism toward a permanent war economy.

Within the span of one generation, America has become the leading industrial society of the world, and at the same time one of the leading military states. The younger military are of course growing up in the atmosphere of the economic-military alliance, but more than that they are being intensively and explicitly educated to carry it on. 'The Industrial College of the Armed Forces,' concerned with the interdependence of economy and warfare, is at the top level of the military educational system.[44]

To the optimistic liberal of the nineteenth century all this would appear a most paradoxical fact. Most representatives of liberalism at that time assumed that the growth of industrialism would quickly relegate militarism to a very minor role in modern affairs. Under the amiable canons of the industrial society, the heroic violence of the military state would simply disappear. Did not the rise of industrialism and the long era of nineteenth-century peace reveal as much? But the classic liberal expectation of men like Herbert Spencer has proved quite mistaken. What the main drift of the twentieth century has revealed is that as the economy has become concentrated and incorporated into great hierarchies, the military has become enlarged and decisive to the shape of the entire economic structure; and, moreover, the economic and the military have become structurally and deeply interrelated, as the economy has become a seemingly permanent war economy; and military men and policies have increasingly penetrated the corporate economy.*

'What officials fear more than dateless war in Korea,' Arthur Krock reported in April of 1953, 'is peace . . . The vision of peace which could lure the free world into letting down its guard, and

---

* For a fuller discussion of these trends, see below, TWELVE: The Power Elite.

demolishing the slow and costly process of building collective security in western Europe while the Soviets maintained and increased their military power, is enough to make men in office indecisive. And the stock market selling that followed the sudden conciliatory overtures from the Kremlin supports the thesis that immediate prosperity in this country is linked to a war economy and suggests desperate economic problems that may arise on the home front.'[45]

5

Scientific and technological development, once seated in the economy, has increasingly become part of the military order, which is now the largest single supporter and director of scientific research in fact, as large, dollar-wise, as all other American research put together. Since World War II, the general direction of pure scientific research has been set by military considerations, its major finances are from military funds, and very few of those engaged in basic scientific research are not working under military direction.

The United States has never been a leader in basic research, which it has imported from Europe. Just before World War II, some $40 million—the bulk of it from industry—was spent for basic scientific research; but $227 million was spent on applied research and 'product development and engineering.'[46] With the Second World War pure scientists were busy, but not in basic research. The atom program, by the time it became governmental, was for the most part an engineering problem. But such technological developments made it clear that the nations of the world were entering a scientific, as well as an armaments, race. In the lack of any political policies for science, the military, first the navy, then the army, began to move into the field of scientific direction and support, both pure and applied. Their encroachment was invited or allowed by corporate officials who preferred military rather than civilian control of governmental endeavors in science, out of fear of 'ideological' views of civilians concerning such things as patents.

By 1954, the government was spending about $2 billion on research (twenty times the prewar rate); and 85 per cent of it was for 'national security.'[47] In private industry and in the larger universities, the support of pure science is now dominantly a military support. Some universities, in fact, are financial branches of the military establishment, receiving three or four times as much money from military as from all other sources combined. During the war, four leading institutions of learning received a total of more than $200 million in research contracts—not including atom research, for which exact figures are lacking.

The general tendency for the militarization of science has continued into the years of peace. That fact, as The National Science Foundation has made clear, is responsible for the relative neglect of 'fundamental science.' Out of the $2 billion scientific budget of 1955, only $120 million (6 per cent) was for basic research, but, as we have said, 85 per cent was for military technology.[48]

The military ascendancy in the world of science is more dramatically revealed by the troubled atmosphere which the military's 'risk system' has brought about. By October of 1954, this had reached the point at which Dr. Vannevar Bush—World War II Chief of the Office of Scientific Research and Development—felt it necessary to assert flatly that the scientific community was 'demoralized.' 'You won't find any strikes . . .' he said, 'but scientists today are discouraged and downhearted and feel that they are being pushed out, and they are.'[49] In the context of distrust, no less a scientist than Albert Einstein publicly asserted: 'If I would be a young man again and had to decide how to make my living, I would not try to become a scientist or scholar or teacher. I would rather choose to be a plumber or a peddler in the hope to find that modest degree of independence still available under present circumstances.'[50]

Although there are perhaps 600,000 engineers and scientists in the United States, only some 125,000 of them are active in research, and of these perhaps 75,000 are researching for industry in its pursuit of new commercial products, and another 40,000 are in developmental engineering. There are only 10,000 scientists engaged in fundamental research in all branches, and informed opinion has it that the top-rate creators number no more than one or two thousand.[51]

It is these senior circles that have become deeply involved in the politics of military decisions, and the militarization of political life. In the last fifteen years, they have moved into the vac-

uum of theoretical military studies, in which strategy and policy
become virtually one. It is a vacuum because, historically—as
Theodore H. White has pointed out—the American warlords
have not concerned themselves with it, being more engaged in
'technique' than 'theory.' Accordingly, as part of the military
ascendancy, there is the felt need of the warlords for theory, the
militarization of science, and the present 'demoralization' of the
scientist in the service of the warlord.[52]

In educational institutions the pursuit of knowledge has been
linked with the training of men to enact special roles in all areas
of modern society. The military, in addition to their own schools,
have used and increasingly use the educational facilities of private and public educational institutions.* As of 1953, almost 40
per cent of the male students of 372 colleges and universities were
enrolled in officer-training programs of army, navy or air force.
The liberal arts institutions involved were devoting about 16 per
cent of their curriculum to the military courses. For the nation as
a whole, about one out of five students were in ROTC units, an
unprecedented proportion for a year of formal peace.[53]

During World War II, the military had begun to use the colleges and universities for specialist training, as well as for the military training of students in accelerated courses. And the specialist
training, as well as the heavy research programs, has continued
after the war.

Today, many colleges and universities are eager to have military programs of training and research established on their cam-

* During the Civil War, land grant colleges were set up in various
states, which included in their curricula military training. In some of
these colleges, between that war and World War I, this training was
voluntary; in others, compulsory for various periods of the college
career. In 1916, the War Department standardized military training as
compulsory for the first two years in the land grant colleges. But in
1923, the Wisconsin legislature successfully challenged this arrangement for its University, a land grant institution, and several other
schools followed suit. During World War I, Reserve Officers Training
Corps units were established in various colleges. These ROTC programs
have been expanded on the campuses of colleges and universities. Universal military training—steadily pressed for by the military—would, of
course, mean the processing of all young men in military skills and appropriate attitudes, for a period half as long and probably twice as intensive as a four-year college course.

puses. It is prestigeful and it is financially sound. Moreover, the list of military men who, most of them without any specific educational qualifications, have come to serve as college administrators, and in other educational capacities, is impressive. General Eisenhower, of course, on his way to the Presidency, was the head of Columbia University, as well as a member of the National Educational Association Policy Commission. And even a casual survey reveals a dozen or so military men in educational positions.*

There has been a good deal of tension between the schools and the military. In the case of the Armed Forces Institute—a correspondence school for men in the service—one clause in the contract with universities gives the military direct power over university personnel, in case they are 'disapproved' by the government: as of August 1953, twenty-eight universities had signed, fourteen had rejected, and five were pending.[55] But in general, the acceptance by the educators of the military has been accomplished without such misunderstandings; it has been accomplished during the war and after it, because many schools need financial support; the federal government has not provided it under civilian control, but the military has had it to provide.

6

It is not only within the higher political and economic, scientific and educational circles that the military ascendancy is apparent. The warlords, along with fellow travelers and spokesmen, are attempting to plant their metaphysics firmly among the population at large.

During World War II, sympathizers of the warlords came out into the open as spokesmen for militarism. The wartime speeches of Mr. Frank Knox, of Mr. Charles E. Wilson (G.E.), and of James Forrestal—for example—were rich in military images of the future held by key men of power, and the images have by no means

---

* For example, Rear Admiral Herbert J. Grassie, chancellor of Lewis College of Science and Technology; Admiral Chester Nimitz, regent of the University of California at Berkeley; Major General Frank Keating, a member of the Ithaca College board of trustees; Rear Admiral Oswald Colcough, dean of the George Washington University Law School; Colonel Melvin A. Casburg, dean of the St. Louis School of Medicine; Admiral Charles M. Cook, Jr., a member of the California State Board of Education.[54]

faded. Since World War II, in fact, the warlords have caused
a large-scale and intensive public-relations program to be carried
out. They have spent millions of dollars and they have employed
thousands of skilled publicists, in and out of uniform, in order to
sell their ideas and themselves to the public and to the Congress.

The content of this great effort reveals its fundamental purpose: to define the reality of international relations in a military
way, to portray the armed forces in a manner attractive to civilians, and thus to emphasize the need for the expansion of military
facilities. The aim is to build the prestige of the military establishment and to create respect for its personnel, and thus to prepare
the public for military-approved policies, and to make Congress
ready and willing to pay for them. There is also, of course, the
intention of readying the public for the advent of war.

To achieve these ends, the warlords of Washington have at hand
extensive means of communication and public relations. Daily, in
war and in peace, they release items and stories to the press and to
the three or four dozen newsmen housed in the newsroom of the
Pentagon. They prepare scripts, make recordings, and take pictures for radio and TV outlets; they maintain the largest motion-
picture studio in the East, bought from Paramount in 1942. They
are ready to serve magazine editors with prepared copy. They
arrange speaking engagements for military personnel and provide
the speeches. They establish liaison with important national organizations, and arrange orientation conferences and field trips for
their leaders, as well as for executives and key people in the business, the educational, the religious, the entertainment worlds.
They have arranged, in some 600 communities, 'advisory committees' which open the way to their messages and advise them
of unfavorable reactions.[56]

Everything that appears in the news or on the air that concerns
the military is summarized and analyzed; and everything which
they release, including the writing of retired warlords, is reviewed
and censored.

The cost of this program varies from year to year, but interested
Senators have estimated it as between $5 million and $12 million.
Such estimates, however, mean little, for the position of the mili-
tary is such that they were able to enjoy, during one twelve-

month period, some $30 million worth of motion pictures, which they co-operated in producing; obtain millions of dollars worth of free time on TV, and, according to *Variety's* estimate, about $6 million of free radio time.

Nor does the 1951 estimate of Senator Harry F. Byrd (of 2,235 military and 787 civilians in publicity, advertising, and public relations) accurately reveal the scale of the program. For it is not difficult to use, at least part-time, many service personnel for public-relations purposes. Top admirals and generals, of course, have their own public-relations men. In 1948, General MacArthur's command included one hundred thirty-five army men and forty civilians assigned to publicity. Eisenhower, when Chief of Staff, had forty-four military and one hundred thirteen civilians.[57] And the warlords themselves have been learning the ways of publicity. Recently the retiring Air Force Chief of Staff, General Hoyt S. Vandenberg, told graduates at an air force base that 'the greatest fraternity on the face of the earth are the people who wear wings . . . You're not just jet jockeys . . . Take up the broader duty of understanding and preaching the role of air power . . . The people who won't face the truth . . . must be told repeatedly, earnestly, logically that air power will save the world from destruction . . .'[58]

It is a delicate problem which the military publicists confront, but there is one great fact that works entirely for their success: in all of pluralist America, there is no interest—there is no possible combination of interests—that has anywhere near the time, the money, the manpower, to present a point of view on the issues involved that can effectively compete with the views presented day in and day out by the warlords and by those whom they employ.[59]

This means, for one thing, that there is no free and wide debate of military policy or of policies of military relevance. But that, of course, is in line with the professional soldier's training for command and obedience, and with his ethos, which is certainly not that of a debating society in which decisions are put to a vote. It is also in line with the tendency in a mass society for manipulation to replace explicitly debated authority, as well as with the fact of total war in which the distinction between soldier and civilian is obliterated. The military manipulation of civilian opinion and the military invasion of the civilian mind are now important ways in which the power of the warlords is steadily exerted.

The extent of the military publicity, and the absence of opposition to it, also means that it is not merely this proposal or that point of view that is being pushed. In the absence of contrasting views, the very highest form of propaganda warfare can be fought: the propaganda for a definition of reality within which only certain limited viewpoints are possible. What is being promulgated and reinforced is the military metaphysics—the cast of mind that defines international reality as basically military. The publicists of the military ascendancy need not really work to indoctrinate with this metaphysics those who count: they have already accepted it.

7

In contrast with the existence of military men, conceived simply as experts in organizing and using violence, 'militarism' has been defined as 'a case of the dominance of means over ends' for the purpose of heightening the prestige and increasing the power of the military.[60] This is, of course, a conception from the standpoint of the civilian who would consider the military as strictly a means for civilian political ends. As a definition, it points to the tendency of military men not to remain means, but to pursue ends of their own, and to turn other institutional areas into means for accomplishing them.

Without an industrial *economy*, the modern army, as in America, could not exist; it is an army of machines. Professional economists usually consider military institutions as parasitic upon the means of production. Now, however, such institutions have come to shape much of the economic life of the United States. *Religion*, virtually without fail, provides the army at war with its blessings, and recruits from among its officials the chaplain, who in military costume counsels and consoles and stiffens the morale of men at war. By constitutional definition, the military is subordinated to *political* authority, and is generally considered, and has generally been, a servant as well as an adviser of civilian politicians; but the warlord is moving into these circles, and by his definitions of reality, influencing their decisions. The *family* provides the army and navy with the best men and boys that it possesses. And, as we have seen, *education* and *science* too are becoming means to the ends sought by the military.

The military pursuit of status, in itself, is no threat of military dominance. In fact, well enclosed in the standing army, such status is a sort of pay-off for the military relinquishment of adventures in political power. So long as this pursuit of status is confined to the military hierarchy itself, it is an important feature of military discipline, and no doubt a major source of much military gratification. It becomes a threat, and it is an indication of the growing power of the military elite today, when it is claimed outside the military hierarchy and when it tends to become a basis of military policy.

The key to an understanding of status is power. The military cannot successfully claim status among civilians if they do not have, or are not thought to have power. Now power, as well as images of it, are always relative: one man's powers are another man's weaknesses. And the powers that have weakened the status of the military in America have been the powers of money and of money-makers, and the powers of the civilian politicians over the military establishment.

American 'militarism,' accordingly, involves the attempt of military men to increase their powers, and hence their status, in comparison with businessmen and politicians. To gain such powers they must not be considered a mere means to be used by politicians and money-makers. They must not be considered parasites on the economy and under the supervision of those who are often called in military circles 'the dirty politicians.' On the contrary, their ends must be identified with the ends as well as the honor of the nation; the economy must be their servant; politics an instrument by which, in the name of the state, the family, and God, they manage the nation in modern war. 'What does it mean to go to war?' Woodrow Wilson was asked in 1917. 'It means,' he replied, 'an attempt to reconstruct a peacetime civilization with war standards, and at the end of the war there will be no bystanders with sufficient peace standards left to work with. There will be only war standards . . .'[61] American militarism, in fully developed form, would mean the triumph in all areas of life of the military metaphysic, and hence the subordination to it of all other ways of life.

There can be little doubt but that, over the last decade, the warlords of Washington, with their friends in the political directorate and the corporate elite, have definitely revealed militaristic tendencies. Is there, then, in the higher circles of America 'a military clique'? Those who argue about such a notion—as Supreme Court Justice William O. Douglas and General of the Army Omar Bradley have recently done[63]—are usually arguing only about the increased influence of the professional military. That is why their arguments, in so far as they bear upon the structure of the elite, are not very definitive and are usually at cross-purposes. For when it is fully understood, the idea of a military clique involves more than the military ascendancy. It involves a coincidence of interests and a co-ordination of aims among economic and political as well as military actors.

Our answer to the question, 'Is there now a military clique?' is: Yes, there is a military clique, but it is more accurately termed the power elite, for it is composed of economic, political, as well as military, men whose interests have increasingly coincided. In order to understand the role of the military within this power elite, we must understand the role of the corporation executive and the politician within it. And we must also understand something of what has been happening in the political sphere of America.

10

The Political Directorate

THE perfect candidate for the Presidency of the United States was born some fifty-four years ago in a modest but ramshackled farm house in the pivotal state of Ohio. Of a sizable family, which arrived from England shortly after the *Mayflower*, he grew up on the farm, performing the traditional chores and thus becoming well acquainted with all farm problems. When he was in high school his father died, the farm was sold, his strong and sensible mother moved the family to a near-by small town, and the struggle began.

The future President worked in his uncle's factory, quickly becoming a practical expert on all labor and management problems, while putting himself through college. He arrived in France during World War I just in time to make clear, for a full six months, that, in another war with more time, he would undoubtedly be a statesman of note. Returning home, he went to the state law school for two years, married his high-school sweetheart, whose grandfathers fought with the Confederate armies, opened his office, and joined the local party club, as well as the Elks, and in due course the Rotary Club, and attended the Episcopalian church. He is having a very busy life now, but he can stand such strains, for it is as if his constitution was built for them. During the 'twenties, he represented a group of small factories in their relations with labor, and was so successful that during the 'thirties there was no labor trouble of any consequence. Other companies, noting this as a remarkable fact, also engaged him, and thus, with the publicity, he became mayor of his city in 1935.

As the soldier-statesman and labor-relations expert took hold of
the reins, both business and labor acclaimed the skill and vigor of
his administration. Although an absolutely regular party man, he
remodeled the city government from top to bottom. Came the
Second World War, and despite his two young sons, he re-
signed his mayoralty to become a lieutenant colonel, and a member of a favored general's staff. He quickly became a statesman
well versed in Asiatic and European affairs and confidently pre-
dicted everything that happened.

A brigadier general, he returned to Ohio after the war and
found himself the overwhelming choice for governor. For two
terms he has been swept into office, his administration being as
efficient as any business, as moral as any church, as warm-hearted
as any family. His face is as honest as any business executive's,
his manner as sincere as any salesman's; in fact, he is something of
both, with a touch of grimness and homely geniality all his own.
And all of this comes through, magnetically, straight to you,
through the lens of any camera and the microphone as well.[1]

1

Some of the features of this portrait are not too different from
the average modern President's to be recognizable, although perhaps their interpretation is somewhat unmeasured. Among those
who have reached the top positions of the American government
one can find at least two or three who represent almost anything
for which one looks. One could endlessly collect biographical anecdotes and colorful images about them—but these would not
add up to any conclusions about the leading types of men and
their usual careers. We must understand how history and biography have interplayed to shape the course of American politics,
for every epoch selects and forms its own representative political men—as well as prevailing images of them.

That is the first point to bear in mind: many of the images
of politicians that prevail today are, in fact, drawn from earlier
epochs. Accordingly, 'The American Politician' is seen as a valuable originator but also a cheap tool, a high statesman but also a
dirty politician, a public servant but also a sly conniver. Our view
is not clear because, as with most of our views of those above us,

we tend to understand our own time in accordance with the confused stereotypes of previous periods.

The classic commentaries of American politics—those of Tocqueville, Bryce, and Ostrogorski—rest upon nineteenth-century experience—generally from Andrew Jackson to Theodore Roosevelt. It is, of course, true that many of the trends that determined the political shape of the long middle period are still at work influencing the type of politician that prevails in our own political times—especially on the middle levels of power, in the Congress. But during the twentieth century, and especially after the First World War, other forces have greatly modified the content and the importance in America of political institutions. The political establishment of the United States has become more tightly knit, it has been enlarged in scope, and has come up closer to virtually all of the social institutions which it frames. Increasingly, crises have arisen that have not seemed resolvable on the old local and decentralized basis; increasingly those involved in these crises have looked to the state to resolve them. As these changes in the shape and practice of the state have increased the power available to those who would gain power and exert it through political institutions, new types of political men have become ascendant.

The higher politicians do not constitute any one psychological type; they cannot be sorted out and understood in terms of any standard set of motives. Like men of other pursuits, politicians, high or low, are sometimes driven by technological love of their activities—of the campaigning and the conniving and the holding of office; more frequently than others, they are drawn to politics by the prestige that their success brings to them; in fact, 'power for power's sake'—a very complicated set of motives—usually involves the feeling of prestige which the exercise of power bestows.[2] Rarely is it the money they receive as officeholders which attracts them.

The only general meaning we can give to 'The Politician' is the man who more or less regularly enacts a role in political institutions and thinks of it as at least among his major activities. Accordingly, since there are two major kinds of political institutions in the United States, there are two major types of 'politicians.'

The party politician's working career is spent inside a specific kind of political organization: he is a party man. There is also the

political professional whose career has been spent in the adminis
trative areas of government, and who becomes 'political' to the
extent that he rises above the civil-service routine and into the
policy-making levels. In the pure type, such a politician is an ex-
bureaucrat.

As types, party politicians and political bureaucrats are the
professionals of modern government, if only in the sense that their
careers are spent mainly within the political orbit. But not all men
who are in politics are professional politicians either in the party
sense or in the bureaucratic sense: in fact, today the men at the
political top are much less likely to be bureaucrats, and rather
less likely to be party politicians than political outsiders.

The political outsider is a man who has spent the major part of
his working life outside strictly political organizations, and who—
as the case may be—is brought into them, or who forces his way
in, or who comes and goes in the political order. He is occupationally formed by nonpolitical experience, his career and his connections have been in other than political circles, and as a psychological type, he is anchored in other institutional areas. In fact, he is
usually considered by the professionals as a representative or as an
agent within the government of some non-governmental interest
or group. The political outsider is by no means confined to the
Republican party. Under the Democrats, he is more likely to be on
the make, striving to become acceptable to the corporate chieftains; whereas, under the Republicans, he is more usually a man
already acceptable and therefore surer of himself and of how his
decisions will be interpreted by those who count. A further consequence is that under the Republicans he can be less hypo-
critical.

Such outsiders, of course, may become bureaucratic experts by
spending much time in administrative work, and thus linking their
careers and their expectations to government; they may become
party politicians by cultivating their role inside a political party,
and coming to base their power and their career upon their party
connections. But they need not make either transition; they may
simply move into an inner circle, as an appointed consultant or
adviser having intimate and trusted access to an official power-
holder, to whom they are beholden for such political power as
they possess.

There are, to be sure, other ways of classifying men as political animals, but these types—the party politician, the professional adiministrator, the political outsider—are quite serviceable in understanding the social make-up and psychological complexion of the political visage of present-day America.

Within American political institutions, the center of initiative and decision has shifted from the Congress to the executive; the executive branch of the state has not only expanded mightily but has come to centralize and to use the very party which puts it into power. It has taken over more initiative in legislative matters not only by its veto but by its expert counsel and advice. Accordingly, it is in the executive chambers, and in the agencies and authorities and commissions and departments that stretch out beneath them, that many conflicts of interests and contests of power have come to a head—rather than in the open arena of politics of an older style.

These institutional changes in the shape of the political pyramid have made the new political command posts worthy of being struggled for. They have also made for changes in the career of the type of political man who is ascendant. They have meant that it is now more possible for the political career to lead directly to the top, thus by-passing local political life. In the middle of the nineteenth century—between 1865 and 1881—only 19 per cent of the men at the top of the government began their political career on the national level; but from 1901 to 1953, about one-third of the political elite began there, and, in the Eisenhower administration, some 42 per cent started in politics at the national level—a high for the entire political history of the United States.*

From 1789 right up to 1921, generation after generation, the proportion of the political elite which has *ever* held local or state offices decreased from 93 to 69 per cent. In the Eisenhower administration, it fell to 57 per cent. Moreover, only 14 per cent of this current group—and only about one-quarter of earlier twentieth-century politicians—have ever served in any *state legislature*. In the Founding Fathers' generation of 1789–1801, 81 per cent of the higher politicians had done so. There has also been a definite decline in the proportions of higher politicians who have ever sat

* Only about 20 per cent of the political elite of 1789–1825 had done so; the historical average as a whole is about 25 per cent.[3]

in the United States House of Representatives or in the Senate.*

The decline in state and local apprenticeships before entering national positions, as well as the lack of legislative experience, tie in with another characteristic trend. Since there are so many more elected positions on the lower and legislative levels and relatively few on the national, the more recent members of the political elite are likely to have reached their position through appointments rather than elections. Once, most of the men who reached the political top got there because people elected them up the hierarchy of offices. Until 1901, well over one-half, and usually more than two-thirds, of the political elite had been elected to all or most of their positions before reaching their highest national office. But of late, in a more administrative age, men become big politically because small groups of men, themselves elected, appoint them: only 28 per cent of the higher politicians in 1933-53 rose largely by means of elective offices; 9 per cent has as many appointed as elected offices, and 62 per cent were appointed to all or most of their political jobs before reaching top position; 1 per cent had held no previous political position. Among the Eisenhower group, 36 per cent were elected to the top; 50 per cent had been appointed more than elected, and 14 per cent had never before held any political office.

For the American statesmen as a group, the median number of years spent in politics was 22.4; in non-political activities, 22.3. Thus, these top members of government have spent about the same time working in politics as in other professions. (For some of these years, of course, they were working at both at the same time.) But this over-all fact is somewhat misleading, for there is a definite historical trend: until the Civil War, the top men spent more time in politics than in non-political pursuits. Since the Civil War, the typical member of the political elite has spent more years working outside of politics than in it. Strictly political careers reached a peak in the generation of 1801-25, with 65 per cent of the total working life spent in politics. Outside activities

---

* In 1801-25, 63 per cent of the political elite had been politicians in the House, 39 per cent; in the Senate; from 1865-1901, the proportions were 32 and 29 per cent; but during the 1933-53 era, only 23 per cent had ever been members of the House of Representatives, 18 per cent of the Senate. For the visible government of the Eisenhower administration, the proportions were 14 and 7 per cent.

reached their peak in the Progressive Era, 1901–21: at that time, professionals and reformers seem briefly to have entered high political positions, 72 per cent of this generation's active working time being taken up by non-political activities. It is not possible to make this calculation for politicians since 1933 for their careers are not yet over.

All these tendencies—(i) for the political elite to begin on the national level and thus to by-pass local and state offices, (ii) never to serve in national legislative bodies, (iii) to have more of an appointed than an elected career, and (iv) to spend less proportions of their total working life in politics—these tendencies point to the decline of the legislative body and to the by-passing of elective offices in the higher political career. They signify the 'bureaucratization' of politics and the decline at the political top of men who are professional politicians in the simple, old-fashioned sense of being elected up the political hierarchy and experienced in electoral politics. They point, in short, to the political outsider. Although this type has prevailed in previous periods, in our time he flourishes, and in the Eisenhower administration he has become ascendant. This administration, in fact, is largely an inner circle of political outsiders who have taken over the key executive posts of administrative command; it is composed of members and agents of the corporate rich and of the high military in an uneasy alliance with selected professional party politicians seated primarily in the Congress, whose interests and associations are spread over a variety of local societies.

2

A small group of men are now in charge of the executive decisions made in the name of the United States of America. These fifty-odd men of the executive branch of the government include the President, the Vice President, and the members of the cabinet; the head men of the major departments and bureaus, agencies and commissions, and the members of the Executive Office of the President, including the White House staff.

Only three of these members of the political directorate* are professional party politicians in the sense of having spent most of their working lives running for and occupying elective offices; and

* As of May 1953.[4]

only two have spent most of their careers as 'behind-the-scenes' political managers or 'fixers.' Only nine have spent their careers within governmental hierarchies—three of them in the military; four as civil servants in civilian government; and two in a series of appointive positions not under the civil-service system. Thus, a total of only fourteen (or about one-fourth) of these fifty-three executive directors have by virtue of their career been 'professionals' of government administration or party politics.

The remaining three-quarters are political outsiders. At one time or another, several of them have been elected to political offices, and some have entered government service for short periods but, for most of their careers, they have generally worked outside the realms of government and politics. Most of these outsiders—thirty of the thirty-nine in fact—are quite closely linked, financially or professionally or both, with the corporate world, and thus make up slightly over half of all the political directors. The remainder have been active in various other 'professional' fields.

The three top policy-making positions in the country (secretaries of state, treasury, and defense) are occupied by a New York representative of the leading law firm of the country which does international business for Morgan and Rockefeller interests; by a Mid-West corporation executive who was a director of a complex of over thirty corporations; and by the former president of one of the three or four largest corporations and the largest producer of military equipment in the United States.

There are four more members of the corporate rich in the cabinet—two more men from General Motors; a leading financier and director of New England's largest bank; and a millionaire publisher from Texas. The positions of Secretaries of Agriculture and Labor are occupied by professional outsiders, leaving only one cabinet member who is an insider to politics and government—the Attorney-General, who has been both a New York State Assemblyman and a partner in the law firm of Lord, Day and Lord, but has, since 1942, been a political manager for Dewey and later Eisenhower.

Although the Attorney-General and Vice-President are the only political professionals, two other cabinet members have at one time held elective state offices and at least five of the cabinet members were active in the political campaign of 1952. None of them are, in any sense that may be given to the term, civil servants; the President is alone among them as a man trained in a governmental (military) bureaucracy.

On the 'second team' of the political directorate, there is a 'Little Cabinet,' whose members stand in for the first and, who, in fact, handle most of the administrative functions of governing. Among the top thirty-two deputies of the agencies, departments, and commissions, twenty-one are novices in government: many of them never held political office, nor in fact even worked in government, before their present positions. These men usually have had fathers who were big businessmen; twelve attended Ivy League colleges; and they themselves have often been business-men or bankers or the salaried lawyers of large corporations or members of the big law firms. Unlike professional politicians, they do not belong to the local jamboree of Elk and Legion; they are more often members of quiet social clubs and exclusive country clubs. Their origins, their careers, and their associations make them representative of the corporate rich.

On this 'second team' there is one Rockefeller as well as a former financial adviser to the Rockefellers; there are working inheritors of family power and textile companies; there are bankers; there is a publisher, an airline executive, and lawyers; a representative from the southwestern affiliate of America's largest corporation; and another man from General Motors. There is also Allen Dulles who spent ten years in the diplomatic service, left it (because a promotion in rank offered him no increase above his $8,000 salary) to join the law firm of Sullivan and Cromwell (about the time that his brother became its senior partner) and then returned to the government as its senior spy. On this second team there are also four men who have not been directly associated with the corporate world.

Only seven of the thirty-two members of the second team have been trained in governmental bureaucracies; only four have had considerable experience in party politics.

In the complex organization of modern government, the need for an 'inner circle' of personal advisers has become increasingly important to the executive, especially if he would be an innovator. In order to originate and carry out his policies, he needs men who are quite wholly in his service. The specific functions that these men may perform are enormously varied; but, in whatever they do and say, they function as the *alter ego* of their commander. These personal lieutenants of power are loyal agents, first of all, of the man to whose inner circle they belong. They may be professional politicians or professional civil servants, but usually they have been neither.

And yet they must mediate between party politicians in the legislative branch and the outsiders in the executive administration—as well as among the various outside pressure groups—and they must maintain public relations with the unorganized public. These men on the White House Staff, therefore, are not in office so much for what they represent as for what they can *do*. They are a variety of skilled men, and they are socially alike in a number of ways: they are quite young; they come from the urban areas of the country, in fact from the East; and they are likely to have attended the Ivy League Colleges.

Of the nine key members of the White House Staff, six are novices in government and politics; there are no civilian civil servants; there is one professional party politician; one professional political manager; and one professional military man. The men of the President's inner circle thus come from Dewey's inner circle, from Henry Luce's, or from the higher levels of the Pentagon. With few exceptions, they are neither professional party politicians nor political bureaucrats.*

* Of 27 men mentioned in recent descriptions of Eisenhower's golf and bridge 'cronies,' only two men could strictly be called 'politicians'; there was also his brother Milton, and there was Bobby Jones, the former golf champion; there was the president of one of the largest advertising agencies and Freeman Gosden, Amos of 'Amos and Andy'; there was a public relations executive and a Washington lawyer; there were two retired Army officers and there was Lucius D. Clay, the retired General of the Army who is now Chairman of Continental Can Company. There were three men identified only as local—to the Augusta National Golf Club—businessmen. All the rest were top officers of various corporations scattered among different industries and usually along the eastern seaboard. Represented on the golf course are Continental Can, Young and Rubicam, General Electric, Cities Service Oil Company, Studebaker, Reynolds Tobacco, Coca Cola, and Republic Steel.[5] Between June 1953 and February 1955, Mr. Eisenhower gave 38 'stag dinners,' at which 'he has entertained 294 businessmen and industrialists, 81 administration officials, 51 editors, publishers, and writers, 30

As a group, the political outsiders who occupy the executive command posts and form the political directorate are legal, managerial, and financial members of the corporate rich. They are members of cliques in which they have shown to their higher-ups that they are trustworthy in economic or military or political endeavors. For corporation executives and army generals, no less than professional politicians, have their 'old cronies.' Neither *bureaucratic advancement* nor *party patronage* is the rule of the political outsider. As in the private corporation, the rule is the *co-optation* of one's own kind by those who have taken over the command posts.

3

The rise of the political outsider within the modern political directorate is not simply one more aspect of the 'bureaucratization' of the state. In fact, as in the case of the military ascendancy, the problem which the rise of the political outsider creates for the democratic theorist has, first of all, to do with the absence of a genuine bureaucracy. For it is partly in lieu of a genuine bureaucracy that the pseudo-bureaucracy of the political outsiders, as well as the regime of the party hacks, has come to prevail.

By a 'genuine' bureaucracy, we refer to an organized hierarchy

---

educators, 23 Republican party leaders. A dozen other groups—farm, labor, charities, sports—have provided smaller numbers of guests.'[6]

Of his various associates, Theodore Roosevelt once remarked: 'I am simply unable to make myself take the attitude of respect toward the very wealthy men which such an enormous multitude of people evidently really feel. I am delighted to show any courtesy to Pierpont Morgan or Andrew Carnegie or James J. Hill, but as for regarding any one of them, as for instance, I regard Professor Bury, or Peary, the Arctic explorer, or Rhodes, the historian—why, I could not force myself to do it, even if I wanted to, which I don't.' Of President Eisenhower's associates, a shrewd observer—Merriman Smith—has remarked: 'It would be unfair to say that he likes the company of kings of finance and industry purely because of their Dun and Bradstreet ratings. He believes that if a man has worked up to become president of the Ford Motor Company, head of the Scripps-Howard newspapers, a college president or an Archbishop, then certainly the man has a lot on the ball, knows his field thoroughly and will be literate and interesting.' To which William H. Lawrence has added: 'This business of working your way up will come as quite a surprise to young Henry Ford or young Jack Howard.'[7]

of skills and authorities, within which each office and rank is restricted to its specialized tasks. Those who occupy these offices do not own the equipment required for their duties, and they, personally, have no authority: the authority they wield is vested in the offices they occupy. Their salary, along with the honor due each rank, is the sole remuneration offered.

The bureaucrat or civil servant, accordingly, is above all an expert whose knowledge and skill have been attested to by qualifying examination, and later in his career, qualifying experience. As a specially qualified man, his access to his office and his advancement to higher offices are regulated by more or less formal tests of competence. By aspiration and by achievement, he is set for a career, regulated according to merit and seniority, within the prearranged hierarchy of the bureaucracy. He is, moreover, a disciplined man, whose conduct can be readily calculated, and who will carry out policies even if they go against his grain, for his 'merely personal opinions' are strictly segregated from his official life, outlook, and duties. Socially, the bureaucrat is likely to be rather formal with his colleagues, as the smooth functioning of a bureaucratic hierarchy requires a proper balance between personal good will and adequate social distance according to rank.

Even if its members only approximate the principled image of such a man, the bureaucracy is a most efficient form of human organization. But such an organized corps is quite difficult to develop, and the attempt can easily result in an apparatus that is obstreperous and clumsy, hide-bound and snarled with procedure, rather than an instrument of policy.

The integrity of a bureaucracy as a unit of a government depends upon whether or not, as a corps of officials, it survives changes of political administration.

The integrity of a professional bureaucrat depends upon whether or not his official conduct, and even his person, embodies the status codes of the official, foremost among them political neutrality. He will serve a new political administration and its policies as faithfully as he did the old. That is the political meaning of genuine bureaucracy. For the bureaucrat as such does not make policy; he provides information relevant to alternative policies and he carries out the alternative that becomes official. As a more or less permanent staff with a more or less permanent hierarchy beneath it, the bureaucracy is loyal only to the policies that are given it to execute. 'It has been recognized almost universally,' Herman Finer asserts, 'that interference with this neutrality [from political parties] means the loss of technical skill to the state as a whole, and only the most extreme minorities of the Left and Right have been ready to sacrifice this neutrality by "purification" of the services.'[8]

The civilian government of the United States never has had and does not now have a genuine bureaucracy. In the civil-service system, established in 1883, people appointed by the President and confirmed by the Senate are not 'required to be classified.' What constitutes 'The Civil Service' can change with changing political administrations. Any rules of competitive recruitment can be by-passed by creating whole new agencies without established precedents; jobs can be classified and declassified in and out of the civil-service tenure and restriction; civil-service tenure can be made meaningless by the wholesale abolition of governmental agencies or parts thereof, not only by the Congress but by the head of the agency or by the Budget Bureau.[9]

Of the late nineteenth-century practice, an English observer noted that 'while appointments to the lower grades were filled on the basis of merit, the pressure for spoils at each change of administration forced inexperienced, political or personal favourites in at the top. This blocked promotions and demoralized the service. Thus, while the general effect of the act was to limit very greatly the number of vicious appointments, at the same time the effect of these exceptions was to confine them to the upper grades, where the demoralizing effects of each upon the service would be a maximum.'[10]

Since then, of course, the proportion of employees covered by the Civil Service has increased. At the end of Theodore Roosevelt's administration (in 1909) some 60 per cent of all federal civilian employees were civil service; at the beginning of Franklin Roosevelt's, about 80 per cent. Much of the New Deal expansion involved 'new agencies which were staffed without competitive civil-service examinations. By 1936 only 60 per cent of Government civilian employees had entered Government through competitive civil-service tests; many of the [remaining] 40 per cent were patronage appointments, and most of them were New Deal enthusiasts.' World War II brought another huge wave of government employees who did not win their jobs competitively. Once in, however, these government workers found civil-service protection; when President Truman left office in 1953, the tenure of 'at least 95 per cent of Government civilian employees' was presumably protected.[11]

Now of the two million or so government employees,[12] perhaps some 1500 can be considered 'key officials': these include the head men of the executive departments, under-secretaries and assistant secretaries, the chiefs of the independent agencies and their deputy and assistant heads, the chiefs of the various bureaus and their deputies, the ambassadors and other chiefs of missions.[13] Occupationally they include lawyers and air force officers, economists and physicians, engineers and accountants, aeronautical experts and bankers, chemists and newspaper men, diplomats and soldiers. Altogether, they occupy the key administrative, technical, military, and professional positions of the federal government.

In 1948, only 32 per cent (502) of such key officials worked in agencies which had a 'formal career service'—such as the foreign service of the Department of State, the military hierarchy, certain appointments in the Public Health Service. The top career men averaged twenty-nine years in government service; over half of them had earned graduate or professional degrees; one-fourth, in fact, attended Harvard, Columbia, Princeton, Yale, MIT, or Cornell. These represented such higher civil service as the government then contained.

Two months before the party nominations for the 1952 elections, Harold E. Talbott—a New York financier, later a Secretary of the Air Force exposed for using his office for private gain—hired a management consulting firm to determine what posts it would be necessary for a Republican administration to take over in order to control the government of the United States. A few days after his election, Eisenhower received a fourteen-volume analysis—including suggested qualifications for appointees and the main problems they would face—of each of the 250 to 300 top policy-making jobs that were found.[14]

More party-minded analysts knew that even under the laws and orders then existing, some 2,000 positions seemed open.[15] Patronage is patronage, and the new administration quickly set about finding ways of increasing it.* In April 1953, Eisenhower by executive order stripped job security from at least 800 'confidential and policy-making' government workers; in June, he released some 54,000 non-veterans from job security.[17]

The exact number of positions that the Republicans declassified is difficult to know with accuracy: one knowledgeable estimate puts the number at 134,000.[18] But the withdrawal of jobs from civil-service coverage is not the only way to get in one's own people. Under a security ruling which rests upon 'a reasonable doubt' of someone's 'security-risk' status, rather than 'proof,' and which places the burden of proof upon the accused, thousands more have been fired or forced to resign from government service. This has been especially damaging to the experienced personnel and morale of the State Department where such attacks have been most prolific and systematic.**

The details at any given time are not important; the over-all fact is: The United States has never and does not now have a genuine civil service, in the fundamental sense of a reliable civil-service career, or of an independent bureaucracy effectively above political party pressure. The fact of the long Democratic tenure (1933–53) had tended to hide the extent to which the civil-service laws had failed to result in the creation of a Civil Service. The changeover of 1953 revealed, further, that the civil-service laws

* 'Some jobs can simply be abolished,' the editors of *Fortune* asserted. 'Other men can be left with their titles while someone else is given the real authority and direct access to the department head. Some of the more notorious Fair Dealers may be shunted off into harmless, boondoggling projects. In government circles there are phrases for such techniques: "letting him dry up on the vine," or "sending him to the reading room." Such methods are wasteful. And yet it is virtually the only way the Eisenhower Administration can be assured of having a force of key careerists whom it can trust . . . The new Administration has to tackle the government personnel problem from two opposite directions at once: on the one hand getting rid of top-grade careerists whose ideologies are overtly or covertly hostile to Republican policies; while on the other hand trying to make government service work, and thereby attracting top-grade men—which is the more important objective in the long run.'[16]

** On the downfall of diplomacy, see above, NINE: The Military Ascendency.

merely make the operation of 'patronage' more difficult and more expensive, and also, as it turned out, somewhat nastier. For there is no real question but that 'security clearance' procedures have been used to cover the replacement of untrustworthy Democrat by trustworthy Republican.

The superior man who might be bent on a professional career in government is naturally not disposed to train himself for such political perils and administrative helplessness.

No intellectually qualified personnel for a genuine bureaucracy can be provided if the Civil Service is kept in a political state of apprehension; for that selects mediocrities and trains them for un-reflective conformity.

No morally qualified personnel can be provided if civil servants must work in a context of universal distrust, paralyzed by suspicion and fear.

And in a society that values money as the foremost gauge of caliber, no truly independent Civil Service can be built—either from upper or middle-class recruits, if it does not provide compensation comparable to that provided by private employment. Pensions and security of job do not make up for the lower pay of civil servants, for private executives, as we have seen, now have such privileges and many more as well. The top civil-service salary in 1954 was only $14,800, and only 1 per cent of all the federal employees earned over $9,000 a year.[19]

The historical check upon the development of an administrative bureaucracy in the United States has been the patronage system of the parties, which as machines use jobs for pay-offs, thus making impossible office discipline and recruitment on the basis of expert qualification. In addition, since government regulation of business has become important, a government job has become important as one link in a business or legal career in the private corporate world. One serves a term in the agency which has to do with the industry one is going to enter. In the regulatory agencies especially, public offices are often stepping stones in a corporate career, and as organizations the agencies are outposts of the private corporate world. And there is also the 'new spoils system' operating as a security measure in the context of distrust.

Magazines for business executives and ghost writers for politicians regularly run pious editorials on the need for a better Civil

Service. But neither executives nor politicians really want a group of expert administrators who are genuinely independent of party considerations, and who, by training and experience, are the depository of the kind of skills needed to judge carefully the consequences of alternative policies. The political and economic meaning of such a corps for responsible government is all too clear.

In the lower ranks of the state hierarchy, from which genuine civil servants might be recruited, there has not been enough prestige or money to attract really first-rate men. In the upper ranks, 'outsiders,' that is, men from outside the bureaucracy, have been called upon. They have served only for relatively short periods and not as a life career, and hence they have not acquired the neutrality and demeanor associated with the ideal civil servant.

There is no civil-service career that is secure enough, there is no administrative corps that is permanent enough, to survive a change-over of political administration in the United States. Neither professional party politicians, nor professional bureaucrats are now at the executive centers of decision. Those centers are occupied by the political directorate of the power elite.

The Theory of Balance

Not wishing to be disturbed over moral issues of the political economy, Americans cling to the idea that the government is a sort of automatic machine, regulated by the balancing of competing interests. This image of politics is simply a carry-over from the official image of the economy: in both, an equilibrium is achieved by the pulling and hauling of many interests, each restrained only by legalistic and amoral interpretations of what the traffic will bear.

The ideal of the automatic balance reached its most compelling elaboration in eighteenth-century economic terms: the market is sovereign and in the magic economy of the small entrepreneur there is no authoritarian center. And in the political sphere as well: the division, the equilibrium, of powers prevails, and hence there is no chance of despotism. 'The nation which will not adopt an equilibrium of power,' John Adams wrote, 'must adopt a despotism. There is no other alternative.'[1] As developed by the men of the eighteenth century, equilibrium, or checks and balances, thus becomes the chief mechanism by which both economic and political freedom were guaranteed and the absence of tyranny insured among the sovereign nations of the world.

Nowadays, the notion of an automatic political economy is best known to us as simply the practical conservatism of the anti-New Dealers of the 'thirties. It has been given new—although quite false —appeal by the frightening spectacle of the totalitarian states of Germany yesterday and Russia today. And although it is quite irrelevant to the political economy of modern America, it is the only rhetoric that prevails widely among the managerial elite of corporation and state.

1

It is very difficult to give up the old model of power as an automatic balance, with its assumptions of a plurality of independent, relatively equal, and conflicting groups of the balancing society. All these assumptions are explicit to the point of unconscious caricature in recent statements of 'who rules America.' According to Mr. David Riesman, for example, during the past half century there has been a shift from 'the power hierarchy of a ruling class to the power dispersal' of 'veto groups.' Now no one runs anything: all is undirected drift. 'In a sense,' Mr. Riesman believes, 'this is only another way of saying that America is a middle-class country . . . in which, perhaps people will soon wake up to the fact that there is no longer a "we" who run things and a "they" who don't or a "we" who don't run things and a "they" who do, but rather that all "we's" are "they's" and all "they's" are "we's." '

'The chiefs have lost the power, but the followers have not gained it,' and in the meantime, Mr. Riesman takes his psychological interpretation of power and of the powerful to quite an extreme, for example: 'if businessmen *feel* weak and dependent, they *are* weak and dependent, no matter what material resources may be ascribed to them.'

'. . . The future,' accordingly, 'seems to be in the hands of the small business and professional men who control Congress: the local realtors, lawyers, car salesmen, undertakers, and so on; of the military men who control defense and, in part, foreign policy; of the big business managers and their lawyers, finance-committee men, and other counselors who decide on plant investment and influence the rate of technological change; of the labor leaders who control worker productivity and worker votes; of the black belt whites who have the greatest stake in southern politics; of the Poles, Italians, Jews, and Irishmen who have stakes in foreign policy, city jobs, and ethnic religious and cultural organizations; of the editorializers and storytellers who help socialize the young, tease and train the adult, and amuse and annoy the aged; of the farmers—themselves warring congeries of cattlemen, corn men, dairymen, cotton men, and so on—who control key departments

and committees and who, as the living representatives of our
inner-directed past, control many of our memories; of the Russians
and, to a lesser degree, other foreign powers who control much of
our agenda of attention; and so on. The reader can complete the
list.'[2]

Here indeed is something that measures up 'to the modern
standards of being fully automatic and completely impersonal.'[3]
Yet there is some reality in such romantic pluralism, even in such
a *pasticcio* of power as Mr. Riesman invents: it is a recognizable,
although a confused, statement of the middle levels of power,
especially as revealed in Congressional districts and in the Congress itself. But it confuses, indeed it does not even distinguish
between the top, the middle, and the bottom levels of power. In
fact, the strategy of all such romantic pluralism, with its image of
a semi-organized stalemate, is rather clear:

You elaborate the number of groups involved, in a kind of be-
wildering, Whitmanesque enthusiasm for variety. Indeed, what
group fails to qualify as a 'veto group'? You do not try to clarify the
hodge-podge by classifying these groups, occupations, strata, organizations according to their political relevance or even according to whether they are organized politically at all. You do not try
to see how they may be connected with one another into a structure of power, for by virtue of his perspective, the romantic conservative focuses upon a scatter of milieux rather than upon their
connections within a structure of power. And you do not consider
the possibility of any community of interests among the top
groups. You do not connect all these milieux and miscellaneous
groups with the big decisions: you do not ask and answer with
historical detail: exactly *what*, directly or indirectly, did 'small
retailers' or 'brick masons' have to do with the sequence of decision
and event that led to World War II? What did 'insurance agents,'
or for that matter, the Congress, have to do with the decision to
make or not to make, to drop or not to drop, the early model of
the new weapon? Moreover, you take seriously the public-rela-
tions-minded statements of the leaders of all groups, strata, and
blocs, and thus confuse psychological uneasiness with the facts
of power and policy. So long as power is not nakedly displayed, it
must not be power. And of course you do not consider the diffi-

culties posed for you as an observer by the fact of secrecy, official and otherwise.

In short, you allow your own confused perspective to confuse what you see and, as an observer as well as an interpreter, you are careful to remain on the most concrete levels of description you can manage, defining the real in terms of the existing detail.

The balance of power theory, as Irving Howe has noted, is a narrow-focus view of American politics.[4] With it one can explain temporary alliances within one party or the other. It is also narrow-focus in the choice of time-span: the shorter the period of time in which you are interested, the more usable the balance of power theory appears. For when one is up-close and dealing journalistically with short periods, a given election, for example, one is frequently overwhelmed by a multiplicity of forces and causes. One continual weakness of American 'social science,' since it became ever so empirical, has been its assumption that a mere enumeration of a plurality of causes is the wise and scientific way of going about understanding modern society. Of course it is nothing of the sort: it is a paste-pot eclecticism which avoids the real task of social analysis: that task is to go beyond a mere enumeration of all the facts that might conceivably be involved and weigh each of them in such a way as to understand how they fit together, how they form a model of what it is you are trying to understand.[5]

Undue attention to the middle levels of power obscures the structure of power as a whole, especially the top and the bottom. American politics, as discussed and voted and campaigned for, have largely to do with these middle levels, and often only with them. Most 'political' news is news and gossip about middle-level issues and conflicts. And in America, the political theorist too is often merely a more systematic student of elections, of who voted for whom. As a professor or as a free-lance intellectual, the political analyst is generally on the middle levels of power himself. He knows the top only by gossip; the bottom, if at all, only by 're-search.' But he is at home with the leaders of the middle level, and, as a talker himself, with their 'bargaining.'

Commentators and analysts, in and out of the universities, thus focus upon the middle levels and their balances because they are closer to them, being mainly middle-class themselves; because these levels provide the noisy content of 'politics' as an explicit and reported-upon fact; because such views are in accord with the folklore of the formal model of how democracy works; and because, accepting that model as good, especially in their current patrioteering, many intellectuals are thus able most readily to satisfy such political urges as they may feel.

When it is said that a 'balance of power' exists, it may be meant that no one interest can impose its will or its terms upon others; or that any one interest can create a stalemate; or that in the course of time, first one and then another interest gets itself realized, in a kind of symmetrical taking of turns; or that all policies are the results of compromises, that no one wins all they want to win, but each gets something. All these possible meanings are, in fact, attempts to describe what can happen when, permanently or temporarily, there is said to be 'equality of bargaining power.' But, as Murray Edelman has pointed out,[6] the goals for which interests struggle are not merely given; they reflect the current state of expectation and acceptance. Accordingly, to say that various interests are 'balanced' is generally to evaluate the *status quo* as satisfactory or even good; the hopeful ideal of balance often masquerades as a description of fact.

'Balance of power' implies equality of power, and equality of power seems wholly fair and even honorable, but in fact what is one man's honorable balance is often another's unfair imbalance. Ascendant groups of course tend readily to proclaim a just balance of power and a true harmony of interest, for they prefer their domination to be uninterrupted and peaceful. So large businessmen condemn small labor leaders as 'disturbers of the peace' and upsetters of the universal interests inherent in business-labor cooperation. So privileged nations condemn weaker ones in the name of internationalism, defending with moral notions what has been won by force against those have-nots whom, making their bid for ascendancy or equality later, can hope to change the *status quo* only by force.[7]

The notion that social change proceeds by a tolerant give and take, by compromise and a network of vetoes of one interest balanced by another assumes that all this goes on within a more or less stable framework that does not itself change, that all issues are subject to compromise, and are thus naturally harmonious or can be made such. Those who profit by the general framework of the *status quo* can afford more easily than those who are dissatisfied under it to entertain such views as the mechanics of social change. Moreover, 'in most fields . . . only one interest is organized, none is, or some of the major ones are not.'[8] In these cases, to speak, as Mr. David Truman does, of 'unorganized interests'[9] is merely to use another word for what used to be called 'the public,' a conception we shall presently examine.*

The important 'pressure groups,' especially those of rural and urban business, have either been incorporated in the personnel and in the agencies of the government itself, both legislative and executive, or become the instruments of small and powerful cliques, which sometimes include their nominal leaders but often do not. These facts go beyond the centralization of voluntary groups and the usurpation of the power of apathetic members by professional executives. They involve, for example, the use of the NAM by dominant cliques to reveal to small-business members that their interests are identical with those of big business, and then to focus the power of business-as-a-whole into a political pressure. From the standpoint of such higher circles, the 'voluntary association,' the 'pressure group,' becomes an important feature of a public-relations program. The several corporations which are commanded by the individual members of such cliques are themselves instruments of command, public relations, and pressure, but it is often more expedient to use the corporations less openly, as bases of power, and to make of various national associations their joint operating branches. The associations are more operational organizations, whose limits of power are set by those who use them, than final arbiters of action and inaction.[10]

Checks and balances may thus be understood as an alternative statement of 'divide and rule,' and as a way of hampering the more direct expression of popular aspiration. For the theory of balance often rests upon the moral idea of a natural harmony of interests, in terms of which greed and ruthlessness are reconciled with justice and progress. Once the basic structure of the American political economy was built, and for so long as it could be tacitly supposed that markets would expand indefinitely, the harmony of interest could and did serve well as the ideology of dominant

* See below, THIRTEEN: The Mass Society

groups, by making their interests appear identical with the interests of the community as a whole. So long as this doctrine prevails, any lower group that begins to struggle can be made to appear inharmonious, disturbing the common interest. 'The doctrine of the harmony of interests,' E. H. Carr has remarked, 'thus serves as an ingenious moral device invoked, in perfect sincerity, by privileged groups in order to justify and maintain their dominant position.'[11]

2

The prime focus of the theory of balance is the Congress of the United States, and its leading actors are the Congressmen. Yet as social types, these 96 Senators and 435 Representatives are not representative of the rank and file citizens. They represent those who have been successful in entrepreneurial and professional endeavors. Older men, they are of the privileged white, native-born of native parents, Protestant Americans. They are college graduates and they are at least solid, upper-middle class in income and status. On the average, they have had no experience of wage or lower salaried work. They are, in short, in and of the new and old upper classes of local society.*

* Nowadays, the typical Senator is a college-educated man of about fifty-seven years of age—although in the 83rd Congress (1954) one was eighty-six years old. The typical Representative, also drawn from the less than 10 per cent of the adult population that has been to college, is about fifty-two—although one was only twenty-six in the latest Congress. Almost all of the Senators and Representatives have held local and state offices; and about half of them are veterans of one of the wars. Almost all of them have also worked in non-political occupations, usually occupations of the upper 15 per cent of the occupational hierarchy: in the 1949–51 Congress, for example, 69 per cent of both Senate and House were professional men, and another 24 per cent of the Senate and 22 per cent of the House were businessmen or managers. There are no wage workers, no low salaried white-collar men, no farm laborers in the Senate, and only one or two in the House.[12]

Their major profession is, of course, the law—which only 0.1 per cent of the people at work in the United States follow, but almost 65 per cent of the Senators and Representatives. That they are mainly lawyers is easy to understand. The verbal skills of the lawyer are not unlike those needed by the politicians; both involve bargaining and negotiation and the giving of advice to those who make decisions in business and politics. Lawyers also often find that—win or lose—politics is useful to their

Some members of the Congress are millionaires, others must scrounge the countryside for expense money. The expenses of office are now quite heavy, often including the maintenance of two homes and traveling between them, the demands of an often busy social life, and the greatly increased costs of getting elected and staying in office. An outside income is now almost indispensable for the Congressmen; and, in fact, four out of five of the Representatives and two out of three of the Senators in 1952 received incomes other than their Congressional salaries 'from businesses or professions which they still maintain in their home

---

profession of law, since it publicizes one's practice. In addition, a private law practice, a business which can be carried in one's briefcase, can be set up almost anywhere. Accordingly, the lawyer as politician has something to fall back upon whenever he is not re-elected as well as something to lean upon if he wishes when he is elected. In fact, for some lawyers, a political term or two is thought of, and is in fact, merely a stepping stone to a larger law practice, in Washington or back home. The practice of law often allows a man to enter politics without much risk and some chance of advantage to a main source of money independent of the electorate's whims.[13]

Most of the members of Congress over the last fifteen years—and probably much longer than that—have originated from the same professional and entrepreneurial occupations as they themselves have followed over the last decade. Between 90 and 95 per cent of them have been sons of professionals or businessmen or farmers—although at the approximate time of their birth, in 1890, only 37 per cent of the labor force were of these entrepreneurial strata, and not all of these were married men with sons.[14]

There have been no Negroes in the Senate over the last half century, and, at any given time, never more than two in the House—although Negroes make up about 10 per cent of the American population. Since 1845, the percentage of the foreign-born in the Senate has never exceeded 8 per cent, and has always been much smaller than the percentage in the population—less than one-half of the representative proportion, for example, in 1949–51. Moreover, both first and second generation Congressmen tend to be of the older, northern and western extraction, rather than of the newer immigration from southern and eastern Europe. Protestant denominations of higher status (Episcopal, Presbyterian, Unitarian, and Congregational) provide twice the number of Congressmen as their representative proportions in the population. Middle-level Protestants (Methodists and Baptists) in the Congress are in rough proportion to the population, but Catholics and Jews are fewer: Catholics in the 81st Congress, for example, having only 16 per cent of the House and 12 per cent of the Senate, but 34 per cent of the 1950 population at large.[15]

communities, or from investments. Independently wealthy men are becoming increasingly common on Capitol Hill . . . For those who are without private means . . . life as a member of Congress can border on desperation.'* 'If Federal law really meant what it seems to mean concerning the uses of cash in election campaigns,' Robert Bendiner has recently remarked, 'more politicians would wind up in Leavenworth than in Washington.'[17]

The political career does not attract as able a set of men as it once did. From a money standpoint, the alert lawyer. who can readily make $25,000 to $50,000 a year, is not very likely to trade it for the perils of the Congressman's position; and, no doubt with exceptions, if they are not wealthy men, it is likely that the candidates for Congress will be a county attorney, a local judge, or a mayor—whose salaries are even less than those of Congressmen. Many observers, both in and out of Congress, agree that the Congress has fallen in public esteem over the last fifty years; and that, even in their home districts and states, the Congressmen are by no means the important figures they once were.[18] How many people, in fact, know the name of their Representative, or even of their Senators?

Fifty years ago, in his district or state, the campaigning Congressman did not have to compete in a world of synthetic celebrities with the mass means of entertainment and distraction. The politician making a speech was looked to for an hour's talk about what was going on in a larger world, and in debates he had neither occasion nor opportunity to consult a ghost writer. He was, after all, one of the best-paid men in his locality and a big man there. But today, the politician must rely on the mass media, and access to these media is expensive.** The simple facts of the costs of the

* From the end of World War II until 1955, the members of Congress received $15,000 annually, including a tax-free expense allowance of $2,500; but the average income—including investments, business, and professions as well as writing and speaking—of a member of the House was, in 1952, about $22,000; and of the Senate, $47,000. As of 1 March 1955, the annual salary for members of Congress was raised to $22,-500.[16]

** One veteran Congressman has recently reported that in 1930, he could make the race for $7,500; today, for $25,000 to $50,000; and in the Senate, it might run to much more. John F. Kennedy (son of multimillionaire Joseph P. Kennedy), Democrat of Massachusetts, was re-

modern campaign clearly tie the Congressman, if he is not personally well-to-do, to the sources of needed contributions, which are,
sensibly enough, usually looked upon as investments from which
a return is expected.

As free-lance law practitioners and as party politicians who must
face elections, the professional politicians have cultivated many
different groups and types of people in their localities. They are
great 'joiners' of social and business and fraternal organizations,
belonging to Masons and Elks and the American Legion. In their
constituencies, the Congressmen deal with organized groups, and
they are supported or approved according to their attitude toward
the interests and programs of these groups. It is in the local baili-
wick that the plunder groups, who would exchange votes for
favors, operate most openly. The politicians are surrounded by
the demands and requests of such groups, large and small, local
and national. As brokers of power, the politicians must compromise one interest by another, and, in the process, they are themselves often compromised into men without any firm line of policy.

Most professional politicians represent an astutely balanced
variety of local interests, and such rather small freedom to act in
political decisions as they have derives from precisely that fact:
if they are fortunate they can juggle and play off these varied local
interests against one another, but perhaps more frequently they
come to straddle the issues in order to avoid decision. Protecting
the interests of his electoral domain, the Congressman remains
attentively loyal to his sovereign locality. In fact, his parochialism
is in some cases so intense that as a local candidate he may even
invite and collect for local display an assortment of out-of-state
attacks upon him, thus turning his campaign into a crusade of the
sovereign locality against national outsiders.[20]

Inside the Congress, as in his constituency, the politician finds
a tangle of interests; and he also finds that power is organized
according to party and according to seniority. The power of the
Congress is centered in the committee; the power of the committee
is usually centered in its chairman, who becomes chairman by
seniority. Accordingly, the politician's chance to reach a position

---

ported to have spent $15,866 in his 1952 campaign, but 'committees on
his behalf for the improvement of the shoe, fishing and other industries
of the state, spent $217,995.'[19]

of power within the Congress often rests upon his ability to stay in office for a long and uninterrupted period, and to do that, he cannot antagonize the important elements in his constituency. Flexible adjustment to these several interests and their programs, the agility to carry several, sometimes conflicting, lines of policy, but to look good doing it, is at a premium. Therefore, by a mechanical process of selection, mediocre party 'regulars,' who for twenty years or more have been firmly anchored in their sovereign localities, are very likely to reach and to remain at the centers of Congressional power.

Even when the politician becomes a chairman—if possible, of a committee affecting the local interests of his district—he will not usually attempt to play the role of the national statesman. For however enjoyable such attendant prestige may be, it is secondary to the achievement of local popularity; his responsibility is not to the nation; it is to the dominant interests of his locality. Moreover, 'better congressional machinery,' as Stanley High has remarked, 'does not cure the evil of localism; indeed it may provide members with more time and better facilities for its practice.'[21]

Nonetheless, the chairman of the major committees are the elite members of the Congress. In their hands rest the key powers of Congress, both legislative and investigative. They can originate, push, halt, or confuse legislation; they are adept at evasion and stall. They can block a White House proposal so that it never reaches the floor for debate, let alone a vote. And they can tell the President what will and what will not gain the approval of the people in their district or of colleagues under their influence in Congress.

In the first and second decades of this century, only a few bills were presented during the six months of the first session or the three months of the second. These bills were considered during the ample time between committee study and their debate on the floor. Debate was of importance and was carried on before a sizable audience in the chamber. Legislation took up most of the member's time and attention. Today hundreds of bills are considered at each session; and since it would be impossible for members even to read them all—or a tenth of them—they have come to rely upon the committees who report the bills. There is little debate and what there is often occurs before an emptied chamber.

The speeches that are made are mainly for the member's locality, and many are not delivered, but merely inserted in the record. While legislation goes through the assembly line, the Congressmen are busy in their offices, administering a small staff which runs errands for constituents and mails printed and typed matter to them.[22]

In the campaigns of the professional politician, insistent national issues are not usually faced up to, but local issues are raised in a wonderfully contrived manner. In the 472 Congressional elections of 1954, for example, no national issues were clearly presented, nor even local issues related clearly to them.* Slogans and personal attacks on character, personality defects, and counter-charges and suspicions were all that the electorate could see or hear, and, as usual, many paid no attention at all. Each candidate tried to dishonor his opponent, who in turn tried to dishonor him. The outraged candidates seemed to make themselves the issue, and on that issue virtually all of them lost. The electorate saw no issues at all, and they too lost, although they did not know it.[24]

As part of the grim trivialization of public life, the American political campaign readily distracts attention from the possible debate of national policy. But one must not suppose that such noise is all that is involved. There are issues, in each district and

---

* In one state, the desegregation issue seemed to matter most; in another, an Italian, married to an Irish woman, used the names of both with due effect. In one state, a tape-recording of a candidate's two-year-old talk about whom policemen tended to marry seemed important; in another, whether or not a candidate had been kind enough, or too kind, to his sister. Here bingo laws were important, and there the big question was whether or not an older man running for the Senate was virile enough. In one key state, twenty-year old charges that a candidate had been tied up with a steamship company which had paid off a judge for pier leases was the insistent issue expensively presented on TV. One of the most distinguished Senators asserted of his opponent—also a quite distinguished man of old wealth—that he 'was either dishonest or dumb or stupid and a dupe.' Another candidate broke down under pressure and confessed that he had been telling detailed lies about his war record. And everywhere, in the context of distrust, it was hinted, insinuated, asserted, guessed that, after all, the opponents were associated with Red spies, if they were not actually in the pay of the Soviet octopus. All over again the Democrats fought the depression; all over again, the Republicans were determined to put Alger Hiss in jail.[23]

state, issues set up and watched by organized interests of local importance. And that is the major implication to be drawn from the character of the campaigns:

There are no national parties to which the professional politicians belong and which by their debate focus national issues clearly and responsibly and continuously.

By definition, the professional politician is a party politician. And yet the two political parties in the United States are not nationally centralized organizations. As semi-feudal structures, they have operated by trading patronage and other favors for votes and protection. The lesser politician trades the votes that are in his domain for a larger share of the patronage and favors. But there is no national 'boss,' much less a nationally responsible leader of either of the parties. Each of them is a constellation of local organizations curiously and intricately joined with various interest blocs. The Congressman is generally independent of the Congressional leaders of his party as far as campaign funds go. The national committees of each major party consist mainly of political nonentities; for, since the parties are coalitions of state and local organizations, each of them develops such national unity as it has only once every four years, for the Presidential election.[25] At the bottom and on the middle levels, the major parties are strong, even dictatorial; but, at the top, they are very weak. It is only the President and the Vice-President whose constituencies are national and who, by their actions and appointments, provide such national party unity as prevails.

The differences between the two parties, so far as national issues are concerned, are very narrow and very mixed up. Each seems to be forty-eight parties, one to each state; and accordingly, the professional politician, as Congressman and as campaigner, is not concerned with national party lines, if any are discernible. He is not subject to any effective national party discipline. He speaks solely for his own locality, and he is concerned with national issues only in so far as they affect his locality, the interests effectively organized there, and the chances of his re-election. That is the major reason why, when he speaks of national matters, the political vocabulary of the politician is such an empty rhetoric. Seated in his sovereign locality, the professional politician is not at the

summit of national, political power: he is on and of the middle
levels.

3

More and more of the fundamental issues never come to any
point of decision before the Congress, or before its most powerful
committees, much less before the electorate in campaigns. The
entrance of the United States into World War II, for example, in so
far as it involved American decision, by-passed the Congress quite
completely. It was never a clearly debated issue clearly focused
for a public decision. Under the executive's emergency power,
the President, in a virtually dictatorial way, can make the decision
for war, which is then presented to the Congress as a fact accomplished. 'Executive agreements' have the force of treaties but
need not be ratified by the Senate: the destroyer deal with Great
Britain and the commitment of troops to Europe under NATO,
which Senator Taft fought so bitterly, are clear examples of that
fact. And in the case of the Formosa decisions of the spring of
1955, the Congress simply abdicated all debate concerning events
and decisions bordering on war to the executive.

When fundamental issues do come up for Congressional debate,
they are likely to be so structured as to limit consideration, and
even to be stalemated rather than resolved. For with no responsible, centralized parties, it is difficult to form a majority in Congress; and—with the seniority system, the rules committee, the
possibility of filibuster, and the lack of information and expertise
—the Congress is all too likely to become a legislative labyrinth. It
is no wonder that firm Presidential initiative is often desired by
Congress on non-local issues, and that, in what are defined as
emergencies, powers are rather readily handed over to the executive, in order to break the semi-organized deadlock. Indeed, some
observers believe that 'congressional abdication and obstruction,
not presidential usurpation, has been the main cause of the shift
of power to the Executive.'[26]

Among the professional politicians there are, of course, common
denominators of mood and interests, anchored in their quite homogeneous origins, careers, and associations; and there is, of course,
a common rhetoric in which their minds are often trapped. In
pursuing their several parochial interests, accordingly, the Con-

gressmen often coincide in ways that are of national relevance. Such interests seldom become explicit issues. But the many little issues decided by local interest, and by bargain, by check and balance, have national results that are often unanticipated by any one of the locally rooted agents involved. Laws are thus sometimes made, as the stalemate is broken, behind the backs of the law-makers involved. For Congress is the prime seat of the middle levels of power, and it is on these middle levels that checks and balances do often prevail.

The truly vested interests are those openly pushed and pro-tected by each Representative and Senator. They are the paro-chial interests of the local societies of each Congressional district and state. In becoming vested in a Senator or a Representative they are compromised and balanced by other parochial interests. The prime search of the Congressman is for the favor he can do for one interest that will not hurt any of the other interests he must balance.

It is not necessary for 'pressure groups' to 'corrupt' politicians in Congress. In fact, lobbyists, in their discrete way, may at times appear as honest men, while Congressmen may appear as lobbyists in disguise. It is not necessary for members of local so-ciety to pay off the professional politician in order to have their interests secured. For by social selection and by political training, he is of and by and for the key groups in his district and state.[27] The Congressmen are more the visible makers of pressure inside the government than the subjects of invisible pressures from the periphery. Fifty years ago, the old muckraker image of the Sena-tor corrupted by money was often true,[28] and money is of course still a factor in politics. But the money that counts now is used mainly to finance elections rather than to pay off politicians di-rectly for their votes and favors.

When we know that before entering politics one of the half dozen most powerful legislators, and chairman of the Ways and Means Committee, gained prominence by promoting and organiz-ing Chambers of Commerce in half a dozen middle-ranking cities of the nation, 'without,' as he says, 'a cent of Federal aid,' we can readily understand why he fought extension of the excess-profits tax without any reference to invisible, behind-the-scenes pres-sures brought to bear upon him.[29] Seventy-eight-year-old Daniel

Reed *is* a man of Puritan-like character and inflexible principle, but principles are derived from and further strengthen character, and character is selected and formed by one's entire career. Moreover, as one member of Congress recently remarked, 'there comes a time in the life of every Congressman when he must rise above principle.'[30] As a political actor, the Congressman is part of the compromised balances of local societies, as well as one or the other of the nationally irresponsible parties. As a result, he is caught in the semi-organized stalemate of the middle levels of national power.

Political power has become enlarged and made decisive, but not the power of the professional politician in the Congress. The considerable powers that do remain in the hands of key Congressmen are now shared with other types of political actors: There is the control of legislation, centered in the committee heads, but increasingly subject to decisive modification by the administrator. There is the power to investigate, as a positive and a negative weapon, but it increasingly involves intelligence agencies, both public and private, and it increasingly becomes involved with what can only be called various degrees of blackmail and counter-blackmail.

In the absence of policy differences of consequences between the major parties, the professional party politician must *invent* themes about which to talk. Historically, this has involved the ordinary emptiness of 'campaign rhetoric.' But since World War II, among frustrated politicians there has come into wider use the accusation and the impugnment of character—of opponents as well as of innocent neutrals. This has, of course, rested upon the exploitation of the new historical fact that Americans now live in a military neighborhood; but it has also rested upon the place of the politician who practices a politics without real issue, a middle-level politics for which the real decisions, even those of patronage, are made by higher ups. Hunting headlines in this context, with less patronage and without big engaging issues, some Congressmen find the way to temporary success, or at least to public attention, in the universalization of distrust.

There is another way of gaining and of exercising power, one which involves the professional politician in the actions of cliques within and between the bureaucratic-like agencies of the administration. Increasingly, the professional politician teams up with the administrator who heads an agency, a commission, or a department in order to exert power with him against other administrators and politicians, often in a cut-and-thrust manner. The traditional distinction between 'legislation' as the making of policy and 'administration' as its realization has broken down from both sides.[31]

In so far as the politician enters into the continuous policy-making of the modern political state, he does so less by voting for or against a bill than by entering into a clique that is in a position to exert influence upon and through the command posts of the executive administration, or by not investigating areas sensitive to certain clique interests.[32] It is as a member of quite complicated cliques that the professional politician, representing a variety of interests, sometimes becomes quite relevant in desisions of national consequence.

If governmental policy is the result of an interplay of group interests, we must ask: what interests outside the government are important and what agencies inside it serve them? If there are *many* such interests and if they conflict with one another, then clearly each loses power and the agency involved either gains a certain autonomy or is stalemated.[33] In the legislative branch, many and competing interests, especially local ones, come to focus, often in a stalemate. Other interests, on the level of national corporate power, never come to a focus but the Congressman, by virtue of what he is as a political and social creature, realizes them. But in the executive agency a number of small and coherent interests are often the only ones at play, and often they are able to install themselves within the agency or effectively nullify its action against themselves. Thus regulatory agencies, as John Kenneth Galbraith has remarked, 'become, with some exceptions, either an arm of the industry they are regulating or servile.'[34] The executive ascendancy, moreover, has either relegated legislative action—and inaction—to a subordinate role in the making of policy or bends it to the executive will. For enforcement' now clearly involves the making of policy, and even legislation itself is often written by members of the executive branch.

In the course of American history, there have been several oscillations between Presidential and Congressional leadership.[35] Congressional supremacy, for example, was quite plain during the last third of the nineteenth century. But in the middle third of the twentieth century, with which we are concerned, the power of the Executive, and the increased means of power at its disposal, is far greater than at any previous period, and there are no signs of its power diminishing. The executive supremacy means the relegation of the legislature to the middle levels of political power; it means the decline of the professional politician, for the major locale of the party politician is the legislature. It is also a prime indicator of the decline of the old balancing society. For—in so far as the old balance was not entirely automatic—it was the politician, as a specialist in balance and a broker of contending pressures, who adjusted the balances, reached compromises, and maintained the grand equilibrium. That politician who best satisfied or held off a variety of interests could best gain power and hold it. But now the professional politician of the old balancing society has been relegated to a position 'among those also present,' often noisy, or troublesome, or helpful to the ascendant outsiders, but not holding the keys to decision. For the old balancing society in which he flourished no longer prevails.[36]

4

Back of the theory of checks and balances as *the* mode of political decision there is the class theory, well-known since Aristotle and held in firm view by the eighteenth-century Founding Fathers, that the state is, or ought to be, a system of checks and balances because the society is a balance of classes, and that society is a balance of classes because its pivot and its stabilizer is the strong and independent middle class.

Nineteenth-century America was a middle-class society, in which numerous small and relatively equally empowered organizations flourished. Within this balancing society there was an economy in which the small entrepreneur was central, a policy in which a formal division of authority was an operative fact, and a political economy in which political and economic orders were quite autonomous. If at times it was not a world of small entrepreneurs, at least it was always a world in which small entrepreneurs had a

real part to play in the equilibrium of power. But the society in
which we now live consists of an economy in which the small
entrepreneurs have been replaced in key areas by a handful of
centralized corporations, of a polity in which the division of
authority has become imbalanced in such a way that the executive
branch is supreme, the legislative relegated to the middle levels
of power, and the judiciary, with due time-lag, to the drift of
policy which it does not initiate; and finally, the new society is
clearly a political economy in which political and economic affairs
are intricately and deeply joined together.[37]

The romantic pluralism of the Jeffersonian ideal prevailed in
a society in which perhaps four-fifths of the free, white population
were in one sense or another, independent proprietors. But in the
epoch following the Civil War, that old middle class of independent proprietors began to decline, as, in one industry after another,
larger and more concentrated economic units came into ascendancy; and in the later part of the progressive era, the independent
middle class of farmers and small businessmen fought politically
—and lost their last real chance for a decisive role in the political
balance.[38] Already appeals to them, as by David Graham Phillips,
were nostalgic deifications of their imagined past, which they
seemed to hope would dispel the world of twentieth-century reality.[39] Such sentiments flared up briefly again in the La Follette
campaign of 1924, and they were one of the sources of the New
Deal's rhetorical strength. But two facts about the middle classes
and one fact about labor—which became politically important during the 'thirties—have become decisive during our own time:

I. The independent middle class became politically, as well as
economically, dependent upon the machinery of the state. It is
widely felt, for example, that the most successful 'lobby' in the
United States is The Farm Bloc; in fact, it has been so successful
that it is difficult to see it as an independent force acting upon the
several organs of government. It has become meshed firmly with
these organs, especially with the Senate, in which, due to the
peculiar geographic principle of representation, it is definitively
over-represented. Ideologically, due to the exploitation of Jeffersonian myths about farming as a way of life, large commercial
farmers as members of an industry are accepted as of that national
interest which ought to be served by very special policies, rather

than as one special interest among others. This special policy is the policy of parity, which holds that the government ought to guarantee to this one sector of the free enterprise system a price level for its products that will enable commercial farmers to enjoy a purchasing power equivalent to the power it possessed in its most prosperous period just prior to World War I. In every sense of the word, this is of course 'class legislation,' but it is 'middle-class legislation,' and it is so wonderfully entrenched as political fact that in the realm of crackpot realism in which such ideas thrive, it is thought of as merely sound public policy.

Well-to-do farmers, who are the chief rural beneficiaries of the subsidized enterprise system, are businessmen and so think of themselves. The hayseed and the rebel of the 'nineties have been replaced by the rural businessmen of the 'fifties. The political hold of the farmer is still strong but, as a demand upon the political top, it is more worrisome than decisive. The farmers, it is true, are taken into account so far as their own special interests are concerned, but these do not include the major issues of peace and war that confront the big political outsiders today, and the issues of slump and boom, to which the farmer is quite relevant, are not now foremost in the political outsiders' attention.

ii. Alongside the old independent middle class, there had arisen inside the corporate society a *new* dependent *middle class* of white-collar employees. Roughly, in the last two generations, as proportions of the middle classes as a whole, the old middle class has declined from 85 to 44 per cent; the new middle class has risen from 15 to 56 per cent. For many reasons, which I have elsewhere tried to make clear—this class is less the political pivot of a balancing society than a rear-guard of the dominant drift towards a mass society.[40] Unlike the farmer and the small businessman—and unlike the wage worker—the white-collar employee was born too late to have had even a brief day of autonomy. The occupational positions and status trends which form the white-collar outlook make of the salaried employees a rear-guard rather than a vanguard of historic change. They are in no political way united or coherent. Their unionization, such as it is, is a unionization into the main drift and decline of labor organization, and serves to incorporate them as hangers-on of the newest interest trying, unsuccessfully, to invest itself in the state.

The old middle class for a time acted as an independent base of power; the new middle class cannot. Political freedom and economic security were anchored in the fact of small-scale and independent properties; they are not anchored in the job world of the new middle class. Scattered properties, and their holders, were integrated economically by free and autonomous markets; the jobs of the new middle class are integrated by corporate authority. The white-collar middle classes do not form an independent base of power: economically, they are in the same situation as propertyless wage workers; politically they are in a worse condition, for they are not as organized.

III. Alongside the old middle class—increasingly invested within the state machinery—and the new middle class—born without independent political shape and developed in such a way as never to achieve it—a new political force came into the political arena of the 'thirties: the force of organized labor. For a brief time, it seemed that labor would become a power-bloc independent of corporation and state but operating upon and against them. After becoming dependent upon the governmental system, however, the labor unions suffered rapid decline in power and now have little part in major national decisions. The United States now has no labor leaders who carry any weight of consequence in decisions of importance to the political outsiders now in charge of the visible government.

Viewed from one special angle, the labor unions have become organizations that select and form leaders who, upon becoming successful, take their places alongside corporate executives in and out of government, and alongside politicians in both major parties, among the national power elite. For one function of labor unions—like social movements and political parties—is to attempt to contribute to the formation of this directorate. As new men of power, the labor leaders have come only lately to the national arena. Samuel Gompers was perhaps the first labor man to become, even though temporarily and quite uneasily, a member of the national power elite. His self-conscious attempt to establish his place within this elite, and thus to secure the labor interest as integral with national interests, has made him a prototype and model for the national labor career. Sidney Hillman was not, of course, the only labor man to take up this course during the 'forties, but his lead during the early war years, his awareness of himself as a member of the national elite, and the real and imagined recognition he achieved as a member ('Clear it with Sidney'), signaled the larger entrance—after the great expansion of the unions during the New Deal—of labor leaders into the political elite. With the advent of Truman's Fair Deal and Eisenhower's Great Crusade, no labor leader can readily entertain serious notions of becoming, formally or informally, a member. The early exit of a minor labor man—Durkin—from his weak cabinet post revealed rather clearly the situation faced by labor leaders as would-be members as well as the position of labor unions as a power bloc. Well below the top councils, they are of the middle levels of power.

Much of the often curious behavior and maneuvers of the labor chieftains over the last two decades is explainable by their search for status within the national power elite. In this context they have displayed extreme sensibility to prestige slights. They feel that they have arrived; they want the status accoutrements of power. In middle and small-sized cities, labor leaders now sit with Chamber of Commerce officials on civic enterprises; and on the national level, they expect and they get places in production boards and price-control agencies.

Their claim for status and power rests on their already increased power—not on property, income, or birth; and power in such situations as theirs is a source of uneasiness as well as a base of operations. It is not yet a solidly bottomed, continuous base having the force of use and wont and law. Their touchiness about prestige matters, especially on the national scene, has been due to (1) their self-made character, and to the fact (2) that their self-making was helped no end by government and the atmosphere it created in the decade after 1935. They are government-made men, and they have feared—correctly, it turns out—that they can be unmade by government. Their status tension is also due to the fact (3) that they are simply new to the power elite and its ways, and (4) that they feel a tension between their publics: their union members—before whom it is politically dangerous to be too big a 'big shot' or too closely associated with inherited enemies—and their newly found companions and routines of life.

Many observers mistake the status accoutrements of labor leaders for *evidence* of labor's power. In a way they are, but in a way they are not. They *are* when they are based on and lead to power. They *are not* when they become status traps for leaders without resulting in power. In such matters, it is well to remember that this is no chicken-and-egg issue. The chicken is power, and comes first, the egg is status.*

* Like the corporate rich, the labor leaders as a group are not wholly unified. Yet the often noted tendency of 'the other side' to regard any move by some unit of one side as having significance in terms of the whole, indicates clearly that in the views, expectations, and demands of these men, they do form, even if unwillingly, blocs. They see one another as members of blocs, and in fact are inter-knit in various and quite intricate ways. Individual unions may lobby for particularistic interests, which is one key to such lack of unity as labor as a bracket displays. But increasingly the issues they face, and the contexts in which they must face them, are national in scope and effect, and so they must co-ordinate labor's line with reference to a national context, on pain of loss of power.

The corporate executive, like the labor leader, is a practical man and an opportunist, but for him enduring means, developed for other purposes, are available for the conduct of his political as well as of his business-labor affairs. The corporation is now a very stable basis of operation; in fact, it is more stable and more important for the continuance of the American arrangement than the lifetime family. The business member of the power elite can rely upon the corporation in the pursuit of his short-term goals and opportunistic maneuvering. But the union is often in a state of protest; it is on the defensive in a sometimes actually and always potentially hostile society. It does not provide such enduring means as are ready-made and at the business elite's disposal. If he wants such means, even for his little goals, the labor leader must himself build and maintain them. Moreover, the great organizing upsurge of the 'thirties showed that officers who were not sufficiently responsive to the demands of industrial workers could lose power. The corporation manager on the other hand, in the context of his corporation, is not an elected official in the same sense. His power does not depend upon the loyalty of the men who work for him and he does not usually lose his job if a union successfully invades his plants. The upsurges of the 'thirties did not oust the managers; their responsibilities are not to the workers whom they employ, but to themselves and their scattered stockholders.

This difference in power situation means that the power of the business leader is likely to be more continuous and more assured than that of the labor leader: the labor leader is more likely to be insecure in his job if he fails to 'deliver the goods.'

However it may be with the corporate and the political elite, there is nothing, it seems to me, in the makeup of the *current* labor leaders as individuals and as a group to lead us to believe that they can or will tran-

During the 'thirties organized labor was emerging for the first time on an American scale; it had little need of any political sense of direction other than the slogan, 'organize the unorganized.' This is no longer the case, but labor—without the mandate of the slump —still remains without political, or for that matter economic, direction. Like small business, its leaders have tried to follow the way of the farmer. Once this farmer was a source of insurgency; in the recent past, labor has seemed to be such. Now the large farmer is a unit in an organized bloc, entrenched within and pressuring the welfare state. Despite its greater objective antagonism to capitalism as a wage system, labor now struggles, unsuccessfully, to go the same way.

5

In the old liberal society, a set of balances and compromises prevailed among Congressional leaders, the executive branch of the government, and various pressure groups. The image of power and of decision is the image of a balancing society in which no unit of power is powerful enough to do more than edge forward a bit at a time, in compromised countervailance with other such forces, and in which, accordingly, there is no unity, much less coordination, among the higher circles. Some such image, combined with the doctrine of public opinion, is still the official view of the formal democratic system of power, the standard theory of most academic social scientists, and the underlying assumption of most literate citizens who are neither political spokesmen nor political analysts.

But as historical conditions change, so do the meanings and political consequences of the mechanics of power. There is nothing magical or eternal about checks and balances. In time of revolution, checks and balances may be significant as a restraint upon

scend the strategy of maximum adaptation. By this I mean that they react more than they lead, and that they do so to retain and to expand their position in the constellation of power and advantage. Certain things could happen that would cause the downfall of the present labor leadership or sections of it, and other types of leaders might then rise to union power; but the current crop of labor leaders is pretty well set up as a dependent variable in the main drift with no role in the power elite. Neither labor leaders nor labor unions are at the present juncture likely to be 'independent variables,' in the national context.[41]

unorganized and organized masses. In time of rigid dictatorship, they may be significant as a technique of divide and rule. Only under a state which is already quite well balanced, and which has under it a balanced social structure, do checks and balances mean a restraint upon the rulers.

The eighteenth-century political theorists had in mind as the unit of power the individual citizen, and the classic economists had in mind the small firm operated by an individual. Since their time, the units of power, the relations between the units, and hence the meaning of the checks and balances, have changed. In so far as there is now a great scatter of relatively equal balancing units, it is on the middle levels of power, seated in the sovereign localities and intermittent pressure groups, and coming to its high point within the Congress. We must thus revise and relocate the received conception of an enormous scatter of varied interests, for, when we look closer and for longer periods of time, we find that most of these middle-level interests are concerned merely with their particular cut, with their particular area of vested interest, and often these are of no decisive political importance, although many are of enormous detrimental value to welfare. Above this plurality of interests, the units of power—economic, political, and military— that count in any balance are few in number and weighty beyond comparison with the dispersed groups on the middle and lower levels of the power structure.

Those who still hold that the power system reflects the balancing society often confuse the present era with earlier times of American history, and confuse the top and the bottom levels of the present system with its middle levels. When it is generalized into a master model of the power system, the theory of balance becomes historically unspecific; whereas in fact, as a model, it should be specified as applicable only to certain phases of United States development—notably the Jacksonian period and, under quite differing circumstances, the early and middle New Deal.

The idea that the power system is a balancing society also assumes that the units in balance are independent of one another, for if business and labor or business and government, for example, are not independent of one another, they cannot be seen as elements of a free and open balance. But as we have seen, the major vested interests often compete less with one another in their effort to promote their several interests than they coincide on many points of interest and, indeed, come together under the umbrella of government. The units of economic and political power not only become larger and more centralized; they come to coincide in interest and to make explicit as well as tacit alliances.

The American government today is not merely a framework within which contending pressures jockey for position and make politics. Although there is of course some of that, this government now has such interests vested within its own hierarchical structure, and some of these are higher and more ascendant than others. There is no effective countervailing power against the coalition of the big businessmen—who, as political outsiders, now occupy the command posts—and the ascendant military men—who with such grave voices now speak so frequently in the higher councils. Those having real power in the American state today are not merely brokers of power, resolvers of conflict, or compromisers of varied and clashing interest—they represent and indeed embody quite specific national interests and policies.

While the professional party politicians may still, at times, be brokers of power, compromisers of interests, negotiators of issues, they are no longer at the top of the state, or at the top of the power system as a whole.

The idea that the power system is a balancing society leads us to assume that the state is a visible mask for autonomous powers, but in fact, the powers of decision are now firmly vested within the state. The old lobby, visible or invisible, is now the visible government. This 'governmentalization of the lobby' has proceeded in both the legislative and the executive domains, as well as between them. The executive bureaucracy becomes not only the center of power but also the arena within which and in terms of which all conflicts of power are resolved or denied resolution. Administration replaces electoral politics; the maneuvering of cliques replaces the clash of parties.

The agrarian revolt of the 'nineties, the small-business revolt that has been more or less intermittent since the 'eighties, the labor revolt of the 'thirties—all of these have failed and all of these have succeeded. They have failed as autonomous movements of small property or of organized workmen which could countervail against the power of the corporate rich, and they have failed as politically

autonomous third parties. But they have succeeded, in varying
degrees, as vested interests inside the expanded state, and they
have succeeded as parochial interests variously seated in particular districts and states where they do not conflict with larger interests. They are well-established features of the *middle* levels of
balancing power.

Among the plurality of these middle powers, in fact, are all those
strata and interests which in the course of American history have
been defeated in their bids for top power or which have never
made such bids. They include: rural small property, urban small
property, the wage-worker unions, all consumers, and all major
white-collar groups. These are indeed still in an unromantic scatter; being structurally unable to unite among themselves, they do
indeed balance one another—in a system of semi-organized stalemate. They 'get in the way' of the unified top, but no one of them
has a chance to come into the top circles, where the political outsiders from corporate institution and military order are firmly in
command.

When the multifarious middle classes are a political balance
wheel, the professional politician is the ascendant decision-maker.
When the middle classes decline as a set of autonomous political
forces, the balancing society as a system of power declines, and
the party politicians of the sovereign localities are relegated to
the middle levels of national power.

These structural trends came to political shape during the period
of the New Deal, which was of course a time of slump. That our
own immediate period has been a time of material prosperity has
obscured these facts, but it has not altered them; and, as facts,
they are important to the understanding of the power elite today.

12

The Power Elite

EXCEPT for the unsuccessful Civil War, changes in the power system of the United States have not involved important challenges to its basic legitimations. Even when they have been decisive enough to be called 'revolutions,' they have not involved the 'resort to the guns of a cruiser, the dispersal of an elected assembly by bayonets, or the mechanisms of a police state.'[1] Nor have they involved, in any decisive way, any ideological struggle to control masses. Changes in the American structure of power have generally come about by institutional shifts in the relative positions of the political, the economic, and the military orders. From this point of view, and broadly speaking, the American power elite has gone through four epochs, and is now well into a fifth.

1

I. During the first—roughly from the Revolution through the administration of John Adams—the social and economic, the political and the military institutions were more or less unified in a simple and direct way: the individual men of these several elites moved easily from one role to another at the top of each of the major institutional orders. Many of them were many-sided men who could take the part of legislator and merchant, frontiersman and soldier, scholar and surveyor.[2]

Until the downfall of the Congressional caucus of 1824, political institutions seemed quite central; political decisions, of great importance; many politicians, considered national statesmen of note. 'Society, as I first remember it,' Henry Cabot Lodge once said,

speaking of the Boston of his early boyhood, 'was based on the old
families; Doctor Holmes defines them in the "Autocrat" as the
families which had held high position in the colony, the province
and during the Revolution and the early decades of the United
States. They represented several generations of education and
standing in the community . . . They had ancestors who had
filled the pulpits, sat upon the bench, and taken part in the government under the crown; who had fought in the Revolution, helped
to make the State and National constitutions and served in the
army or navy; who had been members of the House or Senate in
the early days of the Republic, and who had won success as merchants, manufacturers, lawyers, or men of letters.'[3]

Such men of affairs, who—as I have noted—were the backbone
of Mrs. John Jay's social list of 1787, definitely included political
figures of note. The important fact about these early days is that
social life, economic institutions, military establishment, and
political order coincided, and men who were high politicians also
played key roles in the economy and, with their families, were
among those of the reputable who made up local society. In fact,
this first period is marked by the leadership of men whose status
does not rest exclusively upon their political position, although
their political activities are important and the prestige of politicians high. And this prestige seems attached to the men who occupy Congressional position as well as the cabinet. The elite are
political men of education and of administrative experience, and,
as Lord Bryce noted, possess a certain 'largeness of view and
dignity of character.'[4]

II. During the early nineteenth century—which followed Jefferson's political philosophy, but, in due course, Hamilton's economic principles—the economic and political and military orders
fitted loosely into the great scatter of the American social structure. The broadening of the economic order which came to be
seated in the individual property owner was dramatized by Jefferson's purchase of the Louisiana Territory and by the formation
of the Democratic-Republican party as successor to the Federal-
ists.

In this society, the 'elite' became a plurality of top groups, each
in turn quite loosely made up. They overlapped to be sure, but
again quite loosely so. One definite key to the period, and certainly

to our images of it, is the fact that the Jacksonian Revolution was much more of a status revolution than either an economic or a political one. The metropolitan 400 could not truly flourish in the face of the status tides of Jacksonian democracy; alongside it was a political elite in charge of the new party system. No set of men controlled centralized means of power; no small clique dominated economic, much less political, affairs. The economic order was ascendant over both social status and political power; within the economic order, a quite sizable proportion of all the economic men were among those who decided. For this was the period— roughly from Jefferson to Lincoln—when the elite was at most a loose coalition. The period ended, of course, with the decisive split of southern and northern types.

Official commentators like to contrast the ascendancy in totalitarian countries of a tightly organized clique with the American system of power. Such comments, however, are easier to sustain if one compares mid-twentieth-century Russia with mid-nineteenth-century America, which is what is often done by Tocqueville-quoting Americans making the contrast. But that was an America of a century ago, and in the century that has passed, the American elite have not remained as patrioteer essayists have described them to us. The 'loose cliques' now head institutions of a scale and power not then existing and, especially since World War I, the loose cliques have tightened up. We are well beyond the era of romantic pluralism.

III. The supremacy of corporate economic power began, in a formal way, with the Congressional elections of 1866, and was consolidated by the Supreme Court decision of 1886 which declared that the Fourteenth Amendment protected the corporation. That period witnessed the transfer of the center of initiative from government to corporation. Until the First World War (which gave us an advanced showing of certain features of our own period) this was an age of raids on the government by the economic elite, an age of simple corruption, when Senators and judges were simply bought up. Here, once upon a time, in the era of McKinley and Morgan, far removed from the undocumented complexities of our own time, many now believe, was the golden era of the American ruling class.[5]

The military order of this period, as in the second, was subordinate to the political, which in turn was subordinate to the economic. The military was thus off to the side of the main driving forces of United States history. Political institutions in the United States have never formed a centralized and autonomous domain of power; they have been enlarged and centralized only reluctantly in slow response to the public consequence of the corporate economy.

In the post-Civil-War era, that economy was the dynamic; the 'trusts'—as policies and events make amply clear—could readily use the relatively weak governmental apparatus for their own ends. That both state and federal governments were decisively limited in their power to regulate, in fact meant that they were themselves regulatable by the larger moneyed interests. Their powers were scattered and unorganized; the powers of the industrial and financial corporations concentrated and interlocked. The Morgan interests alone held 341 directorships in 112 corporations with an aggregate capitalization of over $22 billion—over three times the assessed value of all real and personal property in New England.[6] With revenues greater and employees more numerous than those of many states, corporations controlled parties, bought laws, and kept Congressmen of the 'neutral' state. And as private economic power overshadowed public political power, so the economic elite overshadowed the political.

Yet even between 1896 and 1919, events of importance tended to assume a political form, foreshadowing the shape of power which after the partial boom of the 'twenties was to prevail in the New Deal. Perhaps there has never been any period in American history so politically transparent as the Progressive era of President-makers and Muckrakers.

IV. The New Deal did *not* reverse the political and economic relations of the third era, but it did create within the political arena, as well as in the corporate world itself, competing centers of power that challenged those of the corporate directors. As the New Deal directorate gained political power, the economic elite, which in the third period had fought against the growth of 'government' while raiding it for crafty privileges, belatedly attempted to join it on the higher levels. When they did so they found themselves confronting other interests and men, for the places of decision were crowded. In due course, they did come to control and to use for their own purposes the New Deal institutions whose creation they had so bitterly denounced.

But during the 'thirties, the political order was still an instrument of small propertied farmers and businessmen, although they were weakened, having lost their last chance for real ascendancy in the Progressive era. The struggle between big and small property flared up again, however, in the political realm of the New Deal era, and to this struggle there was added, as we have seen, the new struggle of organized labor and the unorganized unemployed. This new force flourished under political tutelage, but nevertheless, for the first time in United States history, social legislation and lower-class issues became important features of the reform movement.

In the decade of the 'thirties, a set of shifting balances involving newly instituted farm measures and newly organized labor unions—along with big business—made up the political and administrative drama of power. These farm, labor, and business groups, moreover, were more or less contained within the framework of an enlarging governmental structure, whose political directorship made decisions in a definitely political manner. These groups pressured, and in pressuring against one another and against the governmental and party system, they helped to shape it. But it could not be said that any of them for any considerable length of time used that government unilaterally as their instrument. That is why the 'thirties was a *political* decade: the power of business was not replaced, but it was contested and supplemented: it became one major power within a structure of power that was chiefly run by political men, and not by economic or military men turned political.

The earlier and middle Roosevelt administrations can best be understood as a desperate search for ways and means, within the existing capitalist system, of reducing the staggering and ominous army of the unemployed. In these years, the New Deal as a system of power was essentially a balance of pressure groups and interest blocs. The political top adjusted many conflicts, gave way to this demand, sidetracked that one, was the unilateral servant of none, and so evened it all out into such going policy line as prevailed from one minor crisis to another. Policies were the result of a political act of balance at the top. Of course, the bal-

4   THE POWER ELITE

mental institutions of capitalism as a type of economy. By his
policies, he subsidized the defaults of the capitalist economy,
which had simply broken down; and by his rhetoric, he balanced
its political disgrace, putting 'economic royalists' in the political
doghouse.

The 'welfare state,' created to sustain the balance and to carry
out the subsidy, differed from the 'laissez-faire' state: 'If the state
was believed neutral in the days of T.R. because its leaders
claimed to sanction favors for no one,' Richard Hofstadter has remarked, 'the state under F.D.R. could be called neutral only in the
sense that it offered favors to everyone.'[7] The new state of the corporate commissars differs from the old welfare state. In fact, the
later Roosevelt years—beginning with the entrance of the United
States into overt acts of war and preparations for World War II—
cannot be understood entirely in terms of an adroit equipoise of
political power.

2

We study history, it has been said, to rid ourselves of it, and
the history of the power elite is a clear case for which this maxim
is correct. Like the tempo of American life in general, the long-
term trends of the power structure* have been greatly speeded up
since World War II, and certain newer trends within and between
the dominant institutions have also set the shape of the power elite
and given historically specific meaning to its fifth epoch:

I. In so far as the structural clue to the power elite today lies
in the political order, that clue is the decline of politics as genuine and public debate of alternative decisions—with nationally
responsible and policy-coherent parties and with autonomous
organizations connecting the lower and middle levels of power
with the top levels of decision. America is now in considerable
part more a formal political democracy than a democratic social
structure, and even the formal political mechanics are weak.

The long-time tendency of business and government to become more intricately and deeply involved with each other has,
in the fifth epoch, reached a new point of explicitness. The two
cannot now be seen clearly as two distinct worlds. It is in terms

* See above, ONE: The Higher Circles.

of the executive agencies of the state that the rapprochement has proceeded most decisively. The growth of the executive branch of the government, with its agencies that patrol the complex economy, does not mean merely the 'enlargement of government' as some sort of autonomous bureaucracy: it has meant the ascendancy of the corporation's man as a political eminence.

During the New Deal the corporate chieftains joined the political directorate; as of World War II they have come to dominate it. Long interlocked with government, now they have moved into quite full direction of the economy of the war effort and of the postwar era. This shift of the corporation executives into the political directorate has accelerated the long-term relegation of the professional politicians in the Congress to the middle levels of power.

II. In so far as the structural clue to the power elite today lies in the enlarged and military state, that clue becomes evident in the military ascendancy. The warlords have gained decisive political relevance, and the military structure of America is now in considerable part a political structure. The seemingly permanent military threat places a premium on the military and upon their control of men, materiel, money, and power; virtually all political and economic actions are now judged in terms of military definitions of reality: the higher warlords have ascended to a firm position within the power elite of the fifth epoch.

In part at least this has resulted from one simple historical fact, pivotal for the years since 1939: the focus of elite attention has been shifted from domestic problems, centered in the 'thirties around slump, to international problems, centered in the 'forties and 'fifties around war. Since the governing apparatus of the United States has by long historic usage been adapted to and shaped by domestic clash and balance, it has not, from any angle, had suitable agencies and traditions for the handling of international problems. Such formal democratic mechanics as had arisen in the century and a half of national development prior to 1941, had not been extended to the American handling of international affairs. It is, in considerable part, in this vacuum that the power elite has grown.

III. In so far as the structural clue to the power elite today lies in the economic order, that clue is the fact that the economy is at once a permanent-war economy and a private-corporation economy. American capitalism is now in considerable part a military capitalism, and the most important relation of the big corporation to the state rests on the coincidence of interests between military and corporate needs, as defined by warlords and corporate rich. Within the elite as a whole, this coincidence of interest between the high military and the corporate chieftains strengthens both of them and further subordinates the role of the merely political men. Not politicians, but corporate executives, sit with the military and plan the organization of war effort.

The shape and meaning of the power elite today can be understood only when these three sets of structural trends are seen at their point of coincidence: the military capitalism of private corporations exists in a weakened and formal democratic system containing a military order already quite political in outlook and demeanor. Accordingly, at the top of this structure, the power elite has been shaped by the coincidence of interest between those who control the major means of production and those who control the newly enlarged means of violence; from the decline of the professional politician and the rise to explicit political command of the corporate chieftains and the professional warlords; from the absence of any genuine civil service of skill and integrity, independent of vested interests.

The power elite is composed of political, economic, and military men, but this instituted elite is frequently in some tension: it comes together only on certain coinciding points and only on certain occasions of 'crisis.' In the long peace of the nineteenth century, the military were not in the high councils of state, not of the political directorate, and neither were the economic men—they made raids upon the state but they did not join its directorate. During the 'thirties, the political man was ascendant. Now the military and the corporate men are in top positions.

Of the three types of circle that compose the power elite today, it is the military that has benefited the most in its enhanced power, although the corporate circles have also become more explicitly intrenched in the more public decision-making circles. It is the professional politician that has lost the most, so much that in examining the events and decisions, one is tempted to speak of a political vacuum in which the corporate rich and the high warlord, in their coinciding interests, rule.

It should not be said that the three 'take turns' in carrying the initiative, for the mechanics of the power elite are not often as deliberate as that would imply. At times, of course, it is—as when political men, thinking they can borrow the prestige of generals, find that they must pay for it, or, as when during big slumps, economic men feel the need of a politician at once safe and possessing vote appeal. Today all three are involved in virtually all widely ramifying decisions. Which of the three types seems to lead depends upon 'the tasks of the period' as they, the elite, define them. Just now, these tasks center upon 'defense' and international affairs. Accordingly, as we have seen, the military are ascendant in two senses: as personnel and as justifying ideology. That is why, just now, we can most easily specify the unity and the shape of the power elite in terms of the military ascendancy.

But we must always be historically specific and open to complexities. The simple Marxian view makes the big economic man the *real* holder of power; the simple liberal view makes the big political man the chief of the power system; and there are some who would view the warlords as virtual dictators. Each of these is an oversimplified view. It is to avoid them that we use the term 'power elite' rather than, for example, 'ruling class.'*

In so far as the power elite has come to wide public attention,

* 'Ruling class' is a badly loaded phrase. 'Class' is an economic term; 'rule' a political one. The phrase, 'ruling class,' thus contains the theory that an economic class rules politically. That short-cut theory may or may not at times be true, but we do not want to carry that one rather simple theory about in the terms that we use to define our problems; we wish to state the theories explicitly, using terms of more precise and unilateral meaning. Specifically, the phrase 'ruling class,' in its common political connotations, does not allow enough autonomy to the political order and its agents, and it says nothing about the military as such. It should be clear to the reader by now that we do not accept as adequate the simple view that high economic men unilaterally make all decisions of national consequence. We hold that such a simple view of 'economic determinism' must be elaborated by 'political determinism' and 'military determinism'; that the higher agents of each of these three domains now often have a noticeable degree of autonomy; and that only in the often intricate ways of coalition do they make up and carry through the most important decisions. Those are the major reasons we prefer 'power elite' to 'ruling class' as a characterizing phrase for the higher circles when we consider them in terms of power.

it has done so in terms of the 'military clique.' The power elite does, in fact, take its current shape from the decisive entrance into it of the military. Their presence and their ideology are its major legitimations, whenever the power elite feels the need to provide any. But what is called the 'Washington military clique' is not composed merely of military men, and it does not prevail merely in Washington. Its members exist all over the country, and it is a coalition of generals in the roles of corporation executives, of politicians masquerading as admirals, of corporation executives acting like politicians, of civil servants who become majors, of vice-admirals who are also the assistants to a cabinet officer, who is himself, by the way, really a member of the managerial elite.

Neither the idea of a 'ruling class' nor of a simple monolithic rise of 'bureaucratic politicians' nor of a 'military clique' is adequate. The power elite today involves the often uneasy coincidence of economic, military, and political power.

3

Even if our understanding were limited to these structural trends, we should have grounds for believing the power elite a useful, indeed indispensable, concept for the interpretation of what is going on at the topside of modern American society. But we are not, of course, so limited: our conception of the power elite does not need to rest only upon the correspondence of the institutional hierarchies involved, or upon the many points at which their shifting interests coincide. The power elite, as we conceive it, also rests upon the similarity of its personnel, and their personal and official relations with one another, upon their social and psychological affinities. In order to grasp the personal and social basis of the power elite's unity, we have first to remind ourselves of the facts of origin, career, and style of life of each of the types of circle whose members compose the power elite.

The power elite is *not* an aristocracy, which is to say that it is not a political ruling group based upon a nobility of hereditary origin. It has no compact basis in a small circle of great families whose members can and do consistently occupy the top positions in the several higher circles which overlap as the power elite. But such nobility is only one possible basis of common origin. That it does not exist for the American elite does not mean that members of this elite derive socially from the full range of strata composing American society. They derive in substantial proportions from the upper classes, both new and old, of local society and the metropolitan 400. The bulk of the very rich, the corporate executives, the political outsiders, the high military, derive from, at most, the upper third of the income and occupational pyramids. Their fathers were at least of the professional and business strata, and very frequently higher than that. They are native-born Americans of native parents, primarily from urban areas, and, with the exceptions of the politicians among them, overwhelmingly from the East. They are mainly Protestants, especially Episcopalian or Presbyterian. In general, the higher the position, the greater the proportion of men within it who have derived from and who maintain connections with the upper classes. The generally similar origins of the members of the power elite are underlined and carried further by the fact of their increasingly common educational routine. Overwhelmingly college graduates, substantial proportions have attended Ivy League colleges, although the education of the higher military, of course, differs from that of other members of the power elite.

But what do these apparently simple facts about the social composition of the higher circles really mean? In particular, what do they mean for any attempt to understand the degree of unity, and the direction of policy and interest that may prevail among these several circles? Perhaps it is best to put this question in a deceptively simple way: in terms of origin and career, who or what do these men at the top represent?

Of course, if they are elected politicians, they are supposed to represent those who elected them; and, if they are appointed, they are supposed to represent, indirectly, those who elected their appointers. But this is recognized as something of an abstraction, as a rhetorical formula by which all men of power in almost all systems of government nowadays justify their power of decision. At times it may be true, both in the sense of their motives and in the sense of who benefits from their decisions. Yet it would not be wise in any power system merely to assume it.

The fact that members of the power elite come from near the top of the nation's class and status levels does not mean that they are necessarily 'representative' of the top levels only. And if they were, as social types, representative of a cross-section of the population, that would not mean that a balanced democracy of interest and power would automatically be the going political fact.

We cannot infer the direction of policy merely from the social origins and careers of the policy-makers. The social and economic backgrounds of the men of power do not tell us all that we need to know in order to understand the distribution of social power. For: (1) Men from high places may be ideological representatives of the poor and humble. (2) Men of humble origin, brightly self-made, may energetically serve the most vested and inherited interests. Moreover (3), not all men who effectively represent the interests of a stratum need in any way belong to it or personally benefit by policies that further its interests. Among the politicians, in short, there are sympathetic *agents* of given groups, conscious and unconscious, paid and unpaid. Finally (4), among the top decision-makers we find men who have been chosen for their positions because of their 'expert knowledge.' These are some of the obvious reasons why the social origins and careers of of the power elite do not enable us to infer the class interests and policy directions of a modern system of power.

Do the high social origin and careers of the top men mean nothing, then, about the distribution of power? By no means. They simply remind us that we must be careful of any simple and direct inference from origin and career to political character and policy, not that we must ignore them in our attempt at political understanding. They simply mean that we must analyze the political psychology and the actual decisions of the political directorate as well as its social composition. And they mean, above all, that we should control, as we have done here, any inference we make from the origin and careers of the political actors by close understanding of the institutional landscape in which they act out their drama. Otherwise we should be guilty of a rather simple-minded biographical theory of society and history.

Just as we cannot rest the notion of the power elite solely upon the institutional mechanics that lead to its formation, so we cannot rest the notion solely upon the facts of the origin and career of its personnel. We need both, and we have both—as well as other bases, among them that of the status intermingling.

But it is not only the similarities of social origin, religious affiliation, nativity, and education that are important to the psychological and social affinities of the members of the power elite. Even if their recruitment and formal training were more heterogeneous than they are, these men would still be of quite homogeneous social type. For the most important set of facts about a circle of men is the criteria of admission, of praise, of honor, of promotion that prevails among them; if these are similar within a circle, then they will tend as personalities to become similar. The circles that compose the power elite do tend to have such codes and criteria in common. The co-optation of the social types to which these common values lead is often more important than any statistics of common origin and career that we might have at hand.

There is a kind of reciprocal attraction among the fraternity of the successful—not between each and every member of the circles of the high and mighty, but between enough of them to insure a certain unity. On the slight side, it is a sort of tacit, mutual admiration; in the strongest tie-ins, it proceeds by intermarriage. And there are all grades and types of connection between these extremes. Some overlaps certainly occur by means of cliques and clubs, churches and schools.

If social origin and formal education in common tend to make the members of the power elite more readily understood and trusted by one another, their continued association further cements what they feel they have in common. Members of the several higher circles know one another as personal friends and even as neighbors; they mingle with one another on the golf course, in the gentleman's clubs, at resorts, on transcontinental airplanes, and on ocean liners. They meet at the estates of mutual friends, face each other in front of the TV camera, or serve on the same philanthropic committee; and many are sure to cross one another's path in the columns of newspapers, if not in the exact cafes from which many of these columns originate. As we have seen, of 'The New 400' of cafe society, one chronicler has named forty-one members of the very rich, ninety-three political leaders, and seventy-nine chief executives of corporations.*

'I did not know, I could not have dreamed,' Whittaker Chambers has written, 'of the immense scope and power of Hiss' politi-

* See above, FOUR: The Celebrities.

cal alliances and his social connections, which cut across all party lines and ran from the Supreme Court to the Religious Society of Friends, from governors of states and instructors in college faculties to the staff members of liberal magazines. In the decade since I had last seen him, he had used his career, and, in particular, his identification with the cause of peace through his part in organizing the United Nations, to put down roots that made him one with the matted forest floor of American upper class, enlightened middle class, liberal and official life. His roots could not be disturbed without disturbing all the roots on all sides of him.'[8]

The sphere of status has reflected the epochs of the power elite. In the third epoch, for example, who could compete with big money? And in the fourth, with big politicians, or even the bright young men of the New Deal? And in the fifth, who can compete with the generals and the admirals and the corporate officials now so sympathetically portrayed on the stage, in the novel, and on the screen? Can one imagine *Executive Suite* as a successful motion picture in 1935? Or *The Caine Mutiny?*

The multiplicity of high-prestige organizations to which the elite usually belong is revealed by even casual examination of the obituaries of the big businessman, the high-prestige lawyer, the top general and admiral, the key senator: usually, high-prestige church, business associations, plus high-prestige clubs, and often plus military rank. In the course of their lifetimes, the university president, the New York Stock Exchange chairman, the head of the bank, the old West Pointer—mingle in the status sphere, within which they easily renew old friendships and draw upon them in an effort to understand through the experience of trusted others those contexts of power and decision in which they have not personally moved.

In these diverse contexts, prestige accumulates in each of the higher circles, and the members of each borrow status from one another. Their self-images are fed by these accumulations and these borrowings, and accordingly, however segmental a given man's role may seem, he comes to feel himself a 'diffuse' or 'generalized' man of the higher circles. a 'broad-gauge' man. Perhaps such inside experience is one feature of what is meant by 'judgment.'

The key organizations, perhaps, are the major corporations themselves, for on the boards of directors we find a heavy overlapping among the members of these several elites. On the lighter side, again in the summer and winter resorts, we find that, in an intricate series of overlapping circles; in the course of time, each meets each or knows somebody who knows somebody who knows that one.

The higher members of the military, economic, and political orders are able readily to take over one another's point of view, always in a sympathetic way, and often in a knowledgeable way as well. They define one another as among those who count, and who, accordingly, must be taken into account. Each of them as a member of the power elite comes to incorporate into his own integrity, his own honor, his own conscience, the viewpoint, the expectations, the values of the others. If there are no common ideals and standards among them that are based upon an explicitly aristocratic culture, that does not mean that they do not feel responsibility to one another.

All the structural coincidence of their interests as well as the intricate, psychological facts of their origins and their education, their careers and their associations make possible the psychological affinities that prevail among them, affinities that make it possible for them to say of one another: He is, of course, one of us. And all this points to the basic, psychological meaning of class consciousness. Nowhere in America is there as great a 'class consciousness' as among the elite; nowhere is it organized as effectively as among the power elite. For by class consciousness, as a psychological fact, one means that the individual member of a 'class' accepts only those accepted by his circle as among those who are significant to his own image of self.

Within the higher circles of the power elite, factions do exist; there are conflicts of policy; individual ambitions do clash. There are still enough divisions of importance within the Republican party, and even between Republicans and Democrats, to make for different methods of operation. But more powerful than these divisions are the internal discipline and the community of interests that bind the power elite together, even across the boundaries of nations at war.[9]

4

Yet we must give due weight to the other side of the case which may not question the facts but only our interpretation of them. There is a set of objections that will inevitably be made to our whole conception of the power elite, but which has essentially to do with only the psychology of its members. It might well be put by liberals or by conservatives in some such way as this:

'To talk of a power elite—isn't this to characterize men by their origins and associations? Isn't such characterization both unfair and untrue? Don't men modify themselves, especially Americans such as these, as they rise in stature to meet the demands of their jobs? Don't they arrive at a view and a line of policy that represents, so far as they in their human weaknesses can know, the interests of the nation as a whole? Aren't they merely honorable men who are doing their duty?'

What are we to reply to these objections?

I. We are sure that they are honorable men. But what is honor? Honor can only mean living up to a code that one believes to be honorable. There is no one code upon which we are all agreed. That is why, if we are civilized men, we do not kill off all of those with whom we disagree. The question is not: are these honorable men? The question is: what are their codes of honor? The answer to that question is that they are the codes of their circles, of those to whose opinions they defer. How could it be otherwise? That is one meaning of the important truism that all men are human and that all men are social creatures. As for sincerity, it can only be disproved, never proved.

II. To the question of their adaptability—which means their capacity to transcend the codes of conduct which, in their life's work and experience, they have acquired—we must answer: simply no, they cannot, at least not in the handful of years most of them have left. To expect that is to assume that they are indeed strange and expedient: such flexibility would in fact involve a violation of what we may rightly call their character and their integrity. By the way, may it not be precisely because of the lack of such character and integrity that earlier types of American politicians have not represented as great a threat as do these men of character?

It would be an insult to the effective training of the military, and to their indoctrination as well, to suppose that military officials shed their military character and outlook upon changing from uniform to mufti. This background is more important perhaps in the military case than in that of the corporate executives, for the training of the career is deeper and more total.

'Lack of imagination,' Gerald W. Johnson has noted, 'is not to be confused with lack of principle. On the contrary, an unimaginative man is often a man of the highest principles. The trouble is that his principles conform to Cornford's famous definition: "A principle is a rule of inaction giving valid general reasons for not doing in a specific instance what to unprincipled instinct would seem to be right." '[10]

Would it not be ridiculous, for example, to believe seriously that, in psychological fact, Charles Erwin Wilson represented anyone or any interest other than those of the corporate world? This is not because he is dishonest; on the contrary, it is because he is probably a man of solid integrity—as sound as a dollar. He is what he is and he cannot very well be anything else. He is a member of the professional corporation elite, just as are his colleagues, in the government and out of it; he represents the wealth of the higher corporate world; he represents its power; and he believes sincerely in his oft-quoted remark that 'what is good for the United States is good for the General Motors Corporation and vice versa.'

The revealing point about the pitiful hearings on the confirmation of such men for political posts is not the cynicism toward the law and toward the lawmakers on the middle levels of power which they display, nor their reluctance to dispose of their personal stock.[11] The interesting point is how impossible it is for such men to divest themselves of their engagement with the corporate world in general and with their own corporations in particular. Not only their money, but their friends, their interests, their training—their lives in short—are deeply involved in this world. The disposal of stock is, of course, merely a purifying ritual. The point is not so much financial or personal interests in a given corporation, but identification with the corporate world. To ask a man suddenly to divest himself of these interests and sensibilities is almost like asking a man to become a woman.

III. To the question of their patriotism, of their desire to serve the nation as a whole, we must answer first that, like codes of honor, feelings of patriotism and views of what is to the whole nation's good, are not ultimate facts but matters upon which there exists a great variety of opinion. Furthermore, patriotic opinions too are rooted in and are sustained by what a man has become by virtue of how and with whom he has lived. This is no simple mechanical determination of individual character by social conditions; it is an intricate process, well established in the major tradition of modern social study. One can only wonder why more social scientists do not use it systematically in speculating about politics.

IV. The elite cannot be truly thought of as men who are merely doing their duty. They are the ones who determine their duty, as well as the duties of those beneath them. They are not merely following orders: they give the orders. They are not merely 'bureaucrats': they command bureaucracies. They may try to disguise these facts from others and from themselves by appeals to traditions of which they imagine themselves the instruments, but there are many traditions, and they must choose which ones they will serve. They face decisions for which there simply are no traditions.

Now, to what do these several answers add up? To the fact that we cannot reason about public events and historical trends merely from knowledge about the motives and character of the men or the small groups who sit in the seats of the high and mighty. This fact, in turn, does not mean that we should be intimidated by accusations that in taking up our problem in the way we have, we are impugning the honor, the integrity, or the ability of those who are in high office. For it is not, in the first instance, a question of individual character; and if, in further instances, we find that it is, we should not hesitate to say so plainly. In the meantime, we must judge men of power by the standards of power, by what they do as decision-makers, and not by who they are or what they may do in private life. Our interest is not in that: we are interested in their policies and in the *consequences* of their conduct of office. We must remember that these men of the power elite now occupy the strategic places in the structure of American society; that they command the dominant institutions of a dominant nation; that, as a set of men, they are in a position to make decisions with terrible consequences for the underlying populations of the world.

5

Despite their social similarity and psychological affinities, the members of the power elite do not constitute a club having a permanent membership with fixed and formal boundaries. It is of the nature of the power elite that within it there is a good deal of shifting about, and that it thus does not consist of one small set of the same men in the same positions in the same hierarchies. Because men know each other personally does not mean that among them there is a unity of policy; and because they do not know each other personally does not mean that among them there is a disunity. The conception of the power elite does not rest, as I have repeatedly said, primarily upon personal friendship.

As the requirements of the top places in each of the major hierarchies become similar, the types of men occupying these roles at the top—by selection and by training in the jobs—become similar. This is no mere deduction from structure to personnel. That it is a fact is revealed by the heavy traffic that has been going on between the three structures, often in very intricate patterns. The chief executives, the warlords, and selected politicians came into contact with one another in an intimate, working way during World War II; after that war ended, they continued their associations, out of common beliefs, social congeniality, and coinciding interests. Noticeable proportions of top men from the military, the economic, and the political worlds have during the last fifteen years occupied positions in one or both of the other worlds: between these higher circles there is an interchangeability of position, based formally upon the supposed transferability of 'executive ability,' based in substance upon the co-optation by cliques of insiders. As members of a power elite, many of those busy in this traffic have come to look upon 'the government' as an umbrella under whose authority they do their work.

As the business between the big three increases in volume and importance, so does the traffic in personnel. The very criteria for selecting men who will rise come to embody this fact. The corporate commissar, dealing with the state and its military, is wiser to choose a young man who has experienced the state and its military than one who has not. The political director, often dependent for his own political success upon corporate decisions and corporations, is also wiser to choose a man with corporate experience. Thus, by virtue of the very criterion of success, the interchange of personnel and the unity of the power elite is increased.

Given the formal similarity of the three hierarchies in which the several members of the elite spend their working lives, given the ramifications of the decisions made in each upon the others, given the coincidence of interest that prevails among them at many points, and given the administrative vacuum of the American civilian state along with its enlargement of tasks—given these trends of structure, and adding to them the psychological affinities we have noted—we should indeed be surprised were we to find that men said to be skilled in administrative contacts and full of organizing ability would fail to do more than get in touch with one another. They have, of course, done much more than that: increasingly, they assume positions in one another's domains.

The unity revealed by the interchangeability of top roles rests upon the parallel development of the top jobs in each of the big three domains. The interchange occurs most frequently at the points of their coinciding interest, as between regulatory agency and the regulated industry; contracting agency and contractor. And, as we shall see, it leads to co-ordinations that are more explicit, and even formal.

The inner core of the power elite consists, first, of those who interchange commanding roles at the top of one dominant institutional order with those in another: the admiral who is also a banker and a lawyer and who heads up an important federal commission; the corporation executive whose company was one of the two or three leading war materiel producers who is now the Secretary of Defense; the wartime general who dons civilian clothes to sit on the political directorate and then becomes a member of the board of directors of a leading economic corporation.

Although the executive who becomes a general, the general who becomes a statesman, the statesman who becomes a banker, see much more than ordinary men in their ordinary environments, still the perspectives of even such men often remain tied to their dominant locales. In their very career, however, they interchange roles within the big three and thus readily transcend the particularity of interest in any one of these institutional milieux. By their very careers and activities, they lace the three types of milieux together. They are, accordingly, the core members of the power elite.

These men are not necessarily familiar with every major arena of power. We refer to one man who moves in and between perhaps two circles—say the industrial and the military—and to another man who moves in the military and the political, and to a third who moves in the political as well as among opinion-makers. These in-between types most closely display our image of the power elite's structure and operation, even of behind-the-scenes operations. To the extent that there is any 'invisible elite,' these advisory and liaison types are its core. Even if—as I believe to be very likely—many of them are, at least in the first part of their careers, 'agents' of the various elites rather than themselves elite, it is they who are most active in organizing the several top milieux into a structure of power and maintaining it.

The inner core of the power elite also includes men of the higher legal and financial type from the great law factories and investment firms, who are almost professional go-betweens of economic, political and military affairs, and who thus act to unify the power elite. The corporation lawyer and the investment banker perform the functions of the 'go-between' effectively and powerfully. By the nature of their work, they transcend the narrower milieu of any one industry, and accordingly are in a position to speak and act for the corporate world or at least sizable sectors of it. The corporation lawyer is a key link between the economic and military and political areas; the investment banker is a key organizer and unifier of the corporate world and a person well versed in spending the huge amounts of money the American military establishment now ponders. When you get a lawyer who handles the legal work of investment bankers you get a key member of the power elite.

During the Democratic era, one link between private corporate organizations and governmental institutions was the investment house of Dillon, Read. From it came such men as James Forrestal and Charles F. Detmar, Jr.; Ferdinand Eberstadt had once been a partner in it before he branched out into his own investment house from which came other men to political and military circles. Republican administrations seem to favor the investment firm of

Kuhn, Loeb and the advertising firm of Batten, Barton, Durstine and Osborn.

Regardless of administrations, there is always the law firm of Sullivan and Cromwell. Mid-West investment banker Cyrus Eaton has said that 'Arthur H. Dean, a senior partner of Sullivan & Cromwell of No. 48 Wall Street, was one of those who assisted in the drafting of the Securities Act of 1933, the first of the series of bills passed to regulate the capital markets. He and his firm, which is reputed to be the largest in the United States, have maintained close relations with the SEC since its creation, and theirs is the dominating influence on the Commission.'[12]

There is also the third largest bank in the United States: the Chase National Bank of New York (now Chase-Manhattan). Regardless of political administration, executives of this bank and those of the International Bank of Reconstruction and Development have changed positions: John J. McCloy, who became Chairman of the Chase National in 1953, is a former president of the World Bank; and his successor to the presidency of the World Bank was a former senior vice-president of the Chase National Bank.[18] And in 1953, the president of the Chase National Bank, Winthrop W. Aldrich, had left to become Ambassador to Great Britain.

The outermost fringes of the power elite—which change more than its core—consist of 'those who count' even though they may not be 'in' on given decisions of consequence nor in their career move between the hierarchies. Each member of the power elite need not be a man who personally decides every decision that is to be ascribed to the power elite. Each member, in the decisions that he does make, takes the others seriously into account. They not only make decisions in the several major areas of war and peace; they are the men who, in decisions in which they take no direct part, are taken into decisive account by those who are directly in charge.

On the fringes and below them, somewhat to the side of the lower echelons, the power elite fades off into the middle levels of power, into the rank and file of the Congress, the pressure groups that are not vested in the power elite itself, as well as a multiplicity of regional and state and local interests. If all the men on the middle levels are not among those who count, they sometimes must be taken into account, handled, cajoled, broken or raised to higher circles.

When the power elite find that in order to get things done they must reach below their own realms—as is the case when it is necessary to get bills passed through Congress—they themselves must exert some pressure. But among the power elite, the name for such high-level lobbying is 'liaison work.' There are 'liaison' military men with Congress, with certain wayward sections of industry, with practically every important element not directly concerned with the power elite. The two men on the White House staff who are *named* 'liaison' men are both experienced in military matters; one of them is a former investment banker and lawyer as well as a general.

Not the trade associations but the higher cliques of lawyers and investment bankers are the active political heads of the corporate rich and the members of the power elite. 'While it is generally assumed that the national associations carry tremendous weight in formulating public opinion and directing the course of national policy, there is some evidence to indicate that interaction between associations on a formal level is not a very tight-knit affair. The general tendency within associations seems to be to stimulate activities around the specific interests of the organization, and more effort is made to educate its members rather than to spend much time in trying to influence other associations on the issue at hand . . . As media for stating and re-stating the over-all value structure of the nation they (the trade associations) are important . . . But when issues are firmly drawn, individuals related to the larger corporate interests are called upon to exert pressure in the proper places at the strategic time The national associations may act as media for co-ordinating such pressures, but a great volume of intercommunication between members at the apex of power of the larger corporate interests seems to be the decisive factor in final policy determination.'[14]

Conventional 'lobbying,' carried on by trade associations, still exists, although it usually concerns the middle levels of power—usually being targeted at Congress and, of course, its own rank and file members. The important function of the National Association of Manufacturers, for example, is less directly to influence policy than to reveal to small businessmen that their interests are the same as those of larger businesses. But there is also 'high-level lobbying.' All over the country the corporate leaders are drawn into the circle of the high military and political through personal friendship, trade and professonal associations and their various subcommittees, prestige clubs, open political affiliation, and customer relationships. 'There is . . . an awareness among these power leaders,' one first-hand investigator of such executive cliques has asserted, 'of many of the current major policy issues before the nation such as keeping taxes down, turning all productive operations over to private enterprises, increasing foreign trade, keeping governmental 'welfare and other domestic activities to a minimum, and strengthening and maintaining the hold of the current party in power nationally.'[15]

There are, in fact, cliques of corporate executives who are more important as informal opinion leaders in the top echelons of corporate, military, and political power than as actual participants in military and political organizations. Inside military circles and inside political circles and 'on the sidelines' in the economic area, these circles and cliques of corporation executives are in on most all major decisions regardless of topic. And what is important about all this high-level lobbying is that it is done within the confines of that elite.

6

The conception of the power elite and of its unity rests upon the corresponding developments and the coincidence of interests among economic, political, and military organizations. It also rests upon the similarity of origin and outlook, and the social and personal intermingling of the top circles from each of these dominant hierarchies. This conjunction of institutional and psychological forces, in turn, is revealed by the heavy personnel traffic within and between the big three institutional orders, as well as by the rise of go-betweens as in the high-level lobbying. The conception of the power elite, accordingly, does *not* rest upon the assumption that American history since the origins of World War II must be understood as a secret plot, or as a great and co-ordinated conspiracy of the members of this elite. The conception rests upon quite impersonal grounds.

There is, however, little doubt that the American power elite—

which contains, we are told, some of 'the greatest organizers in the world'—has also planned and has plotted. The rise of the elite, as we have already made clear, was not and could not have been caused by a plot; and the tenability of the conception does not rest upon the existence of any secret or any publicly known organization. But, once the conjunction of structural trend and of the personal will to utilize it gave rise to the power elite, then plans and programs did occur to its members and indeed it is not possible to interpret many events and official policies of the fifth epoch without reference to the power elite. 'There is a great difference,' Richard Hofstadter has remarked, 'between locating conspiracies *in* history and saying that history *is*, in effect, a conspiracy . . .'[16]

The structural trends of institutions become defined as opportunities by those who occupy their command posts. Once such opportunities are recognized, men may avail themselves of them. Certain types of men from each of the dominant institutional areas, more far-sighted than others, have actively promoted the liaison before it took its truly modern shape. They have often done so for reasons not shared by their partners, although not objected to by them either; and often the outcome of their liaison has had consequences which none of them foresaw, much less shaped, and which only later in the course of development came under explicit control. Only after it was well under way did most of its members find themselves part of it and become gladdened, although sometimes also worried, by this fact. But once the co-ordination is a going concern, new men come readily into it and assume its existence without question.

So far as explicit organization—conspiratorial or not—is concerned, the power elite, by its very nature, is more likely to use existing organizations, working within and between them, than to set up explicit organizations whose membership is strictly limited to its own members. But if there is no machinery in existence to ensure, for example, that military and political factors will be balanced in decisions made, they will invent such machinery and use it, as with the National Security Council. Moreover, in a formally democratic polity, the aims and the powers of the various elements of this elite are further supported by an aspect of the permanent war economy: the assumption that the security of the nation supposedly rests upon great secrecy of plan and in-

tent. Many higher events that would reveal the working of the
power elite can be withheld from public knowledge under the
guise of secrecy. With the wide secrecy covering their operations
and decisions, the power elite can mask their intentions, operations, and further consolidation. Any secrecy that is imposed upon
those in positions to observe high decision-makers clearly works
for and not against the operations of the power elite.

There is accordingly reason to suspect—but by the nature of the
case, no proof—that the power elite is not altogether 'surfaced.'
There is nothing hidden about it, although its activities are not
publicized. As an elite, it is not organized, although its members
often know one another, seem quite naturally to work together,
and share many organizations in common. There is nothing conspiratorial about it, although its decisions are often publicly unknown and its mode of operation manipulative rather than explicit.

It is not that the elite 'believe in' a compact elite behind the
scenes and a mass down below. It is not put in that language. It is
just that the people are of necessity confused and must, like trusting children, place all the new world of foreign policy and
strategy and executive action in the hands of experts. It is just that
everyone knows somebody has got to run the show, and that somebody usually does. Others do not really care anyway, and besides,
they do not know how. So the gap between the two types gets
wider.

When crises are defined as total, and as seemingly permanent,
the consequences of decision become total, and the decisions in
each major area of life come to be integrated and total. Up to a
point, these consequences for other institutional orders can be assessed; beyond such points, chances have to be taken. It is then that
the felt scarcity of trained and imaginative judgment leads to plain-
tive feelings among executives about the shortage of qualified successors in political, military, and economic life. This feeling, in
turn, leads to an increasing concern with the training of successors
who could take over as older men of power retire.[17] In each area,
there slowly arises a new generation which has grown up in an age
of co-ordinated decisions.

In each of the elite circles, we have noticed this concern to
recruit and to train successors as 'broad-gauge' men, that is, as men

capable of making decisions that involve institutional areas other than their own. The chief executives have set up formal recruitment and training programs to man the corporate world as virtually a state within a state. Recruitment and training for the military elite has long been rigidly professionalized, but has now come to include educational routines of a sort which the remnants of older generals and admirals consider quite nonsensical.

Only the political order, with its absence of a genuine civil service, has lagged behind, creating an administrative vacuum into which military bureaucrats and corporate outsiders have been drawn. But even in this domain, since World War II, there have been repeated attempts, by elite men of such vision as the late James Forrestal's, to inaugurate a career service that would include periods in the corporate world as well as in the governmental.[18]

What is lacking is a truly common elite program of recruitment and training; for the prep school, Ivy League College, and law school sequence of the metropolitan 400 is not up to the demands now made upon members of the power elite.*[19] Britishers, such as Field Marshall Viscount Montgomery, well aware of this lack, recently urged the adoption of a system 'under which a minority of high-caliber young students could be separated from the mediocre and given the best education possible to supply the country with leadership.' His proposal is echoed, in various forms, by many who accept his criticism of 'the American theory of public education on the ground that it is ill-suited to produce the "elite" group of leaders . . . this country needs to fulfill its obligations of world leadership.'[20]

In part these demands reflect the unstated need to transcend recruitment on the sole basis of economic success, especially since it is suspect as often involving the higher immorality; in part it reflects the stated need to have men who, as Viscount Montgomery says, know 'the meaning of discipline.' But above all these demands reflect the at least vague consciousness on the part of the power elite themselves that the age of co-ordinated decisions, entailing a newly enormous range of consequences, requires a power elite that is of a new caliber. In so far as the sweep of matters which go into the making of decisions is vast and interrelated, the

* See above, THREE: Metropolitan 400

information needed for judgments complex and requiring particularized knowledge,[21] the men in charge will not only call upon one another; they will try to train their successors for the work at hand. These new men will grow up as men of power within the co-ordination of economic and political and military decision.

7

The idea of the power elite rests upon and enables us to make sense of (1) the decisive institutional trends that characterize the structure of our epoch, in particular, the military ascendancy in a privately incorporated economy, and more broadly, the several coincidences of objective interests between economic, military, and political institutions; (2) the social similarities and the psychological affinities of the men who occupy the command posts of these structures, in particular the increased interchangeability of the top positions in each of them and the increased traffic between these orders in the careers of men of power; (3) the ramifications, to the point of virtual totality, of the kind of decisions that are made at the top, and the rise to power of a set of men who, by training and bent, are professional organizers of considerable force and who are unrestrained by democratic party training.

Negatively, the formation of the power elite rests upon (1) the relegation of the professional party politician to the middle levels of power, (2) the semi-organized stalemate of the interests of sovereign localities into which the legislative function has fallen, (3) the virtually complete absence of a civil service that constitutes a politically neutral, but politically relevant, depository of brainpower and executive skill, and (4) the increased official secrecy behind which great decisions are made without benefit of public or even Congressional debate.

As a result, the political directorate, the corporate rich, and the ascendant military have come together as the power elite, and the expanded and centralized hierarchies which they head have encroached upon the old balances and have now relegated them to the middle levels of power. Now the balancing society is a conception that pertains accurately to the middle levels, and on that level the balance has become more often an affair of intrenched provincial and nationally irresponsible forces and demands than a center of power and national decision.

But how about the bottom? As all these trends have become visible at the top and on the middle, what has been happening to the great American public? If the top is unprecedentedly powerful and increasingly unified and willful; if the middle zones are increasingly a semi-organized stalemate—in what shape is the bottom, in what condition is the public at large? The rise of the power elite, we shall now see, rests upon, and in some ways is part of, the transformation of the publics of America into a mass society.

13

The Mass Society

In the standard image of power and decision, no force is held to be as important as The Great American Public. More than merely another check and balance, this public is thought to be the seat of all legitimate power. In official life as in popular folklore, it is held to be the very balance wheel of democratic power. In the end, all liberal theorists rest their notions of the power system upon the political role of this public; all official decisions, as well as private decisions of consequence, are justified as in the public's welfare; all formal proclamations are in its name.

1

Let us therefore consider the classic public of democratic theory in the generous spirit in which Rousseau once cried, 'Opinion, Queen of the World, is not subject to the power of kings; they are themselves its first slaves.'

The most important feature of the public of opinion, which the rise of the democratic middle class initiates, is the free ebb and flow of discussion. The possibilities of answering back, of organizing autonomous organs of public opinion, of realizing opinion in action, are held to be established by democratic institutions. The opinion that results from public discussion is understood to be a resolution that is then carried out by public action; it is, in one version, the 'general will' of the people, which the legislative organ enacts into law, thus lending to it legal force. Congress, or Parliament, as an institution, crowns all the scattered publics; it is the archetype for each of the little circles of face-to-face citizens discussing their public business.

This eighteenth-century idea of the public of public opinion parallels the economic idea of the market of the free economy. Here is the market composed of freely competing entrepreneurs; there is the public composed of discussion circles of opinion peers. As price is the result of anonymous, equally weighted, bargaining individuals, so public opinion is the result of each man's having thought things out for himself and contributing his voice to the great chorus. To be sure, some might have more influence on the state of opinion than others, but no one group monopolizes the discussion, or by itself determines the opinions that prevail.

Innumerable discussion circles are knit together by mobile people who carry opinions from one to another, and struggle for the power of larger command. The public is thus organized into associations and parties, each representing a set of viewpoints, each trying to acquire a place in the Congress, where the discussion continues. Out of the little circles of people talking with one another, the larger forces of social movements and political parties develop; and the discussion of opinion is the important phase in a total act by which public affairs are conducted.

The autonomy of these discussions is an important element in the idea of public opinion as a democratic legitimation. The opinions formed are actively realized within the prevailing institutions of power; all authoritative agents are made or broken by the prevailing opinions of these publics. And, in so far as the public is frustrated in realizing its demands, its members may go beyond criticism of specific policies; they may question the very legitimations of legal authority. That is one meaning of Jefferson's comment on the need for an occasional 'revolution.'

The public, so conceived, is the loom of classic, eighteenth-century democracy; discussion is at once the threads and the shuttle tying the discussion circles together. It lies at the root of the conception of authority by discussion, and it is based upon the hope that truth and justice will somehow come out of society as a great apparatus of free discussion. The people are presented with problems. They discuss them. They decide on them. They formulate viewpoints. These viewpoints are organized, and they compete. One viewpoint 'wins out.' Then the people act out this view, or their representatives are instructed to act it out, and this they promptly do.

Such are the images of the public of classic democracy which are still used as the working justifications of power in American society. But now we must recognize this description as a set of images out of a fairy tale: they are not adequate even as an approximate model of how the American system of power works. The issues that now shape man's fate are neither raised nor decided by the public at large. The idea of the community of publics is not a description of fact, but an assertion of an ideal, an assertion of a legitimation masquerading—as legitimations are now apt to do—as fact. For now the public of public opinion is recognized by all those who have considered it carefully as something less than it once was.

These doubts are asserted positively in the statement that the classic community of publics is being transformed into a society of masses. This transformation, in fact, is one of the keys to the social and psychological meaning of modern life in America.

I. In the democratic society of publics it was assumed, with John Locke, that the individual conscience was the ultimate seat of judgment and hence the final court of appeal. But this principle was challenged—as E. H. Carr has put it—when Rousseau 'for the first time thought in terms of the sovereignty of the whole people, and faced the issue of mass democracy.'[1]

II. In the democratic society of publics it was assumed that among the individuals who composed it there was a natural and peaceful harmony of interests. But this essentially conservative doctrine gave way to the Utilitarian doctrine that such a harmony of interests had first to be created by reform before it could work, and later to the Marxian doctrine of class struggle, which surely was then, and certainly is now, closer to reality than any assumed harmony of interests.

III. In the democratic society of publics it was assumed that before public action would be taken, there would be rational discussion between individuals which would determine the action, and that, accordingly, the public opinion that resulted would be the infallible voice of reason. But this has been challenged not only (1) by the assumed need for experts to decide delicate and intricate issues, but (2) by the discovery—as by Freud—of the ir-rationality of the man in the street, and (3) by the discovery—as by Marx—of the socially conditioned nature of what was once assumed to be autonomous reason.

IV. In the democratic society of publics it was assumed that after determining what is true and right and just, the public would act accordingly or see that its representatives did so. In the long run, public opinion will not only be right, but public opinion will prevail. This assumption has been upset by the great gap now existing between the underlying population and those who make decisions in its name, decisions of enormous consequence which the public often does not even know are being made until well after the fact.

Given these assumptions, it is not difficult to understand the articulate optimism of many nineteenth-century thinkers, for the theory of the public is, in many ways, a projection upon the community at large of the intellectual's ideal of the supremacy of intellect. The 'evolution of the intellect,' Comte asserted, 'determines the main course of social evolution.' If looking about them, nineteenth-century thinkers still saw irrationality and ignorance and apathy, all that was merely an intellectual lag, to which the spread of education would soon put an end.

How much the cogency of the classic view of the public rested upon a restriction of this public to the carefully educated is revealed by the fact that by 1859 even John Stuart Mill was writing of 'the tyranny of the majority,' and both Tocqueville and Burckhardt anticipated the view popularized in the recent past by such political moralists as Ortega y Gasset. In a word, the transformation of public into mass—and all that this implies—has been at once one of the major trends of modern societies and one of the major factors in the collapse of that liberal optimism which determined so much of the intellectual mood of the nineteenth century.

By the middle of that century: individualism had begun to be replaced by collective forms of economic and political life; harmony of interests by inharmonious struggle of classes and organized pressures; rational discussions undermined by expert decisions on complicated issues, by recognition of the interested bias of argument by vested position; and by the discovery of the effectiveness of irrational appeal to the citizen. Moreover, certain structural changes of modern society, which we shall presently consider, had begun to cut off the public from the power of active decision.

2

The transformation of public into mass is of particular concern to us, for it provides an important clue to the meaning of the power elite. If that elite is truly responsible to, or even exists in connection with, a community of publics, it carries a very different meaning than if such a public is being transformed into a society of masses.

The United States today is not altogether a mass society, and it has never been altogether a community of publics These phrases are names for extreme types; they point to certain features of reality, but they are themselves constructions; social reality is always some sort of mixture of the two. Yet we cannot readily understand just how much of which is mixed into our situation if we do not first understand, in terms of explicit dimensions, the clear-cut and extreme types:

At least four dimensions must be attended to if we are to grasp the differences between public and mass.

I. There is first, the ratio of the givers of opinion to the receivers, which is the simplest way to state the social meaning of the formal media of mass communication. More than anything else, it is the shift in this ratio which is central to the problems of the public and of public opinion in latter-day phases of democracy. At one extreme on the scale of communication, two people talk personally with each other; at the opposite extreme, one spokesman talks impersonally through a network of communications to millions of listeners and viewers. In between these extremes there are assemblages and political rallies, parliamentary sessions, lawcourt debates, small discussion circles dominated by one man, open discussion circles with talk moving freely back and forth among fifty people, and so on.

II. The second dimension to which we must pay attention is the possibility of answering back an opinion without internal or external reprisals being taken. Technical conditions of the means of communication, in imposing a lower ratio of speakers to listeners, may obviate the possibility of freely answering back. Informal rules, resting upon conventional sanction and upon the informal structure of opinion leadership, may govern who can speak, when, and for how long. Such rules may or may not be in congruence with formal rules and with institutional sanctions which govern the process of communication. In the extreme case, we may conceive of an absolute monopoly of communication to pacified media groups whose members cannot answer back even 'in private.' At the opposite extreme, the conditions may allow and the rules may uphold the wide and symmetrical formation of opinion.

III. We must also consider the relation of the formation of opinion to its realization in social action, the ease with which opinion is effective in the shaping of decisions of powerful consequence. This opportunity for people to act out their opinions collectively is of course limited by their position in the structure of power. This structure may be such as to limit decisively this capacity, or it may allow or even invite such action. It may confine social action to local areas or it may enlarge the area of opportunity; it may make action intermittent or more or less continuous.

IV. There is, finally, the degree to which institutional authority, with its sanctions and controls, penetrates the public. Here the problem is the degree to which the public has genuine autonomy from instituted authority. At one extreme, no agent of formal authority moves among the autonomous public. At the opposite extreme, the public is terrorized into uniformity by the infiltration of informers and the universalization of suspicion. One thinks of the late Nazi street-and-block-system, the eighteenth-century Japanese kumi, the Soviet cell structure. In the extreme, the formal structure of power coincides, as it were, with the informal ebb and flow of influence by discussion, which is thus killed off.

By combining these several points, we can construct little models or diagrams of several types of societies. Since 'the problem of public opinion' as we know it is set by the eclipse of the classic bourgeois public, we are here concerned with only two types: public and mass.

In a *public*, as we may understand the term, (1) virtually as many people express opinions as receive them. (2) Public communications are so organized that there is a chance immediately and effectively to answer back any opinion expressed in public. Opinion formed by such discussion (3) readily finds an outlet in effective action, even against—if necessary—the prevailing system of authority. And (4) authoritative institutions do not penetrate the public, which is thus more or less autonomous in its operations. When these conditions prevail, we have the working model of a community of publics, and this model fits closely the several assumptions of classic democratic theory.

At the opposite extreme, in a *mass*, (1) far fewer people express opinions than receive them; for the community of publics becomes an abstract collection of individuals who receive impressions from the mass media. (2) The communications that prevail are so organized that it is difficult or impossible for the individual to answer back immediately or with any effect. (3) The realization of opinion in action is controlled by authorities who organize and control the channels of such action. (4) The mass has no autonomy from institutions; on the contrary, agents of authorized institutions penetrate this mass, reducing any autonomy it may have in the formation of opinion by discussion.

The public and the mass may be most readily distinguished by their dominant modes of communication: in a community of publics, discussion is the ascendant means of communication, and the mass media, if they exist, simply enlarge and animate discussion, linking one *primary public* with the discussions of another. In a mass society, the dominant type of communication is the formal media, and the publics become mere *media markets:* all those exposed to the contents of given mass media.

3

From almost any angle of vision that we might assume, when we look upon the public, we realize that we have moved a considerable distance along the road to the mass society. At the end of that road there is totalitarianism, as in Nazi Germany or in Communist Russia. We are not yet at that end. In the United States today, media markets are not entirely ascendant over primary publics. But surely we can see that many aspects of the public life of our times are more the features of a mass society than of a community of publics.

What is happening might again be stated in terms of the historical parallel between the economic market and the public of public opinion. In brief, there is a movement from widely scattered little powers to concentrated powers and the attempt at monopoly control from powerful centers, which, being partially hidden, are centers of manipulation as well as of authority. The small shop serving the neighborhood is replaced by the anonymity of the national corporation: mass advertisement replaces the personal influence of opinion between merchant and customer. The political leader hooks up his speech to a national network and speaks, with appropriate personal touches, to a million people he never saw and never will see. Entire brackets of professions and industries are in the 'opinion business,' impersonally manipulating the public for hire.

In the primary public the competition of opinions goes on between people holding views in the service of their interests and their reasoning. But in the mass society of media markets, competition, if any, goes on between the manipulators with their mass media on the one hand, and the people receiving their propaganda on the other.

Under such conditions, it is not surprising that there should arise a conception of public opinion as a mere reaction—we cannot say 'response'—to the content of the mass media. In this view, the public is merely the collectivity of individuals each rather passively exposed to the mass media and rather helplessly opened up to the suggestions and manipulations that flow from these media. The fact of manipulation from centralized points of control constitutes, as it were, an expropriation of the old multitude of little opinion producers and consumers operating in a free and balanced market.

In official circles, the very term itself, 'the public'—as Walter Lippmann noted thirty years ago—has come to have a phantom meaning, which dramatically reveals its eclipse. From the standpoint of the deciding elite, some of those who clamor publicly can be identified as 'Labor,' others as 'Business,' still others as 'Farmer.' Those who can *not* readily be so identified make up 'The Public.' In this usage, the public is composed of the unidentified and the non-partisan in a world of defined and partisan interests. It is socially composed of well-educated salaried professionals, especially college professors; of non-unionized employees, especially white-collar people, along with self-employed professionals and small businessmen.

In this faint echo of the classic notion, the public consists of

those remnants of the middle classes, old and new, whose interests are not explicitly defined, organized, or clamorous. In a curious adaptation, 'the public' often becomes, in fact, 'the unattached
expert,' who, although well informed, has never taken a clear-cut,
public stand on controversial issues which are brought to a focus
by organized interests. These are the 'public' members of the
board, the commission, the committee. What the public stands for,
accordingly, is often a vagueness of policy (called open-mindedness), a lack of involvement in public affairs (known as reasonableness), and a professional disinterest (known as tolerance).

Some such official members of the public, as in the field of
labor-management mediation, start out very young and make a
career out of being careful to be informed but never taking a
strong position; and there are many others, quite unofficial, who
take such professionals as a sort of model. The only trouble is that
they are acting as if they were disinterested judges but they do not
have the power of judges; hence their reasonableness, their tolerance, and their open-mindedness do not often count for much in
the shaping of human affairs.

4

All those trends that make for the decline of the politician and
of his balancing society bear decisively upon the transformation of
public into mass.* One of the most important of the structural
transformations involved is the decline of the voluntary association as a genuine instrument of the public. As we have already
seen, the executive ascendancy in economic, military, and political institutions has lowered the effective use of all those voluntary
associations which operate between the state and the economy
on the one hand, and the family and the individual in the primary
group on the other. It is not only that institutions of power have
become large-scale and inaccessibly centralized; they have at the
same time become less political and more administrative, and it
is within this great change of framework that the organized public
has waned.

In terms of *scale*, the transformation of public into mass has
been underpinned by the shift from a political public decisively

*See, especially, the analysis of the decline of the independent middle
classes, ELEVEN: The Theory of Balance.

restricted in size (by property and education, as well as by sex and age) to a greatly enlarged mass having only the qualifications of citizenship and age.

In terms of *organization*, the transformation has been underpinned by the shift from the individual and his primary community to the voluntary association and the mass party as the major units of organized power.

Voluntary associations have become larger to the extent that they have become effective; and to just that extent they have become inaccessible to the individual who would shape by discussion the policies of the organization to which he belongs. Accordingly, along with older institutions, these voluntary associations have lost their grip on the individual. As more people are drawn into the political arena, these associations become mass in scale; and as the power of the individual becomes more dependent upon such mass associations, they are less accessible to the individual's influence.*

Mass democracy means the struggle of powerful and large-scale interest groups and associations, which stand between the big decisions that are made by state, corporation, army, and the will of the individual citizen as a member of the public. Since these middle-level associations are the citizen's major link with decision, his relation to them is of decisive importance. For it is only through them that he exercises such power as he may have.

The gap between the members and the leaders of the mass association is becoming increasingly wider. As soon as a man gets to be a leader of an association large enough to count he readily becomes lost as an instrument of that association. He does so (1) in the interests of maintaining his leading position in, or rather over, his mass association, and he does so (2) because he comes to see himself not as a mere delegate, instructed or not, of the mass association he represents, but as a member of 'an elite' composed of such men as himself. These facts, in turn, lead to (3) the big gap between the terms in which issues are debated and resolved among members of this elite, and the terms in which they are presented

* At the same time—and also because of the metropolitan segregation and distraction, which I shall discuss in a moment—the individual becomes more dependent upon the means of mass communication for his view of the structure as a whole.

to the members of the various mass associations. For the decisions that are made must *take into account* those who are important— other elites—but they must be *sold* to the mass memberships.

The gap between speaker and listener, between power and public, leads less to any iron law of oligarchy than to the law of spokesmanship: as the pressure group expands, its leaders come to organize the opinions they 'represent.' So elections, as we have seen, become contests between two giant and unwieldy parties, neither of which the individual can truly feel that he influences, and neither of which is capable of winning psychologically impressive or politically decisive majorities. And, in all this, the parties are of the same general form as other mass associations.[2]

When we say that man in the mass is without any sense of political belonging, we have in mind a political fact rather than merely a style of feeling. We have in mind (I.) a certain way of belonging (II.) to a certain kind of organization.

I. The way of belonging here implied rests upon a belief in the purposes and in the leaders of an organization, and thus enables men and women freely to be at home within it. To belong in this way is to make the human association a psychological center of one's self, to take into our conscience, deliberately and freely, its rules of conduct and its purposes, which we thus shape and which in turn shape us. We do not have this kind of belonging to any political organization.

II. The kind of organization we have in mind is a voluntary association which has three decisive characteristics: first, it is a context in which reasonable opinions may be formulated; second, it is an agency by which reasonable activities may be undertaken; and third, it is a powerful enough unit, in comparison with other organizations of power, to make a difference.

It is because they do not find available associations at once psychologically meaningful and historically effective that men often feel uneasy in their political and economic loyalties. The effective units of power are now the huge corporation, the inaccessible government, the grim military establishment. Between these, on the one hand, and the family and the small community on the other, we find no intermediate associations in which men feel secure and with which they feel powerful. There is little live political struggle. Instead, there is administration from above, and the political vacuum below. The primary publics are now either so small as to be swamped, and hence give up; or so large as to be merely another feature of the generally distant structure of power, and hence inaccessible.

Public opinion exists when people who are not in the government of a country claim the right to express political opinions freely and publicly, and the right that these opinions should influence or determine the policies, personnel, and actions of their government.[3] In this formal sense there has been and there is a definite public opinion in the United States. And yet, with modern developments this formal right—when it does still exist as a right —does not mean what it once did. The older world of voluntary organization was as different from the world of the mass organization, as was Tom Paine's world of pamphleteering from the world of the mass media.

Since the French Revolution, conservative thinkers have Viewed With Alarm the rise of the public, which they called the masses, or something to that effect. 'The populace is sovereign, and the tide of barbarism mounts,' wrote Gustave Le Bon. 'The divine right of the masses is about to replace the divine right of kings,' and already 'the destinies of nations are elaborated at present in the heart of the masses, and no longer in the councils of princes.'[4] During the twentieth century, liberal and even socialist thinkers have followed suit, with more explicit reference to what we have called the society of masses. From Le Bon to Emil Lederer and Ortega y Gasset, they have held that the influence of the mass in unfortunately increasing.

But surely those who have supposed the masses to be all powerful, or at least well on their way to triumph, are wrong. In our time, as Chakhotin knew, the influence of autonomous collectivities within political life is in fact diminishing.[5] Furthermore, such influence as they do have is guided; they must now be seen not as publics acting autonomously, but as masses manipulated at focal points into crowds of demonstrators. For as publics become masses, masses sometimes become crowds; and, in crowds, the psychical rape by the mass media is supplemented up-close by the harsh and sudden harangue. Then the people in the crowd disperse again—as atomized and submissive masses.

In all modern societies, the autonomous associations standing between the various classes and the state tend to lose their effectiveness as vehicles of reasoned opinion and instruments for the rational exertion of political will. Such associations can be deliberately broken up and thus turned into passive instruments of rule, or they can more slowly wither away from lack of use in the face of centralized means of power. But whether they are destroyed in a week, or wither in a generation, such associations are replaced in virtually every sphere of life by centralized organizations, and it is such organizations with all their new means of power that take charge of the terrorized or—as the case may be—merely intimidated, society of masses.

5

The institutional trends that make for a society of masses are to a considerable extent a matter of impersonal drift, but the remnants of the public are also exposed to more 'personal' and intentional forces. With the broadening of the base of politics within the context of a folk-lore of democratic decision-making, and with the increased means of mass persuasion that are available, the public of public opinion has become the object of intensive efforts to control, manage, manipulate, and increasingly intimidate.

In political, military, economic realms, power becomes, in varying degrees, uneasy before the suspected opinions of masses, and, accordingly, opinion-making becomes an accepted technique of power-holding and power-getting. The minority electorate of the propertied and the educated is replaced by the total suffrage—and intensive campaigns for the vote. The small eighteenth-century professional army is replaced by the mass army of conscripts—and by the problems of nationalist morale. The small shop is replaced by the mass-production industry—and the national advertisement.

As the scale of institutions has become larger and more centralized, so has the range and intensity of the opinion-makers' efforts. The means of opinion-making, in fact, have paralleled in range and efficiency the other institutions of greater scale that cradle the modern society of masses. Accordingly, in addition to their enlarged and centralized means of administration, exploitation, and violence, the modern elite have had placed within their grasp historically unique instruments of psychic management and manipulation, which include universal compulsory education as well as the media of mass communication.

Early observers believed that the increase in the range and volume of the formal means of communication would enlarge and animate the primary public. In such optimistic views—written before radio and television and movies—the formal media are understood as simply multiplying the scope and pace of personal discussion. Modern conditions, Charles Cooley wrote, 'enlarge indefinitely the competition of ideas, and whatever has owed its persistence merely to lack of comparison is likely to go, for that which is really congenial to the choosing mind will be all the more cherished and increased.'[6] Still excited by the break-up of the conventional consensus of the local community, he saw the new means of communication as furthering the conversational dynamic of classic democracy, and with it the growth of rational and free individuality.

No one really knows all the functions of the mass media, for in their entirety these functions are probably so pervasive and so subtle that they cannot be caught by the means of social research now available. But we do now have reason to believe that these media have helped less to enlarge and animate the discussions of primary publics than to transform them into a set of media markets in mass-like society. I do not refer merely to the higher ratio of deliverers of opinion to receivers and to the decreased chance to answer back; nor do I refer merely to the violent banalization and stereotyping of our very sense organs in terms of which these media now compete for 'attention.' I have in mind a sort of psychological illiteracy that is facilitated by the media, and that is expressed in several ways:

1. Very little of what we think we know of the social realities of the world have we found out first-hand. Most of 'the pictures in our heads' we have gained from these media—even to the point where we often do not really believe what we see before us until we read about it in the paper or hear about it on the radio.[7] The media not only give us information; they guide our very experiences. Our standards of credulity, our standards of reality, tend to be set by these media rather than by our own fragmentary experience.

Accordingly, even if the individual has direct, personal experience of events, it is not really direct and primary: it is organized in stereotypes. It takes long and skillful training to so uproot such stereotypes that an individual sees things freshly, in an unstereotyped manner. One might suppose, for example, that if all the people went through a depression they would all 'experience it,' and in terms of this experience, that they would all debunk or reject or at least refract what the media say about it. But experience of such a *structural* shift has to be organized and interpreted if it is to count in the making of opinion.

The kind of experience, in short, that might serve as a basis for resistance to mass media is not an experience of raw events, but the experience of meanings. The fleck of interpretation must be there in the experience if we are to use the word experience seriously. And the capacity for such experience is socially implanted. The individual does not trust his own experience, as I have said, until it is confirmed by others or by the media. Usually such direct exposure is not accepted if it disturbs loyalties and beliefs that the individual already holds. To be accepted, it must relieve or justify the feelings that often lie in the back of his mind as key features of his ideological loyalties.

Stereotypes of loyalty underlie beliefs and feelings about given symbols and emblems; they are the very ways in which men see the social world and in terms of which men make up their specific opinions and views of events. They are the results of previous experience, which affect present and future experience. It goes without saying that men are often unaware of these loyalties, that often they could not formulate them explicitly. Yet such general stereotypes make for the acceptance or the rejection of specific opinions not so much by the force of logical consistency as by their emotional affinity and by the way in which they relieve anxieties. To accept opinions in their terms is to gain the good solid feeling of being correct without having to think. When ideological stereotypes and specific opinions are linked in this way, there is a lowering of the kind of anxiety which arises when loyalty and belief are not in accord. Such ideologies lead to a willingness to accept a given line of belief; then there is no need, emotionally or rationally, to overcome resistance to given items in that line; cumulative selections of specific opinions and feelings become the pre-organized attitudes and emotions that shape the opinion-life of the person.

These deeper beliefs and feelings are a sort of lens through which men experience their worlds, they strongly condition acceptance or rejection of specific opinions, and they set men's orientation toward prevailing authorities. Three decades ago, Walter Lippmann saw such prior convictions as biases: they kept men from defining reality in an adequate way. They are still biases. But today they can often be seen as 'good biases'; inadequate and misleading as they often are, they are less so than the crackpot realism of the higher authorities and opinion-makers. They are the lower common sense and as such a factor of resistance. But we must recognize, especially when the pace of change is so deep and fast, that common sense is more often common than sense. And, above all, we must recognize that 'the common sense' of our children is going to be less the result of any firm social tradition than of the stereotypes carried by the mass media to which they are now so fully exposed. They are the first generation to be so exposed.

II. So long as the media are not entirely monopolized, the individual can play one medium off against another; he can compare them, and hence resist what any one of them puts out. The more genuine competition there is among the media, the more resistance the individual might be able to command. But how much is this now the case? *Do* people compare reports on public events or policies, playing one medium's content off against another's?

The answer is: generally no, very few do: (1) We know that people tend strongly to select those media which carry contents with which they already agree. There is a kind of selection of new opinions on the basis of prior opinions. No one seems to search out such counter-statements as may be found in alternative media offerings. Given radio programs and magazines and newspapers often get a rather consistent public, and thus reinforce their messages in the minds of that public. (2) This idea of playing one medium off against another assumes that the media really have varying contents. It assumes genuine competition, which is not widely true. The media display an apparent variety and competition, but on closer view they seem to compete more in terms of variations on a few standardized themes than of clashing issues.

The freedom to raise issues effectively seems more and more to be confined to those few interests that have ready and continual access to these media.

III. The media have not only filtered into our experience of external realities, they have also entered into our very experience of our own selves. They have provided us with new identities and new aspirations of what we should like to be, and what we should like to appear to be. They have provided in the models of conduct they hold out to us a new and larger and more flexible set of appraisals of our very selves. In terms of the modern theory of the self,[8] we may say that the media bring the reader, listener, viewer into the sight of larger, higher reference groups—groups, real or imagined, up-close or vicarious, personally known or distractedly glimpsed—which are looking glasses for his self-image. They have multiplied the groups to which we look for confirmation of our self-image.

More than that: (1) the media tell the man in the mass who he is—they give him identity; (2) they tell him what he wants to be—they give him aspirations; (3) they tell him how to get that way—they give him technique; and (4) they tell him how to feel that he is that way even when he is not—they give him escape. The gaps between the identity and aspiration lead to technique and/or to escape. That is probably the basic psychological formula of the mass media today. But, as a formula, it is not attuned to the development of the human being. It is the formula of a pseudoworld which the media invent and sustain.

IV. As they now generally prevail, the mass media, especially television, often encroach upon the small-scale discussion, and destroy the chance for the reasonable and leisurely and human interchange of opinion. They are an important cause of the destruction of privacy in its full human meaning. That is an important reason why they not only fail as an educational force, but are a malign force: they do not articulate for the viewer or listener the broader sources of his private tensions and anxieties, his inarticulate resentments and half-formed hopes. They neither enable the individual to transcend his narrow milieu nor clarify its private meaning.

The media provide much information and news about what is happening in the world, but they do not often enable the listener or the viewer truly to connect his daily life with these larger realities. They do not connect the information they provide on public issues with the troubles felt by the individual. They do not increase rational insight into tensions, either those in the individual or those of the society which are reflected in the individual. On the contrary, they distract him and obscure his chance to understand himself or his world, by fastening his attention upon artificial frenzies that are resolved within the program framework, usually by violent action or by what is called humor. In short, for the viewer they are not really resolved at all. The chief distracting tension of the media is between the wanting and the not having of commodities or of women held to be good looking. There is almost always the general tone of animated distraction, of suspended agitation, but it is going nowhere and it has nowhere to go.

But the media, as now organized and operated, are even more than a major cause of the transformation of America into a mass society. They are also among the most important of those increased means of power now at the disposal of elites of wealth and power; morever, some of the higher agents of these media are themselves either among the elites or very important among their servants.

Alongside or just below the elite, there is the propagandist, the publicity expert, the public-relations man, who would control the very formation of public opinion in order to be able to include it as one more pacified item in calculations of effective power, increased prestige, more secure wealth. Over the last quarter of a century, the attitudes of these manipulators toward their task have gone through a sort of dialectic:

In the beginning, there is great faith in what the mass media can do. Words win wars or sell soap; they move people, they restrain people. 'Only cost,' the advertising man of the 'twenties proclaims, 'limits the delivery of public opinion in any direction on any topic.'[9] The opinion-maker's belief in the media as mass persuaders almost amounts to magic—but he can believe mass communications omnipotent only so long as the public is trustful. It does not remain trustful. The mass media say so very many and such competitively exaggerated things; they banalize their message and they cancel one another out. The 'propaganda phobia,' in reaction to wartime lies and postwar disenchantment, does not help matters, even though memory is both short and subject to official distortion. This distrust of the magic of media is translated into a slogan among the opinion managers. Across their banners they write: 'Mass Persuasion Is Not Enough.'

Frustrated, they reason; and reasoning, they come to accept the principle of social context. To change opinion and activity, they say to one another, we must pay close attention to the full context and lives of the people to be managed. Along with mass persuasion, we must somehow use personal influence; we must reach people in their life context and *through* other people, their daily associates, those whom they trust: we must get at them by some kind of 'personal' persuasion. We must not show our hand directly; rather than merely advise or command, we must manipulate.

Now this live and immediate social context in which people live and which exerts a steady expectation upon them is of course what we have called the primary public. Anyone who has seen the inside of an advertising agency or public-relations office knows that the primary public is still the great unsolved problem of the opinion-makers. Negatively, their recognition of the influence of social context upon opinion and public activity implies that the articulate public resists and refracts the communications of the mass media. Positively, this recognition implies that the public is not composed of isolated individuals, but rather of persons who not only have prior opinions that must be reckoned with, but who continually influence each other in complex and intimate, in direct and continual ways.

In their attempts to neutralize or to turn to their own use the articulate public, the opinion-makers try to make it a relay network for their views. If the opinion-makers have so much power that they can act directly and openly upon the primary publics, they may become authoritative; but, if they do not have such power and hence have to operate indirectly and without visibility, they will assume the stance of manipulators.

Authority is power that is explicit and more or less 'voluntarily' obeyed; manipulation is the 'secret' exercise of power, unknown to those who are influenced. In the model of the classic democratic society, manipulation is not a problem, because formal authority resides in the public itself and in its representatives who are made or broken by the public. In the completely authoritarian society, manipulation is not a problem, because authority is openly identified with the ruling institutions and their agents, who may use authority explicitly and nakedly. They do not, in the extreme case, have to gain or retain power by hiding its exercise.

Manipulation becomes a problem wherever men have power that is concentrated and willful but do not have authority, or when, for any reason, they do not wish to use their power openly. Then the powerful seek to rule without showing their powerfulness. They want to rule, as it were, secretly, without publicized legitimation. It is in this mixed case—as in the intermediate reality of the American today—that manipulation is a prime way of exercising power. Small circles of men are making decisions which they need to have at least authorized by indifferent or recalcitrant people over whom they do not exercise explicit authority. So the small circle tries to manipulate these people into willing acceptance or cheerful support of their decisions or opinions—or at least to the rejection of possible counter-opinions.

Authority *formally* resides 'in the people,' but the power of initiation is in fact held by small circles of men. That is why the standard strategy of manipulation is to make it appear that the people, or at least a large group of them, 'really made the decision.' That is why even when the authority is available, men with access to it may still prefer the secret, quieter ways of manipulation.

But are not the people now more educated? Why not emphasize the spread of education rather than the increased effects of the mass media? The answer, in brief, is that mass education, in many respects, has become—another mass medium.

The prime task of public education, as it came widely to be understood in this country, was political: to make the citizen more knowledgeable and thus better able to think and to judge of public affairs. In time, the function of education shifted from the political to the economic: to train people for better-paying jobs and thus to get ahead. This is especially true of the high-school movement, which has met the business demands for white-collar skills at the public's expense. In large part education has become merely vocational; in so far as its political task is concerned, in many schools, that has been reduced to a routine training of nationalist loyalties.

The training of skills that are of more or less direct use in the vocational life is an important task to perform, but ought not to be mistaken for liberal education: job advancement, no matter on what levels, is not the same as self-development, although the two are now systematically confused.[10] Among 'skills,' some are more and some are less relevant to the aims of liberal—that is to say, liberating—education. Skills and values cannot be so easily separated as the academic search for supposedly neutral skills causes us to assume. And especially not when we speak seriously of liberal education. Of course, there is a scale, with skills at one end and values at the other, but it is the middle range of this scale, which one might call sensibilities, that are of most relevance to the classic public.

To train someone to operate a lathe or to read and write is pretty much education of skill; to evoke from people an understanding of what they really want out of their lives or to debate with them stoic, Christian and humanist ways of living, is pretty much a clear-cut education of values. But to assist in the birth among a group of people of those cultural and political and technical sensibilities which would make them genuine members of a genuinely liberal public, this is at once a training in skills and an education of values. It includes a sort of therapy in the ancient sense of clarifying one's knowledge of one's self; it includes the imparting of all those skills of controversy with one's self, which we call thinking; and with others, which we call debate. And the end product of such liberal education of sensibilities is simply the self-educating, self-cultivating man or woman.

The knowledgeable man in the genuine public is able to turn his personal troubles into social issues, to see their relevance for his community and his community's relevance for them. He understands that what he thinks and feels as personal troubles are very often not only that but problems shared by others and indeed not subject to solution by any one individual but only by modifications of the structure of the groups in which he lives and sometimes the structure of the entire society.

Men in masses are gripped by personal troubles, but they are not aware of their true meaning and source. Men in public confront issues, and they are aware of their terms. It is the task of the liberal institution, as of the liberally educated man, continually to translate troubles into issues and issues into the terms of their human meaning for the individual. In the absence of deep and wide political debate, schools for adults and adolescents could perhaps become hospitable frameworks for just such debate. In a community of publics the task of liberal education would be: to keep the public from being overwhelmed; to help produce the disciplined and informed mind that cannot be overwhelmed; to help develop the bold and sensible individual that cannot be sunk by the burdens of mass life. But educational practice has not made knowledge directly relevant to the human need of the troubled person of the twentieth century or to the social practices of the citizen. This citizen cannot now see the roots of his own biases and frustrations, nor think clearly about himself, nor for that matter about anything else. He does not see the frustration of idea, of intellect, by the present organization of society, and he is not able to meet the tasks now confronting 'the intelligent citizen.'

Educational institutions have not done these things and, except in rare instances, they are not doing them. They have become mere elevators of occupational and social ascent, and, on all levels, they have become politically timid. Moreover, in the hands of 'professional educators,' many schools have come to operate on an ideology of 'life adjustment' that encourages happy acceptance of mass ways of life rather than the struggle for individual and public transcendence.*

There is not much doubt that modern regressive educators have adapted their notions of educational content and practice to the idea of the mass. They do not effectively proclaim standards of cultural level and intellectual rigor; rather they often deal in the trivia of vocational tricks and 'adjustment to life'—meaning the

---

* If the schools are doing their job,' A. E. Bestor has written, 'we should expect educators to point to the significant and indisputable achievement in raising the intellectual level of the nation—measured perhaps by larger per capita circulation of books and serious magazines, by definitely improved taste in movies and radio programs, by higher standards of political debate, by increased respect for freedom of speech and of thought, by marked decline in such evidences of mental retardation as the incessant reading of comic books by adults.'[11]

slack life of masses. 'Democratic schools' often mean the further-
ance of intellectual mediocrity, vocational training, nationalistic
loyalties, and little else.

6

The structural trends of modern society and the manipulative
character of its communication technique come to a point of coincidence in the mass society, which is largely a metropolitan society.
The growth of the metropolis, segregating men and women into
narrowed routines and environments, causes them to lose any firm
sense of their integrity as a public. The members of publics in
smaller communities know each other more or less fully, because
they meet in the several aspects of the total life routine. The members of masses in a metropolitan society know one another only as
fractions in specialized milieux: the man who fixes the car, the
girl who serves your lunch, the saleslady, the women who take
care of your child at school during the day. Prejudgment and
stereotype flourish when people meet in such ways. The human
reality of others does not, cannot, come through.

People, we know, tend to select those formal media which confirm what they already believe and enjoy. In a parallel way, they
tend in the metropolitan segregation to come into live touch with
those whose opinions are similar to theirs. Others they tend to
treat unseriously. In the metropolitan society they develop, in
their defense, a blasé manner that reaches deeper than a manner.
They do not, accordingly, experience genuine clashes of viewpoint, genuine issues. And when they do, they tend to consider it
mere rudeness.

Sunk in their routines, they do not transcend, even by discussion, much less by action, their more or less narrow lives. They do
not gain a view of the structure of their society and of their role
as a public within it. The city is a structure composed of such little
environments, and the people in them tend to be detached from
one another. The 'stimulating variety' of the city does not stimulate the men and women of 'the bedroom belt,' the one-class suburbs, who can go through life knowing only their own kind. If they
do reach for one another, they do so only through stereotypes
and prejudiced images of the creatures of other milieux. Each
is trapped by his confining circle; each is cut off from easily identi-

fiable groups. It is for people in such narrow milieux that the mass media can create a pseudo-world beyond, and a pseudo-world within themselves as well.

Publics live in milieux but they can transcend them—individually by intellectual effort; socially by public action. By reflection and debate and by organized action, a community of publics comes to feel itself and comes in fact to be active at points of structural relevance.

But members of a mass exist in milieux and cannot get out of them, either by mind or by activity, except—in the extreme case—under 'the organized spontaneity' of the bureaucrat on a motor-cycle. We have not yet reached the extreme case, but observing metropolitan man in the American mass we can surely see the psychological preparations for it.

We may think of it in this way: When a handful of men do not have jobs, and do not seek work, we look for the causes in their immediate situation and character. But when twelve million men are unemployed, then we cannot believe that all of them suddenly 'got lazy' and turned out to be 'no good.' Economists call this 'structural unemployment'—meaning, for one thing, that the men involved cannot themselves control their job chances. Structural unemployment does not originate in one factory or in one town, nor is it due to anything that one factory or one town does or fails to do. Moreover, there is little or nothing that one ordinary man in one factory in one town can do about it when it sweeps over his personal milieu.

Now, this distinction, between social structure and personal milieu, is one of the most important available in the sociological studies. It offers us a ready understanding of the position of 'the public' in America today. In every major area of life, the loss of a sense of structure and the submergence into powerless milieux is the cardinal fact. In the military it is most obvious, for here the roles men play are strictly confining; only the command posts at the top afford a view of the structure of the whole, and moreover, this view is a closely guarded official secret. In the division of labor too, the jobs men enact in the economic hierarchies are also more or less narrow milieux and the positions from which a view of the production process as a whole can be had are centralized, as men are alienated not only from the product and the tools of their labor, but from any understanding of the structure and the processes of production. In the political order, in the fragmentation of the lower and in the distracting proliferation of the middle-level organization, men cannot see the whole, cannot see the top, and cannot state the issues that will in fact determine the whole structure in which they live and their place within it.

This loss of any structural view or position is the decisive meaning of the lament over the loss of community. In the great city, the division of milieux and of segregating routines reaches the point of closest contact with the individual and the family, for, although the city is not the unit of prime decision, even the city cannot be seen as a total structure by most of its citizens.

On the one hand, there is the increased scale and centralization of the structure of decision; and, on the other, the increasingly narrow sorting out of men into milieux. From both sides, there is the increased dependence upon the formal media of communication, including those of education itself. But the man in the mass does not gain a transcending view from these media; instead he gets his experience stereotyped, and then he gets sunk further by that experience. He cannot detach himself in order to observe, much less to evaluate, what he is experiencing, much less what he is not experiencing. Rather than that internal discussion we call reflection, he is accompanied through his life-experience with a sort of unconscious, echoing monologue. He has no projects of his own: he fulfills the routines that exist. He does not transcend whatever he is at any moment, because he does not, he cannot, transcend his daily milieux. He is not truly aware of his own daily experience and of its actual standards: he drifts, he fulfills habits, his behavior a result of a planless mixture of the confused standards and the uncriticized expectations that he has taken over from others whom he no longer really knows or trusts, if indeed he ever really did.

He takes things for granted, he makes the best of them, he tries to look ahead—a year or two perhaps, or even longer if he has children or a mortgage—but he does not seriously ask, What do I want? How can I get it? A vague optimism suffuses and sustains him, broken occasionally by little miseries and disappointments that are soon buried. He is smug, from the standpoint of those who think something might be the matter with the mass style of life in the metropolitan frenzy where self-making is an externally busy branch of industry. By what standards does he judge himself and his efforts? What is really important to him? Where are the models of excellence for this man?

He loses his independence, and more importantly, he loses the desire to be independent: in fact, he does not have hold of the idea of being an independent individual with his own mind and his own worked-out way of life. It is not that he likes or does not like this life; it is that the question does not come up sharp and clear so he is not bitter and he is not sweet about conditions and events. He thinks he wants merely to get his share of what is around with as little trouble as he can and with as much fun as possible.

Such order and movement as his life possesses is in conformity with external routines; otherwise his day-to-day experience is a vague chaos—although he often does not know it because, strictly speaking, he does not truly possess or observe his own experience. He does not formulate his desires; they are insinuated into him. And, in the mass, he loses the self-confidence of the human being —if indeed he has ever had it. For life in a society of masses implants insecurity and furthers impotence; it makes men uneasy and vaguely anxious; it isolates the individual from the solid group; it destroys firm group standards. Acting without goals, the man in the mass just feels pointless.

The idea of a mass society suggests the idea of an elite of power. The idea of the public, in contrast, suggests the liberal tradition of a society without any power elite, or at any rate with shifting elites of no sovereign consequence. For, if a genuine public is sovereign, it needs no master; but the masses, in their full development, are sovereign only in some plebiscitarian moment of adulation to an elite as authoritative celebrity. The political structure of a democratic state requires the public; and, the democratic man, in his rhetoric, must assert that this public is the very seat of sovereignty.

But now, given all those forces that have enlarged and centralized the political order and made modern societies less political and more administrative; given the transformation of the old middle classes into something which perhaps should not even be called middle class; given all the mass communications that do not truly communicate; given all the metropolitan segregation that is not community; given the absence of voluntary associations that really connect the public at large with the centers of power—what is happening is the decline of a set of publics that is sovereign only in the most formal and rhetorical sense. Moreover, in many countries the remnants of such publics as remain are now being frightened out of existence. They lose their will for rationally considered decision and action because they do not possess the instruments for such decision and action; they lose their sense of political belonging because they do not belong; they lose their political will because they see no way to realize it.

The top of modern American society is increasingly unified, and often seems willfully co-ordinated: at the top there has emerged an elite of power. The middle levels are a drifting set of stalemated, balancing forces: the middle does not link the bottom with the top. The bottom of this society is politically fragmented, and even as a passive fact, increasingly powerless: at the bottom there is emerging a mass society.

14

The Conservative Mood

IF we are to suppose that modern America ought to be a democratic society, we must look to the intellectual community for knowledge of the power elite and of their decisions. For democracy implies that those who bear the consequences of decisions have enough knowledge—not to speak of power—to hold the decision-makers accountable. Everyone must depend upon knowledge provided by others, for no man can know by his own experience more than a small portion of the social worlds that now affect him. Most of our experience is indirect and, as we have seen, subject to much distortion. The opinion-makers of every age have provided images of the elite of their time and place. Like the realities they are supposed to represent, these images change; in our own immediate time, in fact, many old images have been revised and many new ones invented.

Of late, this work has occurred less as an effort to know reality better than to serve a strangely conservative mood that has come to prevail among the image-makers. The images they now offer us are not those of an elite in irresponsible command of unprecedented means of power and manipulation, but of a scatter of reasonable men overwhelmed by events and doing their best in a difficult situation. The mood out of which these images have arisen serves less to justify the real power of the real elite, or the intelligence of its decisions, than to sustain their spokesmen. The images we are expected to take most seriously are either irrelevant to the facts of power and of the power elite or they are simply private fantasies serving more as emotional cushions for small

coteries of comfortable writers, paid and unpaid, than as a dia-
gram of all those forces which in our time come to such obvious
climax in the American power elite.

Yet scholars, knowingly and unknowingly, have been seeking
suitable ideas about this elite. They have not found them and they
have not managed to create them. What they have found is an
absence of mind and of morality in the public life of our times,
and what they have managed to create is a mere elaboration of
their own conservative mood. It is a mood quite appropriate to
men living in a material boom, a nationalist celebration, a political vacuum. At its heart there is a knowledge of powerlessness
without poignancy, and a feeling of pseudo-power based on mere
smugness. By its softening of the political will, this mood enables
men to accept public depravity without any private sense of out-
rage, and to give up the central goal of western humanism, so
strongly felt in nineteenth-century American experience: the presumptuous control by reason of man's fate.

1

Those who grope for ideologies with which to explain their
conservative mood would anchor this mood—as well as themselves
—in some solid tradition. They feel that they have somehow been
tricked by liberalism, progressivism, radicalism, and they are a
little frightened. What many of them want, it would seem, is a
society of classic conservatism.

Conservatism in its classic form is of course traditionalism
become self-conscious and elaborated, argumentative and ration-
alized.[1] It also involves some 'natural aristocracy.' Sooner or later
all those who relax the grand tension of human rationality must
take up the neo-Burkeian defense of a traditional elite, for in the
end, such an elite is the major premise of a genuinely conservative
ideology.

The more explicit—and hence the less successful—attempts to
find or to invent a traditional elite for America today seem upon
examination to be merely hopeful assertions, and as little relevant
to modern realities as they are usable guides to political conduct.
The conservative—Mr. Russell Kirk tells us—believes that (1)
'divine intent rules society,' man being incapable of grasping by
his reason the great forces that prevail. Accordingly, change must

be slow, for 'Providence is the proper instrument for change,' and the test of a statesman is his 'cognizance of the real tendency of Providential social forces.' The conservative (2) has an affection for 'the variety and mystery of traditional life,' perhaps most of all because he believes that 'tradition and sound prejudice' check man's presumptuous will and archaic impulse. Moreover (3), 'Society longs for leadership,' and the conservative holds that there are 'natural distinctions' among men which form a natural order of classes and powers.[2]

Tradition is sacred; through it the real social tendencies of Providence are displayed; therefore, tradition must be our guide. Whatever is traditional represents the accumulated wisdom of the ages, and more: it exists by 'divine intent.'

Naturally we must ask how we are to know which traditions are instruments of Providence? Which of the events and changes all around us are by divine intent? At what moment did the highly conscious contrivances of the Founding Fathers become traditional and thus sanctified? And must one believe that society in the United States—before the progressive movement and before the New Deal reforms—represented anything akin to what the classic conservative would call orders and classes based on 'natural distinctions'? If not, then what and where is the model which the classic conservative would have us cherish? And do those who now man the political and economic institutions of the United States represent the Providential intent which is sought? And how are we to know if they do or do not?

The conservative defends the irrationality of tradition against the powers of human reason; he denies the legitimacy of man's attempt individually to control his own fate and collectively to build his own world. How then can he bring in reason as a means of choosing among traditions and men, as a means of deciding which changes are Providential and which are evil forces? He cannot provide any rational guide in our choice of which leaders grasp Providence and act it out and which are reformers and levelers. There is within this view no guide-line to help us decide which contenders for this natural distinction are genuine.

And yet the answer, although not always clear, is always there: if we do not destroy the natural order of classes and the hierarchy of powers, we shall have superiors and leaders to tell us. If we uphold these natural distinctions, and in fact resuscitate older ones, the leaders will decide. In the end, the classic conservative is left with this single principle: the principle of gratefully accepting the leadership of some set of men whom he considers a sanctified elite. If such men were there for all to recognize, then the conservative could at least be socially clear. Then the yearning for a classic tradition and a conservative hierarchy could be satisfied. For they would be visibly anchored in the authority of an aristocracy, and this aristocracy would be tangible to the senses as the very model of private conduct and public decision.

It is just here that American publicists of the conservative mood have become embarrassed and confused. Their embarrassment is in part due to a fear of confronting the all-pervading liberal rhetoric; their confusion is mainly due to two simple facts about the American upper classes in general, and the higher circles of power in particular:

Those who are on high are not suitable as models of conservative excellence. Nor do they themselves uphold any ideology truly suitable for public use.

The very rich in America have been culturally among the very poor; the only kinds of experience for which they have been models are the material ones of money-getting and money-keeping. Material success is their sole basis of authority. One might, of course, be nostalgic for the old families and their last resorts, but such images are not generally supposed to count for much, being more of a tinsel past than of the serious present. Alongside the old rich and supplanting them are the synthetic celebrities of national glamour who often make a virtue out of cultural poverty and political illiteracy. By their very nature the professional celebrities are transient figures of the mass means of distraction rather than people who carry the prestige of authority because they embody the continuity of tradition. And of the new rich, the big rich of Texas are too unsophisticated, and the corporate rich too much involved in what we shall call the higher immorality. As for the chief executives of the corporations, ideologies—conservative or otherwise—are much too fancy for them: besides, their hired men can and do talk easily in the liberal patter—why then should they take on the burden of conservative principles? Furthermore, is it not virtually a condition of success in the American political economy that one learn to use, and use frequently, the liberal rhetoric which is the common denominator of all proper and successful spokesmanship?[3]

There are, accordingly, no highly placed social figures whom conservative scholars might celebrate as models of excellence, who stand in contrast with the liberal confusion they would deplore, and who are ready, able, and eager to adopt new conservative creeds. There are no pre-capitalist, pre-liberal elites which they can draw upon, even in fond remembrance; they cannot, as European writers have been able to do, contrast such holdovers from feudalism, however modified, with the vulgarity of the successful of capitalist society.

Consequently, the greatest problem of the spokesmen for an American conservatism is simply to locate the set of people whose interests the conservative ideology would serve, and who, in turn, would accept it. Classic conservativism has required the spell of tradition among such surviving elements of pre-industrial societies as an aristocracy of noble men, a peasantry, a petty-bourgeoisie with guild inheritances; and these are precisely what America has never had. For in America, the bourgeoisie has been predominant from its beginnings—in class, in status, and in power. In America, there has not been and there can be no conservative ideology of the classic type.

The high and the mighty in America espouse no acceptable conservative ideas and actually abhor conservative rhetoric. In so far as one can find a clue to the basic impulse of conservative spokesmen, it is the attempt to sacrifice politics as an autonomous sphere of men's will to the free and arbitrary dominance of corporate institutions and their key personnel. They have no connection with those fountainheads of modern conservative thought with which many American intellectuals have been so hopefully seeking to associate them. Neither Burke nor Locke is the source of such ideology as the American elite have found truly congenial. Their ideological source is Horatio Alger.[4] The maxims of work-and-win, of strive-and-succeed have sustained them in their noble game of grab. They have not elaborated such awareness of their newer power into any conscious ideology. They have not had to confront any opposition based upon ideas that stand in challenging contrast to the liberal rhetoric which they too employ as standard public relations. Perhaps it is easiest to be 'conservative' when there is no true sense of the conservative present as one alternative to what the future might be. If one cannot say that American conservatism, as represented by men of wealth and power, is unconsciousness, certainly conservatives are often happily unconscious.

Accordingly, even less than the radical writers of the 'thirties have conservative writers of the 'forties and 'fifties been in close touch with the leaders or policy-makers they would influence or justify.[5] On the right and in the center, public relations fills any need for 'ideology,' and public relations are something you hire. Just now, the elite of wealth and power do not feel in need of any ideology, much less an ideology of classic conservatism.

Yet, despite this, one may go ahead and defend the American elite and the upper classes in general and the system within which they are successful. This is no longer so popular among writers who are neither hired publicists nor academic hacks, although every little tendency or chance to follow it is promptly seized upon by those who are. Moreover, notions of trusteeship are still well received, especially among the chief executives of the corporate world, and every week by poll and by chart it is conclusively proved that the American economy is the very best in the world. Such an explicit defense, however, does not satisfy those who yearn for classic conservatism; to be useful, such defense must make out the elite as dynamic and hence no anchor for tradition. On the contrary, the capitalist elite must always be composed of self-making men who smash tradition to rise to the top by strictly personal accomplishments.

2

If classic conservatism, anchored in a recognized elite, is not quite possible today in America, that does not mean that scholars with conservative yearnings have not found other ways to realize themselves. In their need for an aristocracy, they often become grandly vague about the aristocrat. Generalizing the notion, they make it moral rather than socially firm and specific. In the name of 'genuine democracy' or 'liberal conservatism' they stretch the meaning of aristocracy—the 'natural aristocracy' has nothing to do with existing social orders, classes, or hierarchies of power; the aristocracy becomes a scatter of morally superior persons rather than a socially recognizable class. Such notions are now quite popular, for they satisfy the conservative mood without requiring allegiance to the current crop of 'aristocrats.' So it is with Ortega y Gasset and so it is with Peter Viereck. The latter, for example, writes that it is not 'the aristocratic class' that is valuable but 'the aristocratic spirit'—which, with its decorum and *noblesse oblige,* is 'open to all, regardless of class.'[6] Some have tried to find a way to hold onto such a view, almost secretly, not stating it directly, but holding it as a latent assumption while talking about, not the elite, but 'the mass.' That, however, is dangerous, for again, it goes against the liberal rhetoric which requires a continual flattery of the citizens.

Generalizing the aristocratic ethos and emptying it of social content are not really satisfactory because they provide no widely accepted criteria for judging who is elite and who is not. A self-selecting elite can be no anchor. Moreover, such a generalization does not have to do with the existing facts of power and hence is politically irrelevant.

Both outright defense of those who are ascendant within the *status quo,* and defense of an imaginary aristocratic ethos, in fact, end up not with an elite that is fixed in tradition and hierarchy, but with a dynamic and ever-changing elite continually struggling to the top in an expanding society. There is simply no socially, much less politically, recognized traditional elite and there is no tradition that can be imaginatively elaborated around such an elite. Moreover, whatever else it may be, tradition is something one cannot create; one can only uphold it when it exists. There is today no magic spell of unbroken tradition upon which modern society is or can be steadily based. Accordingly, greatness cannot be confused with mere duration, nor the competition of values decided by an endurance contest.

3

But the conservative mood is strong, almost as strong as the pervasive liberal rhetoric, and there is a way to satisfy them both. One refuses to recognize and confront the top as it is, and one refuses to imagine a more defensible one. One simply denies that there is any elite or even any upper class, or at any rate asserts that in so far as such exist they do not really count in the American way of life. If this can be held firmly to be the case, then one can indulge the conservative mood without having to associate it with the actual elite or with any imaginary aristocracy.

When they write of the upper classes, conservatives of the painless school of liberalism often confuse wishful image with reality. Either they tend to relegate the elite to the past or they diversify its elements in the present. In the nineteenth century, leaning into the future, liberals relegated the elite to the past; in the twentieth century, being heavy with the insistent present, they have considered elites to be diversified to the point of powerlessness.* So far as power is concerned, nobody really makes the decisions; let us fall back upon official and formal images of representative government. So far as wealth or high income is concerned, that is after all without decisive consequence, although perhaps it does affect the tone of society at large. Besides, everybody in America is rich nowadays. This unserious liberalism is the nerve-center of the present-day conservative mood.

Perhaps nothing is of more importance, both as cause and as effect, to the conservative mood than the rhetorical victory and the intellectual and political collapse of American liberalism. It is of course obvious that the kind of 'liberalism' that prevailed in the 'thirties has lost the political initiative in the postwar era. In the economic boom and the military terror of this era, a small group of political primitives, on the middle levels of power, have exploited the new American jitters, emptied domestic politics of rational content, and decisively lowered the level of public sensi-bility. They have attacked the policies of the New and Fair Deals; tried to rewrite the history of these administrations; and impugned the very biographies of those who took part in them. They have done all this in a manner that reveals clearly their appeal to the rankling status resentment of those newly prosperous classes which, having achieved considerable wealth during and after World War II, have not received the prestige or gained the power they have felt to be their due.**

The petty right have appealed less to the economically discon-

---

* I have already presented and analyzed this romantic pluralism. See above ELEVEN: The Theory of Balance.

** See above, TWO: Local Society.

tented than to the status frustrated. They have done so by attack-
ing the symbols, the men, and the institutions of established
prestige.[7] At the very beginning of their push, they almost succeeded in destroying one of the inner citadels of the old upper
class—the Foreign Service—and at one high point of their drive,
their leading member, having told off an army general, enabled
a nation-wide public to witness the Secretary of the Army, who
was also a man of older family wealth, being disgraced in a public
brawl with unestablished nihilists.

They have brought to wide attention a new conception of national loyalty, as loyalty to individual gangs who placed themselves above the established legitimations of the state and invited
its personnel to do likewise. They have made clear the central
place now achieved in the governmental process by secret police
and secret 'investigations,' to the point where observant men
speak realistically of a shadow cabinet based in considerable part
upon new ways of power which include the wire tap, the private
eye, the use and threat of blackmail. They have dramatized the
hollowing out of sensibility among a population which for a generation has been steadily and increasingly subjected to the
shrill trivialization of the mass means of entertainment and distraction. They have brought into public view the higher immorality as well as the mindlessness of selected upper and middle circles. And they have revealed a decayed and frightened liberalism
weakly defending itself from the insecure and ruthless fury of
political gangsters.

As the liberalism-of-the-'thirties sat in its postwar hearing, liberals became aware, from time to time, of how near they were to
the edge of mindlessness. The status edifice of established
bourgeois society was under attack, but since in America there is
nothing from the past above that edifice, and since those of once
liberal and left persuasion see nothing in the future below it, they
have become terribly frightened by the viciousness of the attack,
and their political lives have been narrowed to the sharp edge
of defensive anxiety.

Postwar liberalism has been organizationally impoverished: the
prewar years of liberalism-in-power devitalized independent liberal groups, drying up the grass roots, making older leaders dependent upon the federal center and not training new leaders

round the country. The New Deal left no liberal organization to carry on any liberal program; rather than a new party, its instrument was a loose coalition inside an old one, which quickly fell apart so far as liberal ideas are concerned. Moreover, the New Deal used up the heritage of liberal ideas, made them banal as it put them into law; turned liberalism into a set of administrative routines to defend rather than a program to fight for.[8]

In their moral fright, postwar liberals have not defended any left or even any militantly liberal position: their defensive posture has, first of all, led them to celebrate the 'civil liberties,' in contrast with their absence from Soviet Russia. In fact, many have been so busy celebrating the civil liberties that they have had less time to defend them; and, more importantly, most have been so busy defending civil liberties that they have had neither the time nor the inclination to *use* them. 'In the old days,' Archibald MacLeish remarked at the end of the 'forties, freedom 'was something you used . . . [it] has now become something you save—something you put away and protect like your other possessions—like a deed or a bond in a bank.'[9]

It is much safer to celebrate civil liberties than to defend them; it is much safer to defend them as a formal right than to use them in a politically effective way. Even those who would most willingly subvert these liberties usually do so in their very name. It is easier still to defend someone else's right to have used them years ago than to have something yourself to say *now* and to say it now forcibly. The defense of civil liberties—even of their practice a decade ago—has become the major concern of many liberal and once leftward scholars. All of which is a safe way of diverting intellectual effort from the sphere of political reflection and demand.

The defensive posture of the postwar liberals has also involved them in the very nervous center of elite and plebeian anxieties about the position of America in the world today. At the root of these anxieties is not simply international tension and the terrible, helpless feeling of many that there is no alternative to another war. There is also a specific worry with which many Americans are seriously concerned. The United States is now engaged with other nations, in particular Russia, in a full-scale competition for cultural prestige based on nationality. In this competition, at issue are American music, literature, and art and, in a somewhat higher meaning than is usually given the term, The American Way of Life. The economic, military and political power of the United States greatly exceeds its cultural spell. What America has abroad is power; what it does not have at home or abroad is cultural prestige. This fact has led many liberals into the new American celebration,[10] which rests not only upon their felt need to defend themselves in nationalist terms against the petty right but also upon the urgent compulsion to uphold the cultural prestige of America abroad.

But the defensive posture and the organizational impoverishment are not the full story of what has happened to make American liberalism painless to the rich and the powerful. Over the past half century, liberalism has been undergoing a moral and intellectual decline of serious proportion. As a proclamation of *ideals,* classic liberalism, like classic socialism, remains part of the secular tradition of the western society. But as a *rhetoric,* liberalism's key terms have become the common denominators of the political vocabulary; in this rhetorical victory, in which the most divergent positions are all proclaimed and defended in the same liberal terms, liberalism has been stretched beyond any usefulness as a way of defining issues and stating policies.

The great range and variety of life in America does not include a great range and variety of political statement, much less of political alternative. In their rhetoric, spokesmen of all interests share much more than they differ. Although only the liberals are captured by it, all of them use the liberal rhetoric. The stereotype of America as essentially a progressive and even a radical country finds its anchorage only in its technological sphere,* and in strange ways, in the fashions of its entertainment and amusement industries. These have been so 'dynamic' and 'radical' that they have led to the characteristic American trait of animated distraction. These two surface areas of life have often been misinterpreted, at home and abroad, as America the dynamic and progressive, instead of what is the fact: America is a conservative country without any conservative ideology. The intellectual slackness of its political life is such that it does very well with the liberal rhetoric.

* I do not mean to imply that the United States *does* lead in technological ingenuity; in fact, I believe that its products generally do not compare in design or in quality with those of Germany and England.

If, as a rhetoric, liberalism has become a mask of all political positions, as a theory of society it has become irrelevant, and in its optative mood, misleading. No revision of liberalism as a *theory* of the mechanics of modern social change has overcome the trademark of the nineteenth century that is stamped upon it. Liberalism as a social theory rests on the notion of a society in automatic balance.[11]

The idea of the great balance, in all its various forms, is now the prevailing common-sense view of public affairs. It is also the theory of power held by most academic social scientists; and it is the resting place of the conservative mood, as sustained by the liberal intelligentsia. This mood cannot be articulated as classic conservatism; it cannot rest upon a pre-capitalist, much less upon a pre-industrial, base; and it cannot employ the image of a society in which authority is legitimated by traditionalism as interpreted by a recognized aristocracy.

As an intellectual articulation, the conservative mood is merely a reformulation of classic liberalism in the entirely unclassical age of the twentieth century; it is the image of a society in which authority is at a minimum because it is guided by the autonomous forces of the magic market. The 'providence' of classic conservatism becomes liberalism's generalization of the 'unseen hand' of the market, for, in secular guise, Providence refers to a faith that the unintended consequences of many wills form a pattern, and that this pattern ought to be allowed to work itself out. Accordingly, it can be said that there is no elite, that there is no ruling class, that there are no powerful centers which need defense. Instead of justifying the power of an elite by portraying it favorably, one denies that any set of men, any class, any organization has any really consequential power. American liberalism is thus readily made to sustain the conservative mood. It is, in fact, because of the dominance of such liberal terms and assumptions that no need is felt by the elite of power and wealth for an explicitly conservative ideology.

4

The greatest appeal of romantic pluralism* to those of conservative yearning is that it makes unnecessary any explicit justi-

* See above, ELEVEN: The Theory of Balance.

fication of the men who are ostensibly in charge of public affairs. For if they are all in balance, each of them really quite impotent, then no one set of higher circles and no manageable set of institutional arrangements can be held accountable for the events and decisions of our time. Therefore, all serious political effort is really a delusion which sensible men may observe with interest but which they certainly do not allow to engage them morally.

That is the political meaning of the conservative mood of today; in the end, it is an irresponsible style of pretentious smugness. Curiously enough, for a conservative mood, it is not a snobbery linked with nostalgia, but, on the contrary, with what is just one-step-ahead-of-the-very-latest-thing, which is to say that it is a snobbery based not on tradition but on fashion and fad.[12] Those involved are not thinking for a nation, or even about a nation; they are thinking of and for themselves. In self-selected coteries, they confirm one another's mood, which thus becomes snobbishly closed—and quite out of the main stream of the practice of decision and the reality of power.

One may thus suppose, quite correctly, that the conservative mood is a playful little fashion toyed with in a period of material prosperity by a few comfortable writers. Certainly it is not a serious effort to work out a coherent view of the world in which we live and the demands we might make upon it as political men—conservative, liberal or radical. Neither an intellectual community nor a set of liberal publics is providing the terms of those issues and conflicts, decisions and policies that make up the history of our time. The combination of the liberal rhetoric and the conservative mood, in fact, has obfuscated hard issues and made possible historical development without benefit of idea. The prevalence of this mood and this rhetoric means that thought, in any wide meaning of the term, has become largely irrelevant to such politics as have been visible, and that in postwar America mind has been divorced from reality.

The petty conservatives, of course, have no more won political power than administrative liberals have retained it. While these two camps have been engaged in wordy battle on the middle levels of power, on the upper levels, less noisy and more sophisticated conservatives have assumed political power. Accordingly, in their imbroglio with the noisy right, liberal and once-left forces have in effect defended these established conservatives, even as they have been absorbed by conflict with their own leftward pasts, and have lost any point of effective defense against the outrageous accusations of the petty right. The elite of corporation, army, and state have benefited politically and economically and militarily by the antics of the petty right, who have become, often unwittingly, their political shocktroops.

It is in this context of material prosperity, with the demagogic right setting the tone of public sensibility; the more sophisticated conservatives silently achieving established power in a largely undebated victory; with liberal ideas made official in the 'thirties, now stolen and banalized by·alien use; with liberal hopes carefully adjusted to mere rhetoric by thirty years of rhetorical victory; with radicalism deflated and radical hope stoned to death by thirty years of defeat—it is in this context that the conservative mood has set in among the observant scholars. Among them there is no demand and no dissent, and no opposition to the monstrous decisions that are being made without deep or widespread debate, in fact with no debate at all. There is no opposition to the undemocratically impudent manner in which policies of high military and civilian authority are simply turned out as facts accomplished. There is no opposition to public mindlessness in all its forms nor to all those forces and men that would further it. But above all— among the men of knowledge there is little or no opposition to the divorce of knowledge from power, of sensibilities from men of power, no opposition to the divorce of mind from reality.* Contemporary men of power, accordingly, are able to command without any ideological cloak, political decisions occur without benefit of political discussion or political ideas, and the higher circles of America have come to be the embodiment of the American system of organized irresponsibility.

5

It should not be supposed that such few and small publics as still exist, or even the American masses, share the conservative mood of the intellectuals. But neither should it be supposed that they have firmly in mind adequate images of the American elite. Their images are ambiguous; they are mainly in terms of status

* See below, FIFTEEN: The Higher Immorality.

and wealth rather than of power; and they are quite moral in a politically petty way.

Moral distrust of the high and mighty is of course an old American custom. Sometimes, as during the 'thirties, it is primarily of the corporate rich—then called economic royalists; sometimes, as between wars, of admirals and generals; and, all the time it is, at least a little bit, of the politicians.

One must, of course, discount the wonderful make-believe and easy accusation of campaign oratory. And yet, the rather persistent attention paid to such matters as 'corruption' in business and government expresses a widespread concern with public morality and personal integrity in high places, and signifies that it has been an underlying worry in almost every area of American life.

These areas include military and political as well as directly economic institutions; they include the elite as the heads of these major institutions as well as the elite as a set of private individuals. Many little disclosures, spurring the moral worry of those still capable of such concern, have indicated how widespread public immorality might be.*

* A few years ago at West Point—center of the higher military life in America—some of the carefully selected young men were caught cheating to get by examinations. In other schools of higher learning college men have played dishonest basketball at the moneyed requests of crooked gamblers. In New York City, girls from quite respectable homes have been bought, for a few hundred dollars, by holidaying corporate executives from playboys of very rich families in the business of procuring. In Washington, as well as in other major cities, men in high places have accepted bribes and yielded to pull. By September 1954, some 1400 cases of windfall profits, appropriated during the later 'forties, had been turned up: corporations that had built for or invested in the Federal Housing Administration's rental housing got mortgages for more than the cost of the building, pocketing the difference, which came to hundreds of millions.[13] Government officials and business contractors, as well as party girls—three for $400—and paid-for fishing trips were part of the operating procedure. During the late war, of course, anyone with smart money and the right connections could have all the black-market meat and gasoline he cared for. And in one recent Presidential campaign, public distrust reached a shrill and cynical tone, when, in an unprecedented gesture, each of the leading candidates for the highest offices in the land felt it necessary to make public an accounting of his personal income.

In illegal enterprises, the small investment with the quick, fantastic return flourishes. Dozens of such industries flourish in the boomtown flush of the post-Korean crime increase. The world bankers have formed an association to fight the rise of embezzlement: 'Put bluntly,' reports *The New York Times*, 'more people are stealing more money from banks.'[14] Narcotics and hijacking, embezzlements and counterfeiting, tax cheating and shoplifting—all have paid off handsomely.

Put bluntly, crime, if organized on a proper business-like basis, pays. American gangsters, we now know, are the specialized personnel of nationwide businesses, having syndicated connections with one another and with local public authorities. But more important than the fact that illegal businesses are now well-organized industries is the fact that the 'hoods' of the 'twenties have in the 'forties and 'fifties become businessmen who own hotels and distilleries, resorts and trucking companies. Among such members of the fraternity of success, to have a police record means merely that you did not know the right people.[15]

Organized crime in the underworld raises to an extreme the individualistic philosophy of predatory success, the indifference to the public weal, the fetish of the profit motive and of the laissez-faire state. As an integral part of American culture, the 'underworld . . . serves to meet demands for goods and services which are defined as illegitimate, but for which there is nevertheless a strong demand from respectable people . . . It is implicit in our economic, political, legal and social organization . . . It is in this sense that we have the criminals we deserve.'[16]

For the New Jersey banker, Harold G. Hoffman, crime paid. He became mayor, Congressman, Governor of his state; only upon his death in 1954 was it discovered that for over a decade he had gotten away with $300,000 of state funds and in addition, in the morality play of state politics, had been deep in a network of corruption involving respected banks, insurance companies and highly placed individuals. Army Px's have sold 'such unmilitary items as mink coats and expensive jewelry' at prices well below retail levels. Charities have been discovered to be rackets for private profit. Eighteen persons and seven corporations were indicted in February 1954 on charges of defrauding the government in surplus ship deals, among them Julius C. Holmes, former Minister in the United States embassy in London and special assistant to the Secretary of State. Czars of local labor unions have enriched themselves by extortion and shakedown, by bribery and the union welfare fund. Respected administrators of private hospitals have bought aspirin in wholesale lots for $9.83, selling it to patients for $600. Major General Roderick Allen in March 1954 caused $1,200 of army money to be spent on a dog house for his Siberian Huskies. Those who read business manuals, in addition to newspapers, know that, by 1954, some 214 internal revenue employees and friends of the middle 'forties had been indicted, 100 convicted—including the head tax-collector of the Federal government.[17] And all over the country, upper-middle and upper-class tax dodgers personally treat each spring as an invitation to a game of ingenious lying and skillful deception. Revelations from the upper depths reached some sort of climax during the spring of 1954 when the Secretary of the

What element of the higher circles—what would-be element—
has such immorality not touched? Perhaps all those cases that
come briefly to public attention are but marginal—or, at any rate,
those that were caught. But then, there is the feeling that the
bigger you are, the less likely you are to be caught. There is the
feeling that all the petty cases seem to signify something grander,
that they go deeper and that their roots are now well organized in
the higher and middle American ways of life. But among the mass
distractions this feeling soon passes harmlessly away. For the
American distrust of the high and mighty is a distrust without
doctrine and without political focus; it is a distrust felt by the
mass public as a series of more or less cynically expected disclosures. Corruption and immoralities, petty and grand, are facts
about the higher circles, often even characteristic facts about many
of them. But the immoral tone of American society today also involves the lack of public sensibility when confronted with these
facts. Effective moral indignation is not evoked by the corrupt
public life of our time; the old middle-class moralities have been
replaced in America by the higher immorality.

The exploiting plutocrat and the corrupted machine of the
'nineties were replaced in public imagery by the uncultivated
philistine and provincial of the 'twenties, who, in turn, were replaced by the economic royalists and their cohorts of the 'thirties.
All these were negative images; the first of urban greed as seen
through an indignant and rural moral optic; the second of mindless Babbitry as seen by urban strata for whom moral principles
have been replaced by big-city ways; and the third, somewhat less
clearly, of the old plutocrat turned more systematic and impersonal.

But the corporate rich of the 'forties and 'fifties, in their economic and in their political aspects—there are no such stereotypes
of them; they are rather cynically accepted, and even secretly ad-
mired by members of the mass society. No negative stereotype
has been widely formed of the corporate rich and the political

Army and his assistants tangled with a Senator and his assistants: the
McCarthy-Army hearings, as we have already noted, stripped from high
officials and a number of Senators all dignity and status. All the official
masks were ripped off and two sets of top circles were shown to be
prime examples of the petty immorality, the substantial charges of both
appearing as quite true.

outsider; and if one or two should crop up in popular imagery, they are soon vanquished by the 'forward-looking,' energetic, clean-cut American boy as executive.

Given the state of the mass society, we should not expect anything else. Most of its members are distracted by status, by the disclosures of pettier immortalities, and by that Machiavellianism-for-the-little-man that is the death of political insurgency. Perhaps it might be different were the intellectual community not so full of the conservative mood, not so comfortably timid, not so absorbed by the new gentility of many of its members. But given these conditions of mass society and intellectual community, we can readily understand why the power elite of America has no ideology and feels the need of none, why its rule is naked of ideas, its manipulation without attempted justification. It is this mindlessness of the powerful that is the true higher immorality of our time; for, with it, there is associated the organized irresponsibility that is today the most important characteristic of the American system of corporate power.

15

The Higher Immorality

THE higher immorality can neither be narrowed to the political sphere nor understood as primarily a matter of corrupt men in fundamentally sound institutions. Political corruption is one aspect of a more general immorality; the level of moral sensibility that now prevails is not merely a matter of corrupt men.[1] The higher immorality is a systematic feature of the American elite; its general acceptance is an essential feature of the mass society.

Of course, there may be corrupt men in sound institutions, but when institutions are corrupting many of the men who live and work in them are necessarily corrupted. In the corporate era, economic relations become impersonal—and the executive feels less personal responsibility. Within the corporate worlds of business, war-making and politics, the private conscience is attenuated—and the higher immorality is institutionalized. It is not merely a question of a corrupt administration in corporation, army, or state; it is a feature of the corporate rich, as a capitalist stratum, deeply intertwined with the politics of the military state.

From this point of view, the most important question, for instance, about the campaign funds of ambitious young politicians is not whether the politicians are morally insensitive, but whether or not any young man in American politics, who has come so far and so fast, could very well have done so today without possessing or acquiring a somewhat blunted moral sensibility. Many of the problems of 'white-collar crime' and of relaxed public morality, of high-priced vice and of fading personal integrity, are problems of *structural* immorality. They are not merely the problem of the small character twisted by the bad milieu. And many people are at least vaguely aware that this is so. As news of higher immoralities breaks, they often say, 'Well, another one got caught today,' thereby implying that the cases disclosed are not odd events involving occasional characters but symptoms of a widespread condition. There is good probative evidence that they are right. But what is the underlying condition of which all these instances are symptoms?

1

The moral uneasiness of our time results from the fact that older values and codes of uprightness no longer grip the men and women of the corporate era, nor have they been replaced by new values and codes which would lend moral meaning and sanction to the corporate routines they must now follow. It is not that the mass public has explicitly rejected received codes; it is rather that to many of the members these codes have become hollow. No moral terms of acceptance are available, but neither are any moral terms of rejection. As individuals they are morally defenseless; as groups, they are politically indifferent. It is this generalized lack of commitment that is meant when it is said that 'the public' is morally confused.

But, of course, not only 'the public' is morally confused in this way. 'The tragedy of official Washington,' James Reston has commented, 'is that it is confounded at every turn by the hangover of old political habits and outworn institutions but is no longer nourished by the ancient faith on which it was founded. It clings to the bad things and casts away the permanent. It professes belief but does not believe. It knows the old words but has forgotten the melody. It is engaged in an ideological war without being able to define its own ideology. It condemns the materialism of an atheistic enemy, but glorifies its own materialism.'[2]

In economic and political institutions the corporate rich now wield enormous power, but they have never had to win the moral consent of those over whom they hold this power. Every such naked interest, every new, unsanctioned power of corporation, farm bloc, labor union, and governmental agency that has risen in the past two generations has been clothed with morally loaded slogans. For what is *not* done in the name of the public interest?

As these slogans wear out, new ones are industriously made up, also to be banalized in due course. And all the while, recurrent economic and military crises spread fears, hesitations, and anxieties which give new urgency to the busy search for moral justifications and decorous excuses.

'Crisis' is a bankrupted term, because so many men in high places have evoked it in order to cover up their extraordinary policies and deeds; as a matter of fact, it is precisely the absence of crises that is a cardinal feature of the higher immorality. For genuine crises involve situations in which men at large are presented with genuine alternatives, the moral meanings of which are clearly opened to public debate. The higher immorality, the general weakening of older values and the organization of irresponsibility have not involved any public crises; on the contrary, they have been matters of a creeping indifference and a silent hollowing out.

The images that generally prevail of the higher circles are the images of the elite seen as celebrities. In discussing the professional celebrities, I noted that the instituted elites of power do not monopolize the bright focus of national acclaim. They share it nationally with the frivolous or the sultry creatures of the world of celebrity, which thus serves as a dazzling blind of their true power. In the sense that the volume of publicity and acclaim is mainly and continuously upon those professional celebrities, it is not upon the power elite. So the social visibility of that elite is lowered by the status distraction, or rather public vision of them is through the celebrity who amuses and entertains—or disgusts, as the case may be.

The absence of any firm moral order of belief makes men in the mass all the more open to the manipulation and distraction of the world of the celebrities. In due course, such a 'turnover' of appeals and codes and values as they are subjected to leads them to distrust and cynicism, to a sort of Machiavellianism-for-the-little-man. Thus they vicariously enjoy the prerogatives of the corporate rich, the nocturnal antics of the celebrity, and the sad-happy life of the very rich.

But with all this, there is still one old American value that has not markedly declined: the value of money and of the things money can buy—these, even in inflated times, seem as solid and enduring as stainless steel. 'I've been rich and I've been poor,' Sophie Tucker has said, 'and believe me, rich is best.'[3] As many other values are weakened, the question for Americans becomes not 'Is there anything that money, used with intelligence, will not buy?' but, 'How many of the things that money will *not* buy are valued and desired more than what money *will* buy?' Money is the one unambiguous criterion of success, and such success is still the sovereign American value.

Whenever the standards of the moneyed life prevail, the man with money, no matter how he got it, will eventually be respected. A million dollars, it is said, covers a multitude of sins. It is not only that men want money; it is that their very standards are pecuniary. In a society in which the money-maker has had no serious rival for repute and honor, the word 'practical' comes to mean useful for private gain, and 'common sense,' the sense to get ahead financially. The pursuit of the moneyed life is the commanding value, in relation to which the influence of other values has declined, so men easily become morally ruthless in the pursuit of easy money and fast estate-building.

A great deal of American corruption—although not all of it—is simply a part of the old effort to get rich and then to become richer. But today the context in which the old drive must operate has changed. When both economic and political institutions were small and scattered—as in the simpler models of classical economics and Jeffersonian democracy—no man had it in his power to bestow or to receive great favors. But when political institutions and economic opportunities are at once concentrated and linked, then public office can be used for private gain.

Governmental agencies contain no more of the higher immorality than do business corporations. Political men can grant financial favors only when there are economic men ready and willing to take them. And economic men can seek political favors only when there are political agents who can bestow such favors. The publicity spotlight, of course, shines brighter upon the transactions of the men in government, for which there is good reason. Expectations being higher, publics are more easily disappointed by public officials. Businessmen are supposed to be out for themselves, and if they successfully skate on legally thin ice, Americans generally honor them for having gotten away with it. But in a civilization so thoroughly business-penetrated as America, the rules of business are carried over into government—especially when so many businessmen have gone into government. How many executives would really fight for a law requiring a careful and public accounting of all executive contracts and 'expense accounts'? High income taxes have resulted in a network of collusion between big firm and higher employee. There are many ingenious ways to cheat the spirit of the tax laws, as we have seen, and the standards of consumption of many high-priced men are determined more by complicated expense accounts than by simple take-home pay. Like prohibition, the laws of income taxes and the regulations of wartime exist without the support of firm business convention. It is merely illegal to cheat them, but it is smart to get away with it. Laws without supporting moral conventions invite crime, but much more importantly, they spur the growth of an expedient, amoral attitude.

A society that is in its higher circles and on its middle levels widely believed to be a network of smart rackets does not produce men with an inner moral sense; a society that is merely expedient does not produce men of conscience. A society that narrows the meaning of 'success' to the big money and in its terms condemns failure as the chief vice, raising money to the plane of absolute value, will produce the sharp operator and the shady deal. Blessed are the cynical, for only they have what it takes to succeed.

2

In the corporate world, in the political directorate, and increasingly in the ascendant military, the heads of the big hierarchies and power machines are seen not only as men who have succeeded, but as wielders of the patronage of success. They interpret and they apply to individuals the criteria of success. Those immediately below them are usually members of their clique, of their clientele, sound men as they themselves are sound. But the hierarchies are intricately related to one another, and inside each clique are some whose loyalties are to other cliques. There are personal loyalties as well as official ones, personal as well as impersonal criteria for advancement. As we trace the career of the individual member of various higher circles, we are also tracing the history of his loyalties, for the first and overshadowing fact about the higher circles, from the standpoint of what it takes to succeed within them, is that they are based upon self-co-optation. The second fact about these hierarchies of success is that they do not form one monolithic structure; they are a complex set of variously related and often antagonistic cliques. The third fact we must recognize is that, in any such world, younger men who would succeed attempt to relate themselves to those in charge of their selection as successes.

Accordingly, the American literature of practical aspiration—which carries the great fetish of success—has undergone a significant shift in its advice about 'what it takes to succeed.' The sober, personal virtues of will power and honesty, of high-mindedness and the constitutional inability to say 'yes' to The Easy Road of women, tobacco, and wine—this later nineteenth-century image has given way to 'the most important single factor, the effective personality,' which 'commands attention by charm,' and 'radiates self-confidence.' In this 'new way of life,' one must smile often and be a good listener, talk in terms of the other man's interests and make the other feel important—and one must do all this sincerely. Personal relations, in short, have become part of 'public relations,' a sacrifice of selfhood on a personality market, to the sole end of individual success in the corporate way of life.[4] Being justified by superior merit and hard work, but being founded on co-optation by a clique, often on quite other grounds, the elite careerist must continually persuade others and himself as well that he is the opposite of what he actually is.

It is the proud claim of the higher circles in America that their members are entirely self-made. That is their self-image and their well-publicized myth. Popular proof of this is based on anecdotes; its scholarly proof is supposed to rest upon statistical rituals whereby it is shown that varying proportions of the men at the top are sons of men of lower rank. We have already seen the proportions of given elite circles composed of the men who have risen. But what is more important than the proportions of the sons of wage workers among these higher circles is the criteria of admission to them, and the question of who applies these criteria. We cannot from upward mobility infer higher merit. Even if the rough figures that now generally hold were reversed, and 90 per cent of the elite were sons of wage workers—but the criteria of co-optation by the elite remained what they now are—we could not from that mobility necessarily infer merit. Only if the criteria of the top positions were meritorious, and only if they were self-applied, as in a purely entrepreneurial manner, could we smuggle merit into such statistics—from any statistics—of mobility. The idea that the self-made man is somehow 'good' and that the family-made man is not good makes moral sense only when the career is independent, when one is on one's own as an entrepreneur. It would also make sense in a strict bureaucracy where examinations control advancement. It makes little sense in the system of corporate co-optation.

There is, in psychological fact, no such thing as a self-made man. No man makes himself, least of all the members of the American elite. In a world of corporate hierarchies, men are selected by those above them in the hierarchy in accordance with whatever criteria they use. In connection with the corporations of America, we have seen the current criteria. Men shape themselves to fit them, and are thus made by the criteria, the social premiums that prevail. If there is no such thing as a self-made man, there is such a thing as a self-used man, and there are many such men among the American elite.

Under such conditions of success, there is no virtue in starting out poor and becoming rich. Only where the ways of becoming rich are such as to require virtue or to lead to virtue does personal enrichment imply virtue. In a system of co-optation from above, whether you began rich or poor seems less relevant in revealing what kind of man you are when you have arrived than in revealing the principles of those in charge of selecting the ones who succeed.

All this is sensed by enough people below the higher circles to lead to cynical views of the lack of connection between merit and mobility, between virtue and success. It is a sense of the immorality of accomplishment, and it is revealed in the prevalence of such views as: 'it's all just another racket,' and 'it's not what you know but who you know.' Considerable numbers of people now accept the immorality of accomplishment as a going fact.

Some observers are led by their sense of the immorality of ac-complishment to the ideology, obliquely set forth by academic social science, of human relations in industry;[5] still others to the solace of mind provided by the newer literature of resignation, of peace of mind, which in some quietened circles replaces the old literature of frenzied aspiration, of how to get ahead. But, regard-less of the particular style of reaction, the sense of the immorality of accomplishment often feeds into that level of public sensibility which we have called the higher immorality. The old self-made man's is a tarnished image, and no other image of success has taken its once bright place. Success itself, as the American model of excellence, declines as it becomes one more feature of the higher immorality.

3

Moral distrust of the American elite—as well as the fact of or-ganized irresponsibility—rests upon the higher immorality, but also upon vague feelings about the higher ignorance. Once upon a time in the United States, men of affairs were also men of sensi-bility: to a considerable extent the elite of power and the elite of culture coincided, and where they did not coincide they often over-lapped as circles. Within the compass of a knowledgeable and ef-fective public, knowledge and power were in effective touch; and more than that, this public decided much that was decided.

'Nothing is more revealing,' James Reston has written, 'than to read the debate in the House of Representatives in the Eigh-teen Thirties on Greece's fight with Turkey for independence and the Greek-Turkish debate in the Congress in 1947. The first is dignified and eloquent, the argument marching from principle through illustration to conclusion; the second is a dreary garble of debating points, full of irrelevancies and bad history.'[6] George Washington in 1783 relaxed with Voltaire's 'letters' and Locke's 'On Human Understanding'; Eisenhower read cowboy tales and detective stories.[7] For such men as now typically arrive in the higher political, economic and military circles, the briefing and the memorandum seem to have pretty well replaced not only the serious book, but the newspaper as well. Given the immorality of accomplishment, this is perhaps as it must be, but what is some-what disconcerting about it is that they are below the level on which they might feel a little bit ashamed of the uncultivated style of their relaxation and of their mental fare, and that no self-cultivated public is in a position by its reactions to educate them to such uneasiness.

By the middle of the twentieth century, the American elite have become an entirely different breed of men from those who could on any reasonable grounds be considered a cultural elite, or even for that matter cultivated men of sensibility. Knowledge and power are not truly united inside the ruling circles; and when men of knowledge do come to a point of contact with the circles of powerful men, they come not as peers but as hired men. The elite of power, wealth, and celebrity do not nave even a passing acquaintance with the elite of culture, knowledge and sensibility; they are not in touch with them—although the ostentatious fringes of the two worlds sometimes overlap in the world of the celebrity.

Most men are encouraged to assume that, in general, the most powerful and the wealthiest are also the most knowledgeable or, as they might say, 'the smartest.' Such ideas are propped up by many little slogans about those who 'teach because they can't *do*,' and about 'if you're so smart, why aren't you rich?'* But all that such wisecracks mean is that those who use them assume that power and wealth are sovereign values for all men and especially for men 'who are smart.' They assume also that knowledge always pays off in such ways, or surely ought to, and that the test of genuine knowledge is just such pay-offs. The powerful and the wealthy *must* be the men of most knowledge, otherwise how could they be where they are? But to say that those who succeed to power must be 'smart,' is to say that power *is* knowledge. To say that those who succeed to wealth must be smart, is to say that wealth *is* knowledge.

The prevalence of such assumptions does reveal something that is true: that ordinary men, even today, are prone to explain and

* Bernard Baruch, an adviser to Presidents, has recently remarked, 'I think economists as [a] rule . . . take for granted they know a lot of things. If they really knew so much, they would have all the money and we would have none.' And again he reasons: 'These men [economists] can take facts and figures and bring them together, but their predictions are not worth any more than ours. If they were, they would have all the money and we would not have anything.'[8]

to justify power and wealth in terms of knowledge or ability. Such assumptions also reveal something of what has happened to the kind of experience that knowledge has come to be. Knowledge is no longer widely felt as an ideal; it is seen as an instrument. In a society of power and wealth, knowledge is valued as an instrument of power and wealth, and also, of course, as an ornament in conversation.

What knowledge does to a man (in clarifying what he is, and setting him free)—that is the personal ideal of knowledge. What knowledge does to a civilization (in revealing its human meaning, and setting it free)—that is the social ideal of knowledge. But today, the personal *and* the social ideals of knowledge have coincided in what knowledge does *for* the smart guy—it gets him ahead; and for the wise nation—it lends cultural prestige, sanctifying power with authority.

Knowledge seldom lends power to the man of knowledge. But the supposed, and secret, knowledge of some men-on-the-make, and their very free use thereof, has consequence for other men who have not the power of defense. Knowledge, of course, is neither good nor bad, nor is its use good or bad. 'Bad men increase in knowledge as fast as good men,' John Adams wrote, 'and science, arts, taste, sense and letters, are employed for the purpose of injustice as well as for virtue.'⁹ That was in 1790; today we have good reason to know that it is so.

The problem of knowledge and power is, and always has been, the problem of the relations of men of knowledge with men of power. Suppose we were to select the one hundred most powerful men, from all fields of power, in America today and line them up. And then, suppose we selected the one hundred most knowledgeable men, from all fields of social knowledge, and lined them up. How many men would be in *both* our line-ups? Of course our selection would depend upon what we mean by power and what we mean by knowledge—especially what we mean by knowledge. But, if we mean what the words seem to mean, surely we would find few if any men in America today who were in both groups, and surely we could find many more at the time the nation was founded than we could find today. For, in the eighteenth century, even in this colonial outpost, men of power pursued learning, and men of learning were often in positions of power. In these respects we have, I believe, suffered grievous decline.[10]

There is little union in the same persons of knowledge and power; but persons of power do surround themselves with men of some knowledge, or at least with men who are experienced in shrewd dealings. The man of knowledge has not become a philosopher king; but he has often become a consultant, and moreover a consultant to a man who is neither king-like nor philosophical. It is, of course, true that the chairman of the pulp writers section of the Authors' League helped a leading senator 'polish up the speeches he delivered in the 1952 senatorial campaign.'[11] But it is not natural in the course of their careers for men of knowledge to meet with those of power. The links between university and government are weak, and when they do occur, the man of knowledge appears as an 'expert' which usually means as a hired technician. Like most others in this society, the man of knowledge is himself dependent for his livelihood upon the job, which nowadays is a prime sanction of thought control. Where getting ahead requires the good opinions of more powerful others, their judgments become prime objects of concern. Accordingly, in so far as intellectuals serve power directly—in a job hierarchy—they often do so unfreely.

The democratic man assumes the existence of a public, and in his rhetoric asserts that this public is the very seat of sovereignty. Two things are needed in a democracy: articulate and knowledgeable publics, and political leaders who if not men of reason are at least reasonably responsible to such knowledgeable publics as exist. Only where publics and leaders are responsive and responsible, are human affairs in democratic order, and only when knowledge has public relevance is this order possible. Only when mind has an autonomous basis, independent of power, but powerfully related to it, can mind exert its force in the shaping of human affairs. This is democratically possible only when there exists a free and knowledgeable public, to which men of knowledge may address themselves, and to which men of power are truly responsible. Such a public and such men—either of power or of knowledge—do not now prevail, and accordingly, knowledge does not now have democratic relevance in America.

The characteristic member of the higher circles today is an

intellectual mediocrity, sometimes a conscientious one, but still a mediocrity. His intelligence is revealed only by his occasional realization that he is not up to the decisions he sometimes feels called upon to confront. But usually he keeps such feelings private, his public utterances being pious and sentimental, grim and brave, cheerful and empty in their universal generality. He is open only to abbreviated and vulgarized, predigested and slanted ideas. He is a commander of the age of the phone call, the memo, and the briefing.

By the mindlessness and mediocrity of men of affairs, I do not, of course, mean that these men are not sometimes intelligent— although that is by no means automatically the case. It is not, however, primarily a matter of the distribution of 'intelligence'—as if intelligence were a homogeneous something of which there may be more or less. It is rather a matter of the type of intelligence, of the quality of mind that is selected and formed. It is a matter of the evaluation of substantive rationality as the chief value in a man's life and character and conduct. That evaluation is what is lacking in the American power elite. In its place there are 'weight' and 'judgment' which count for much more in their celebrated success than any subtlety of mind or force of intellect.

All around and just below the weighty man of affairs are his technical lieutenants of power who have been assigned the role of knowledge and even of speech: his public relations men, his ghost, his administrative assistants, his secretaries. And do not forget The Committees. With the increased means of decision, there is a crisis of understanding among the political directorate of the United States, and accordingly, there is often a commanding indecision.

The lack of knowledge as an experience among the elite ties in with the malign ascendancy of the expert, not only as fact but as legitimation. When questioned recently about a criticism of defense policies made by the leader of the opposition party, the Secretary of Defense replied, 'Do you think he is an expert in the matter?' When pressed further by reporters he asserted that the 'military chiefs think it is sound, and I think it is sound,' and later, when asked about specific cases, added: 'In some cases, all you can do is ask the Lord.'[12] With such a large role so arrogantly given to God and to experts, what room is there for political leadership? Much less for public debate of what is after all every bit as much a political and a moral as a military issue. But then, from before Pearl Harbor, the trend has been the abdication of debate and the collapse of opposition under the easy slogan of bi-partisanship.

Beyond the lack of intellectual cultivation by political personnel and advisory circle, the absence of publicly relevant mind has come to mean that powerful decisions and important policies are not made in such a way as to be justified or attacked; in short, debated in any intellectual form. Moreover, the attempt to so justify them is often not even made. Public relations displace reasoned argument; manipulation and undebated decisions of power replace democratic authority. More and more, since the nineteenth century, as administration has replaced politics, the decisions of importance do not carry even the panoply of reasonable discussion, but are made by God, by experts, and by men like Mr. Wilson.

More and more the area of the official secret expands, as well as the area of the secret listening in on those who might divulge in public what the public, not being composed of experts with Q clearance, is not to know. The entire sequence of decisions concerning the production and the use of atomic weaponry has been made without any genuine public debate. and the facts needed to engage in that debate intelligently have been officially hidden, distorted, and even lied about. As the decisions become more fateful, not only for Americans but literally for mankind, the sources of information are closed up, and the relevant facts needed for decision (even the decisions made!) are, as politically convenient 'official secrets,' withheld from the heavily laden channels of information.

In those channels, meanwhile, political rhetoric seems to slide lower and lower down the scale of cultivation and sensibility. The height of such mindless communications to masses, or what are thought to be masses, is probably the demagogic assumption that suspicion and accusation, if repeated often enough, somehow equal proof of guilt—just as repeated claims about toothpaste or brands of cigarettes are assumed to equal facts. The greatest kind of propaganda with which America is beset, the greatest at least in terms of volume and loudness, is commercial propaganda for soap and cigarettes and automobiles; it is to such things, or rather to Their Names, that this society most frequently sings its loudest praises. What is important about this is that by implication and ommission, by emphasis and sometimes by flat statement, this astounding volume of propaganda for commodities is often un-truthful and misleading; and is addressed more often to the belly or to the groin than to the head or to the heart. Public communica-tions from those who make powerful decisions, or who would have us vote them into such decision-making places, more and more take on those qualities of mindlessness and myth which com-mercial propaganda and advertising have come to exemplify.

In America today, men of affairs are not so much dogmatic as they are mindless. Dogma has usually meant some more or less elaborated justification of ideas and values, and thus has had some features (however inflexible and closed) of mind, of intellect, of reason. Nowadays what we are up against is precisely the absence of mind of any sort as a public force; what we are up against is a disinterest in and a fear of knowledge that might have liberating public relevance. What this makes possible are decisions having no rational justifications which the intellect could confront and engage in debate.

It is not the barbarous irrationality of dour political primitives that is the American danger; it is the respected judgments of Sec-retaries of State, the earnest platitudes of Presidents, the fearful self-righteousness of sincere young American politicians from sunny California. These men have replaced mind with platitude, and the dogmas by which they are legitimated are so widely ac-cepted that no counter-balance of mind prevails against them. Such men as these are crackpot realists: in the name of realism they have constructed a paranoid reality all their own; in the name of practicality they have projected a utopian image of capitalism. They have replaced the responsible interpretation of events with the disguise of events by a maze of public relations; respect for public debate with unshrewd notions of psychological warfare; intellectual ability with agility of the sound, mediocre judgment; the capacity to elaborate alternatives and gauge their conse-quences with the executive stance.

4

Despite—perhaps because of—the ostracism of mind from public affairs, the immorality of accomplishment, and the general
prevalence of organized irresponsibility, the men of the higher
circles benefit from the total power of the institutional domains
over which they rule. For the power of these institutions, actual
or potential, is ascribed to them as the ostensible decision-makers.
Their positions and their activities, and even their persons, are
hallowed by these ascriptions; and, around all the high places of
power, there is a penumbra of prestige in which the political
directorate, the corporate rich, the admirals and generals are
bathed. The elite of a society, however modest its individual member, embodies the prestige of the society's power.* Moreover, few
individuals in positions of such authority can long resist the temptation to base their self-images, at least in part, upon the sounding
board of the collectivity which they head. Acting as the representative of his nation, his corporation, his army, in due course,
he comes to consider himself and what he says and believes as
expressive of the historically accumulated glory of the great institutions with which he comes to identify himself. When he speaks
in the name of his country or its cause, its past glory also echoes
in his ears.

Status, no longer rooted primarily in local communities, follows the big hierarchies, which are on a national scale. Status
follows the big money, even if it has a touch of the gangster about
it. Status follows power, even if it be without background. Below,
in the mass society, old moral and traditional barriers to status
break down and Americans look for standards of excellence among

* John Adams wrote in the late eighteenth century: 'When you rise
to the first ranks, and consider the first men; a nobility who are known
and respected at least, perhaps habitually esteemed and beloved by a
nation; Princes and Kings, on whom the eyes of all men are fixed, and
whose every motion is regarded, the consequences of wounding their
feelings are dreadful, because the feelings of an whole nation, and
sometimes of many nations, are wounded at the same time. If the small-
est variation is made in their situation, relatively to each other; if one
who was inferior is raised to be superior, unless it be by fixed laws,
whose evident policy and necessity may take away disgrace, nothing but
war, carnage and vengeance has ever been the usual consequence of
it . . .'[13]

the circles above them, in terms of which to model themselves and judge their self-esteem. Yet nowadays, it seems easier for Americans to recognize such representative men in the past than in the present. Whether this is due to a real historical difference or merely to the political ease and expediency of hindsight is very difficult to tell.* At any rate it is a fact that in the political assignments of prestige there is little disparagement of Washington, Jefferson, and Lincoln, but much disagreement about current figures. Representative men seem more easily recognizable after they have died; contemporary political leaders are merely politicians; they may be big or little, but they are not great, and increasingly they are seen in terms of the higher immorality.

Now again status follows power, and older types of exemplary figures have been replaced by the fraternity of the successful— the professional executives who have become the political elite, and who are now the *official* representative men. It remains to be seen whether they will become representative men in the images

* In every intellectual period, some one discipline or school of thought becomes a sort of common denominator. The common denominator of the conservative mood in America today is American history. This is the time of the American historian. All nationalist celebration tends, of course, to be put in historical terms, but the celebrators do not wish to be relevant merely to the understanding of history as past event. Their purpose is the celebration of the present. (1) One reason why the American ideology is so historically oriented is that of all the scholarly community it is the historians who are most likely to create such public assumptions. For, of all the scholarly writers, the historians have been the ones with the literate tradition. Other 'social scientists' are more likely to be unacquainted with English usage and moreover, they do not write about large topics of public concern. (2) The 'good' historians, in fulfilling the public role of the higher journalists, the historians with the public attention and the Sunday acclaim, are the historians who are the quickest to re-interpret the American past with relevance to the current mood, and in turn, the cleverest at picking out of the past, just now, those characters and events that most easily make for optimism and lyric upsurge. (3) In truth, and without nostalgia, we ought to realize that the American past is a wonderful source for myths about the American present. That past, at times, did indeed embody quite a way of life; the United States has been extraordinarily fortunate in its time of origin and early development; the present is complicated, and, especially to a trained historian, quite undocumented. The general American ideology accordingly tends to be of history and by historians.[4]

and aspirations of the mass public, or whether they will endure any
longer than the displaced liberals of the 'thirties. Their images
are controversial, deeply involved in the immorality of accomplishment and the higher immorality in general. Increasingly, literate
Americans feel that there is something synthetic about them. Their
style and the conditions under which they become 'big' lend themselves too readily to the suspicion of the build-up; the shadows of
the ghost writer and the make-up man loom too large; the slick-
ness of the fabrication is too apparent.

We should, of course, bear in mind that men of the higher circles
may or may not seek to impose themselves as representative upon
the underlying population, and that relevant public sectors of the
population may or may not accept their images. An elite may try
to impose its claims upon the mass public, but this public may
not cash them in. On the contrary, it may be indifferent or even
debunk their values, caricature their image, laugh at their claim
to be representative men.

In his discussion of models of national character, Walter Bagehot does not go into such possibilities;[15] but it is clear that for our
contemporaries we must consider them, since precisely this reaction has led to a sometimes frenzied and always expensive practice of what is known as 'public relations.' Those who have both
power and status are perhaps best off when they do not actively
have to seek acclaim. The truly proud old families will not seek
it; the professional celebrities are specialists in seeking it actively.
Increasingly, the political, economic, and military elite—as we
have seen—compete with the celebrities and seek to borrow their
status. Perhaps those who have unprecedented power without
the aura of status, will always seek it, even if uneasily, among
those who have publicity without power.

For the mass public, there is the status distraction of the celebrity, as well as the economic distraction of war prosperity; for the
liberal intellectual, who does look to the political arena, there is
the political distraction of the sovereign localities and of the middle levels of power, which sustain the illusion that America is still
a self-balancing society. If the mass media focus on the professional celebrities, the liberal intellectuals, especially the academic social scientists among them, focus upon the noisy middle levels. Professional celebrities and middle-level politicians

are the most visible figures of the system; in fact, together they tend to monopolize the communicated or public scene that is visible to the members of the mass society, and thus to obscure and to distract attention from the power elite.

The higher circles in America today contain, on the one hand, the laughing, erotic, dazzling glamour of the professional celebrity, and, on the other, the prestige aura of power, of authority, of might and wealth. These two pinnacles are not unrelated. The power elite is not so noticeable as the celebrities, and often does not want to be; the 'power' of the professional celebrity is the power of distraction. America as a national public is indeed possessed of a strange set of idols. The professionals, in the main, are either glossy little animals or frivolous clowns; the men of power, in the main, rarely seem to be models of representative men.

Such moral uneasiness as prevails among the American elite themselves is accordingly quite understandable. Its existence is amply confirmed by the more serious among those who have come to feel that they represent America abroad. There, the double-faced character of the American celebrity is reflected both by the types of Americans who travel to play or to work, and in the images many literate and articulate Europeans hold of 'Americans.' Public honor in America tends now to be either frivolous or grim; either altogether trivial or portentous of a greatly tightened-up system of prestige.

The American elite is not composed of representative men whose conduct and character constitute models for American imitation and aspiration. There is no set of men with whom members of the mass public can rightfully and gladly identify. In this fundamental sense, America is indeed without leaders. Yet such is the nature of the mass public's morally cynical and politically unspecified distrust that it is readily drained off without real political effect. That this is so, after the men and events of the last thirty years, is further proof of the extreme difficulty of finding and of using in America today the political means of sanity for morally sane objectives.

America—a conservative country without any conservative ideology—appears now before the world a naked and arbitrary power, as, in the name of realism, its men of decision enforce their often crackpot definitions upon world reality. The second-rate mind is in command of the ponderously spoken platitude. In the liberal rhetoric, vagueness, and in the conservative mood, irrationality, are raised to principle. Public relations and the official secret, the trivializing campaign and the terrible fact clumsily accomplished, are replacing the reasoned debate of political ideas in the privately incorporated economy, the military ascendancy, and the political vacuum of modern America.

The men of the higher circles are not representative men; their high position is not a result of moral virtue; their fabulous success is not firmly connected with meritorious ability. Those who sit in the seats of the high and the mighty are selected and formed by the means of power, the sources of wealth, the mechanics of celebrity, which prevail in their society. They are not men selected and formed by a civil service that is linked with the world of knowledge and sensibility. They are not men shaped by nationally responsible parties that debate openly and clearly the issues this nation now so unintelligently confronts. They are not men held in responsible check by a plurality of voluntary associations which connect debating publics with the pinnacles of decision. Commanders of power unequaled in human history, they have succeeded within the American system of organized irresponsibility.

Acknowledgments

NEITHER the very top nor the very bottom of modern society is a normal part of the world of those who read and write books; we are more familiar with the middle ranks. To understand the middle classes we have only to *see* what is actually around us, but to understand the very top or the very bottom, we must first seek to discover and describe. And that is very difficult to do: the very top of modern society is often inaccessible, the very bottom often hidden.

The terms of such national surveys as are undertaken are far too gross to catch such numerically fine groups as make up the American elite; much public information about their character and their activities is systematically misleading; and they are themselves busy and aloof and even secretive. Were we to select our field of study according to the ready availability of much unworked material, we should never choose the elite. And yet, if we are trying to understand something of the true nature of the society in which we live, we cannot allow the impossibility of rigorous proof to keep us from studying whatever we believe to be important. We must expect fumbles when, without authority or official aid, we set out to investigate something which is in part organized for the purpose of causing fumbles among those who would understand it plainly. Yet, by asserting what we can under such conditions, we may engage them and their agents in controversy, and thus learn more.

Our desire for tight proof and our genuine need for facts do not at all mean that reasoning together is not still a very important part of the proper way of arriving at the truth. A book of this sort consists of three conversations: There is the conversation which the writer has with himself and with imaginary persons, which is here recorded. Underneath this, there is going on, whether the writer knows it or not, a conversation between certain influential thinkers and observers whose views have filtered into his mind and into the minds of his readers. And also, in the minds of his readers there is going on another unspoken conversation with themselves and with him—a conversation in which each confronts what is written here with what he has experienced or found out. One of the jobs of the writer, accordingly, is to try to get as much of these two unspoken conversations as he can into his written work. In reasoning together with his readers, he does more than set forth his views.

He also clarifies them, and in doing so, becomes aware of ideas he did not even know he had.

We do not want to so busy ourselves with details that we take the world in which they exist for granted. We neither take the world for granted nor believe it to be a simple fact. Our business is with facts only in so far as we need them to upset or to clinch our ideas. Facts and figures are only the beginning of the proper study. Our main interest is in making sense of the facts we know or can readily find out. We do not want merely to take an inventory, we want to discover meanings, for most of our important questions are questions of meaning.

We have, of course, gotten outside the dialogue by which we reason together and found out what we could by various kinds of special study, the results of which we have introduced into the conversation going on in 'our inner city.' There are good reasons why we should adopt just this essay-like way of reasoning together—especially for such a sprawling and controversial topic. In a convenient, and I hope fruitful, way it enables us to bring together an effective variety of viewpoints and skills, and it allows us to invite the reader to become a member of our dialogue about the higher circles of America.

Funds for the research that has gone into this book were provided by Columbia University's Social Science Research Council and I am glad to thank my colleagues for their aid. Funds were also supplied by The Oxford University Press, New York, which has in fact gone beyond the ordinary office of publisher in helping me get on with this as well as other books. A first draft of the materials was completed while in residence as a visitor at Brandeis University during the spring of 1953 and I wish to thank my friends of that institution for their many kindnesses. During the summer of 1954, my wife and I were resident fellows at the Huntington Hartford Foundation of Pacific Palisades, California, and I am grateful to the fellows of that foundation for making the summer's work both pleasant and profitable.

My wife, Ruth Harper Mills, as chief researcher and editorial adviser, has shaped much of the book. Walter Klink, Paul Lucas, and William Taber have assisted me by writing research memoranda. I wish also to thank Mrs. Katherine Stanton for her secretarial services; without her there would be no book but only a chaotic file of manuscript.

Several individuals who know at first hand the Federal government, the military, or large corporations have helped me enormously. Without their help this book would be much the poorer, which makes all the more onerous to me the fact that at their request I cannot acknowledge their help by name.

Other friends who have generously given me the benefit of their advice include: Lewis Coser, Louis Friedland, Herbert Gold, Richard Hofstadter, Irving Howe, Floyd Hunter, Paolo Milano, Harry L. Miller, William Miller, Irving Sanes, Ben Seligman, Kenneth M. Stampp, and Harvey Swados.

Notes

1. The Higher Circles

1. Jacob Burckhardt, *Force and Freedom* (New York: Pantheon Books, 1943), pp. 303 ff.

2. Cf. Hans Gerth and C. Wright Mills, *Character and Social Structure* (New York: Harcourt, Brace, 1953), pp. 457 ff.

3. The statistical idea of choosing some value and calling those who have the most of it an elite derives, in modern times, from the Italian economist, Pareto, who puts the central point in this way: 'Let us assume that in every branch of human activity each individual is given an index which stands as a sign of his capacity, very much the way grades are given in the various subjects in examinations in school. The highest type of lawyer, for instance, will be given 10. The man who does not get a client will be given 1—reserving zero for the man who is an out-and-out idiot. To the man who has made his millions—honestly or dishonestly as the case may be—we will give 10. To the man who has earned his thousands we will give 6; to such as just manage to keep out of the poor-house, 1, keeping zero for those who get in . . . So let us make a class of people who have the highest indices in their branch of activity, and to that class give the name of *elite*.' Vilfredo Pareto, *The Mind and Society* (New York: Harcourt, Brace, 1935), par. 2027 and 2031. Those who follow this approach end up not with one elite, but with a number corresponding to the number of values they select. Like many rather abstract ways of reasoning, this one is useful because it forces us to think in a clear-cut way. For a skillful use of this approach, see the work of Harold D. Lasswell, in particular, *Politics: Who Gets What, When, How* (New York: McGraw-Hill, 1936); and for a more systematic use, H. D. Lasswell and Abraham Kaplan, *Power and Society* (New Haven: Yale University Press, 1950).

4. The conception of the elite as members of a top social stratum, is, of course, in line with the prevailing common-sense view of stratification. Technically, it is closer to 'status group' than to 'class,' and has been very well stated by Joseph A. Schumpeter, 'Social Classes in an Ethically Homogeneous Environment,' *Imperialism and Social Classes* (New

York: Augustus M. Kelley, Inc., 1951), pp. 133 ff., especially pp. 137–47. Cf. also his *Capitalism, Socialism and Democracy*, 3rd ed. (New York: Harper, 1950), Part II. For the distinction between class and status groups, see *From Max Weber: Essays in Sociology* (trans. and ed. by Gerth and Mills; New York: Oxford University Press, 1946). For an analysis of Pareto's conception of the elite compared with Marx's conception of classes, as well as data on France, see Raymond Aron, 'Social Structure and Ruling Class,' *British Journal of Sociology*, vol. I, nos. 1 and 2 (1950).

5. The most popular essay in recent years which defines the elite and the mass in terms of a morally evaluated character-type is probably José Ortega y Gasset's, *The Revolt of the Masses*, 1932 (New York: New American Library, Mentor Edition, 1950), esp. pp. 91 ff.

6. 'The American elite' is a confused and confusing set of images, and yet when we hear or when we use such words as Upper Class, Big Shot, Top Brass, The Millionaire Club, The High and The Mighty, we feel at least vaguely that we know what they mean, and often do. What we do not often do, however, is connect each of these images with the others; we make little effort to form a coherent picture in our minds of the elite as a whole. Even when, very occasionally, we do try to do this, we usually come to believe that it is indeed no 'whole'; that, like our images of it, there is no one elite, but many, and that they are not really connected with one another. What we must realize is that until we *do* try to see it as a whole, perhaps our impression that it may not be is a result merely of our lack of analytic rigor and sociological imagination.

The first conception defines the elite in terms of the sociology of institutional position and the social structure these institutions form; the second, in terms of the statistics of selected values; the third, in terms of membership in a clique-like set of people; and the fourth, in terms of the morality of certain personality types. Or, put into inelegant shorthand: what they head up, what they have, what they belong to, who they really are.

In this chapter, as in this book as a whole, I have taken as generic the first view—of the elite defined in terms of institutional position—and have located the other views within it. This straight-forward conception of the elite has one practical and two theoretical advantages. The practical advantage is that it seems the easiest and the most concrete 'way into' the whole problem—if only because a good deal of information is more or less readily available for sociological reflection about such circles and institutions.

But the theoretical advantages are much more important. The institutional or structural definition, first of all, does not force us to prejudge by definition that we ought properly to leave open for investigation. The elite conceived morally, for example, as people having a certain type of character is not an ultimate definition, for apart from being rather morally arbitrary, it leads us immediately to ask *why* these people have this or that sort of character. Accordingly, we should leave open the type of characters which the members of the elite in fact turn out to have, rather than by definition select them in terms of one type or another. In a similar way, we do not want, by mere definition, to prejudge whether or not the elite are conscious members of a social class. The second theoretical advantage of defining the elite in terms of major institutions, which I hope this book as a whole makes clear, is the fact that it allows us to fit the other three conceptions of the elite into place in a systematic way: (1) The institutional positions men occupy throughout their lifetime determine their chances to get and to hold selected values. (2) The kind of psychological beings they become is in large part determined by the values they thus experience and the institutional roles they play. (3) Finally, whether or not they come to feel that they belong to a select social class, and whether or not they act according to what they hold to be its interests—these are also matters in large part determined by their institutional position, and in turn, the select values they possess and the characters they acquire.

7. As in the case, quite notably, of Gaetano Mosca, *The Ruling Class* (New York: McGraw-Hill, 1939). For a sharp analysis of Mosca, see Fritz Morstein Marx, 'The Bureaucratic State,' *Review of Politics*, vol. I, 1939, pp. 457 ff. Cf. also Mills, 'On Intellectual Craftsmanship,' April 1952, mimeographed, Columbia College, February 1955.

8. Cf. Karl Löwith, *Meaning in History* (Chicago: University of Chicago Press, 1949), pp. 125 ff. for concise and penetrating statements of several leading philosophies of history.

9. Some of these items are taken from Gerth and Mills, *Character and Social Structure*, pp. 405 ff. On role-determined and role-determining men, see also Sidney Hook's discussion, *The Hero in History* (New York: John Day, 1943).

10. I have taken the idea of the following kind of formulation from Joseph Wood Krutch's presentation of the morality of choice. See *The Measure of Man* (Indianapolis: Bobbs-Merrill, 1954), p. 52.

2. Local Society

1. Much of this chapter is based upon my own observations and interviews in some dozen middle-sized cities in the Northeast, the Middle-West, and the South. Some results of this work have appeared in 'Small Business and Civic Welfare, Report of the Smaller War Plants Corporation to the Special Committee to Study Problems of American Small Business,' (with Melville J. Ulmer), *Senate Document* No. 135, 79th Cong., 2nd Session, Washington, 1946; 'The Middle Classes in Middle-sized Cities,' *American Sociological Review*, October 1946; and *White Collar: The American Middle Classes* (New York: Oxford University Press, 1951). I have also used field notes made during the course of an intensive study of a city of 60,000 in Illinois during the summer of 1945. Unless otherwise noted, all quotations in this chapter are from my own research.

I have also drawn upon a memorandum, prepared for me by Mr. J. W. Harless, in which all statements about local upper classes appearing in the following studies were organized: Robert S. Lynd and Helen M. Lynd, *Middletown* (New York: Harcourt, Brace, 1929) and *Middletown in Transition* (New York: Harcourt, Brace, 1937); Elin L. Anderson, *We Americans* (Cambridge, Mass.: Harvard University Press, 1938); Hortense Powdermaker, *After Freedom* (New York: The Viking Press, 1939); John Dollard, *Caste and Class in a Southern Town*, 2nd ed. (New York: Harper, 1950); W. Lloyd Warner and Paul S. Lunt, *The Social Life of a Modern Community* (New Haven: Yale University Press, 1941), volume I of the Yankee City Series; Allison Davis and Burleigh B. Gardner and Mary R. Gardner, *Deep South* (Chicago: University of Chicago Press, 1941); Liston Pope, *Millhands and Preachers* (New Haven: Yale University Press, 1942); John Useem, Pierre Tangent, and Ruth Useem, 'Stratification in a Prairie Town,' *American Sociological Review*, July 1942; James West, *Plainville, U.S.A.* (New York: Columbia University Press, 1950); Harold F. Kaufman, *Defining Prestige in a Rural Community* (New York: Beacon House, 1946); Evon Z. Vogt, Jr., 'Social Stratification in the Rural Midwest: A Structural Analysis,' *Rural Sociology*, December 1947; August B. Hollingshead, *Elmtown's Youth* (New York: John Wiley, 1949); W. Lloyd Warner, *et al*, *Democracy in Jonesville* (New York: Harper, 1949); M. C. Hill and Bevode C. McCall, 'Social Stratification in "Georgiatown,"' *American Sociological Review*, December 1950; and Alfred Winslow Jones, *Life, Liberty and Property* (Philadelphia: J. B. Lippincott, 1941).

Most local community studies of prestige, so often the unit of sociological study, are of merely local interest. One cannot even say that they are of interest beyond that because of the methodological innovations they make possible, for in truth most of these methodological advancements are suitable only for what they have been worked out for—local community studies.

It is interesting to notice that in examining the small American city, both novelist and sociologist have, each in his own way, been interested in similar details and reached quite similar conclusions. They have both generally been more interested in status than in power. The novelist has been more interested in manners and in the frustrating effects of small-town life on human relations and personality; the sociologist has not paid very full attention to the small city as a structure of power, much less as a unit in a system of power that is nation-wide. The similarity of their descriptive effects is revealed by the fact that, despite the rituals of proof they contain, the endless 'community studies' of the sociologists often read like badly written novels; and the novels, like better-written sociology.

2. See Allison Davis, *et al*, op. cit. p. 497.

3. I have drawn in this section from various parts of Floyd Hunter's

first-hand study, *Community Power Structure* (Chapel Hill: University of North Carolina Press, 1953).

4. Cf. ibid. pp. 172–4.

5. See Richard Hofstadter, *The Age of Reform* (New York: Knopf, 1955), pp. 46 ff.

6. See Hollingshead, op. cit. p. 59. On farm ownership in a southern county, see Allison Davis, op. cit. p. 276.

7. On urban ownership of farm land in a Middle-Western county, see Evon Vogt, op. cit.

8. Compare, on the small city and the national corporation, Mills and Ulmer, 'Small Business and Civic Welfare,' op. cit.

9. For an example of the confusion of small town with nation to the point of caricature, see W. Lloyd Warner, *American Life: Dream and Reality* (Chicago: University of Chicago Press, 1953).

3. Metropolitan 400

1. Cf. Dixon Wecter, *The Saga of American Society* (New York: Scribner's, 1937), pp. 199 ff., which is the standard work on the history of American 'Society.' The best examinations of the 'Societies' of particular big cities are Cleveland Amory, *The Proper Bostonians* (New York: E. P. Dutton, 1947); and Edward Digby Baltzell Jr., *The Elite and the Upper Class in Metropolitan America: A Study of Stratification in Philadelphia,* (Ph.D. thesis, Columbia University, 1953), both of which I have used.

2. Mrs. John King Van Rensselaer, *The Social Ladder* (New York: Henry Holt, 1924), pp. 30–32.

3. Dixon Wecter, op. cit. pp. 294–5.

4. Cf. J. L. Ford, 'New York of the Seventies,' *Scribner's Magazine*, June 1923, p. 744.

5. Mrs. John King Van Rensselaer, op. cit. pp. 53–4.

6. W. J. Mills, 'New York Society,' *Delineator*, November 1904. Cf. also Ralph Pulitzer, 'New York Society at Work,' *Harper's Bazaar*, December 1909.

7. Cf. Harvey O'Connor, *The Astors* (New York: Knopf, 1941), p. 197.

8. Wecter, op. cit. pp. 209-10.

9. Ibid. pp. 212, 214.

10. Cited in ibid. p. 215.

11. See FIVE: The Very Rich, and notes to that chapter.

12. Wecter, op. cit. pp. 232–3.

13. See Mona Gardner, 'Social Register Blues,' *Collier's*, 14 December 1946 and G. Holland, 'Social Register,' *American Mercury*, June 1932. On the volumes of *The Social Register* published up to 1925, see Wecter, op. cit. p. 233.

14. Wecter, op. cit. p. 234.

15. As of 1940. Cf. Baltzell Jr., op. cit. Table 2.

16. See ibid. Table 14, pp. 89 ff.

17. Wecter, op. cit. pp. 235, 234.

18. Thorstein Veblen, *The Theory of the Leisure Class*, 1899 (New York: New American Library, Mentor Edition, 1953), p. 162. Cf. also my Introduction to that edition for a fuller criticism of Veblen's theory.

19. *Time*, 26 October 1953.

20. See 'Boston,' *Fortune*, February 1933, p. 27.

21. *Business Week*, 5 June 1954, pp. 92–3.

22. From private estimations. Cf. Baltzell Jr., op. cit. p. 178.

23. Cf. ibid. footnote 5, p. 172.

24. 'Miss Chapin's, Miss Walker's, Foxcroft, Farmington,' *Fortune*, August 1931, p. 38.

25. See Porter Sargent, *A Handbook of Private Schools*, 25th ed. (Boston: Porter Sargent, 1941); 'Schools for Boys,' *Fortune*, May 1944, pp. 165 ff.; 'St. Paul's, St. Mark's, Groton, Andover, *et al*,' *Fortune*, September 1931, pp. 76 ff. Cf. also George S. Counts, 'Girls' Schools,' *Fortune*, August 1931 and 'Twelve of The Best American Schools,' *Fortune*, January 1936, pp. 48 ff.

26. 'Schools for Boys,' op. cit. p. 165. Cf. also 'Boys' Prep School,' *Life*, 1 March 1954, which deals with Hotchkiss. Compare Eleanor Roosevelt's feelings upon sending her youngest son, John, to Groton, as reported by her in *This I Remember* (New York: Harper, 1949), p. 43.

27. Cf. Frank D. Ashburn, *Peabody of Groton* (New York: Coward McCann, 1944), pp. 30, 67–8.

28. 'St. Paul's, St. Mark's, Groton, Andover, *et al*,' op. cit. p. 76.

29. Cf. Allan Heely, *Why the Private School?* (New York: Harper, 1951).

30. Cf. John P. Marquand, *H. M. Pulham Esquire* (New York: Bantam Edition, 1950), pp. 76, 60; and W. M. Spackman, *Heyday* (New York: Ballantine Edition, 1953), p. 12.

31. Cf. Baltzell Jr., op. cit. pp. 218–20.

4. The Celebrities

1. See 'The Yankee Doodle Salon,' *Fortune*, December 1937; and, for a recent account, George Frazier, 'Cafe Society: Wild, Wicked and Worthless,' *Coronet*, August 1954. Cf. also Elsa Maxwell, *R.S.V.P., Elsa Maxwell's Own Story* (Boston: Little, Brown, 1954).

2. Cf. *Business Week*, 12 January 1953, pp. 58, 64.

3. 'The U.S. Debutante,' *Fortune*, December 1938, pp. 48 ff.; and 'The Yankee Doodle Salon,' op. cit. pp. 128–9.

4. Cf. ibid. p. 127; and Mrs. John King Van Rennselaer, 'Entertaining Royalty,' *Ladies' Home Journal*, May 1925, p. 72.

5. 'The Yankee Doodle Salon,' op. cit. pp. 124–5.

6. Jack Gould, 'Television in Review,' *The New York Times*, 6 April 1954. Cf. also Jack Gould, 'TV Techniques on the Political Stage,' *The New York Times Magazine*, 25 April 1954, pp. 12 ff.

7. Cf. Igor Cassini, 'The New 400,' *Esquire*, June 1953. On Cassini, see *Who's Who in America*, vol. 27; *Time*, 5 November 1945, pp. 69–70; and *Newsweek*, 3 September 1945, p. 68.

8. I did not feel that Cassini's list warranted exhaustive analysis; in a cursory way, I was able to classify only 342 of the 399 names he listed: 102 professional celebrities; 41 of the metropolitan 400; and 199 institutional leaders (93 in government and 79 in business).

9. 'By and large, branch by branch, family by family, the Bostonian of today has withdrawn from productive enterprise. He has lost the active management of his industries. He has lost the political control of his city. He is no longer a figure, as he was a dominant figure a hundred years ago, in the government of the nation. He no longer leads either in public opinion or in private thought. And he has so completely lost his leadership in the arts that his former influence has become a subject for satire.' But 'no great Boston family of the first rank has lost either means or position. No real break has been made in the city's ruling class. And all the laws of economic determinism seem to have been violated in that fact. . . . At present, by the supplementary device of giving trustees discretion to pay or not to pay income as they see the necessity, a Massachusetts estate may be tied up beyond the reach of any power but the Communist International. But it was already possible three generations ago to expedite one's fortune safely into eternity—or into so much of eternity as the Rule Against Perpetuities left open. And Boston families early formed the habit—a habit in which the highly reputed Suffolk County Bar and the helpful provisions of the Massachusetts laws on trustee investments confirmed them. Fortunately—or unfortunately—for Boston they formed the habit in the days of their wealth . . . Time cannot wither nor custom stale their infinite variety of sound investments. Social power is theirs. Civilization is theirs. But should they attempt to strike back through the mirror into the world of actual power they would bleed to death. Farther forward and in the focus of living authority is the great banking unity, the First National. Below it in various relations of financial dependence are the Boston industries. Above it, in a somewhat shadowy perspective, are the individuals who control it . . . To the side, and in no apparent relation either to the financial web or to the social, stands the political hierarchy . . . And above the political hierarchy but in no apparent relation to it other than the relation established by a common blood and a common religion stands the Irish Catholic hierarchy of the city . . . There are doubtless mysterious threads and channels which lead from one focus of power to another. Certainly there are rumors enough of such connectives . . . There is no agreement. Or if there is agreement it is agreement upon the single point that no threads of power, save the threads which bind Harvard College to the sterns of the clipper ships, lead to the Bostonians.' 'Boston,' *Fortune*, February 1933, pp. 27 ff.

10. For example, Mrs. J. Borden Harriman wrote that 'The Four Hundred have grown to four thousand. Perhaps I exaggerate, but cer-

tainly there are a dozen sets, each sufficient unto itself, and yet interlocking, like directorates, that set the fashions in New York today . . .'
'Hither and Yon,' *The Century Magazine*, September 1923, p. 881.
And Alice-Leone Moats made it clear that 'the cold nose' was not sufficient: 'One must have the showmanship to put it across, to make it
obvious that the possession of the coldest nose entitles one to a position
of eminence. But the person who can go into a restaurant, be instantly
recognized and given the best table in the room has cafe value. In
other words, the outstanding social figures are all Diamond Jim Bradys.'
'Cafe Value,' *The Saturday Evening Post*, 3 August 1935, p. 12.

11. See 'The Yankee Doodle Salon,' op. cit. pp. 183, 186.

12. *Time*, 31 January 1955, p. 57.

13. See *Time*, 18 January 1954, p. 30.

14. Perhaps it is also revealed by two contrasting stories recently
carried in a national news magazine: (1) Upon her death in 1953, no less
a Society Lady than Mrs. Cornelius Vanderbilt is treated as a quaint
sort of curiosity (Cf. *Time*, 19 January 1953, p. 21). (2) About the same
time, we read of Prince Mike Romanoff, probably born one Harry F.
Gerguson in Brooklyn, of cafe society fame. In the account of his personality, Harry F. Gerguson is treated with due deference and quite
some jolly admiration for being such a successful fake. Cf. *Time*, 9 June
1952, p. 41.

15. Dixon Wecter, *The Saga of American Society* (New York: Scribner's, 1937), pp. 227, 226, 228.

16. 'The U.S. Debutante,' op. cit. pp. 48, 52. Cf. also Alida K. L.
Milliken, 'This Debutante Business,' *North American Review*, February
1930.

17. Elsa Maxwell, 'Society—What's Left of It,' *Collier's*, March 1939,
p. 101.

18. Cf., for example, the Woodbury ad in the *Ladies' Home Journal*,
February 1939, p. 45.

19. Cf. *Life*, 25 December 1950, p. 67.

20. 'Yankee Doodle Salon,' op. cit. p. 126.

21. *Business Week*, 3 October 1953, p. 184. Cf. also Anonymous,
'Piloting a Social Climber,' *Ladies' Home Journal*, August 1927.

22. Maude Parker, 'The New Four Hundred of New York,' *The Saturday Evening Post*, 2 April 1927, p. 214.

23. Mona Gardner, 'Social Register Blues,' *Collier's*, 14 December
1946, p. 97. Cf. also 'Society,' *Literary Digest*, 16 January 1937, p. 22;
and Bennett Schiff, 'Inside Cafe Society: The Debutantes,' *New York
Post*, 20 April 1955, pp. 4 ff.

24. For various recent images of 'The All-American Girl,' see Elizabeth Hardwick, 'The American Woman as Snow-Queen,' *Commentary*,
December 1951, pp. 546 ff.; Parker Tyler, *The Hollywood Hallucina-
tion* (New York: Creative Age Press, 1944); and Bennett Schiff, 'Inside
Cafe Society,' *New York Post*, 19 April 1955, pp. 4 ff.

25. On the relation between night clubs and businessmen on expense

accounts, cf. *Business Week,* 12 January 1952, pp. 58 ff. On the 'expense-account girls,' see reports of the Micky Jelke hearings, especially *Life,* 2 March 1953, pp. 29 ff. On cafe-society morality in general, see Mills, 'Public Morality: Girls Using Vice To Help Careers,' *New York Journal-American,* 31 August 1952, p. 4-L.

26. In 1946, one important Washington social list, it is said, had 3,000 changes out of 5,000. Jane Eads, 'Washington Playground,' *Collier's,* 13 April 1946, p. 52. There is, in Washington, of course, a metropolitan 400 known as 'The Cave Dwellers,' the families whose members have resided in Washington for at least two or three generations, and who live by the engagement book. But, competing with them are the 'great hostesses,' not all of them familied to any notable degree, who are rather professional in the strategy of status; and the wealthy, although temporary, residents whose entertaining is frequent and socially successful. And, as in other cities, there are the climbers who have the money of the new upper classes, as well as the social inclination, but not the accomplished status.

27. Cf. John K. Galbraith, *American Capitalism* (Boston: Houghton Mifflin, 1952).

28. Ida M. Tarbell, *Owen D. Young* (New York: Macmillan, 1932), pp. 211–12.

29. Quoted in *Fortune,* March 1931, pp. 92, 94.

30. *The Secret Diary of Harold L. Ickes, Vol. II: The Inside Struggle, 1936–1939* (New York: Simon and Schuster, 1954), p. 644.

31. 'Last year [1954] Wisconsin's Republican Senator Alexander Wiley impressed himself on the folks back home by posing for photographs with his gavel about to descend on the bald dome of New Jersey's G. O. P. Senator H. Alexander Smith; this year New Jersey's 320-lb. Democratic Representative T. James Tumulty made a big impression by posing in his underpants.

'During this session, while the 84th Congress has been deliberating on the state of the U. S., Maine's Republican Senator Margaret Chase Smith has been seen on Edward R. Murrow's television program as she traipsed around the globe—e.g., to Formosa, India, Spain. A pixy TV program called *Masquerade Party* has achieved a clown's gallery of Senators, e.g., Indiana's Republican Senator Homer Capehart came with a Roman toga draped around his aldermanic figure, South Dakota's Republican Senator Karl Mundt and his wife appeared as Wild Bill Hickok and Calamity Jane, Alabama's Democratic Senator John Sparkman (his party's 1952 nominee for Vice President) showed up disguised as a fireman.' *Time,* 4 April 1955, p. 17. See also Douglas Cater's excellent analysis, 'Every Congressman a Television Star,' *The Reporter,* 16 June 1955, pp. 26 ff.

On the status of businessmen, compare the 1907 presidential address of Jeremiah W. Jenks, 'The Modern Standard of Business Honor,' to the American Economic Association (Third Series, vol. III), pp. 1–22, with comments to be found in Sigmund Diamond's *The Reputation of the*

American Businessman (Cambridge: Harvard University Press, 1955). See also 'Corporation Life Gets a Literature,' *Business Week,* 5 June 1954, p. 79.

32. Gustave Le Bon, *The Crowd,* 1896 (London: Ernest Benn, 1952), pp. 129, 130, 131.

33. In this section, I have drawn upon Harold Nicolson's *The Meaning of Prestige* (Cambridge, England: Cambridge University Press, 1937).

34. Gustave Le Bon, op. cit. p. 140.

35. Cf. Thorstein Veblen, *The Theory of the Leisure Class,* 1899 (New York: New American Library, Mentor Edition, 1953).

36. Cf. John Adams, *Discourses on Davila* (Boston: Russell and Cutler, 1805), especially pp. 26–7, 30–34, 48–9. The subsequent quotations are from pp. 40, 28–9, and 18.

37. But see Rene Sedillot, 'Now Medals for Civilians, Too,' *The New York Times Magazine,* 24 April 1955, pp. 22 ff., for recent attempts to have honor more officially recognized.

38. Winthrop Rockefeller. Cf. *The New York Times,* 27 December 1953, and the *New York Post,* 16 October 1953.

39. Haroldson L. Hunt. Cf. *The New York Times Magazine,* 8 March 1953.

40. Barbara Sears Rockefeller. See *Time,* 28 June 1954 and *The New York Times,* 4 August 1954.

41. Dorothy Taylor di Frasso. Cf. *The New York Herald Tribune,* 5 January 1954, p. 9 and *Time,* 18 January 1954, p. 88.

5. The Very Rich

1. Cf. Joseph A. Schumpeter, *Capitalism, Socialism and Democracy* 3rd ed. (New York: Harper, 1950), pp. 81 ff.

2. For a careful and revealing analysis of the attitudes and connections of the Presidents and the commissioners involved in anti-trust action during the crucial Progressive Era, see Meyer H. Fishbein, *Bureau of Corporations: An Agency of the Progressive Era* (MA thesis, American University, 1954), esp. pp. 19–29, 100–119.

3. Frederick Lewis Allen, *The Lords of Creation* (New York: Harper, 1935), pp. 9–10.

4. Ibid. p. 12.

5. Cf. *Time,* 10 August 1953, p. 82.

6. Report of the Smaller War Plants Corporation to the Special Committee to Study Problems of American Small Business, U.S. Senate, *Economic Concentration and World War II,* 79th Congress, 2nd Session, Senate Committee Print No. 6 (Washington, D.C.: U.S. Government Printing Office, 1946). pp. 37, 39, 40.

7. On wealth in Colonial America, see Dixon Wecter, *The Saga of American Society* (New York: Scribner's, 1937), chap. 2; and Gustavus Myers, *History of the Great American Fortunes,* 1907 (revised Modern Library edition, 1936), pp. 55–6, 59, 85. On the estate of George Wash-

ington, see ibid. p. 49. On the multi-millionaires in the early 1840's, see
A. Forbes and J. W. Greene, *The Rich Men of Massachusetts* (Boston:
Fetridge & Co., 1851); Moses Yale Beach, *Wealth and Pedigree of the
Wealthy Citizens of New York City* (New York: Compiled with much
care and published at the Sun Office, 1842), 4th ed.; and 'Wealth and
Biography of the Wealthy Citizens of Philadelphia,' by a Member of the
Philadelphia Bar, 1845. On the New York multi-millionaires in the mid-
dle 1850's, see Moses Yale Beach, 'The Wealthy Citizens of the City
of New York,' 12th ed. (New York: Published at the Sun Office, 1855).
On the coinage of the word 'millionaire,' see Wecter, op. cit. p. 113.

8. See The New York Tribune, *Tribune Monthly,* June 1892. Sidney
Ratner has recently edited a book, *New Light on the History of Great
American Fortunes* (New York: Augustus M. Kelley, 1953), which reprints two listings of American millionaires—from the *Tribune Monthly,*
June 1892 and the *World Almanac, 1902*. These lists are of little use in
the attempt to list the very rich (see footnote 9 below) since only rarely
is an estimate of the exact size of the fortune given; examination of this
list shows that hundreds of 'mere millionaires' appear alongside John D.
Rockefeller and Andrew Carnegie.

9. In a country which, as Ferdinand Lundberg once remarked, 'literally flaunts a chaos of statistics about subjects of little general interest,'
there are no precise figures on the great fortunes. To list the names of
the richest people of three generations, I have had to do the best that I
could with such unsystematic sources as are available. I have, of course,
availed myself of all the histories of great fortunes in the United States,
as well as the biographies of those who possessed them. Twice in the
twentieth century—1924 and 1938—rather systematic information has
been published on large incomes or big properties (see below); and
there is an intermittent stream of information and myth appearing in
newspapers and magazines, the facts of a probated will, the tax scandal,
the anecdote about rich individuals.

I began with a list of all persons mentioned in the books listed below
who were born after 1799 and who were stated to have ever possessed
$30 million or more. In many cases, the size of the fortune was not
estimated in the source of the name; but taking note of all possible
names, we searched all the sources at hand for estimations of the size
of fortune. The general criterion of $30 million is mainly a matter of
convenience. We found that such a criterion will yield 371 names: since
it was necessary to compile detailed information about the fortune and
the career of each of these individuals, our resources did not permit us
to handle a larger list. Here are the sources used:

(I) Gustavus Myers, *History of the Great American Fortunes,* 1907
(revised Modern Library edition, 1936). (II) Gustavus Myers, *The
Ending of Hereditary Fortunes* (New York: Julian Messner, 1939).
(III) Matthew Josephson, *The Robber Barons* (New York: Harcourt,
Brace, 1934). (IV) Frederick Lewis Allen, *The Lords of Creation* (New
York: Harper, 1935). (V) Ferdinand Lundberg, *America's 60 Families,*

1937 (New York: The Citadel Press, 1946)—our cautious use of this book is discussed below in (xi). (vi) Dixon Wecter, *The Saga of American Society* (New York: Scribner's 1937). (vii) 'Richest U.S. Women,' *Fortune,* November 1936 (viii) Stewart H. Holbrook, *The Age of the Moguls* (New York: Doubleday, 1953). Based in considerable detail upon Myers' work and those of other historians, this work is mainly a popularization of earlier work. (ix) 'Noted Americans of the Past: American Industrial Leaders, Financiers and Merchants,' *World Almanac,* 1952, p. 381, and 1953, p. 783. Does not include estimates of fortunes. (x) Cleveland Amory, *The Last Resorts* (New York: Harper, 1952). There are naturally many duplications of people mentioned in these sources; but each one of them has yielded information unmentioned by all the others.

Three further sources require more detailed discussion:

(xi) In 1924 and again in 1925, a temporary law allowed the release of information on the size of income-tax payments made on incomes for 1923 and 1924. Journalists were admitted to various offices of the Bureau of Internal Revenue and there copied names with the taxes paid by each. The release of this data was so administratively sloppy that one paper published data about a man whom another paper ignored, some errors were printed, and in some cases all journalists missed the names of people who were known to have paid large taxes. (There were, of course, some wealthy people whose entire income was tax free. Selecting the 1924 income tax list for study, we took everyone who had paid $200,000 or more in taxes as listed in either or in both *The New York Times* or *The New York Herald Tribune,* 2 to 15 September 1925.

The average tax at this time and at these levels resulted in a payment of about 40 per cent of the gross income; so a payment of $200,000 reveals an annual income during 1924 of about $500,000. Since most such high incomes are derived from investments, an overall figure of 5 per cent return on investment would mean that for one to obtain a half million dollars from investments, the capital owned would have to be about $10 million. It has been presumed that only about one-third of most entire fortunes were at that time in taxable sources; hence, the over-all fortune owned would be three times larger than the taxable fortune. (These are the calculations Ferdinand Lundberg made on the 1924 returns in his book cited above. He comments that 'in individual instances the multiplication by three of the net fortune upon whose income a tax was paid may result in some distortion, but this appears to be the only way in which to obtain a general approximation; and as the method gives generally accurate results, the picture as a whole is not overdrawn. Rather it is very conservative.' (p. 25.) I think this is so.) By these calculations, then, a tax of $200,000 indicates an income of $500,000, a taxable fortune of 10 million, and an entire fortune of 30 million.

Most evidence from those estates that were probated shortly after 1924 shows that these calculations are reasonably accurate. For instance, according to these calculations, the $434,000 tax payment of Richard Teller Crane, Jr., indicated a total fortune of $64.8 million; he died in 1931 leaving an estate of 50 million. Ogden Mills' tax payment of $372,000 would indicate a fortune of 55.5 million in 1924; he died in 1929 leaving 41 million. There are, of course, cases in which people's estates were much less, but they usually were known to have *lost* their money (such as grain speculator Arthur W. Cutten who was wiped out in the 1929 crash) or given it away before their death. I included such people as long as they were at any one time in possession of $30 million.

I know of no systematic use of these names. Ferdinand Lundberg, in 1937, compiled a list of '60 families' which, in fact, are not all families and which number—as 'families'— not 60, but about 74. But he does not analyze them systematically. By 'systematic' I understand that similar information is compiled for each person on the list and generalizations made therefrom.

What Lundberg does is (1) generalize blood relations –sometimes cousinhood only—into power and financial cliques. We do not wish to confuse the two. In addition (2), we cannot go along with the list he has abstracted from *The New York Times,* which is not uniformly made up of families or individuals or companies but is a miscellany.

Of the so-called 60 families, there are 37 'families' represented by more than one member's tax payments. There are eight unrelated men included along with the Morgans; and there is another group of seven families forming his 38th 'family' (this is the 'Standard Oil Group'). The list is filled out with 22 individuals paying 1924 taxes ranging from $188,608 to $791,851. Thus, if 'family' is to mean a blood tie, there are many more than 60 families on his list; but the list is not even a full account of these families, since only those paying a tax under the *family name* were included. Moreover, there are a number of people (e.g. J. H. Brewer, L. L. Cooke) who paid much higher taxes in 1924 than many of the people named by Lundberg but who are not included in his listing of '60 families.' Some, but not all, of these are not listed in *The New York Times,* but are in *The New York Herald Tribune,* which Mr. Lundberg seems to have ignored.

More importantly for the purpose of obtaining a list of the top richest *persons* is the fact that some of the families in Lundberg's list of the top 60 do not even appear among the very rich when individuals are concerned. The Deerings, for instance: Lundberg uses three Deerings; the tax payment of all three adds up to $315,701. We do not include the Deerings on our list of the 'very rich' since James Deering paid a tax of only $179,896; Charles, only $139,341; the third Deering, some $7,000. The same type of procedure holds for the Tafts, Lehmans, and deForests. They are all undoubtedly rich people, but not to the same degree as the people in whom we are interested.

(xii) A more recent systematic source of information regarding size of private fortunes is the Temporary National Economic Committee's Monograph No. 29: 'The Distribution of Ownership in the 200 Largest

Non-Financial Corporations' (Washington: U.S. Government Printing Office, 1940). This monograph gives the 20 largest stockholders of record in each of the 200 largest non-financial corporations, along with the stockholdings of the directors and officers of these corporations, as of 1937 or 1938. Although it does contain most of the well-known fortunes that are based upon industrial ownership, the list is not complete: it does not cover money held in government or local bonds, in real estate or in financial houses. Moreover, in a number of instances ownership even of industrial corporations is disguised by the practice of recording the ownership of a block of stock under various investment houses which do not divulge the names of the actual owners. Nevertheless, this TNEC list represents the best we have found for the later period. Compared with the scattered case studies available for the nineteenth century, the wealthy it discloses are a rather stable set of men.

From this source I have taken each person for whom the total value of all shares owned in all companies listed was equal to $10 million or more in 1937 or 1938. Multiplying this figure by three (assuming again that the taxable wealth represents only one-third of the total fortune owned), gives us all those people owning $30 million or more in the late 'thirties.

(XIII) None of the sources above provide really up-to-date information about the very rich. Many of the people named in the various books, and in the 1924 and 1938 lists, are, of course, still alive; and we have found living heirs to people now dead—through obituaries, we tried to trace the fortunes of all names selected, and included in our list all those heirs whom we have found to have inherited $30 million or more.

(XIV) In order to obtain information about people now alive, the following agencies and government bureaus were contacted—various officials in each of them gave us such information as they could, none of it 'official,' and none of much use to us: the Federal Reserve Board of New York; the Securities Exchange Commission; U.S. Department of Commerce, Bureau of Domestic Commerce; and the Bureau of Internal Revenue's Statistical Division and Information Division. Individuals were also contacted in the following private organizations: Dun & Bradstreet; The National Industrial Conference Board's Division of Business Economics; *The Wall Street Journal; Barron's; Fortune;* The Russell Sage Foundation; *U.S. News and World Report;* Brookings Institution; Bureau of National Affairs, Federal Savings and Loan; and two private investment houses. People seen in these organizations could only refer us to sources of which we were already aware. Some had never thought much about the problem, others seemed slightly shocked at the idea of 'finding out' about the top wealthy people, others were enchanted with the idea but helpless as to sources. I am grateful to Professor Fred Blum for making most of these contacts for us, and for his helpful comments on this whole problem.

(xv) During the post-World War II years, I have been searching current papers and periodicals for any mention of other multi-millionaires. From magazines such as *Business Week*, *Look* and *Life* and *Time* and from *The New York Times*, I have picked up additional names, mainly of the new crop of Texans. In this search for additional names, I have had the benefit of about two dozen interested students and friends.

Because of the necessarily miscellaneous character of the collection of names, we cannot be certain, and I do not claim, that the list includes *all* the richest people in America over the last 100 years; nor that all the people whom we have included in our list have, in proven fact, possessed at one time or another, $30 million.

Two things, however, can be said with reasonable surety: (1) There is fairly good evidence for the accuracy of the $30 million figure. In cases of people who have died, I have checked by probate of will and found that these estimations seem quite accurate. (2) Even though the list cannot be proved to exhaust the richest—including every single person who has owned the prescribed amounts—all of these people are undoubtedly among the richest people in the United States by any reasonable definition. Undoubtedly in our listing we have missed some who should have been included, and have included others who should not have been. But we have included all those people about whom printed information is available to us, and it is our opinion that such errors as might occur do not materially affect the picture. In short, no exact and proven list seems to us possible; this list seems to us a quite reasonable approximation of the most prominent very rich people in America over the last one hundred years.

The foregoing outline of procedure, along with a preliminary listing of the names selected, and a secondary listing of people we had designated as being of lesser wealth, were sent, for suggestions and criticisms to the following: Dr. John M. Blair of the Bureau of Industrial Economics, Federal Trade Commission; Professor Thomas Cochran of the University of Pennsylvania; Professor Shepard Clough of Columbia University; Professors Arthur Cole, Leland H. Jenks, and Sigmund O. Diamond of the Research Center of Entrepreneurial History at Harvard University; Professors Joseph Dorfman and Robert S. Lynd of Columbia University; Professor Frank Freidel of Stanford University; Frank Fogarty of *Business Week;* Ernest Dale of the School of Business, Columbia University; and Max Lerner of the *New York Post* and Brandeis University. I wish to thank these people for their time, consideration and help on this problem, although they are in no way responsible for any errors of fact or judgement.

Of the 371 names, I was unable to find, from a search of biographical sources, the books mentioned above, and newspaper files, any information about the life of 69 of them. More than half of these names came from the 1924 tax lists where we had only the last name and first initials to go by. The speculative nature of many large incomes during the 'twenties would lead me to believe that the chances were high that many of these incomes did not represent durable great fortunes; and our concern with the 'most prominent' very rich in America makes it feasible to omit these 69 people from the Very Rich. At any rate it was necessary.

In an effort to make some allowance for the variance in the value of the dollar over the periods in which we are interested, I ranked the members of each of our three generations by the estimated sizes of their fortunes. Economic historians whom I consulted have indicated that they 'do not know of any satisfactory device for reducing a given amount of money to purchasing power equivalents over a long period of time ' (Letter to the author from Sigmund O. Diamond and Leland H. Jenks, 30 March 1954). Of course, when one gets into the multi-million-dollar categories, the cost of living—which is usually the purpose of establishing relative purchasing power—is not a matter of concern.

For each generation I took the 90 rich*est* people. We are thus considering the 90 or so *most prominent* and rich*est* in each of the three historical epochs. This gives us a total of 275 cases for concentrated analysis, which is the upper 74 per cent of the 371 cases mentioned by all sources known to us.

Of the 90 cases selected as Group I, the median year of birth is 1841; the median years of death, 1912. The year when the median age is 60 is therefore 1901; hereafter Group I is identified as the 1900 generation.

Of the 95 cases selected from Group II, the median year of birth is 1867; the median year of death, 1936. The year when the median age is 60 is therefore 1927; Group II thus consists of the 1925 generation.

Of the 90 cases in Group III, the median year of birth is 1887; and most of these were still alive in 1954. On the average they were 60 in 1947; Group III is thus the 1950 generation.

10. On John D. Rockefeller, see Wecter, op. cit. pp. 141–2, 482; Frederick Lewis Allen, op. cit. pp. 4–7; *The New York Times*, 24 May 1937 and 6 June 1937; and, for further references, John T. Flynn, *God's Gold* (New York: Harcourt, Brace, 1932). On Henry O. Havemeyer, see *Dictionary of American Biography;* Myers, *History of the Great American Fortunes,* pp 697 ff.; and *The New York Times*, 5 December 1907. On Henrietta Green, see *Dictionary of American Biography; The New York Times,* 4 July 1916, p. 1 and 9 July 1916, magazine section; and Boyden Sparkes and Samuel Taylor Moore, *The Witch of Wall Street: Hetty Green* (Garden City, N.Y.: Doubleday Doran, 1935). On George F. Baker, Jr., see *Who Was Who, 1897–1942;* and *The New York Times,* 31 May 1937.

11. On Hunt and Cullen, see *The New York Times,* 21 November 1952 and the magazine section of 8 March 1953; *The Washington Post,* 15 through 19 February 1954; and other reports of the United Press Survey such as those of Preston McGraw in the *Long Island Star-Journal,* 4 and 5 August 1954 and Gene Patterson, 'World's Richest Man is a Texan,' *Pacific Coast Business and Shipping Register,* 16 August 1954.

12. The figure on the proportion of foreign-born adult U.S. males in

1900 was calculated from the U.S. Department of Commerce, *Historical Statistics of the U.S.,1789–1945*, p. 32. On the foreign-born white population in the United States in 1950, cf. *The World Almanac, 1954*, p. 266.

13. See *Historical Statistics of the U.S., 1789–1945*, p. 29.

14. The general figures on religion cannot be given with more precision for religious faith is unknown for a good many of the very rich. The censuses are likewise inaccurate on religious denominations for most periods of U.S. history, thus also prohibiting comparison of any one group with the general population.

15. For instance, Eleanor Rice, who was the daughter of William L. Elkins and at one time the wife of George D. Widener, gave millions to a variety of artistic and educational organizations and her last husband was a physician and geographer who was famed for expeditions to South America to study tropical diseases and native tribes. See *The New York Herald Tribune*, 5 October 1951. At her palatial home in California, Mary Virginia McCormick had a permanent staff of musicians and imported entire symphony orchestras for parties and concerts. See *The New York Times*, 26 May 1951.

16. On Anita McCormick Blaine, see *The New York Times*, 13 February 1954; on Hetty Sylvia Green Wilks, see *The New York Times*, 6 February 1951, p. 27

17. Even in 1900, when only 39 per cent of the very rich were recruited from the upper classes, some 25 per cent of the very rich were economic men of this family-manager type. William Henry Vanderbilt, son of the Commodore and dead by 1900, became a conservative manager of the Vanderbilt enterprises, and, in fact, was head of them when they reached their financial high point. It is, of course, difficult to know whether this was a result of his management—which was neither speculative nor extravagant—or a result of objective changes resulting in the increased value of railroad securities. The indolence of his sons, who spent more time in Europe playing a game of fashion, was perhaps less a cause of the relative decline of the Vanderbilt fortune than the downswing of the railroad economy. Cf. Wayne Andrews, *The Vanderbilt Legend*, New York: Harcourt, Brace, 1941. George D. Widener, son of P. A. B. Widener, became a stockholder in 23 companies and was president and director of 18. He was an active type of economic man in that he was involved in 1902 in a suit for fraud for praising a weak company so that he could sell his stock in it and get out before it failed. Cf. *Philadelphia Public Ledger*, 2 April 1912 and *Philadelphia Press*, 23 September 1902.

Of the modern-day family managers there is, for instance, Vincent Astor—the great-grandson of John Jacob Astor—who may be an enthusiast for yachting and automobile racing, but he disappointed society editors in their search for the idle life of scandal when, at the death of his father, he quit Harvard and, at the age of 21, began to improve the value of the Astor land in New York City. Young Vincent changed the

NOTES

management policy by abolishing many tenements and attempting to bring middle and upper-class clientele to Astor land, thus, of course, increasing its value to him. Cf. Harvey O'Connor, *The Astors*, New York: Knopf, 1941, p. 336. And the daily decisions of John D. Rockefeller III involve the disposition of millions of dollars; he has a full-time job for which he was trained: philanthropic work on an international scope. Moreover, he has been active as a director in many American corporations, including the New York Life Insurance Company and the Chase National Bank.

18. See *The New York Times*, 1 August 1954, pp. 1, 7.

19. On the vicious circle of poverty and the withdrawal from success, see Mills, *White Collar* (New York: Oxford University Press, 1951), pp. 259 ff.

20. See Myers, *History of the Great American Fortunes*, pp. 634 ff.; Lewis Corey, *The House of Morgan* (New York: G. Howard Watt, 1930); and John K. Winkler, *Morgan the Magnificent* (New York: The Vanguard Press, 1930).

21. See Harvey O'Connor, *How Mellon Got Rich* (New York: International Pamphlets, 1933) and *Mellon's Millions* (New York: John Day, 1933); Frank R. Denton, *The Mellons of Pittsburgh* (New York: Newcomen Society of England, American Branch, 1948); and *The New York Times*, 30 August 1937, p. 16.

22. Quoted in *Time*, 1 June 1953, p. 38.

23. See *The New York Times*, 2 February 1944, p. 15.

24. See *The New York Times*, 7 June 1948, p. 19.

25. See Wallace Davis, *Corduroy Road* (Houston: Anson Jones Press, 1951).

See also the testimony of James D. Stietenroth, former chief financial officer of the Mississippi Power & Light Co., in regard to the Dixon-Yates contract, reported in the Interim Report of the Subcommittee of the Committee on the Judiciary on Antitrust and Monopoly on Investigation Into Monopoly in the Power Industry, *Monopoly in the Power Industry*, U.S. Senate, 83d Congress, 2nd Session (Washington, D.C., U.S. Government Printing Office, 1955), pp. 12 ff.

26. Cf. Frederick Lewis Allen, op. cit. p. 85.

6. The Chief Executives

1. See Mills, *White Collar: The American Middle Classes* (New York: Oxford University Press, 1951), Chapters 2 and 3.

2. Calculated from Bureau of the Census, *1951 Annual Survey of Manufacturers* and 'The Fortune Directory of the 500 Largest U.S. Industrial Corporations,' *Fortune*, July 1955, Supplement and p. 96.

3. John Kenneth Galbraith, *American Capitalism: The Concept of Countervailing Power* (New York: Houghton Mifflin, 1952), p. 58; see also pp. 115 ff. and 171 ff.

4. For substantiation, with recent data, of the Gardiner Means view of price rigidity in the corporate economy, see John M. Blair, 'Economic

Concentration and Depression Price Rigidity,' *American Economic Review,* vol. XLV, May 1955, pp. 566–82.

5. Cf. Ferdinand Lundberg, *America's 60 Families,* 1937 (New York: The Citadel Press, 1946), Appendix E.

6. The number of stockholders in 1952, and the proportion they represent of the various occupational groups and income levels which follow, are from a study by Lewis H. Kimmel, *Share Ownership in the United States* (Washington: The Brookings Institution, 1952). Cf. also '1955 Survey of Consumer Finances' *Federal Reserve Bulletin,* June 1955, which reveals that only two percent of 'the spending units' hold $10,000 worth or more in stock. On the adult population in 1950, see *The World Almanac, 1954,* p. 259.

7. Between these polar groups of stockholders there are the farmers, 7 per cent of whom own some stock. Cf. Kimmel, op. cit.

8. Back in 1936 only about 55,000 people—lesss than 1 per cent of all the stockholders—received as much as $10,000 a year in dividends. Cf. 'The 30,000 Managers,' *Fortune,* February 1940, p. 108. In 1937, people with incomes of $20,000 or more—excluding capital gains and losses—collected between 40 and 50 per cent of all corporate dividends, and represented less than 1 per cent of all stockholders. See Temporary National Emergency Committee, 'Final Report to the Executive Secretary,' p. 167.

9. Furthermore, 13 per cent of the corporate dividends received in 1949 went to people who had either no taxable income or income of less than $5,000 a year. Calculated from the U.S. Treasury Department, Bureau of Internal Revenue, 'Statistics of Income for 1949, Part I,' pp. 16, 17.

10. Cf. Floyd Hunter, *Community Power Structure* (Chapel Hill: University of North Carolina Press, 1953); and Robert A. Brady, *Business as a System of Power* (New York: Columbia University Press, 1943).

11. Cf. Mills, *The New Men of Power* (New York: Harcourt, Brace, 1948), pp. 23–7.

12. For details on interlocking directorship in 1938, see TNEC Monograph No. 29: 'The Distribution of Ownership in the 200 Largest Non-financial Corporations,' pp. 59, 533 ff.; cf. also TNEC Monograph No. 30: 'Survey of Shareholdings in 1710 Corporations with Securities Listed on a National Securities Exchange.' In 1947, the story for the broader base of U.S. corporations, financial and non-financial, was practically the same as among the director-owners of the top 200 non-financial corporations in 1938: Of the 10,000 persons who were directors in the 1,600 leading corporations, some 1,500 had seats on more than one board. Since 1914 it has been illegal for a person to be the director of two or more corporations if those corporations are in competition; in 1951, the Federal Trade Commission argued that it wanted the law amplified to include two or more corporations of a certain size regardless of whether or not they are in competition. 'The present law is . . .

unduly limited in its conception of the competition that may be pre-
vented by interlocking directorates. The law applies only where there is
or has been competition between the interlocked companies. It does
not apply where these companies might readily become competitors and
probably would do so but for the effect of the interlock . . . [The law]
is applicable only to direct interlocks among competitors, whereas there
are competition-reducing potentialities in indirect interlocks as well.'
See *Report of The Federal Trade Commission on Interlocking Directorates* (Washington: U.S. Government Printing Office, 1951), esp. pp.
14–15.

In 1950 there were 556 positions as director in the 25 largest corporations in America. One man (Winthrop W. Aldrich), who is now the
Ambassador to Great Britain, held directorships in four of these companies (Chase National Bank, American Telephone and Telegraph
Company, New York Central Railroad, and Metropolitar Life Insurance Company). Seven men each held directorships in three of these
companies; 40, in two companies; and 451 men held directorships in
only one company. Thus, 105 of the 556 seats on the boards of these 25
companies were held by 48 men. See the table prepared for Congressman Emanuel Celler, Chairman of the House Committee on the Judiciary, by the Legislative Reference Service of the Library of Congress,
*Hearings Before the Subcommittee on the Study of Monopoly Power of
the Committee on the Judiciary,* House of Representatives, Eighty-
second Congress, First Session, Serial No. 1, Part 2 (U.S. Government
Printing Office, 1951), p. 77, Exhibit A.

The concentration of corporation power and the informal co-ordination of the business world—with and without interlocking directorships
—has become such that the Department of Labor estimates that only
some 147 employers really bargain out their wage terms with their labor
forces. These bargains set the pattern of wage contracts; thousands of
other employers may go through the motions of bargaining, but the odds
are high that they will end up according to the pattern set by the few
giant deals. See *Business Week*, 18 October 1952, p. 148; Frederick H.
Harbison and Robert Dubin, *Patterns of Union-Management Relations*
(Chicago: Science Research Associates, 1947); Mills, *The New Men of
Power*, pp. 233 ff. and Frederick H. Harbison and John R. Coleman,
Goals and Strategy in Collective Bargaining (New York: Harper,
1951), pp. 125 ff.

13. 'Special Report to Executives on Tomorrow's Management,'
Business Week, 15 August 1953, p. 161.

14. John M. Blair, 'Technology and Size,' *American Economic Review*, vol. xxxviii, May 1948, Number 2, pp. 150–51. Blair argues
that present-day technology, unlike that of the nineteenth and the early
twentieth century, is a force leading toward decentralization rather than
consolidation. For new techniques—such as the replacement of steam by
electricity and the replacement of iron and steel by light metals, alloys,
plastics, and plywood—reduce the scale of operations at which dimin-

ishing returns set in. Given these new technological developments, the maximum profitability of a plant will be reached at a much lower scale of operations than heretofore. 'In summary . . . it may be expected that the increased substitution of these new materials will reduce the amount of capital required per unit of product and thereby tend to result in the establishment of newer, smaller, and more efficient plants.' Ibid. p. 124.

15. Cf. Galbraith, op. cit.; and *American Economic Review,* vol. XLIV, May 1954 for criticisms of Galbraith.

16. Cf. A. A. Berle, Jr., *The 20th Century Capitalist Revolution* (New York: Harcourt, Brace, 1954) and Ben B. Seligman's perceptive review of it in *Dissent,* Winter 1955, pp. 92 ff.

17. F. W. Taussig and C. S. Joslyn broke the ground by obtaining information from about 7,000 businessmen listed in Poor's 1928 Register of Directors: *American Business Leaders: A Study in Social Origins and Social Stratification* (New York: Macmillan, 1932).

Mills analyzed 1,464 'eminent American businessmen' whose biographies appeared in *The Dictionary of American Biography* and who were born between 1570 and 1879: 'The American Business Elite: A Collective Portrait,' *The Tasks of Economic History,* Supplement V to *The Journal of Economic History,* December 1945.

William Miller has made the chief and the best collection of biographies of business leaders. He has personally analyzed these materials and published four articles on them: 'American Historians and the Business Elite,' *Journal of Economic History,* vol. IX, No. 2, November 1949, which compares 190 business leaders of 1903 with their 188 political contemporaries; 'The Recruitment of the Business Elite,' *Quarterly Journal of Economics,* vol. LXIV, No. 2, May 1950, which deals with the social origins of the business leaders of 1903 as compared with the general population; 'American Lawyers in Business and Politics,' *Yale Law Journal,* vol. LX, No. 1, January 1951, which compares the social characteristics of the lawyers found among the business leaders of 1903 with those found among the politicians; and 'The Business Bureaucracies: Careers of Top Executives in the Early Twentieth Century,' *Men in Business: Essays in the History of Entrepreneurship* (Edited by William Miller) (Cambridge: Harvard University Press, 1952), which discusses the business careers of the businessmen of 1903. Mr. Miller also gathered biographical material on 412 business leaders of 1950.

Under the direction of Miller at the Research Center in Entrepreneurial History at Harvard University, a similar study was undertaken on industrial leaders of 1870–1879: see Frances W. Gregory and Irene D. Neu, 'The American Industrial Elite in the 1870's: Their Social Origins,' *Men in Business.*

An analysis of all three of these generations has been written by Suzanne I. Keller, 'Social Origins and Career Lines of Three Generations of American Business Leaders,' Columbia University Ph.D. Thesis, 1954. Using an approach similar to that of Miller, *Fortune* magazine analyzed a group of 900 top executives in 1952—the three highest paid men in the 250 largest industrial corporations, the 25 largest railroads and the 20 largest utilities: 'The Nine Hundred,' *Fortune*, November 1952, pp. 132 ff., which consists of the largest contemporary sample available, good materials not adequately analyzed. Cf. also Mabel Newcomer, 'The Chief Executives of Large Business Corporations,' *Explorations in Entrepreneurial History*, Vol. V (Cambridge: Research Center for Entrepreneurial History at Harvard University, 1952–3), pp. 1–34, which deals with the chief executives of corporations in 1899, 1923, and 1948.

All such studies of career-lines, as well as others used in this book, are, however, readily liable to many technical difficulties of interpretation, the information needed is often very hard to come by, and one may quite easily be misled. For example, the superficial 'social origin' of Senator Clifford Case of New Jersey, judged by his father's occupation, is 'pleasant but not prosperous': he is the son of a Protestant minister who died when Clifford was sixteen. His uncle, however, was a state senator and, for 23 years, a state supreme court justice. (See *Time*, 18 October 1954, p. 21.) On the dangers inherent in using such career-line statistical studies as predictions of the course of social events, see Richard H. S. Crossman, 'Explaining the Revolution of Our Time: Can Social Science Predict Its Course?' *Commentary*, July 1952, pp. 77 ff.

The figures used in Sections 2 and 3 of this chapter are, unless otherwise noted, from Keller's analysis of Miller's data; in no case is this data used unless it is commensurate with other relevant studies: we may thus take those figures presented in the text as representing a general consensus of all the relevant studies done.

18. 'The Nine Hundred,' op. cit., p. 235.

19. As you extend the sample to more executives, the proportion of the top 900 executives in 1952 who graduated from college is roughly the same (about 65 per cent), but only about one-third of these have had post-graduate training. Of the youngest group of present-day executives—those under 50 years of age—84 per cent have graduated from college. See 'The Nine Hundred,' op. cit., p. 135.

20. See ibid., p. 133.

21. See the study of 127 executives in 57 leading companies reported by *Business Week*, 31 May 1952, pp. 112 ff. Seventy-two of the 127 executives received these extra benefits in addition to their salaries.

22. Cf. *Business Week*, 23 May 1953, pp. 110 ff.

23. We do not know exactly for an adequate sample how long or how hard the executives work, but we do have a few recent facts about a small group of West Coast executives, all of whom received salaries of $35,000 or more; we are not given data on how much they own or get from dividends. Some 37 out of this group of 111 men got to work at about 10 a.m., quit around 3 p.m., 'took three-hour lunches, played golf or went fishing two or three times a week, often stretched their weekends to four or five days. All but five of this group owned their

own companies or were officers of small local businesses.' Only 10 men
(nine per cent) worked a straight 40-hour week. But 64 (some 58 per
cent) worked very hard indeed: 'They were almost all employees of
large national corporations . . . They worked from 69 hours a week to
as high as 112, and I mean all work . . . Most were in the office by 8,
left at 6:30 with a pile of homework; when they went out to dinner (an
average of three times a week), it was always on business.' From a
study done by Arthur Stanley Talbott, as reported in *Time*, 10 November 1952, p. 109.

24. *The New York Times*, 10 April 1955, p. 74.

25. See 'Why Don't Businessmen Read Books?' *Fortune*, May 1954.

26. William Miller, 'American Lawyers in Business and Politics,' op.
cit. p. 66.

27. Since they were about 29 when they first joined their companies,
and have been in them about the same length of time—29 years—and
have been in the present job 6 years, it took them an average of 23 years
to reach the top. These and the figures in the two paragraphs of the
text, are from, or re-classified from, "The Nine Hundred,' op. cit.

28. Robert A. Gordon, *Business Leadership in the Large Corporation* (Washington: Brookings Institution, 1945), p. 71.

29. On the 'Number Two' executives, see, for example, *Business
Week*, 2 January 1954 on the du Pont set-up.

30. See *Business Week*, 16 May 1953.

31. John L. McCaffrey in a speech of 10 June 1953 before the graduating class of the University of Chicago's two-year Executive Program, reprinted as 'What Corporation Presidents Think About at
Night,' *Fortune*, September 1953, pp. 128 ff.

32. Cf. *Business Week*, 3 October 1953.

33. See Gordon, op. cit. p. 91; and Peter F. Drucker, *The Practice
of Management* (New York: Harper, 1954).

34. Both the letters of Lammot du Pont and Alfred P. Sloan were reprinted in *The New York Times*, 7 January 1953, pp. 33, 35.

35. The facts and quotation concerning Robert R. Young's fight to
get control of the New York Central are from John Brooks, 'The Great
Proxy Fight,' *The New Yorker*, 3 July 1954, pp. 28 ff. See also *Business
Week*, 24 July 1954, p. 70.

36. See *Business Week*, 15 May 1954.

37. See *The New York Post*, 16 April 1954.

38. Cf. Robert Coughlin, 'Top Managers in Business Cabinet,' *Life*,
19 January 1953, pp. 111, 105.

39. The quotation concerning a high executive of the world's largest
oil company is from *Business Week*, 17 April 1954, p. 76. On the self-
perpetuation of executives like those already at the top, see Melville
Dalton, 'Informal Factors in Career Achievements,' *American Journal
of Sociology*, vol. LVI, No. 5 (March 1951), p. 414.

40. See Keller, op. cit. pp. 108–111.

41. See 'The 30,000 Managers,' op. cit.; and Robert W. Wald, 'The

Top Executive—a First Hand Profile,' *Harvard Business Review*, August 1954.

42. A recent survey by Booz, Allen & Hamilton showed that half of 50 major companies studied used only one man's opinion in rating executives; 30 per cent 'used several persons' opinions to evaluate ability, and only 20 per cent tried more scientific methods.' *Business Week*, 2 April 1955, p. 88.

43. *Business Week*, 3 November 1951, p. 86. Cf. also Mills, *White Collar*, pp. 106 ff.; and William H. Whyte, Jr., and the editors of *Fortune, Is Anybody Listening?* (New York: Simon and Schuster, 1952).

44. 'The Crown Princes of Business,' *Fortune*, October 1953, p. 152.

45. 'The Nine Hundred,' op. cit. p. 135.

46. The quotations and facts in these two paragraphs are from 'The Crown Princes of Business,' op. cit. pp. 152–3.

47. Ibid. p. 264.

48. The quotation from *Fortune* is from ibid. p. 266; and that from the executive is from an anonymous 'president of a well-known corporation,' loc. cit.

49. Ida M. Tarbell, *Owen D. Young* (New York: Macmillan, 1932), pp. 232, 113, 229–30, 121, and 95–6.

7. The Corporate Rich

1. On 'the managerial revolution,' see James Burnham, *The Managerial Revolution: What is Happening in the World* (New York: John Day, 1941); for a detailed comment on Burnham's view, see H. H. Gerth and C. Wright Mills, 'A Marx For the Managers,' *Ethics*, vol. LII, No. 2, January 1942. For the theory of the leading families, see Ferdinand Lundberg, *America's 60 Families*, 1937 (New York: The Citadel Press, 1946).

2. For the income distribution of 1951 compared with that of 1929, see *Business Week*, 20 December 1952, pp. 122–3; the income for both 1929 and 1951 is in terms of 1951 dollars. Cf. also *Business Week*, 18 October 1952, pp. 28–9.

3. For discussions of some of the general economic facts behind the changed income distribution, see Frederick Lewis Allen, *The Big Change* (New York: Harper, 1952), and *Business Week*, 25 October 1952, p. 192.

4. U.S. Department of Commerce, Bureau of the Census, 'Current Population Reports: Consumer Income,' Series P-60, No. 12, June 1953, p. 4.

5. The figures on declared income for 1949 and its sources are computed from U.S. Treasury Department, Bureau of Internal Revenue, 'Statistics of Income for 1949, Part I, Preliminary Report of Individual Income Tax Returns and Taxable Fiduciary Income Tax Returns filed in 1950' (Washington, D.C., U.S. Government Printing Office, 1952), pp. 16–19.

6. Corporate dividends made up the largest share of those 81 people who received from one to 1.9 million dollars (42 and 45 per cent). Estates and trusts made up the largest share (48 per cent) of the money received by the 20 people in the 2 to 2.9 million-dollar income group. Capital gains accounted for 49 per cent of the money received by those earning three million or more. Dividends were, however, secondary sources in these two last highest groups—39 and 43 per cent. See ibid. pp. 16–19.

7. Ibid. pp. 45–7.

8. Historical figures on million-dollar incomes from 1917 to 1936 have been compiled by the Joint Committee on Internal Revenue Taxation of the Congress of the United States, 'Million-dollar Incomes' (Washington, D.C.: U.S. Government Printing Office, 1938). In the years prior to 1944, individual incomes were not separated from estates and trusts. If one were to include these in the 1949 returns to make them comparable with the 513 in 1929, there would be 145 million-dollar incomes in 1949. On the proportion of families with incomes of less than $2,000 in 1939, see *The New York Times,*' (5 March 1952) presentation of Bureau of Census data.

9. 'Preliminary Findings of the 1955 Survey of Consumer Finances,' *Federal Reserve Bulletin,* March 1955, page 3 of reprint.

10. Simon Kuznets, an expert with tax-derived data, finds that the share in total income after taxes of the richest 1 per cent (which goes down to families earning a mere $15,000) of the population has decreased from 19.1 per cent in 1928 to 7.4 per cent in 1945; but he carefully adds: 'It must be evident from our presentation that we encountered considerable difficulty in contructing estimates with a high degree of reliability and in unearthing data for checking the several hypotheses.' Yet, his are the figures upon which the great 'leveling up' and the 'decline of the rich' theories are popularly based. These figures involve a certain amount of 'estimates' and 'adjustments' which could be debated in great detail; but, the important debate ought to concern the data from which they are 'estimated.' From what we know—and we know only a small part—of the legal and the illegal ways of the heavily taxed, we seriously wonder if the drop from 19.1 to 7.4 per cent is as much an illustration of how well the corporate rich have learned to keep information about their income from the government than of an 'income revolution.' No one, however, will ever really know. For the kind of official investigation required is not politically feasible. See Simon Kuznets, 'Shares of Upper Income Groups in Income and Savings,' National Bureau of Economic Research, Inc., Occasional Paper No. 35, pp. 67 and 59; and Simon Kuznets, assisted by Elizabeth Jenks, *Shares of Upper Income Groups in Income and Savings* (New York: National Bureau of Economic Research, Inc., 1953). For one debate over the methods employed by Kuznets by means of a different interpretation of tax data, see J. Keith Butters, Lawrence E. Thompson and

Lyn L. Bollinger, *Effects of Taxation: Investment by Individuals* (Cambridge: Harvard University Press, 1953), especially p. 104.

Incidentally, the proportion of income that goes for taxation of *all kinds*—which members of the several income levels pay—has not recently been studied with care. During the New Deal, however, the results of such a study by Gerhard Colm and Helen Tarasov for the TNEC (Monograph No. 3: 'Who Pays theTaxes?' see especially p. 6) revealed that a person earning from $1,500 to $2,000 a year paid 17.8 per cent of his income in taxes, and was only able to save 5.8 per cent; while someone earning ten times that income ($15,000 to $20,000) had just less than twice as high proportion of his income taken away by taxes (31.7 per cent) and was able to save over five times as high a proportion (32.3 per cent).

11. Such cost deductions in any given year reduce the amount of 'depletion allowance' since they reduce the size of the net income; but they do not affect the percentage allowed for depletion. See Roy Blough, *The Federal Taxing Process* (New York: Prentice-Hall, 1952) p. 318.

All businesses were given a depletion boost as of 31 July 1954: instead of amortizing the cost of capital equipment bought equally over its entire useful life, two-thirds may now be deducted in the first half of its life. See *The New York Times*, 22 July 1954, pp. 1, 10.

12. See *Time*, 2 November 1953, p. 98.

13. On the gift tax, see *Business Week*, 7 August 1954, pp. 103–104; and 13 November 1954, p. 175.

14. *Business Week*, 7 March 1953, p. 143.

15. Loc. Cit. On family trusts, see also *Business Week*, 9 October 1954, pp. 175 ff.

16. These facts and quotations concerning foundations are from *Business Week*, 19 June 1954, pp. 167–9, 173.

17. *Business Week*, 17 May 1952. A survey of some 164 representative corporations in 1952 revealed that only 8 per cent of them pay their executives by salary alone—cited by Richard A. Girard, 'They Escape Income Taxes—But *You* Can't!' *American Magazine*, December 1952, p. 16.

18. Girard, op. cit. p. 89.

19. At present such stock options are only open to executives who own less than 10 per cent of the company's stock; but there is talk of liberalizing the option to include big owners, although at prices slightly higher than the market prices, so that the owner-executive can retain control of the company's stock when new stock issues are floated. On executive stock options, see *Business Week*, 4 April 1953, pp. 85–8; and 17 July 1954, pp. 52, 54.

20. *Business Week*, 25 December 1954.

21. Ibid. 19 July 1952.

22. *The New York Times*, 17 October 1954, p. F3.

23. Group life insurance, health, accident, disability, and pension plans are increasingly popular among the corporate rich. On new trends

in group life insurance and disability, see *Business Week,* 14 February 1953, pp. 78, 83; 26 September 1953, pp. 120, 122; and 24 July 1954; p. 65. On 'split-dollar' life insurance, see *Business Week,* 24 July 1954, pp. 64, 65.

24. Cf. *Business Week,* 20 June 1953, p. 183.

25. William H. Whyte, Jr., 'The Cadillac Phenomenon,' *Fortune,* February 1955, p. 178.

26. Cf. *Business Week,* 11 June 1955, p. 168 and 9 July 1955, pp. 40 ff.

27. Ernest Haveman, 'The Expense Account Aristocracy,' *Life,* 9 March 1953. Some 73 per cent of one sample of companies recently studied pay all or part of their key executives' club expenses—see Girard, op. cit. p. 88.

28. *The New York Times,* 22 February 1953, News of the Week Section, 'Journeys' End.'

29. See *Business Week,* 15 May 1954.

30. See *Business Week,* 16 October 1954.

31. See *Business Week,* 9 January 1954.

32. Girard, op. cit. p. 89. Sf. also *Business Week,* 29 August 1953.

33. Marya Mannes, 'Broadway Speculators,' *The Reporter,* 7 April 1955, p. 39.

34. Ernest Haveman, op. cit.

35. Honore de Balzac, *The Thirteen* (New York: Macmillan, 1901), p. 64.

36. Quoted in *Look,* 9 February 1954.

37. Honore de Balzac, op. cit.

38. See, for example, 'Hearings before the Subcommittee on Study of Monopoly Power of the Committee on the Judiciary,' House of Representatives, Eighty-first Congress, First Session, Serial No. 14, Part 2-A (Washington: U.S. Government Printing Office, 1950), pp. 468–9.

39. Theodore H. White, 'Texas: Land of Wealth and Fear,' *The Reporter,* 25 May 1954, pp. 11 and 15. On Hugh Roy Cullen, see also *The Washington Post,* 14 February 1954.

40. *The New York Times,* 11 October 1953, p. 65. 'The Hatch Political Activities Act,' *The New York Times* continues, 'makes it illegal to give more than $5,000 to any one national group. But it allows an individual to give up to that amount to each of any number of separate organizations and permits each member of a family to make separate donations.'

41. Harry Carman and Harold C. Syrett, *A History of the American People* (New York: Knopf, 1952), vol. II, p. 451.

42. Jonathan Stout, 'Capital Comment,' *The New Leader,* 5 December 1942.

43. Quoted in *The Reporter,* 25 October 1954, p. 2.

44. John Knox Jessup, 'A Political Role for the Corporation,' *Fortune,* August 1952.

8. The Warlords

1. Cf. Gaetano Mosca, *The Ruling Class* (Translated by Hannah D. Kahn) (New York: McGraw-Hill, 1939), especially pp. 226 ff, and Livingston's Introduction, pp. xxii ff.

2. John Adams, *Discourses on Davila* (Boston: Russell and Cutler, 1805), pp. 36–7.

3. Cf. Ray Jackson, 'Aspects of American Militarism' *Contemporary Issues*, Summer 1948, pp. 19 ff.

4. 'Why An Army?' *Fortune*, September 1935, p. 48.

5. See Stanislaw Andrzejewski, *Military Organization and Society* (London: Routledge & Kegan Paul, 1954), pp. 68 ff. The best book on 'militarism' in the west is undoubtedly Alfred Vagts, *A History of Militarism* (New York: Norton, 1937).

6. The generals and admirals selected for detailed study were taken, in formal rank order—from top down—from official army, navy, and air force registers. The 1900 army men appear in the registers from 1895 through 1905, and include the following fifteen Major Generals: Nelson A. Miles, Thomas H. Ruger, Wealy Merritt, John R. Brooke, Elwell S. Otis, Samuel B. M. Young, Adna R. Chaffee, Arthur MacArthur, Lloyd Wheaton, Robert P. Hughes, John C. Bates, James F. Wade, Samuel S. Sumner, Leonard Wood, George L. Gillespie.

Of the some 64 rear admirals appearing in the registers from 1895 to 1905, only those who appeared for at least three years were taken. This yielded 18 admirals, about the number appearing in any given year: George Brown, John G. Walker, Francis M. Ramsay, William A. Kirkland, Lester A. Beardslee, George Dewey, John A. Howell, William T. Sampson, John C. Watson, Francis J. Higginson, Frederick Rodgers, Albert S. Barker, Charles S. Cotton, Silas Terry, Merrill Miller, John J. Read, Robley D. Evans, Henry Glass.

I wish to thank Henry Barbera for use of material from his M.A. thesis at Columbia University, 1954, in connection with the data on military careers of 1900 and 1950.

7. Gordon Carpenter O'Gara, *Theodore Roosevelt and the Rise of the Modern Navy* (Princeton: Princeton University Press, 1943), p. 102.

8. Cf. for example, *Business Week*, 26 September 1953, p. 38.

9. Lieutenant Colonel Melvin B. Voorhees, *Korean Tales* (New York: Simon and Schuster, 1952), cited in *Time*, 3 August 1953, p. 9, as is the comment by *Time*.

10. The following factual information on the Pentagon is from a report in *Time*, 2 July 1951, pp. 16 ff.

11. The Hoover Commission, cited in Harold D. Lasswell, *National Security and Individual Freedom* (New York: McGraw-Hill, 1950), p. 23.

12. See Hanson W. Baldwin, 'The Men Who Run the Pentagon,' *The New York Times Magazine*, 14 February 1954, pp. 10 ff.

13. Cf. 'The New Brass,' *Time*, 25 May 1953, p. 21; 'New Pentagon Team,' *The New York Times Magazine*, 26 July 1953, pp. 6, 7; and Elie Abel, 'The Joint Chiefs,' *The New York Times Magazine*, 6 February 1955, pp. 10 ff.

14. Secretary Robert B. Anderson and Rear Admiral Homer N. Wallin. Admiral Wallin was removed from a top position in the Pentagon to the Puget Sound Navy Yard in Bremerton, Washington; the Admiral had, in effect, told Anderson to be content 'with broad policy and leave the details to the admirals.' See *Time*, 10 August 1953, p. 18.

15. See Hanson W. Baldwin, '4 Army "Groupings" Noted,' *The New York Times*, 9 May 1951.

16. 'New Joint Chiefs,' *Business Week*, 16 May 1953, pp. 28–9.

17. Hanson W. Baldwin, 'Skill in the Services,' *The New York Times*, 14 July 1954, p. 10C.

18. 'Insuring Military Officers,' *Business Week*, 15 August 1953, p. 70.

19. S. L. A. Marshall, *Men Against Fire* (New York: Wm. Morrow, 1947), pp. 50 ff.

20. See note 6 above. The army registers from 1942 to 1953 yielded 36 men, each of whom is a 4 or a 5 star general: George C. Marshall, Douglas MacArthur, Malin Craig, Dwight D. Eisenhower, Henry H. Arnold, Joseph W. Stilwell, Walter W. Krueger, Brehon B. Somervell, Jacob L. Devers, Mark W. Clark, Omar N. Bradley, Thomas T. Handy, Courtney H. Hodges, Jonathan M. Wainwright, Lucius D. Clay, Joseph L. Collins, Waide H. Haislip, Matthew B. Ridgway, Walter B. Smith, John E. Hull, James A. Van Fleet, Alfred M. Gruenther, John R. Hodge, Carl Spaatz, Hoyt S. Vandenberg, Muir S. Fairchild, Joseph T. McNarney, George C. Kenny, Lauris Norstad, Benjamin Chidlaw, Curtis E. LeMay, John K. Cannon, Otto P. Weyland.

The typical general of 1950 was born in the mean year of 1893 of American parents and is of British ancestry. It took him 35 years, from the first year at the academy or the service, to reach his top command status or generalcy at the age of 52. His father was a professional and from the upper-middle class, and probably had political friendships or connections. The typical general graduated from West Point, besides graduating from four schools in the Army. If he is religious, he is probably Protestant and maybe Episcopalian. He has married (endogomously) an upper-middle class girl and her father might have been a General, a professional, or a businessman. He belongs to about three clubs, e.g., the Army-Navy, Army-Navy Country, and the Masons. He has written about two books and someone has written something about him. He has also received two honorary degrees and probably expects to receive more.

The 25 navy admirals and fleet admirals of 1950 selected were: Harold R. Stark, Ernest J. King, Chester W. Nimitz, Royal E. Ingersoll, William F. Halsey, Raymond A. Spruance, William D. Leahy, Jonas H. Ingram, Frederick J. Horne, Richard S. Edwards, Henry K. Hewitt,

Thomas C. Kinkaid, Richoon K. Turner, John H. Towers, Dewitt C. Ramsey, Louis E. Denfield, Charles M. Coke, Richard L. Conolly, William H. P. Blandy, Forrest P. Sherman, Arthur W. Radford, William M. Fechteler, Robert B. Carney, Lynde D. McCormick, Donald B. Duncan.

The Admiral of 1950 was born in the mean year of 1887, of American parents and is of British ancestry. It took 40 years to reach the top command post from the year he entered the Naval Academy, and he was 58·when this occurred. He was born somewhere in the Eastern-North-Central section of the U.S. and grew up in the middle Atlantic region. He was born in an urban area and his father was a military man when the admiral was about 17 years old. The father's class level at this time was upper-middle and the family might have had some key political connections. He graduated from the Naval Academy and had some college previously. While in service he graduated, also, from a specialty school, e.g., the Naval War College (the top school for commanders and captains). His religion is Episcopalian and his father-in-law is from the upper-middle class and is either in the professional or the business world. He has possibly written one book or is now writing one. He may have received an honorary degree, if not, anticipates one soon.

21. 'Who's in the Army Now?' *Fortune*, September 1935, p. 39.

22. Katharine Tupper Marshall, *Together* (New York: Tupper and Love, Inc., 1946), pp. 8, 17, 22. See also Anne Briscoe Pye and Nancy Shea, *The Navy Wife* (New York: Harper, 1949).

23. Helen Montgomery, *The Colonel's Lady* (New York: Farrar & Rinehart, 1943), pp. 207, 151, 195.

24. *Time*, 2 June 1952, pp. 21–2.

25. *Business Week*, 15 August 1954.

26. 'You'll Never Get Rich,' *Fortune*, March 1938, p. 66.

27. Thorstein Veblen, *The Theory of the Leisure Class* (New York: Macmillan, 1898), pp. 247–9.

28. H. Irving Hancock, *Life at West Point* (New York: Putnam, 1903), pp. 222–3, 228.

29. Out of the 465 men who had held the rank of general officer in the regular army for at least one year between 1898 and 1940, 68 per cent were West Point graduates, most of the remainder serving during the first decade of the century. Two per cent were of working-class origin; 27 per cent were the sons of professional men; 21 per cent, of businessmen; 22 per cent, of farmers; 14 per cent, of public officials; and 14 per cent, of military men. Sixty-three per cent were either Episcopalians or Presbyterians; 28 per cent were other types of Protestants; and 9 per cent were Catholics. See R. C. Brown, 'Social Attitudes of American Generals, 1898–1940,' University of Wisconsin Ph.D. Thesis, 1951.

30. For excellent accounts of professional military indoctrination, see Sanford M. Dornbusch, 'The Military Academy as an Assimilating Institution,' *Social Forces*, May 1955; and M. Brewster Smith's description of the Officer Candidate School of World War II, which is described

'mainly as an attack on the candidate's personality' and the 'building up of a positive officer's personality.' S. A. Stouffer, *et. al. The American Soldier* (Princeton: Princeton University Press, 1949), vol. I, pp. 389–90.

31. 'At the outbreak of World War I, West Pointers constituted 43 per cent of the Regular officers of the army. At its close they occupied the principal positions of responsibility . . . All army commanders, and 34 out of 38 division and corps commanders came from the Academy. At the time of World War II, although West Pointers were only about 1 per cent of the total officer corps, at the close of the war they held 57 per cent of the division and higher combat commands.' Major General Maxwell D. Taylor, *West Point: Its Objectives and Methods* (West Point, November 1947), pp. 16–17.

32. Quoted in Ralph Earle, *Life at the U.S. Naval Academy* (New York: Putnam, 1917), p. 167.

33. Earle, op. cit. pp. 165, 79, 162–3.

34. Cf. John P. Marquand, 'Inquiry Into the Military Mind,' *The New York Times Magazine,* 30 March 1952, pp. 9 ff.

35. Cf. C. S. Forester, *The General* (New York: Bantam Edition, 1953), p. 168.

9. The Military Ascendancy

1. For example, John K. Galbraith, review of John W. Wheeler-Bennett, *The Nemesis of Power: The German Army in Politics* in *The Reporter,* 27 April 1954, pp. 54 ff.

2. 'The U.S. Military Mind,' *Fortune,* February 1952, p. 91.

3. See *Time,* 18 August 1952, p. 14.

4. Hanson W. Baldwin, *The New York Times,* 21 February 1954, p. 2. Cf. also the article by James Reston, ibid. p. 1.

5. *Time,* 7 July 1954, p. 22.

6. Hanson W. Baldwin, 'Army Men in High Posts,' *The New York Times,* 12 January 1947.

7. *The New York Times,* 15 November 1954 and 9 November 1954.

8. See the editorial, 'The Army in Politics,' *The New Leader,* 11 March 1944, p. 1.

9. Hanson W. Baldwin, *The New York Times,* 2 April 1952.

10. Cf. *The New York Times,* 15 November 1954.

11. General MacArthur, speaking in New York in March 1953, and in Boston in 1951, quoted in *The Reporter,* 16 December 1954, p. 3.

12. Mark Skinner Watson, *The War Department; Vol. I: Chief of Staff, Pre-War Plans and Preparations* (Washington: Historical Division of the Department of the Army, 1950); Maurice Matloff and Edwin M. Snell, *The War Department, Vol. II: Strategic Planning for Coalition Warfare, 1941–42* (Washington: Office of the Chief of Military History, Dept. of the Army, 1953); R. S. Cline, *The War Department,*

Vol. III: Washington Command Post: The Operations Division (Washington: Office of the Chief of Military History, Dept. of the Army, 1954,. These three volumes are the best sources on the details of the military ascendancy in the political realm just before and during World War II.

13. Edward L. Katzenbach, Jr., 'Information as a Limitation on Military Legislation: A Problem in National Security,' *Journal of International Affairs*, vol. III, No. 2, 1954, pp. 196 ff.

14. Robert Bendiner, *The Riddle of the State Department* (New York: Farrar & Rinehart, 1942), p. 135. On the foreign service in general, see also the article prepared by the staff of the Foreign Service, 'Miscellaneous Staff Studies Pertaining to the Foreign Service,' *Foreign Affairs Task Force*, Appendix VIIA, 1 September 1948; J. L. McCamy, *The Administration of American Foreign Affairs* (New York: Knopf, 1950); *The Diplomats: 1919–1939* (Edited by Gordon A. Craig and Felix Gilbert) (Princeton: Princeton University Press, 1953); C. L. Sulzberger in *The New York Times*, 8 November 1954; and Henry M. Wriston, 'Young Men and the Foreign Service,' *Foreign Affairs*, October 1954, pp. 28–42.

15. Based upon a study of the careers of the 20 top ambassadors of 1899 who earned salaries of $10,000 or more. On two of these men (Hart and Townsend) we could not find adequate information. The 20 men and the 23 countries included are as follows: Argentina—William I. Buchanan; Austria—Addison C. Harris; Belgium—Lawrence Townsend; Chile—Henry L. Wilson; Brazil—Charles Page Bryan; China—Edwin H. Conger; Colombia—Charles Burdett Hart; Costa Rica, Nicaragua and Salvador—William L. Merry; France—Horace Porter; Germany—Andrew D. White; Great Britain—Joseph H. Choate; Guatemala and Honduras—W. Godfrey Hunter; Italy—William F. Draper; Japan—Alfred E. Buck; Mexico—Powell Clayton; Peru—Irving B. Dudley; Russia—Charlemagne Tower; Spain—Bellamy Storer; Turkey—Oscar S. Straus; Venezuela—Francis Loomis. I wish to thank Mr. Friedman for his research on this project.

16. Of the 53 British Ambassadors from 1893–1930, 76 per cent came from the Foreign Service. Cf. D. A. Hartman, 'British and American Ambassadors: 1893–1930,' *Economica*, vol. XI, August 1931, pp. 328 ff., especially p. 340.

17. Data compiled from the U.S. State Department, *Foreign Service List* by Sylvia Feldman and Harold Sheppard in a course on the "Sociology of the Professions,' at the University of Maryland, Spring 1943.

18. *The New York Times*, 7 February 1954, p. 27.

19. Walter H. Waggoner, *The New York Times*, 3 December 1952, p. 12.

20. We selected for study the men in the 25 countries judged to be either the more powerful countries in the world or to be centers of interest because of location or natural resources for the more powerful countries. Those selected were: Greece—Cavendish W. Cannon; Yugo-

slavia—James W. Riddleberger; Egypt—Jefferson Caffrey; Indonesia—
Hugh S. Comming Jr.; Portugal—Robert M. Guggenheim; England—
Winthrop W. Aldrich; Spain—James Clement Dunn; Mexico—Francis
White; U.S.S.R.—Charles E. Bohlen; India—George V. Allen; Canada—
R. Douglas Stuart; France—C. Douglas Dillon; Czechoslovakia—George
Wadsworth; Union of South Africa—Waldemar J. Gullman; Italy—Clare
Booth Luce; Korea—Ellis O. Briggs; Formosa—Karl L. Rankin; Iran—
Loy W. Henderson; Israel—Monnett B. Davis; Japan—John M. Allison;
Austria—Llewellyn E. Thompson; Poland—Joseph Flack; Australia—
Amos J. Peaslee; Vietnam—Donald R. Heath; Turkey—Aura M. Warren.

In England, still the most coveted diplomatic post, Winthrop W. Aldrich is a millionaire banker and brother-in-law of John D. Rockefeller
II. In France, C. Douglas Dillon is a graduate of Groton and, like Aldrich, of Harvard, the son of the founder'of the banking firm of Dillon,
Read & Co. Mid-west banking and business interests are represented in
Canada by R. Douglas Stuart; Amos J. Peaslee, Ambassador to Australia, is an expert in international law, prominent Republican, son of a
banker and a descendant of an old colonial family; Robert M. Guggenheim in Portugal is the son of one of the founders of the Guggenheim
fortune; and in Italy, Mrs. Clare Booth Luce.

The countries to which the career diplomats were appointed were:
Japan, Korea, Israel, Poland, the Union of South Africa, Vietnam, India,
Greece, Egypt, Turkey, Formosa, Czechoslovakia, Mexico, Indonesia,
Iran, Yugoslavia, Spain and Austria. In only one important country—
Russia—is there a career diplomat, Charles E. Bohlen—and his appointment was very nearly not confirmed by the Senate. Like most of the
career men in the Foreign Service, Bohlen came from an upper-class
family—his father being a 'well-known sportsman'; Bohlen was educated
at St. Paul's School and was a member of the Porcellian Club at Harvard. See *The New York Post*, 8 March 1953.

21. Cf. Marquis Childs in *The New York Post*, 16 January 1955; and
William V. Shannon, *The New York Post*, 13 March 1955, pp. 5, 8.

22. Quoted by C. L. Sulzberger, 'Foreign Affairs,' *The New York
Times*, 8 November 1954.

23. Charlotte Knight, 'What Price Security,' *Collier's*, 9 July 1954,
p. 65.

24. Theodore H. White, *Fire in the Ashes* (New York: William
Sloane Associates, 1953), p. 375.

25. See *The New York Times*, 7 November 1954, p. 31, and 13 and
14 December 1954; and *The Manchester Guardian*, 11 November 1954,
p. 2.

26. Louis J. Halle, in a letter to the editors of *The New York Times*,
14 November 1954, p. 8E.

27. George F. Kennan, cited in *The New York Post*, 16 March 1954.

28. The information and quotations on military attachés in both the
text and the footnote are from Hanson W. Baldwin, 'Army Intelligence
—I,' *The New York Times*, 13 April 1952, p. 12.

29. See Burton M. Sapin and Richard C. Snyder, 'The Role of the Military in American Foreign Policy' (New York: Doubleday & Co., 1954), pp. 33–4.

30. *The Economist*, 22 November 1952.

31. See Edgar Kemler, 'No. 1 Strong Man,' *The Nation*, 17 July 1954, pp. 45 ff.

32. See *Time*, 23 August 1954, p. 9.

33. See Thomas J. Hamilton, *The New York Times*, 15 August 1954, p. E3.

34. Arthur Maass, *Muddy Waters: The Army Engineers and the Nation's Rivers* (New York: Harper, 1951), p. 6. Cf. also his article with Robert de Roos, 'The Lobby That Can't Be Licked,' *Harpers*, August 1949.

35. C. E. and R. E. Merriam, *The American Government* (New York: Ginn & Co., 1954), pp. 774, 775.

36. Eric Sevareid's column in *The Reporter*, 10 February 1955. Cf. *The New York Times*, 14 February 1954. By 1954, The Strategic Air Command alone represented 'a direct fixed capital investment of upwards of $8.5 billion. This covers mainly the cost of its aircraft and bases. The largest U.S. industrial corporation in point of assets is Standard Oil of New Jersey, with its approximately $5.4 billion. And SAC's 175,000 "employees" are not too far from Jersey Standard's 119,000 in employee-assets ratio. Like oilmen, SAC men operate a lot of expensive equipment. (The extreme case is the B-47 crew of three taking up more than $2 million worth.) The assets comparison cannot be pressed very far, however, for the $8.5 billion figure is only a part of SAC's true cost, a complete accounting of which would include a pro rata share of the equipment and installations of other commands (United States Air Forces in Europe, Military Air Transport, Air Material Command, Research and Development, and others) contributory to SAC's operation. A true figure would run well above $10 billion.' John McDonald, 'General LeMay's Management Problem' *Fortune*, May 1954, p. 102.

37. Levin H. Campbell, *The Industry-Ordnance Team* (New York: Whittlesey House, 1946), pp. 3–4.

38. 'The S.O.S.,' *Fortune*, September 1942, p. 67.

39. Major General Lucius D. Clay, General Staff Corps, Assistant Chief of Staff for Material, 'The Army Supply Program,' *Fortune*, February 1943, p. 96.

40. 'The U.S. Military Mind,' *Fortune*, February 1952, p. 91.

41. For details on the coincidence of military and economic views of reconversion, see Bruce Catton, *The Warlords of Washington* (New York: Harcourt, Brace, 1948), esp. pp. 245–88.

42. 'Generals—Then and Now,' *The New York Times Magazine*, 7 March 1954, pp. 78–79; U.S. Atomic Energy Commission, *In the Matter of J. Robert Oppenheimer: Transcript of Hearing Before Personnel Security Board*, 12 April 1954 through 6 May 1954 (U.S. Government Printing Office, 1954), pp. 163 and 176; *The New York Times*, 20

August 1954 and 15 February 1955; *Business Week,* 19 December 1953, 9 October 1954, 27 June 1955; For many other names and positions, see 'The Military Businessmen,' *Fortune,* September 1952, p. 128 f.

43. See loc. cit. and *Business Week,* 9 August 1952.

44. 'The U.S. Military Mind,' op. cit.

45. Arthur Krock, *The New York Times,* 5 April 1953, News of the Week section.

46. John Blair, *et al. Economic Concentration and World War II* (Washington: U.S. Government Printing Office, 1946), pp. 51 ff. See also 'Special Report to Executives: Science Dons a Uniform,' *Business Week,* 14 September 1946, pp. 19 ff; and 'The New World of Research,' *Business Week,* 28 May 1954, pp. 105 ff.

47. *The New York Times,* 5 October 1954.

48. See 'Government and Science,' *The New York Times,* 18 October 1954, p. 24.

49. Quoted in *The New York Times,* 19 October 1954, p. 12.

50. In a letter to the Editor of *The Reporter,* 18 November 1954, p. 8.

51. See Theodore H. White, 'U.S. Science: The Troubled Quest—II,' *The Reporter,* 23 September 1954, pp. 26ff. For a comparison with the number of scientists in Russia, see *The New York Times,* 8 November 1954.

52. See Theodore H. White, 'U.S. Science: The Troubled Quest—II,' op. cit., pp. 27 ff; and Philip Rieff, 'The Case of Dr. Oppenheimer,' *The Twentieth Century,* August and September 1954.

53. Benjamin Fine, 'Education in Review,' *The New York Times,* 8 March 1953, News of the Week Section.

54. See John M. Swomley Jr., 'Militarism in Education' (Washington, D.C.: National Council Against Conscription, February 1950), pp. 65–7.

55. See *The New York Times,* 22 August 1953, p. 7.

56. See John M. Swomley Jr., 'Press Agents of the Pentagon' (Washington, D.C.: National Council Against Conscription, July 1953), pp. 16–18.

57. Ibid. pp. 13 and 9.

58. Quoted in *Time,* 29 June 1953.

59. On factors working for the success of the military publicists, see Swomley Jr., 'Press Agents of the Pentagon,' op. cit. pp. 53–4.

60. Alfred Vagts, *The History of Militarism* (New York: Norton, 1937).

61. Quoted in Samuel E. Morison and Henry S. Commager, *Growth of the American Republic,* 4th ed. (New York: Oxford University Press, 1951), vol. 2, p. 468.

62. Wm. O. Douglas and Omar N. Bradley, 'Should We Fear the Military?' *Look,* II March 1952.

10. The Political Directorate

1. The lead to this chapter is adapted from Robert Bendiner, 'Portrait of the Perfect Candidate,' *The New York Times Magazine,* 18 May 1952, pp. 9 ff.

2. On power as the politician's major motive, see Harold D. Lasswell. *Power and Personality* (New York: Norton, 1948) p. 20.

3. Unless otherwise cited, all statistical data presented in section 1 of this chapter come from an original study of the origins and careers of the occupants of the positions cited below between 1789 and June 1953. For an earlier release of materials from this study, which did not include the Eisenhower administration, see C. Wright and Ruth Mills, 'What Helps Most in Politics,' *Pageant,* November 1952. Cf. also H. Dewey Anderson, 'The Educational and Occupational Attainments of our National Rulers,' *Scientific Monthly,* vol. xxxx, pp. 511 ff; and Richard B. Fisher, *The American Executive* (Hoover Institute and Library on War, Revolution and Peace; Stanford University Press)

If we would understand the higher politician, we must collect information about not one or two, or even fifty, but about the several hundred statesmen who have occupied the highest political offices, and in that simple sense, are the political elite. The statistics presented in this note concern the 513 men who between 1789 and June 1953 occupied the following positions: President, Vice-President, Speaker of the House of Representatives, Cabinet Member, and Supreme Court Justice. To call any selection of men 'the statesmen' or 'the political elite' is to invite disagreement about their selection. In this selection, I have tried to include only the very pinnacles of the American government. The major ommission involves the legislators: even to include the committee chairmen of the House and Senate over such a long period was beyond my means of research. Yet such men are the prototypes of 'the politician.' In this section, however, I am not interested in the American politician at large, but in those who have been at the formal head of the government. Whether they are party politicians or not is one thing I am trying to find out. It is quite true that at times leading members of the Senate, and even governors of key states, have exercised *national political* power without ever having served in one of the top governmental positions studied here. But many senators and governors are caught in the net which I have thrown: of the 513 men, 94 have been governors and 143 have been United States Senators. I do not contend, of course, that those who occupied these positions and who later occupied one of the positions from which I have selected the 513 statesmen were the most powerful and important senators and governors. 'Party politicians' as such are discussed in ELEVEN: The Theory of Balance.

Six out of ten of the 500-odd men who have come to the top of the government during the course of United States history have come from quite prosperous family circumstances, being comfortable boys whose fathers were usually the prosperous and often the wealthy men of local

society. Their families—which were among the upper 5 or 6 per cent of
the American population—could well afford to give them distinct advantages in the selection and pursuit of their careers: 28 per cent are
from the distinctly upper class of landed wealth, big merchants, industrialists, financiers of nation-wide prominence, or professional families
of great wealth and national standing; 30 per cent are from the prosperous upper-middle class of businessmen, farmers, and professionals,
who, although not of national stature, nevertheless were quite successful and prominent in their respective localities.

Two or three out of ten (24 per cent) have come from that middle
class which is neither rich nor poor; their fathers were generally respected businessmen or farmers, or were in the professions of law and
medicine—or were dead at the time the future statesmen left school,
leaving their otherwise prosperous families in less comfortable, but manageable, circumstances.

The final two out of ten (18 per cent) originate in lower-class families—13 per cent from small-business or small-farming families that did
not do so well, but could readily hold their heads above dire poverty;
and 5 per cent from the class of wage workers or destitute small businessmen and farmers.

Occupationally, in each and every generation, the statesmen have
come from business and professional families in much greater proportions than the proportions of such families in the population at large.
Professional men in the occupied population have never exceeded 7 per
cent, and over the years have averaged about 2 per cent; but 44 per
cent of this political elite have come from such fathers' homes. Businessmen have never exceeded 10 per cent of the total American labor force,
but 25 per cent of the political elite have been sons of businessmen.
Farmers have never dropped below 18 per cent and have averaged over
50 per cent of the working force, but only 27 per cent of the political
elite come from farmsteads. Moreover, the 'farmers' whose sons have entered the political elite have been much more often prosperous than not.

It has seldom been a disadvantage for a man bent on entering politics
to have a father who is the governor of the state or a senator in Washington. Even an uncle or a father-in-law in such positions can be very
helpful. At least 25 per cent of these higher politicians have had fathers
who were in some kind of political office about the time the sons left
school, and when the political connections of all relatives are considered, we find that at least 30 per cent of the statesmen *are known* to
have had such political connections at the time they were setting out on
their careers. In this there is some decrease: before the end of the Civil
War, about four out of ten, after the Civil War, about three out of ten,
had political connections among relatives.

There have been, of course, political dynasties in American politics.
Yet, it can safely be said that throughout United States history well over
half of the higher politicians have come from families *not* previously
connected with political affairs. They come more frequently from fam-

ilies highly placed in terms of social and economic position than political influence.

Since so many of the higher politicians come from families with distinct advantages to offer, it is not surprising that no less than 67 per cent of them have graduated from college. Even today—the historical peak of American education—only 6 or 7 per cent of all the people in the United States old enough to have gone, have, in fact, gone to college. But in the first quarter of the nineteenth century, when very few people indeed were college-educated, 54 per cent of the men then holding high political positions had graduated from college. Generally, each generation of the higher politicians has included larger proportions of college graduates, thus paralleling, on a much higher level, the educational history of Americans at large.

Moreover, the colleges they attended have more often been of the Ivy League than is the case for the ordinary college graduate. Harvard and Princeton lead with about 8 per cent each of all the higher politicians among their alumni; Yale is third with about 6 per cent. Slightly over one-quarter attended Ivy League schools, and well over one-third of those who went to any college went to Ivy League schools. If one includes such famous schools as Dartmouth and Amherst, then one-third of all the higher politicians, and 44 per cent of those who ever spent any time in college, went to top-notch eastern schools.

Over half of these men grew up on the Atlantic seaboard, and were educated in the East. That the proportion is so large in spite of the western expansion is largely a reflection of the national hold the densely populated Middle Atlantic states of New York, Pennsylvania, and New Jersey have held in the origins of top politicians. Despite the immigration to the United States of 40 million foreign-born between 1820 and 1953, only 4 per cent of the American statesmen have been foreign-born. Only 2 per cent of them grew up outside the United States—and most of this handful are of The Founding Fathers' generation.

The higher politicians in America have not only been politicians; in fact, only five of these 513 followed no careeer other than politics before entering their top positions. During the entire history of the United States, about three-fourths of them have been lawyers; almost one-fourth have been businessmen; a handful—some 4 per cent—have followed other careers. The industrialization of the American economy is directly reflected in the fact that over three times as many were businessmen immediately after the Civil War as just before it. Since then that fact has remained more or less constant: nearly one-third of the higher politicians since World War I have been businessmen; over 40 per cent of the most recent men, those of the Eisenhower administration, have been.

4. The following are the men and positions included as those 'in charge of executive decisions,' as of 2 May 1953: President Dwight D. Eisenhower; Vice-president Richard M. Nixon. The Cabinet: Secretary

of State John Foster Dulles; Secretary of the Treasury George M. Humphrey; Secretary of Defense Charles Erwin Wilson; Attorney General Herbert Brownell, Jr.; Postmaster General Arthur Sommerfield; Secretary of the Interior Douglas McKay; Secretary of Agriculture Ezra Taft Benson; Secretary of Commerce Sinclair Weeks; Secretary of Labor Martin P. Durkin; Secretary of Health, Education and Welfare Oveta Culp Hobby.

Sub-Cabinet—The Departments: Under Secretary of State Walter Bedell Smith; Director of the Policy Planning Staff of the State Department Robert R. Bowie; Counselor to the Department of State Douglas MacArthur II; Deputy Under Secretary of State H. Freeman Matthews; Assistant Secretary of State for Congressional Relations Thurston B. Morton; Under Secretary of the Treasury Marion B. Folsom; Deputy Secretary of Defense Roger M. Keyes; Assistant Secretary of Defense for Legislative Affairs Fred Seaton; Secretary of the Army Robert T. Stevens; Under Secretary of the Army Earl D. Johnson; Secretary of the Navy Robert B. Anderson; Under Secretary of the Navy Charles S. Thomas; Secretary of the Air Force Harold E. Talbott; Under Secretary of the Air Force James H. Douglas Jr.; Deputy Attorney General William P. Rogers; Director of the Federal Bureau of Investigation John Edgar Hoover; Deputy Postmaster General Charles R. Hook Jr.; Under Secretary of the Interior Ralph A. Tudor; Under Secretary of Agriculture True D. Morse; Under Secretary of Commerce W. Walter Williams; Under Secretary of Labor Lloyd A. Mashburn; Under Secretary of Health, Education and Welfare Nelson A. Rockefeller; Chairman of the Atomic Energy Commission Lewis Strauss; Chairman of the Civil Service Commission Philip Young; Director of Mutual Security Agency Harold E. Stassen.

Sub-Cabinet—Executive Office of the President: Director of the Bureau of the Budget Joseph M. Dodge; Deputy Director of the Bureau of the Budget Percival F. Brundage; Director of the Office of Defense Mobilization Arthur S. Fleming; Deputy Director of the Office of Defense Mobilization Victor E. Cooley; Chairman of the Council of Economic Advisers Arthur F. Burns; Director of the Central Intelligence Agency Allen W. Dulles; Chairman of the National Security Resources Board Jack Gorrie.

White-House Staff: Assistant to the President Sherman Adams; Deputy Assistant to the President Wilton B. Persons; Secretary to the President Thomas E. Stephens; Press Secretary to the President James C. Hagerty; Special Counsel to the President Bernard M. Shanley; Special Assistant to the President for National Security Affairs Robert Cutler; Special Assistant to the President C. D. Jackson; Administrative Assistant to the President Gabriel S. Hauge; Administrative Assistant to the President Emmet J. Hughes.

In obtaining information about these men, I have relied most consistently upon the sketches concerning them appearing in the various

monthly issues of *Current Biography* in the early months of 1953. I wish
to thank Mr. Roy Shotland for a preliminary memorandum concerning
these men.

5. See Fletcher Knebel, 'Ike's Cronies,' *Look*, 1 June 1954, p. 61.

6. 'What goes on at Ike's Dinners,' *U.S. News and World Report*, 4
February 1955.

7. Theodore Roosevelt as quoted by Matthew Josephson, in *The
President-Makers* (New York: Harcourt, Brace, 1940), p. 142; see also
William H. Lawrence's review of Merriman Smith, *Meet Mister Eisenhower* (New York: Harper, 1955) in *The New York Times Book Review*, 10 April 1955, p. 3.

8. Herman Finer, 'Civil Service,' *Encyclopedia of the Social Sciences*,
vol. III, p. 522.

9. The departments of the civilian government vary considerably as
to whether or not they are covered by the existing civil-service regulations. Some agencies—such as the Forest Service, the Federal Bureau of
Investigation, the Bureau of Standards, the Interstate Commerce Commission—are highly professionalized. 'As a general rule, the more professional the agency, the more secure its personnel against job-hungry
politicians.' See James MacGregor Burns, 'Policy and Politics of Patronage,' *The New York Times Magazine*, 5 July 1953, p. 24. The exception
to this rule, of course, is now the State Department. Furthermore, promotion under civil service is supposed to proceed according to merit
which is measured by progress reports. 'This system fails, however, to
exclude personal favor inasmuch as a superior officer is still the judge.'
Finer, op. cit. p. 521.

10. *Encyclopedia Britannica*, Eleventh Edition, vol. 6, p. 414.

11. Some 88 per cent of all government employees had tenure under
the civil-service regulations; some of the remaining seven per cent were
protected by a 1947 Executive Order to the effect that if an employee,
after having been under civil service, had taken a non-civil-service job,
his protection from removal was to be continued; others had been appointed for terms of office overlapping the new administration. *Time*,
20 July 1953, p. 14. Cf. also Burns, op. cit. p. 8; and 'On U.S. Jobhold-
ers,' *The New York Times*, 28 June 1953.

12. In 1953 there were 2.1 million full-time civilian employees in the
United States and almost 200,000 employed outside the continental
domain. About 1.2 million of these civilian employees worked in the Department of Defense; a half million in the Post Office Department, with
the next largest group (178,402) employed in the Veterans Administration, followed by the Department of the Treasury (85,490) and the
Department of Agriculture (78,097). Cf. *The World Almanac 1954*, p.
64.

13. On the 1500 'key officials' in the government, see the study made
of them by Jerome M. Rosow, *American Men in Government* (Washington, D.C.: Public Affairs Press, 1949). The data on these 1500 men
are from this study.

14. See *Time*, 12 January 1953, p. 18.

15. *Business Week*, 27 September 1952, p. 84.

16. See the remarkably forthright article, 'The Little Oscars and Civil Service,' *Fortune*, January 1953, pp. 77 ff.

17. See *Time*, 20 July 1953, p. 14. Not only career men who had risen through civil service to jobs not covered by it lost their job security—but also a miscellanea of government workers such as Coast Guard lamplighters and Hindi interpreters who 'do not fit into the regular civil-service merit system.'

18. Burns, op. cit. p. 8.

19. *Business Week*, 23 October 1954, p. 192.

11. The Theory of Balance

1. John Adams, *Discourses on Davila* (Boston: Russell and Cutler, 1805), pp. 92–3.

2. David Riesman, in collaboration with Reuel Denney and Nathan Glazer, *The Lonely Crowd* (New Haven: Yale University Press, 1950), pp. 234–9, 260, 281, 250, 254–5.

3. George Graham, *Morals in American Politics* (New York: Random House, 1952), p. 4.

4. Cf. Irving Howe, 'Critics of American Socialism,' *New International*, May–June 1952, p. 146.

5. For such an approach, cf. Gerth and Mills, *Character and Social Structure* (New York: Harcourt, Brace, 1953).

6. Murray Edelman, 'Government's Balance of Power in Labor-Management Relations,' *Labor Law Journal*, January 1951, p. 31.

7. See E. H. Carr, *The Twenty Years' Crisis* (London: Macmillan, 1949), pp. 82–3.

8. Edelman, op. cit. p. 32.

9. Cf. David B. Truman, *The Governmental Process* (New York: Knopf, 1951), pp. 506 ff.

10. See Floyd Hunter, 'Structures of Power and Education,' *Conference Report: Studying the University's Community* (New Orleans: Center for the Study of Liberal Education for Adults, April 1954), for the composition of such cliques in a single city, and preliminary notes on his forthcoming book on the national scene.

11. E. H. Carr, op. cit. p. 80.

12. On the members of the 83rd Congress (1954), see Cabell Phillips, 'A Profile of Congress,' *The New York Times Magazine*, 10 January 1954, pp. 16 ff. On the members of the 1949–51 Congress, see Donald R. Matthews, *The Social Background of Political Decision-Makers* (Garden City, New York: Doubleday, 1954), p. 29. See also Madge M. McKinney, 'The Personnel of the Seventy-seventh Congress,' *The American Political Science Review*, vol. xxxvi (1942), pp. 67 ff.

13. Matthews, op. cit. pp. 30 and 23. Cf. also Mills, *White Collar* (New York: Oxford University Press, 1951), pp. 127–8.

14. Matthews, op. cit.

15. Ibid. pp. 24 and 26–27. Catholics were only 9 per cent of the Senators in the 83rd Congress. See the report of the National Council of Churches, cited in *Time*, 19 January 1953.

16. The quotation in the text is from Cabell Phillips, 'The High Cost of our Low-Paid Congress,' *The New York Times Magazine*, 24 February 1952, pp. 42, 44. Franklin Delano Roosevelt has even said of political office in general, that 'either the individual should have enough money of his own safely invested to take care of him when not holding office . . . or else he should have business connections, a profession or a job to which he can turn from time to time.' In a magazine article in 1932, reprinted by Harold F. Gosnell, *Champion Campaigner: Franklin D. Roosevelt* (New York: Macmillan, 1952) and cited in *The New York Times*, 15 October 1952. Cf. also George B. Galloway, *The Legislative Process in Congress* (New York: Crowell, 1953).

On the average total income of members of Congress in 1952, see Phillips, 'The High Cost of Our Low-Paid Congress,' op. cit.; and, on the raising of the annual salaries of Congressmen in 1955, see 'Congress Take-Home,' *The New York Times*, 6 March 1955, p. 2E.

17. Robert Bendiner, Spotlight on a Giant Hoax,' *The Progressive*, June 1955, p. 5.

18. See, for example, Martin Dies, Congressman-at-large from Texas, 'The Truth About Congressmen,' *Saturday Evening Post*, 30 October 1954, pp. 31 ff.

18. See Martin Dies, op. cit. p. 138; on John F. Kennedy, see *The New York Times*, 1 December 1952, p. 16.

In the campaign of 1952, the late Senator from Michigan, 'Blair Moody and several committees working for him reported having raised $98,940. The Senator's personal report listed expenses of $37,224, while the Wayne County Committee for his campaign spent $36,224.' In all their campaigns of 1952, New York State Republicans reported that they had spent $227,290 with the Batten, Barton, Dustine and Osborne advertising agency and an additional $20,844 with other agencies. (Loc. cit.)

20. Fifty years ago, the Senator, even though he might be the 'representative from the railroads,' was a virtual patriarch in comparison with the Representative; for he was responsible to interests powerful enough to influence decisively the state legislature which elected him. But, since 1913, the directly-elected Senator has also had to maneuver among the multiplicity of interests which so often fragment the attention and compromise the policy of the Representative.

On the parochialism of the professional politician, in general, see the excellent book by James MacGregor Burns, *Congress on Trial: The Legislative Process and the Administrative State* (New York: Harper, 1949), pp. 8, 14, 59, 142, 143.

21. Stanley High, quoted in Stephen K. Bailey and Howard D. Samuel, *Congress at Work* (New York: Henry Holt, 1952), p. 8.

22. There is an excellent description of a typical day in the life of a big senator and a key representative in Bailey and Samuel, op. cit.

23. For a good summary of the local 'issues' in the campaign of 1954, see *Life*, 1 November 1954, pp. 30, 20, and 21. The Senator who called his opponent 'dishonest or dumb or stupid and a dupe' was Irving Ives, quoted in *The New York Times*, 29 October 1954, p. 22.

24. Sixty per cent of the electorate were reported not to have thought about the 1954 campaign at all. Gallup poll of 4 October 1954, reported in *Business Week*, 30 October 1954, p. 29.

25. See Burns, op. cit. pp. 198 and 36. Not Norman Thomas, but Arthur Krock has said that 'the mix-up has gone so far that in some states and on some national issues, the voters have great difficulty in finding the major parties' dividing line . . . one outstanding reason is . . . that administrations and major party platforms designate as national positions what are not national in fact . . . because in large sections of the country those under the same party label oppose these positions of the national majority.' *The New York Times*, 15 June 1954.

26. Burns, op. cit. p. 181. Cf. also pp. 123, 124, 182.

27. Cf. ibid. pp. 18, 19, 24.

28. See David G. Phillips, *The Treason of the Senate*, 1906 (Stanford, California: Academic Reprints, 1953).

29. See John D. Morris, 'The Ways and Means of Dan Reed,' *The New York Times Magazine*, 5 July 1953, p. 29.

30. Anonymous member of Congress, quoted by Dies, op. cit. p. 141.

31. See Murray Edelman, 'Government's Balance of Power in Labor-Management Relations.' op. cit. p. 35; and 'Governmental Organization and Policy,' *Public Administration Review*, vol. xii, No. 4, Autumn 1952, pp. 276 ff.

32. See the excellent account of the Senate Judiciary Anti-Monopoly Subcommittee, scheduled to undertake the Dixon-Yates and power inquiry by Elizabeth Donahue, 'The Prosecution Rests,' *New Republic*, 23 May 1955, pp. 11 ff.

33. See Edelman, 'Governmental Organization and Public Policy,' op. cit. pp. 276–83.

34. John K. Galbraith, *The Great Crash* (Boston: Houghton Mifflin, 1955), p. 171.

35. For one statement of presidential and congressional leadership, see Burns, op. cit. pp. 166 ff.

36. Cf. Otto Kirchheimer, 'Changes in the Structure of Political Compromise,' *Studies in Philosophy and Social Science* (Institute of Social Research, New York City), 1941, pp. 264 ff.

37. Those who would understand the present power system as a balancing society must accordingly either (1) smuggle in the old, decentralized society or (2) attempt to find a new equilibrium on the higher level within the new. For comments concerning (2), see six: 'The Chief Executives' and twelve: 'The Power Elite.'

38. Cf. Mills, *White Collar* (New York: Oxford University Press, 1951), pp. 54 ff.

39. Cf. Kenneth S. Lynn, *The Dream of Success* (Boston: Little Brown, 1955), pp. 148 ff.

40. Cf. Mills, op. cit. p. 65 and Chapters 13, 14, 15.

41. Cf. Mills, 'The Labor Leaders and the Power Elite,' *Industrial Conflict* (Edited by Arthur Kornhauser, Robert Dubin, and Arthur M. Ross) (New York: McGraw-Hill, 1954), pp. 144 ff; and Mills, *The New Men of Power: America's Labor Leaders* (New York: Harcourt, Brace, 1948). See also Saul D. Alinsky, *Reveille for Radicals* (Chicago: University of Chicago Press, 1946).

12. The Power Elite

1. Cf. Elmer Davis, *But We Were Born Free* (Indianapolis: Bobbs-Merrill, 1953), p. 187.

2. For points used to characterize the first and second of these phases, I have drawn from Robert Lamb, 'Political Elites and the Process of Economic Development,' *The Progress of Underdeveloped Areas* (Edited by Bert Hoselitz) (Chicago: The University of Chicago Press, 1952).

3. Henry Cabot Lodge, *Early Memoirs,* cited by Dixon Wecter, *The Saga of American Society* (New York: Scribner's, 1937), p. 206.

4. Lord James Bryce, *The American Commonwealth* (New York: Macmillan, 1918), vol. i, pp. 84–5. In pre-revolutionary America, regional differences were of course important; but see: William E. Dodd, *The Cotton Kingdom* (Volume 27 of the Chronicles of America Series, edited by Allen Johnson) (New Haven: Yale University Press, 1919), p. 41; Louis B. Wright, *The First Gentlemen of Virginia* (Huntington Library, 1940), Chapter 12; Samuel Morison and Henry S. Commager, *The Growth of the American Republic* (New York: Oxford University Press, 1950), pp. 177–8; James T. Adams, *Provincial Society, 1690–1763* (New York: Macmillan, 1927), p. 83.

5. Cf., for example, David Riesman, in collaboration with Reuel Denney and Nathan Glazer, *The Lonely Crowd* (New Haven: Yale University Press, 1950).

6. See the Hearings of the Pujo Committee, quoted in Richard Hofstadter, *The Age of Reform* (New York: Knopf, 1955), p. 230; and Louis D. Brandeis, *Other People's Money* (New York: Stokes, 1932), pp. 22–3.

7. Richard Hofstadter, op. cit., p. 305.

8. Whittaker Chambers, *Witness* (New York: Random House, 1952), p. 550.

9. For an excellent introduction to the international unity of corporate interests, see James Stewart Martin, *All Honorable Men* (Boston: Little Brown, 1950).

10. Gerald W. Johnson, 'The Superficial Aspect,' *New Republic,* 25 October 1954, p. 7.

11. See the Hearings before the Committee on Armed Services,

United States Senate, Eighty-third Congress, First Session, On Nomi-
nees Designate Charles E. Wilson, Roger M. Keyes, Robert T. Stevens,
Robert B. Anderson, and Harold E. Talbott, 15, 16, and 23 January
1953 (Washington, D.C.: U.S. Government Printing Office, 1953).

12. Hearings before the Subcommittee on Study of Monopoly Power
of the Committee on the Judiciary, House of Representatives, Eighty-
first Congress, First Session, Serial No. 14, Part 2-A (Washington, D.C.:
U.S. Government Printing Office, 1950), p. 468.

13. Cf. *The New York Times,* 6 December 1952, p. 1.

14. Floyd Hunter, 'Pilot Study of National Power and Policy Structures.' Institute for Research in Social Science, University of North
Carolina, Research Previews, vol. 2, No. 2, March 1954 (mimeo), p. 8,

15. Ibid. p. 9.

16. Richard Hofstadter, op. cit., pp. 71–2.

17. Cf. Gerth and Mills, *Character and Social Structure* (New York:
Harcourt, Brace, 1953).

18. Cf. Mills, 'The Conscription of America,' *Common Sense,* April
1945, pp. 15 ff.

19. Cf. 'Twelve of the Best American Schools,' *Fortune,* January
1936, p. 48.

20. Speech of Field Marshall Viscount Montgomery at Columbia
University as reported in *The New York Times,* 24 November 1954, p.
25.

21. Cf. Dean Acheson, 'What a Secretary of State Really Does,'
Harper's, December 1954, p. 48.

13. The Mass Society

1. See E. H. Carr, *The New Society* (London: Macmillan, 1951),
pp. 63–6, on whom I lean heavily in this and the following paragraphs.

2. On elections in modern formal democracies, E. H. Carr has concluded: 'To speak today of the defence of democracy as if we were defending something which we knew and had possessed for many decades
or many centuries is self-deception and sham—mass democracy is a new
phenomenon—a creation of the last half-century—which it is inappropri-
ate and misleading to consider in terms of the philosophy of Locke or of
the liberal democracy of the nineteenth century. We should be nearer
the mark, and should have a far more convincing slogan, if we spoke of
the need, not to defend democracy, but to create it.' (ibid. pp. 75–6).

3. Cf. Hans Speier, *Social Order and The Risks of War* (New York:
George Stewart, 1952), pp. 323–39.

4. Gustave Le Bon, *The Crowd* (London: Ernest Benn Ltd., 1952—
first English edition, 1896), pp. 207. Cf. also pp. 6, 23, 30, 187.

5. Sergei Chakhotin, *The Rape of the Masses* (New York: Alliance,
1940), pp. 289–91.

6. Charles Horton Cooley, *Social Organization* (New York: Scribner's, 1909), p. 93. Cf. also Chapter IX.

7. See Walter Lippmann, *Public Opinion* (New York: Macmillan, 1922), which is still the best account of this aspect of the media. Cf. especially pp. 1–25 and 59–121.

8. Cf. Gerth and Mills, *Character and Social Structure* (New York: Harcourt, Brace, 1953), pp. 84 ff.

9. J. Truslow Adams, The Epic of America (Boston: Little, Brown, 1931) p. 360.

10. Cf. Mills, 'Work Milieu and Social Structure,' a speech to 'The Asilomar Conference' of the Mental Health Society of Northern California, March 1954, reprinted in their bulletin, *People At Work: A Symposium,* pp. 20 ff.

11. A. E. Bestor, *Educational Wastelands* (Urbana, Ill.: University of Illinois, 1953), p. 7. Cf. also p. 80.

14. The Conservative Mood

1. Cf. Karl Mannheim, *Essays on Sociology and Social Psychology* (Edited and translated by Paul Kecskemeti) (New York: Oxford University Press, 1953), Chapter II: 'Conservative Thought,' pp. 74 ff.

2. See Russell Kirk, *The Conservative Mind* (Chicago: Henry Regnery, 1953), especially Chapter One. For a further discussion of Mr. Kirk, see Mills, 'The Conservative Mood,' *Dissent,* Winter 1954. For a sympathetic guide to *Conservatism in America* see the book by that title by Clinton Rossiter (New York: Knopf, 1955).

3. Cf. Mills, *The New Men of Power: America's Labor Leaders* (New York: Harcourt, Brace, 1948), Chapter Six: 'The Liberal Rhetoric,' pp. 111 ff.

4. Cf. Kenneth S. Lynn, *The Dream of Success* (Boston: Little, Brown, 1955), p. 216.

5. When Senator Taft, before his death, was asked if he had read Russell Kirk's book, he replied that he did not have much time for books. See 'Robert Taft's Congress' and 'Who Dares to Be a Conservative?' *Fortune,* August 1953, pp. 95, 136.

6. See Peter Viereck, *Conservatism Revisited* (New York: Scribner's, 1950); and José Ortega y Gasset, *The Revolt of the Masses,* 1932 (New York: New American Library, 1950).

7. Although the interpretation of 'McCarthyism' as having its roots in the status frustrated is now widely published, Paul Sweezy's and Leo Huberman's original article remains the most forthright account of it: 'The Roots and Prospects of McCarthyism,' *Monthly Review,* January 1954. See also articles by Peter Viereck, for example, 'Old Slums plus New Rich: The Alliance Against the Elite' and 'The Impieties of Progress,' *The New Leader,* 24 January and 31 January 1955. For a more sophisticated statement, see Richard Hofstadter, 'The Pseudo-Conservative Revolt,' *The American Scholar,* Winter 1954–55. On the general theme of middle-class status, see Chapter Eleven: 'The Status Panic,' in Mills, *White Collar* (New York: Oxford University Press, 1951).

8. See Robert Bendiner's excellent article, 'The Liberals' Political Road Back,' *Commentary*, May 1953, pp. 431 ff.

9. Archibald MacLeish, 'Conquest of America,' *The Atlantic Monthly*, August 1949.

10. Examples of The American Celebration are embarrassingly available. Unfortunately no one of them is really worth examining in detail: in order that the sort of thing I have in mind may be clear, by all means see Jacques Barzun, *God's Country and Mine* (Boston: Little, Brown, 1954). For a less flamboyant example, see Daniel J. Boorstin, *The Genius of American Politics* (Chicago: University of Chicago Press, 1953); for a scatter of celebrants, see *America and The Intellectuals* (New York: Partisan Review Series, Number Four, 1953).

11. Cf. Mills, 'Liberal Values in the Modern World,' *Anvil and Student Partisan*, Winter 1952.

12. See the definitive examination of David Riesman and his work by Elizabeth Hardwick, 'Riesman Considered,' *Partisan Review*, September–October, 1954, pp. 548 ff.

13. See *Business Week*, 18 September 1954, p. 32; and *Time*, 12 July 1954, pp. 80–81.

14. *The New York Times*, 7 December 1952, p. 3F.

15. On big-time illegal enterprises, see various reports of the Kefauver hearings in 1950, especially *Third Interim Report of the Special Committee to Investigate Organized Crime in Interstate Commerce*, 82nd Congress, 1st Session, Report 307.

16. Alfred R. Lindesmith, 'Organized Crime,' *Annals of the American Academy of Political and Social Science*, September 1941, as abridged and adapted in Leonard Broom and Philip Selznick, *Sociology: A Text with Adapted Readings* (Evanston, Illinois and White Plains, New York: Row, Peterson, 1955), p. 631.

17. For the above items, see: *Time*, 28 June 1954, pp. 21–2; *The New York Times*, 19 September 1954, pp. 1, 8; ibid. 20 February 1954, pp. 1, 15; ibid. 24 February 1954, pp. 1, 15; and *Time*, 3 March 1952; *Look*, 9 March 1954, pp. 38 ff; *The New York Times*, 12 February 1954, pp. 1, 17; ibid. 16 March 1954; *Time*, 12 July 1954, p. 24 and *The New York Times*, 26 June 1954, p. 1, and 30 June 1954, pp. 1, 28.

15. The Higher Immorality

1. Cf. Mills, 'A Diagnosis of Our Moral Uneasiness,' *The New York Times Magazine*, 23 November 1952.

2. James Reston, *The New York Times*, 10 April 1955, p. 10E.

3. Sophie Tucker, as quoted in *Time*, 16 November 1953.

4. Cf. Mills, *White Collar;* (New York: Oxford University Press, 1951), pp. 259 ff.

5. Cf. Mills, 'The Contribution of Sociology to Industrial Relations,' Proceedings of the First Annual Conference of the Industrial Relations Research Association, December 1948.

6. James Reston, *The New York Times*, 31 January 1954, section 4, p. 8.

7. *The New York Times Book Review*, 23 August 1953. But see also *Time*, 28 February 1955, pp. 12 ff.

8. *Hearings Before the Committee on Banking and Currency*, United States Senate, Eighty-fourth Congress, First Session (U.S. Government Printing Office, Washington, 1955), p. 1001.

9. John Adams, *Discourses on Davila* (Boston: Russell and Cutler, 1805).

10. In *Perspectives, USA*, No. 3, Mr. Lionel Trilling has written optimistically of 'new intellectual classes.' For an informed account of new cultural strata by a brilliantly self-conscious insider, see also Louis Kronenberger, *Company Manners* (Indianapolis: Bobbs-Merrill, 1954).

11. Leo Egan, 'Political "Ghosts" Playing Usual Quiet Role as Experts,' *The New York Times*, 14 October 1954, p. 20.

12. Charles E. Wilson, quoted in *The New York Times*, 10 March 1954, p. 1.

13. John Adams, op. cit. pp. 57–8.

14. Cf. William Harlan Hale, 'The Boom in American History,' *The Reporter*, 24 February 1955, pp. 42 ff.

15. See Walter Bagehot, *Physics and Politics* (New York: D. Appleton, 1912), pp. 36, 146–7, 205–6.

Index

Note: This index does not include names or titles appearing in the NOTES, pp. 365–412.